CINEMA APPROACHING REALITY

CINEMA APPROACHING REALITY

Locating Chinese Film Theory

VICTOR FAN

MINNESOTA

University of Minnesota Press
Minneapolis
London

A different version of chapter 1 previously appeared as "Approaching Reality: Epistemic Distance, Political Crises, and Temporal Imaginations in the Sino-French Dialogue on Cinema Ontology," *World Picture*, no. 7 (2012).

Published by the University of Minnesota Press

111 Third Avenue South, Suite 290
Minneapolis, MN 55401-2520
http://www.upress.umn.edu

Library of Congress Cataloging-in-Publication Data

Fan, Victor.
Cinema approaching reality : locating Chinese film theory / Victor Fan.
Includes bibliographical references and index.
ISBN 978-0-8166-9355-9 (hc : alk. paper)
ISBN 978-0-8166-9357-3 (pb : alk. paper)
1. Motion pictures—Philosophy. 2. Film criticism—China—History. 3. Motion pictures—China—History. I. Title.
PN1995.F27 2015 791.4301—dc23

2014019921

Printed in the United States of America on acid-free paper

21 20 19 18 17 16 15 10 9 8 7 6 5 4 3 2 1

TO MY GRANDMOTHER CHOI MO-KIT
AND MY COMPANION PUPAZZO

CONTENTS

ACKNOWLEDGMENTS

This book is, in truth, the result of many conversations, crisis managements, and unconditional encouragements offered to me by my former colleagues from McGill University, Thomas Lamarre, Grace Fong, and Robin Yates, and my mentors from Yale University, Dudley Andrew, Thomas Elsaesser, and Haun Saussy. I am also exceptionally grateful for the mentorship and confidence given to me by my senior colleagues at King's College London, especially Chris Berry and Sarah Cooper. Financially, the completion of this project would not be possible without the generous support from the Samuel K. Bushnell Fellowship from Yale University and the Fonds de recherche sur la société et la culture from Québec. Equally important, many of the materials of this book came from the Hong Kong Film Archive, where Research Officer Po Fung and Assistant Librarian of the Resource Centre Kat Lai have been offering me, year after year, their untiring and admirably professional assistance. And undoubtedly, I would not be able to survive without the intellectual and spiritual support from my friends Brian Bergstrom, Tyler Cohen, Yuriko Furuhata, Christine LaMarre, Li Yang, Brent Lester Lue, Olivier Marin, James Mudge, Luke Robinson, Tim Sedo, Marc Steinberg, Olga Solovieva, Debbie Wong, and Xie Jingjing.

Of course, the idea of writing a book on opening a comparative space between Chinese and Euro-American film theories came from my senior cohorts at the Permanent Seminar on the Histories of Film Theories, especially my coeditors in the Chinese Film Theory Translation Project Jason McGrath and Guo-Juin Hong, and cofounders Francesco Casetti, Aaron Gerow, and Markus Nornes. It was also a pleasure to discuss parts of my project with Yiman Wang in numerous conferences. I must also thank my colleagues at KCL, Belén Vidal and Erica Carter, who have opened up my mind to many new ideas in European film theories. In addition, I owe a lot to the immense care, nurturing, and mentoring from my wonderful teachers at Yale, John McKay, Charles Musser, and Brigitte Peucker, at the University of Southern California, David E. James, and at the University of Rochester, David N. Rodowick and Mark Betz. Last but not least, I want to thank my parents Samuel Fan and Jackie Mak, my partner John Christiansen and my former partner Robert Burr, my cats Pupazzo (2000–14) and Sabina, and a very special teacher of mine, Robin Lister from Malvern College. I am forever indebted to their unconditional support, patience, and cultivation.

NOTE ON TRANSLITERATION

In principle, the pinyin transliteration system for Chinese words is used throughout this book. However, exceptions are made with respect to historical and regional circumstances:

1. In cases where political institutions, organizations, and persons whose names were historically or customarily transliterated in alternative systems, a pinyin transliteration will be provided when a name first appears in the text, followed by its historical or customary transliteration. Such a name will appear in its historical or customary form in its subsequent appearances in the text. For example, the Guomindang (Kuomintang or Nationalist Party) or Chen Gongbo (Ch'en Kung-po).
2. Place names between 1906 and 1949 will first appear in their pinyin formats, with their Postal Map Romanizations (PMR) included in parentheses. In the rest of the text, the PMR versions will be used in reference to their historical circumstances during the Republican period (1911–49). For example, Guangzhou (Canton) or Nanjing (Nanking).
3. Film companies and political institutions during the Republican period often had official English names or preferred transliteration formats, for example, the Lianhua Film Company (United Photoplay Service or UPS) or the Yihua (Yee Hwa) Film Company. Again, both the pinyin and their preferred English or alternative transliterations are introduced first. The historical formats will be used in subsequent appearances.
4. The same rule applies to Cantonese terms, place names, and persons, for example, Yueju (Jyutkek or Cantonese theater) or Xue Juexian (Sit Koksin). For Cantonese terms, the Jyutping system will be used, while for names of persons, the Hong Kong Government system will be used.

In chapter 2, many of the terms being discussed are loanwords from Japan during the Republican period. These terms will often appear in Japanese, Chinese, and English simultaneously in order to highlight the translational gaps between these languages, for example, *mokuteki ishiki* (*mudi yishi* or directed consciousness). Variations will apply in accordance with the context of the discussion.

Finally, in certain parts of this book, I use Lydia Liu's concept of the "super-sign" (see the introduction for its definition). In her works, Liu prefers highlighting the way new semiological differences are created in the process of translation by using a slash between the two different languages in question, e.g. *rensheng*/human life.

INTRODUCTION

EURO-AMERICAN FILM THEORIES have for many years been treated as a lingua franca in the field of cinema studies. Even countries like the People's Republic of China (PRC), where scholars have made deliberate efforts to recenter the discourse on film theory around the work of Chinese filmmakers, writers, and intellectuals, an alternative perspective can be hard to achieve. As many film theorists and historians who work in China and other parts of East Asia were trained in Europe and North America or are well acquainted with "Western" methodologies, key concepts in Euro-American film theories still form the underlying assumptions in their discussions.[1]

Increasingly, however, film scholars have tried to reclaim a proper position for the theoretical discourses on cinema outside Europe and America, and to use ideas and concepts previously ignored in the Euro-American debate to work through some of its problematics and aporias. This phenomenon was largely prompted by what film scholars would consider an ontological crisis and a disciplinary crisis. On the one hand, the emergence of the digital image in cinema, which is often seen as changing the relationship between the cinematographic image and reality, has motivated a number of scholars to rework Bazinian ontology by seeking inspirations from non-Western film theories.[2] On the other hand, as Dudley Andrew argues, film scholars have historically faced a disciplinary paradox: film studies has always been interdisciplinary; yet by the same token, it constantly requires theorists and historians to redefine its disciplinary boundaries before or while it "disappears" into neighboring terrains such as media, communication, and literary studies.[3] In this regard, learning how filmmakers, critics, and intellectuals outside Europe and North America have discussed cinema since the late nineteenth century allows film scholars today to understand how the discursive and institutional domains of cinema and its studies have been debated, especially as they come face-to-face with other technological, sociopolitical, and scholarly crises.

In response to these demands, new work is emerging. Yet, in the excitement of introducing theories from what some may regard as uncharted terrain into our established debate, film scholars have yet to find an effective means to transpose theories from different parts of the world into a comparative dialogue and consider what we can learn from it. Despite the fact that we have never managed to agree on how this comparative space can be approached, however, the demand for more knowledge about non-Western film theories continues to grow. In 2012 the Permanent Seminar on Histories of Film Theories devoted itself to global research in East Asian film theories, with the aim of producing anthologies of Chinese and Japanese film theories in translation.[4] Kim Soyoung from the Korean National University of Arts has been working tirelessly to foster a discursive space among scholars in East Asian film theories, specific to the historical, linguistic, cultural, and sociopolitical conditions of the region.[5] Aaron Gerow from Yale University has completed a book manuscript and published a number of articles on Japanese film theory since 2010,[6] and cinema and media studies programs around the world are actively expanding the scope of their teachings to include East Asian theories. Opening a comparative colloquy between Chinese and Euro-American film theories is recognized as an urgent need in our discipline today, and demands a serious discussion of the methods of comparison and the key issues at stake.

As most film scholars would agree, the task of rethinking film theory as a global discourse is not simply a matter of adding more works from other parts of the world—in our case, China—to the Euro-American canon. Likewise, one cannot assume that filmmakers, critics, and intellectuals from Shanghai and Hong Kong during the Republican period (1911–49), who lived and worked under a linguistic, social, cultural, and political environment that had already undergone a complex process of negotiation with their Japanese and Euro-American counterparts, would have constructed a fundamentally pure and unified "Chinese" body of knowledge. Rather, Chinese filmmakers and critics between the 1920s and 1940s always conceived of their works as part of a cross-cultural dialogue with their peers in Japan, Europe, and America, an understanding that has, unfortunately, never been reciprocated.

The task of this book is therefore to restore an interregional conversation that was meant to be there in the first place, and allow those of us who work in this field to reevaluate how key concepts in cinema studies can be reconfigured. A global understanding of film theory, I argue, requires actively rewriting our approaches to major issues by highlighting conceptual and intellectual connections among major theorists around the world. In this sense, a sincere and honest cross-cultural exchange can only be restored and fully illuminated by relinquishing the idea that "Eastern" and "Western" film theories and their studies are essentially different. Critical discourses on cinema in Shanghai and Hong Kong were in fact constructed through an intricate process of negotiation between Japan, Euro-America, and China via acts of translation, intellectual critique, and vernacular mediation. In other words, what we may call "Chinese film theory" (the historical and conceptual contestability of this term will be discussed later) is in itself a comparative space, and we can only fully reappraise its position in the history of film theories by adjudicating on its connective points with its Euro-American counterparts.

This book undertakes the task of restoring and reconfiguring this cross-cultural discourse by examining how Chinese and Euro-American film theorists think about reality and cinema, focusing especially on how Chinese film theories between the 1920s and 1940s can help film scholars rework the aporia in Bazinian ontology, one that Bazin himself has painstakingly negotiated in his body of works: the delicate relationship—or in fact, distance—between the cinematographic image and reality. This aporia can be summed up as follows: on the one hand, the cinematographic image is a trace of reality, and is indeed apprehended as an image-consciousness in the same way other images are grasped in one's physical reality; on the other hand, reality is absent in the cinematographic image, and the cinema makes present the absence of a reality that is at once concealed and revealed by the image.[7] The difficulty, as I mentioned earlier, is triggered by a crisis in our perception of cinematographic reality. The digital image, which can be entirely or partially constructed, altered, and manipulated, no longer guarantees any direct relationship between the image-consciousness the viewer apprehends and the reality to which it refers. This challenges the Bazinian assumption that a cinematographic image is a trace of reality. In response, scholars look for new inspirations to reconfigure Bazinian ontology, that is, to think "retrospectively and retroactively" with our knowledge of the digital image at hand.[8]

In the process of "opening Bazin," however, one needs to beware of an epistemological pitfall.[9] Scholars of Euro-American film theories often treat Bazinian ontology as a gold standard and hope to recruit Chinese and other East Asian film theories to reconsolidate it, instead of opening Bazinian theory, in all its vulnerability, to locate the aporia at the heart of his struggle to conceptualize cinema.[10] Meanwhile, researchers in Chinese film theories, in equal deference to Bazin, are not always ready to challenge his established authority. In the end, most merely report their archival findings, which are then appropriated as "new discoveries" by scholars in Euro-American film studies to prove that Bazin was right all along. This, in a sense, replicates the colonial mode of knowledge-production: "native informants" provide the raw materials that Euro-American theorists use to reaffirm a body of knowledge that has always been considered unchallengeable.

In order to circumvent this problem, I choose as my point of departure and comparative common ground a conundrum with which both Bazin and his Chinese compeers grappled, encapsulated in a unique term popularly employed by the Chinese film critics between the 1920s and 1940s: *bizhen*. Often translated as "lifelike," *bizhen* is best understood as "approaching reality."[11] Originally, it meant that the cinematographic image, within its technological limits, was not yet a form of total reality, though it could allow the spectators to apprehend an affect as though they had been there when the event actually happened. This idea corresponds to what Andrew calls the "*Cahiers* axiom," which interprets Bazinian ontology thusly: "cinema has a rapport with the real and yet the real is not the represented."[12] For Bazin, before "total cinema"—that is, a mythological state of total indistinction between cinema and reality—emerges, a film engages the spectators in a state of suspension between reality and its illusion.[13] In other words, the cinematographic image in its imperfect state can be understood as a *potentiality* that can drive the spectators towards total reality, without fully actualizing it. In this light, the digital image, I argue, still navigates between reality and its *not-yet* by reconfiguring or even short-circuiting the relationship between what the body's sense-perception believes to be real and the degree of referentiality within the image to the physical reality within human perception.

What Is Chinese Film Theory?

Retrospectively and retroactively labeling a set of critical writings on cinema "film theory" may risk imposing a Euro-American method of ratiocination, knowledge building, and categorization on intellectual debates that were developed out of a more colloquial or at times leisurely process. In the 2012 meeting of the Permanent Seminar, for example, scholars of Chinese cinema reached a consensus that between the 1920s and 1940s, the discourse on cinema among filmmakers and critics in Shanghai and Hong Kong was best described by the term they used, *pinglun* (critical discussion), instead of a term that we now use, *lilun* (theory). In fact, because of its relatively late appearance in film studies and criticisms, the term *lilun* is often misrecognized as a translation or even a loanword from its Japanese counterpart *riron.*

In fact the term *lilun* is neither a translation nor a loanword. It is found in the *Bei shi* [History of the Northern Dynasties] by Li Daishi and Li Yanshou, which was written in the mid seventh century and describes scholar Cui Liang as "*you hao lilun*" (especially fond of discussing *li*).[14] Here, the term *li* indicates those principles of life, social relationships, politics, and ethics derived from the classics written between the Warring States period (circa 481, 475 or 403–221 BCE) and the Han dynasty (206 BCE–220 CE). Hence, the term *lilun,* in this context, connotes the idea of presenting an argument well-substantiated by reasoning and references to the classical texts, a concept analogous to the Euro-American understanding of theory today. During the imperial period, however, the term *lilun* was rarely used in criticisms of art, poetry, and *xi* (play, drama, or theater). As screenwriter, director, and theater artist Mai Xiaoxia (Mak Siu-ha, d. 1941) argued, academic scholars considered the play, drama, or theater as a *xiaodao* (minor vehicle) of *li,* which was not serious enough to merit any formal debates.[15] In this light, critical writings on the theater, and later, on cinema, were largely written avocationally by intellectual elites in the forms of *tan* (discussion), *hua* (talk), *pi* (commentary), *ping* (critique), and *pu* (catalogue). During the Republican period, film criticisms also appeared as *fansi* (reflection), *zuiyan* (critique), and *zatan* (miscellaneous talk), which, as Charles Laughlin would argue, can be considered variations of the *xiaopin wen* (essays of leisure).[16]

The word *pinglun* therefore implies a process of critiquing, commenting, and discussing with fellow intellectuals. It emphasizes the interactivity and intersubjectivity in the circulation and mediation of opinions. While some *pinglun* can be casual and conversational, others can be conducted by means of formal reasoning. In other words, *lilun* is best considered a method of *pinglun*; but while *lilun* was historically associated with scholarly argumentation, *pinglun* was understood as a form of vernacular mediation. In fact, it was along this historically constructed difference between the academic and the vernacular that *pinglun* and *lilun* began to be distinguished. In 1942 the University of Nanking in Chengdu opened a joint program with New York University in film and radio studies, headed by film and television educator Sun Mingjing (1911–92); the program also published an academic journal titled *Dianying yu boyin* [*Film & Radio*]. This journal features both original and translated essays on what Sun called *meijie lilun* (media theory), which covers both critical and scientific discussions on film, television, radio, radar, electronic memory, aerospace engineering, the concept of time, and other forms of media.[17] Here, in a fully academic and scientific context, the term *lilun* is used in the way one would understand it today: theory.

During the Communist revolutionary years (1949–76), film columns in Mainland newspapers and journals employed the terms *piping* (criticism) and *pipan* (critique and judgment) to evaluate films, often as precursors of larger cultural and political critiques and persecutions.[18] In Hong Kong, the term *pinglun* (*pingleon*) continued to be used regularly.[19] The effort of systematizing a body of knowledge about cinema as theory, one may argue, was not formally proposed in academic circles until the end of the Cultural Revolution in the Mainland, and with the emergence of film studies in the 1970s in Hong Kong. At that time film scholars were motivated by a desire to construct a canon of film theory parallel to its Euro-American counterpart. In 1990, George Semsel, Xia Hong, and Hou Jianping published a concise volume of translations of post-1976 Chinese film theory.[20] However, this translated volume was published at a time when film scholars in North America and Europe knew very little about the history of Chinese cinema. As a result, most readers found these articles inadequately contextualized, and they appeared to lack originality and points of connectivity with Euro-American film theories.

This situation has changed drastically in the last twenty years in two respects. First, as reprints of Republican film magazines and archival materials are becoming more readily available, scholars including Bao Weihong, Guo-Juin Hong, Jason McGrath, Yiman Wang, Yingjin Zhang, and Zhang Zhen have been actively uncovering exciting theoretical debates held between the 1920s and 1940s (many of which are discussed in this book).[21] Second, there has been an increasing effort in Mainland China to anthologize and canonize theoretical writings, although they have yet to reach a wider global audience.[22] Still, after close to four decades of investigation and canonization, film scholars can claim a collection of writings that can roughly be called Chinese film theory. However, conceptually, the act of canonizing a body of writings as theory without asking what theory means in the context of the intellectual history of Chinese cinema is simply, as Lydia Liu argues, an act of "throwing together" two signs that have their own respective semantic fields as a super-sign: *lilun*/theory.[23] It does little more than claim: "China too has theory!"

When confronting a similar question in Japan, Gerow borrows Andrew's idea, arguing that theory conceptualizes the cinematic practice as a whole, whereas criticism is more interested in the discussion of individual films.[24] Yet such an imaginary boundary is frequently crossed in the writings published in Shanghai and Hong Kong before 1949. This problem is nonetheless not unique in East Asia. Early film criticisms in Paris and Berlin, for example, were mostly published in newspapers and fan magazines in a variety of journalistic forms and genres. From the French perspective, for instance, film theorists and historians tend to attribute the gradual formation of the concept "film theory" to the founding of the Institut des Hautes Études Cinématographique (IDEC) in October 1943 and the *filmologie* movement under the leadership of Gilbert Cohen-Séat (b. 1907). Cohen-Séat published his grand plan of institutionalizing the studies of cinema in his book *Essai sur les principes d'une philosophie du cinéma* in 1946.[25] With the support of Sorbonne, he founded the Association Française pour la Recherche Filmologie, and published the journal *Revue international de filmologie* the following year. The institutionalization of film studies, however, did not mean that it created film theory as an academic discipline; instead, it opened up "film theory" as a set of *problèmatiques* for further debates and redefinitions. In fact, as Andrew argues, the *filmologie* movement sought to marginalize the more spontaneous form of film criticism practiced by Bazin and the *Cahiers du cinéma* group.[26] In other words, Cohen-Séat's act of institutionalization had the effect of creating a division between academic film "theory" and journalistic film "criticism."

In China, Europe, and North America, the term "theory" can, I would argue, be best understood as a conceptual framework that may not be articulated in the same manner as contemporary scholarly debates. A theory, nevertheless, often emerges out of a line of discussions that employs a common paradigm either because a group of writers were conversing with each other in the same publication or setting, or they subscribed to a shared sociopolitical, aesthetic, or ethical belief. In this sense, individual essays provide case studies, criticisms, and instances of conceptualization, whereas we as film scholars look at these writings and inquire into how a theoretical discourse, as an epistemological space, emerges out of a network of debates. For example, screenwriters Liu Na'ou (1905–40) and Huang Jiamo (1916–2004) wrote a series of essays on film and spectatorship (discussed in chapter 3) in their magazine *Xiandai dianying* [*Modern Screen*] in 1933–34. Though historians today call these essays collectively the *ruanxing dianying lun*, or soft film theory, they were not first presented as a system of theoretical thoughts.[27] Nonetheless, theoretical concepts emerge in their process of developing ideas and conducting analyses. To take another example, Cantonese filmmakers in the 1930s and 1940s did not write anything overtly theoretical, but a theory took shape as they began to employ certain common terms in discussing their works and industry.[28] Understanding theory this way helps us not only organize the various trains of thought among the intellectuals in Shanghai and Hong Kong during the Republican period, but also connect their conceptual frameworks with those of film theorists with similar interests in Europe and North America.

Theoretical Interventions

In this book we will endeavor to deduce and reconstruct a theoretical space from the critical debates in Shanghai and Hong Kong between the 1920s and 1940s, and to open up a comparative framework between Chinese and Euro-American film theories by following four interrelated lines of investigation. First, archaeologically: we will excavate major works of Chinese film theory and criticism from the Republican period and analyze them closely to make them accessible to both specialists in Chinese cinema and scholars and film students in general. Second, comparatively: we will put these Chinese notions of cinema in conversation with the contemporaneous classical film theory of the West—in particular André Bazin's, but also other ideas from Japan, France, Germany, Italy, and the Soviet Union. Third, retrospectively and retroactively: we will reframe Chinese film theory before 1949 in a way that can contribute to our further understanding of film theory today. In particular, we will redevelop the idea of cinematographic potentiality as proposed by thinkers such as Gilles Deleuze and Giorgio Agamben, who have had such great influence on recent theoretical discussions in the Euro-American academy. Fourth, theoretically: we will activate a critical discussion on the status of digital cinema and its ontological consequences, based on the notion of approaching reality.[29]

The first chapter, "Approaching Reality: Chinese Ontology and the Potentiality of Time," retraces the history of the debate between Chinese and Euro-American scholars on the subject of cinema ontology and defines the meanings of the term "approaching reality." An attempt to put Bazinian ontology into conversation with Chinese film theory was initiated between 1985 and 1986, when two Beijing-based scholars, Chen Xihe (b. 1949) and Zhong Dafeng (b. 1955), retroactively labeled a discussion from the 1920s between screenwriters Gu Kenfu (circa 1890s–1932) and Hou Yao (1903–42) as the *yingxi* (shadow play) theory. According to Chen and Zhong, the ontology propounded by Gu and Hou is fundamentally different from Bazin's: that the cinema, instead of being a trace of reality, is a form of *xiju* (play-drama).[30] Yet by declaring a priori that these two systems of thoughts are essentially divergent, Chen and Zhong effectively shut down any further dialogues between them.

To circumvent this impasse, I suggest that we focus on a peculiar term that Gu and Hou employed, which has been overlooked in Chen and Zhong's version of Chinese ontology: *bizhen* (approaching reality). This term connects Gu and Hou's theory with Bazinian ontology based on a common ground: that the cinema, in its state of imperfection, is a potentiality that can approach reality but never fully actualize it.[31] For Bazin, cinema ontology is not about photographic indexicality; rather, it is about the cinema's potentiality to actualize life in all its presence by preserving a moment of temporal change snatched from an actual life-process. Thus the cinematographic image is a suspended state between life and death, presence and absence—or in Bazin's words, *la momie du changement* (change mummified).[32] The digital image, I argue, complicates such a state by introducing new temporal variations that were beyond Bazin's imagination in the 1940s: transposition, transference, reflection, inflection, inversion, reversion, shuffling, recomposition, counterpoint, and resequencing. Hence, the digital image does not fundamentally change cinematographic potentiality; rather, it unveils and reconfigures previously concealed relationships between human sense-perception and time.

The second chapter, "Cinema of Thought: Directed Consciousness in Chinese Marxist Film Theory," discusses the Marxist turn that took place in Chinese film theory in the 1930s. Based on Lenin's differentiation between spontaneous and revolutionary consciousnesses, Marxist film critics in Shanghai argued that the potentiality of the cinematographic image to actualize reality is inflected by its political modality.[33] But Lenin's ideas arrived in Shanghai via a complex process of translation and reinterpretation. In 1927, they inspired Japanese literary critic Aono Suekichi (1800–1961) to coin the term *mokuteki ishiki* (directed consciousness), repurposed the following year for film criticism by Iwasaki Akira (1903–81) to describe a mode of consciousness configured by capitalism.[34] In 1930, Lu Xun (pseudonym of Zhou Shuren, 1881–1936) adopted this term directly from Japanese (pronounced in Mandarin as *mudi yishi*), and further modified it in keeping with the semicolonial condition of Shanghai.[35] It then became the core of debate among left-wing film critics in the 1930s. For these writers, the essence of the argument was not only that both filmmakers and spectators share a political consciousness shaped by capitalism, imperialism, and feudalism, but that the film itself also has a consciousness: it thinks, feels, and actively instills its consciousness in the sentient bodies of the viewers.[36]

In this chapter, I contextualize the sociopolitical, intellectual, and industrial background of this Marxist film debate, and work through the term *yishi* (consciousness) as a pluralistic semantic field through the writings of Lu Xun, screenwriter and director Shen Xiling (1904–40), and contributors to the magazine *Mingxing yuebao* [Star monthly].[37] Constructed as a super-sign, the term *yishi*/consciousness indicates a liminal space between awareness and consciousness. Such liminality affects the way these critics understood how the cinematographic image approaches reality, how a film actively instills its consciousness in the spectators' sensoria, and how a socially conscious film can activate a political action. Read in relation to Marxist film criticisms from the Soviet Union, France, and Italy, and with Deleuze's discussion on cinema of thought, I illustrate how these Chinese intellectuals reconfigured the concept of approaching reality in political terms.

The third chapter, "Soft Film Theory: Life in All Its Presence and Concreteness," considers the soft film theory proposed by Liu Na'ou and Huang Jiamo in their magazine *Modern Screen* between 1933 and 1934, originally as a retort against their Marxist counterparts. The soft-film theorists regarded the cinematographic image as an aesthetic experience during which the spectator and the object would become one. In such a state, the boundary between the subject and the object would be tentatively dissolved; meanwhile, life, immanent in this oneness, would manifest itself in all its presence and concreteness.[38] This line of thinking has its root in Kantian aesthetics. It was reconfigured in Buddhist terms between the 1890s and the 1910s by philologist Wang Guowei (1877–1927), and later in cinematographic terms in the 1920s and 1930s by the Weimar film critics and the French film theorists.[39] Yet, Republican intellectuals, through a complex process of cross-linguistic and intercultural debate, maintained three interrelated notions of life: (1) *rensheng* (human life), a force of life; (2) *shengtai* (life form), an organic and biological life that evolves in time; (3) *minsheng* (national life), a collection of political lives that partake of a shared national consciousness. Within such a discursive space, the soft-film theorists believed that the cinema was an aesthetic experience in which these three kinds of life would be reconfigured and negotiated.

In this chapter, I investigate the multiple cultural, linguistic, and philosophical deposits that constructed this composite concept of life by first contextualizing the soft film theory in the intellectual discourse on life between the 1890s and the 1930s and then using their composite understanding of life to illuminate how Liu Na'ou and Huang Jiamo theorized cinema as an aesthetic experience. I reconfigure and repurpose the soft film theory via a philosophical conversation that underlines these two writers' presuppositions: Immanuel Kant's aesthetics, and its reconfiguration through Buddhism by Wang Guowei. Finally, I put this definition of life in a retroactive and retrospective dialogue with Gilles Deleuze's definition of life in its pure immanence (and cinematographically, the crystal image) in order to push further our discussion on the relationship between the cinematographic image, life, and temporality.[40]

The fourth chapter, "Fey Mou: The Presence of An Absence," discusses the theory of cinematic immanence proposed by poet-director Fei Mu (Fey Mou, 1906–51). Fey started his career as a director in 1930; he is now best remembered for his 1946 classic *Xiaocheng zhi chun* [*Spring in a Small Town*, Wenhua or Wen Hwa Film Company].[41] This film is about the unrequited love between a young doctor, Zhang Zhichen (Li Wei), and his former lover Zhou Yuwen (Wei Wei) now the wife of his best friend, Dai Liyan (Shi Yu). What could have been a melodrama was shot and edited in a highly lyrical style, with a series of long takes, elegant camera movements, and deep staging. In his writing, Fey claims that his techniques were inspired by the Chinese theater, which uses highly abstract forms to approach an affective reality.[42] He believed that by being absorbed into the characters' everyday lives, the spectators would gradually give up following the narrative and instead "breathe in" the characters' unfulfilled desires as *kongqi* (air).[43] This is because desire is always there, but is not present as a visual or bodily sensation until the possibility of its not being fulfilled is made tangible in the flow of the quotidian. In this sense, desire is made present out of the spectators' cognitive inferences: its absence is also made present as the viewers are drawn into a state of *xuanxiang* (suspension-imagination) when the narrative no longer offers anything out of the ordinary for them to follow.[44]

To many scholars, cinema for Fey Mou is also a vehicle that impresses upon his viewers his Confucian concept of *ren*. *Ren* is often interpreted as benevolence: the highest ethical principle in all social and political relations. But without taking away this level of meaning, *ren*, homonymous, and probably during the Warring States period, synonymous, with the word *ren* (human), can also be understood as "being human," an ontological order that is instantiated in all human relationships. As a mediating force that negotiates human relationships, *ren* measures and regulates the difference between the imaginary poles between good and evil, excess and deprivation; either extreme would be considered a cause of social, political, or even cosmological imbalance and disorder.[45] In this sense, cinema can be understood as a site where *ren*, and the human and political relationships that instantiate it, could be managed by carefully stabilizing the tension between *qing* (affection, emotion, sensation, or desire) and *li* (rites of mutual respect and self-regulation) that put excessive *qing* in check).[46]

In this chapter, I analyze Fey Mou's writings on cinema as well as his film works *Spring in a Small Town* and a recently rediscovered and restored film from 1940, *Kongfuzi* [*Confucius* or *Master Kung*] (Minhua or Min Hwa Film Company), to examine how for him, cinema conveys a *xingshi guan* (view of [cinematic] forms), *rensheng guan* (view of life), and *zhengzhi guan* (view of politics).[47] I shall do so by comparing his theoretical writings with those of David Bordwell, Kristin Thompson, Christian Metz, and André Bazin on the relationship between art and reality.[48] I argue that Fey's ontological view is based in his belief in cinema's ability to make present an absence, that is to allow life, its ontological order, and its regulating principles to manifest themselves without either preaching them rhetorically or encouraging the viewers to infer them causally. Rather, they become palpable when the film image reveals the profound mundaneness of life, in which desire, longing, hope, and their attendant frustration and desolation obstinately hover around the cinematographic image as reality.

The fifth chapter, "Cinema of Ideation; Cinema of Play: The Early Cantonese Sound Film" examines a unique cinematographic phenomenon in Hong Kong between 1930 and 1949. During this time the Cantonese theater and sound film were regarded as *zhengyou* (*zangjau*): a term that describes companions who are so intimate that they are not afraid to offer straightforward advice to one another.[49] Yet it also indicates that the two art forms were seen as *tongchu yichuang* (*tungceot jatcoeng*)—coming out of the same school.[50] This does not immediately support the shadow play theory of Chen Xihe and Zhong Dafeng. Rather, it would be more appropriate to say that both the theater and cinema could be traced back to the same ontological root during this historical period as they both shared the same mode of approaching reality. According to theater artist and historian Mak Siu-ha, the Cantonese theater and cinema approach reality not by means of *xieshi* (*sesat*), i.e. describing reality or mimesis, but by means of *xieyi* (*seji*), sketching ideation.

In this chapter I argue that the early Cantonese sound film is best understood as a cinema of ideation: it sketches an outline of life that invokes an affective state, which in turn invites the viewers to engage in life themselves—not in its appearance, but in the very potentiality of life and its process of becoming.[51] However, unlike the soft-film theorists, the Cantonese filmmakers did not try to elevate the cinema as an aesthetic experience; instead, they saw it as setting life, together with its ontological and political existence, at play. In fact, both the theater and cinema were, and still are, known in the Cantonese-speaking regions as *xi* (*hei* or play), not only in the sense of drama, but also of a game, or simply, something that is capable of putting serious human relationships, social conventions, and political matters at play. To illustrate this I first contextualize the companionship between the Cantonese theater and cinema from the 1900s to the 1930s and then examine the attempt made by the Shanghai filmmakers and the Nanjing (Nanking) policymakers between 1936 and 1937 to ban the Cantonese sound film, based on their accusation that as a dialect cinema, it was premodern, vulgar, and coarsely produced.[52] After this historical contextualization, I will look closely at the ontological and historical discourses between Mak Siu-ha and Ouyang Yuqian (1889–1962), as well as the critical writings and films of Cantonese theater artist and film director Xue Juexian (Sit Kok-sin, 1904–56).[53] I will show how theories of music and performance in the Cantonese theater insinuated themselves into the early Cantonese sound films and became systematized as a film style. I then demonstrate how all of these thoughts converge on the very notion of the Cantonese cinema as an art of ideation, which puts life and its political existence into a state of play. In conclusion, I investigate how the theoretical defense of the Cantonese film as a dialect cinema was formulated by emphasizing the way it makes visible the inconsistencies, contingencies, playfulness, and gleefulness of life by providing a forum for interplay between politics and life, good and evil.[54]

The term "approaching reality" is a way to understand the cinematographic image as a potentiality, a way of thinking of our cinematic experience as a state of suspension between reality and virtuality, life and death, and good and evil. In the conclusion of this book, I will use this newly fostered comparative theoretical space to discuss the ontological, teleological, and ethical implications of the digital image, and especially how it helps film and media scholars today explore concepts of temporality, subjectivity, individuality, and of course, reality; ideas that have been previously overlooked within the epistemic boundaries of Bazinian ontology.[55] Finally, I will conclude our ontological reconfiguration by trying to imagine how one may think about cinema ontology in Buddhist terms. To the question "What is cinema?" a Buddhist philosopher would probably answer, "*ru shi*" (like/is; as is).[56] This phrase is both a riddle and not a riddle. It is a riddle because it leaves the difference between likeness and being indiscernible and indeterminable. It is not a riddle because it is often simply interpreted as "The way it is." If we think through these two seemingly contradictory interpretations we will discover that they are indeed the same answer. Accepting the cinema as "the way it is" is to accept its very indeterminacy and its potential to approach reality in all its immanence.

Potentialities

The term "approaching reality" will provide the basis of our comparison between Bazinian ontology and Chinese film theories from the 1920s through the 1940s. This allows us to address an urgent need to look for new ways to understand cinema ontology in the digital age, and also provides a theoretical framework, methodology, and grounds of discussion for a topic that scholars are eager to explore today. Before I formally launch my discussion, however, perhaps I would remind us that Bazin never aimed at having the last word on the question of cinema ontology. Rather, like many of his contemporaries and successors, he was constantly in the process of exploring, with utmost fascination, the various potentialities brought about by the image. With this in mind, opening a dialogue between Euro-American and Chinese film theories is best carried out with this same intellectual curiosity, one that explores not only the boundaries between the subject and the object, but the way we apprehend the cinematographic image, which can potentially break down the barrier between the self and the other, and produce infinitely new possibilities for understanding life.

1 APPROACHING REALITY

Chinese Ontology and the Potentiality of Time

IN RECENT YEARS, film scholars have become increasingly interested in setting up a dialogue between Bazinian ontology and a similar line of discussion among the Shanghai filmmakers in the 1920s. The desire to open up a comparative space in cinema ontology is motivated by a growing interest in theoretical traditions outside the Euro-American canon, and by a hope to find inspirations for reconfiguring established notions of cinema ontology in response to the digital image. Yet, how one conducts such a dialogue and to what end one does so are precarious problems. Searching for a conceptual alternative in a discourse outside European and American traditions is often based on the assumption that "China" and "the West" are fundamentally different; in the end, instead of putting two bodies of knowledge into a conversation, scholars sometimes inadvertently reproduce such an imagined epistemic distance by too eagerly asserting their differences.[1] In addition, by holding to Bazinian ontology as the gold standard in the course of comparison, it is often tempting to use Chinese theoretical writings to "improve" Bazin or vice versa, instead of locating an aporia with which these two seemingly distantiated discussions might have been grappling in their respective ways.

Attempts to open a discursive space between Bazin and the Shanghai film critics of the 1920s came to the fore in the mid-1980s. Between 1985 and 1986, two film scholars from Beijing, Chen Xihe and Zhong Dafeng, set out to find an alternative concept of ontology specific to the history of Chinese cinema. "Does China have its own system of film theory?" asked Chen. "In comparison with the state of theoretical discourses in the West, is the state of theoretical discourses in China complete? If incomplete, in what sense is it incomplete? Can we follow another specific logic to understand the state of theoretical discourses in China?"[2] In an attempt to answer these questions, Chen and Zhong argued that Chinese thinking on cinema ontology was not based on the image as a trace of reality, but on the relationship between drama, representation, and life.[3] This seemed to present an exciting possibility back in the mid-1980s: the breakthrough idea that film scholars could identify a notion of cinema ontology that was not built upon Bazin's writings.[4] Yet from today's perspective, the desire to find a theoretical alternative in the name of opening a comparative space is based precisely on an assumption that "China" is posited outside the rest of "the World," as though these two cultural discourses, no matter how closely they converse with each other, are fundamentally discreet. Hence, despite the fact that Chen and Zhong managed to construct a whole system of ontological thinking out of the theoretical writings from the 1920s, what their discussion does is simply maintain the imaginary distance between China and the World.

By focusing so much on building an epistemic distance between China and the imagined West, Chen, Zhong, and a whole generation of film theorists who worked along this line missed a potentially more interesting intersection between Bazinian ontology and the early thinking among the Shanghai critics: their shared fascination with a delicate distance between the cinematographic image and reality. In many film writings in the 1920s, Shanghai critics have the tendency to use a peculiar term to describe such distance: *bizhen*—often translated as "lifelike," but more properly understood as "approaching reality." This ambiguously defined term is important for film scholars today because it hints that the Shanghai critics were as interested in the question of reality as Bazin himself was. Equally interesting is the distance between the image and reality that such a term adamantly maintains, which may help film theorists today work through an aporia that fascinated Bazin himself. For Bazin, on the one hand, the cinematographic image is an imprint of reality, or as Dudley Andrew would put it, a spectral presence that both envelops and reveals reality.[5] In this sense, Bazin, not unlike his Shanghai counterparts, seems to maintain a distance between the image that is mechanically registered and the reality into which it is capable of drawing the spectator. On the other hand, in the cinema, the spectator apprehends the image-consciousness in its totality and immediacy, a "here and now" that seems to be perceptually indistinguishable from reality itself.[6]

I shall demonstrate that filmmakers, screenwriters, and critics in Shanghai during the Republican period negotiated this delicate distance between image and reality via the term "approaching reality." Yet how we, as film scholars, researchers, and students, should approach this distance and the epistemic difference it implies is a serious problem. On the one hand, it is tempting to align our new discovery with the Bazinian paradigm and try to prove that above all, these historical theories could be reconfigured in accordance with the critical language to which we are accustomed. On the other hand, it is equally tempting to simply use the Shanghai film theory as a tool to "improve" Bazin, in order to create a version of Bazinian ontology that "had long predicted" the digital image.[7] Thomas Elsaesser has proposed a methodology we can usefully consider: seeing each historical attempt to propose a theory on cinema ontology as a symptom of a crisis—be that cinematic, sociopolitical, or philosophical. By so doing, we can map our current crisis in relating cinematographic reality to the digital image, a crisis based on the assumption that the digitally produced or manipulated image is no longer a mechanical trace of reality. What I suggest here—as Elsaesser did—is not that the digital image has actively transformed the ontology of the moving image, but that it inspires us to think retrospectively and retroactively that the methods used to define the cinema were themselves limited by certain historical imaginations. In the following intervention, I argue that the very term "approaching reality" can offer us an insight into the delicate distance, configured as a temporal difference, between the image-consciousness cinema spectators apprehend and the reality near which it draws them. But if what is at stake in the cinematographic image's approach to reality is a question of temporality, perhaps the digital crisis is best understood not as a problem of indexicality, but a crisis of our own limitations in understanding time beyond such binary concepts as distance and boundary, beginning and end, progression and regression—temporal potentialities that are currently opened up by the digital image.

The Myth of Chinese Ontology

The effort to identify a line of thinking that can be called Chinese ontology emerged out of a sociopolitical crisis in the mid-1980s. Chen Xihe and Zhong Dafeng belonged to the first generation of graduate students trained after the Cultural Revolution at the Beijing Film Academy (BFA) Department of Literature (equivalent to critical studies). Studying film theory and criticism in the late 1970s and early 1980s in Beijing was an adventure. On the one hand, volumes of film magazines and entertainment newspapers from the 1920s and 1930s that had been banned—if not partially destroyed—during the Cultural Revolution were once again made available to researchers. On the other hand, as Cecile Lagesse points out, discussions on Bazinian theory by film theorists and makers resurfaced in academic journals between 1979 and 1980, with the publication of "Tantan mengtaiqi de fazhan" [Discussion on the evolution of montage, 1979] by BFA professor Bai Jingsheng and "Yige zhide zhongshi de dianying meixue xuepai—guanyu 'chang jingtou lilun'" [A school of thought on film aesthetics worth paying attention to: on the "long take theory," 1980] by screenwriter Li Tuo (b. 1939).[8] Yet, as Li and his partner Zhang Nuanxin (director, 1940–1995) suggest, film scholars and makers at the time were not only excited by the possibility of learning about what had happened in the capitalist sphere, but also eager to be inspired by Euro-American and Japanese film theories to come up with technical innovations that could be used to represent and negotiate those sexual desires, social ambitions, economic anxieties, and identity crises experienced by the post-revolutionary generation.[9]

Nonetheless, the blossoming interest in Euro-American theory and Bazinian ontology also encountered some constraints. One was methodological. In the 1980s, the fascination with Bazin was coupled with a revived interest in pre-1966 socialist theories, namely Soviet montage and the Frankfurt school of film criticism. As Lagesse argues, this complicates the discursive contour of the discussions on film theory in several ways. First, Li and Zhang were influenced by Brian Henderson's article "Two Types of Film Theory" (1975), which had the effect of persuading Chinese readers to see Soviet montage and Bazinian ontology as two dichotomized schools of thought based on film forms.[10] As a result, Bazinian ontology was reduced to a formal fascination with the long take and a preoccupation with the French bourgeoisie of the 1940s. Because of this impression, Bazin's line of thought met with a certain resistance from the scholastic circle, as the slowly changing official cultural policy—with its own internal inconsistencies and political contestations—was still hanging on to the protocol of safeguarding the *shehui zhuyi jingshen wenming* (socialist spiritual civilization).[11] This did not mean that Bazin was banned in the academic discourse; it only meant that his works were studied and critiqued within an epistemic space informed by the socialist spiritual civilization.

One solution, as Lagesse points out, was found in the translation of Siegfried Kracauer's *Theory of Film: The Redemption of Physical Reality* (1960) by Shao Mujun.[12] In the translation, Shao uses the term *xieshi zhuyi* (the principle of describing reality) instead of *xianshi zhuyi* (the principle of reality) to translate Kracauer's term "realism." Lagesse, following the view of Hao Jian, argues that "this term might help erect a bridge between Bazin's realism and an earlier Chinese social realism—translated as *shehui xieshizhuyi* (social realism)—that characterized most of Shanghai film production from the 1920s to the 1940s."[13] The term was not in use between the 1920s and 1940s; it was retroactively imposed upon Shanghai cinema during this period by the film historians of the 1950s, and was publicized—if not coined—by Mao Zedong (1945–76) in his Yan'an Talks in 1942.[14] It was then widely discussed and disseminated during the Seventeen Years period (1949–66) by screenwriter and theorist Xia Yan (1900–95).[15] Shao's gesture of connecting Kracauer's notion of realism (and as a result of that, Bazin's) with the Yan'an view was idiomatic of the cultural policy during the reign of Hua Guofeng (1921–2008), Chairman of the Chinese Communist Party (CCP) from 1976 to 1981, who, despite significant public doubts and contestations, suggested that peace, social order, and prosperity would be restored as long as the CCP would turn the clock back to the Seventeen Years period.[16]

Chen and Zhong faced another methodological constraint in that film theory in 1980s China was discussed based on a scientific model. Euro-American discussions of ontology involve a critique of the critical language itself, and an examination of how linguistic definitions and ratiocination work hand-in-hand with the human construction of knowledge and understanding. In this sense, ontology is not supposed to be derived from a series of observations without an active critique of the language itself, for human observation takes place within an epistemic space. Chen and Zhong used methodologies from the natural and social sciences, so their discussions are based primarily on observations of actual film productions and practices. Hence, their theory determines "what cinema is"—understood by Bazin in his essay "Le mythe de cinéma total" ["The Myth of Total Cinema," 1946] as a potentiality that has been gradually actualized and redefined historically—as a sum observation of the characteristics instantiated in individual productions. This is in sharp contrast to Bazin's idea that *[l]e cinéma n'est pas encore inventé* (cinema has not yet been invented), that is, that cinema as a potentiality is still in the historical process of being actualized as a human praxis.[17]

On top of these methodological problems was a sociopolitical one: the re-emergence of the question of *minzu xing* (national character). The search for a national character in Chinese cinema was not new. In the

1920s, for example, Gu Kenfu (circa 1890s–1932), a film critic and studio executive at the Da Zhonghhua Baihe (Great China Lilium) Film Company, and screenwriter Hou Yao (1903–42) of the Minxin Studio (China Sun Motion Picture Co.), were deeply concerned with rectifying the image of Chinese characters and cultures in Hollywood and European films.[18] In 1930, Lu Xun (1881–1936) was in fact the first intellectual to point out that Hollywood representations of Chinese characters and cultures cannot be easily "corrected" for three reasons: (1) the representations are informed by the capitalist and imperialist ideology; hence, one cannot change the cinematic representation without changing the deep-structural social relations under capitalism and imperialism; (2) the desire to change Hollywood is symptomatic of these critics' belief that the only way to represent the social reality of China is to convince the colonial powers to change their own beliefs; (3) Hollywood films attract the Shanghai audience not simply because they produce the affects of enjoying capitalist pleasures, but also because they produce a longing for those pleasures that are meant to be enjoyed by the colonizer only—a form of masochistic pleasure in misrecognizing one's political impotence as an enjoyment.[19] Lu Xun's follower Zheng Zhengqiu (1889–1935), a studio executive and producer at the Mingxing Studio (Star Motion Picture Co.), argued further that such masochistic pleasures were not necessarily imposed by means of Euro-American imperialism, but by the feudal infrastructure of the Chinese economy that made capitalism and imperialism possible (these ideas will be discussed in detail in chapter 2).[20] In 1949, Ye Yiqun (1911–66) proposed that the only way to allow the national character to present itself on screen would be to permit the cinema to represent truthfully the social reality of China.[21] Likewise, in the 1950s, Xia Yan proposed a thorough study of folk narrational forms and theatrical performances not only because they were supposedly indigenous to local cultures, but also because they stemmed from the everyday life of the workers and farmers.[22]

These quests for a national character can be understood as part of film critics' and makers' search for a way to represent reality that was critical of what they deemed the bourgeois ideology. Yet in the 1980s, the question of national character carried a more transcendental tenor. As Wang Hui argues, after the Cultural Revolution and in light of Mao's successor Hua Guofeng's policy of critiquing the Gang of Four while still recognizing the philosophical ingenuity of Mao Zedong, it was, and still is, impossible to critique CCP's policy during the 1960s and 1970s.[23] For Wang, what the CCP did in the late 1970s and 1980s was to avoid positing itself as the ultimate moral authority; but by still drawing a certain transcendental power from Mao, the public maintained a desire for a fetish that stands for the missing authority. Wang argues that with the power of Mao increasingly questioned, the transcendental and nebulous notion of the "nation"—as an imagined community built upon a collective trauma of the Cultural Revolution—replaced Mao and the CCP as the fetish.[24] Seen this way, Chen and Zhong's desire to come up with a Chinese ontology was in fact symptomatic of an eagerness to replace a class-based notion of the imagined community, promoted by Marxist intellectuals and the CCP between the early 1930s and the late 1970s, with a transcendental one that the Party adopted in the early 1980s.

The Shadow Play Theory

The ontological system that Chen and Zhong came up with between 1985 and 1986 is called the shadow play theory. In his article "Lun 'Yingxi' " [On the shadow play, 1985], Zhong Dafeng argues that between the introduction of Lumière's *cinématographe* to Shanghai in August 1896 and the rise of the "left-wing" film movement in 1932, cinema was commonly known as the shadow play, a reference to the popular entertainment of the same name, which, according to Zhong, emerged around the Song (960–1279) and Yuan (1271–1368) dynasties.[25] As a result, intellectuals and filmmakers who wrote about the cinema in Shanghai in the 1920s built their theories upon the various meanings and implications of the term. For example, Zhong cites the memoir of novelist and screenwriter Bao Tianxiao (1875–1973)—one of the major figures in the *Yuanyang hudie pai* (Mandarin Ducks and Butterfly school) of modern melodrama: "When the *dianying* [electric shadows: the common nomination for film and cinema, especially since the 1930s] first arrived in China, it was also called the shadow play. We all used to say, 'Let's go see a shadow play.' From this, we can deduce that the origin of cinema is the *xi-ju* [play-drama]."[26] Zhong also quotes Hou Yao: "The shadow play is a kind of play-drama. A shadow play contains everything that a play-drama contains."[27] Another Mandarin Ducks and Butterfly school novelist and screenwriter, Xu Zhuodai (1880–1958), likewise argues, "The shadow play is . . . after all, a play-drama. Although there are many forms of play, the play-drama is always a unified artistic [concept]."[28] From these claims made by film critics, writers, and directors in the 1920s, Zhong thus suggests that cinema between 1896 and 1932 was imagined not as a newly invented machine that radically transformed its spectator's perception of reality; rather, cinema was considered as a variation of the art of shadow play, a new form of play, drama, or theater that employed a modern technology to tell stories.

The way Zhong establishes his argument is, to say the least, highly ambiguous. First of all, his definition of the *xi-ju* is equivocal. Notice that in my translation above, I tried to retain the ambiguity of the term by hyphenating *xi* (play) and *ju* (drama). The former opens up a discursive space of playfulness, craft, game, imitation, mimesis, identification, affection, and sensation, while the latter leads us to discussions on representation, action, form, structure, signification, and semantics.[29] Also, as a term upon which cinema ontology is supposed to be founded, it is unclear whether we should focus on the level of the text, performance, theatrical architecture, spectatorship, or social institution. Or on a more basic level, it is arguable whether we should understand *xi* as the play itself or the theater. At first glance, then, Zhong does not seem to be clear whether the shadow play theory is about the ontology of the moving image or the institution of cinema itself. To complicate matters, Hou Yao's categorization of the cinema in relation to play and drama (an idea that would be further developed by Chen Xihe) is a highly debatable one. "A shadow play contains everything that a play-drama contains" does not also mean the reverse: "a play-drama contains everything a shadow play contains."[30] In other words, a shadow play contains something that belongs to a different order: the photographic image.

To circumvent this problem, Zhong has to explain why these film critics in the 1920s did not seem to be interested in the photographic image. Such thought should be quite familiar to Bazinian scholars, for Bazin pondered a similar question in his essay "Théatre et cinéma" ["Theater and Cinema," 1951]. In the course of his discussion, Bazin agrees that both the cinema and theater represent reality, but that cinema, unlike the theater, is a photographic image. Hence, in the theater, the immediate presence of the actor often draws a boundary between the spectators and the dramatized or represented reality, and the spectators are drawn nearer or pushed further from such reality by an alternation between absorption and distantiation in their viewing process. The photographic image in the cinema, however, is immediately apprehended as a form of consciousness. It does not represent reality; rather, it draws the spectators into reality without any human mediation.[31]

Zhong is aware of the logical pitfall in his own argument. To address this problem, he proposes to study the shadow play theory not as a transhistorical system of thoughts, but as a way of thinking about cinema specific to the semicolonial conditions in Shanghai in the 1920s. For Zhong, the shadow play theory does not explain what cinema is or has always been, but it does tell us how film critics and makers in the 1920s thought about what cinema was, which in turn affected the way film forms were developed in Shanghai. In this sense, by imposing such a conceptual framework upon the cinema, Chinese cinema in the 1920s was turned into the shadow play when filmmakers "borrowed the stage play's methods of narration and visual representation" and used them in the cinema. For Zhong, the Shanghai film critics collectively overlooked the photographic image for a reason. He argues that these writers did acknowledge that the shadow play, unlike the stage play, uses the "image, not staged actions, as a means of representation." Yet, the Shanghai critics concentrated less on cinema's specificity than on those traits that are common to both the cinema and theater, that is, the textual, performative, and aesthetic mediations that go into the realistic representation of life. In this light, the photographic image was not regarded as a trace of reality; rather, it was a *jiqiao* (*technē*), a new technology that filmmakers could utilize to describe reality.[32]

The resulting ontology, according to Zhong and Chen, is called the *xiju benti lun* (ontology based on the play-drama), as opposed to the *yingxiang benti lun* (ontology based on the [photographic] image) that Bazin proposed. For Zhong, Bazinian ontology is based on more than a century of the Euro-American fascination with reality, representation, and simulacrum, and hence, cinema for Bazin is primarily a machine that reproduces reality, which happens to be used commercially as a narrational medium. Meanwhile, cinema in China was introduced as a commodity of semicolonialism and feudalism, and hence, cinema for those film critics and makers in Shanghai in the 1920s was nothing but a form of entertainment.[33]

Zhong's argument may sound awkward to us, but it is symptomatic of the socialist methodology that persuades him to find an ontological system that is not necessarily universal, but is instead historically conditioned. It also allows him to establish a connection between his claim and the left-wing political film writing in the 1930s—commonly known as the *yingxing dianying lilun* or hard film theory. The hard film theory can be traced back to Lu Xun's translation and commentary on Iwasaki Akira's

(1903–81) article "Xiandai dianying yu youchan jieji" [Modern cinema and the bourgeoisie, 1930], but is more commonly used to refer to a theoretical debate among the members of the Star (Mingxing) Film Company and the pro-CCP Chinese Association of Film Culture, or CAFC (*Zhongguo dianying wenhua xiehui*).[34] In his 1930 article, Iwasaki argues that Hollywood and Japanese fiction films appear to be only "entertainment," but such entertainment produces a pleasurable affect among the spectators, which arouses in them a desire to consume those material and ideological pleasures that are represented on screen and to continue supporting the capitalist system that makes such pleasures accessible.[35] Lu Xun argues that Shanghai's semicolonial condition complicated Iwasaki's reading. For Lu Xun, those material and sexual pleasures represented by Hollywood and Japanese films were meant to be enjoyed by the colonizing powers only; they were in fact inaccessible to the Shanghai spectators who were posited as the subaltern in this asymmetrical political relationship. Hence, the Shanghai viewers were encouraged to enjoy not only those pleasures that were denied them by their colonizers, but also to turn their sense of shame and impotence—and the perpetual sense of longing for something unattainable—into a form of enjoyment.[36] In this light, Zhong suggests that as cultural producers under imperialism, European, American, and Japanese filmmakers and critics could afford to philosophize the cinema in terms of representation, reality, and simulacrum. In semicolonial Shanghai, though, the cinema was nothing but a commodity for public entertainment—one that in fact turned the displeasure of being colonized into a form of pleasure.

In fact, between the late nineteenth and early twentieth centuries, writers from the Mandarin Ducks and Butterfly school were attracted to the cinema precisely because they could use it as a new medium to entertain their audience. It also attracted writers and directors from the *xinju* (new theater, also known as *wenming xi* or civilized play), a form of melodrama that emerged around the early twentieth century and combined forms and performing techniques from local operas and European dramas. For these writers, Zhong argues, literature and cinema help the readers or spectators to cultivate their *quwei* (taste), that is, the cultivation of quotidian, pleasurable, and leisurely interests that appear to be detached from politics and the rest of the society, but are in fact made possible by the availability of excessive time (outside material labor) under capitalism. As a consequence, film critics and makers in the 1920s, including Hou Yao and Gu Kenfu (who came from the new theater), and

Xu Zhuodai and Bao Tianxiao (who were Mandarin Ducks and Butterfly writers), were primarily interested in perfecting the narrational devices and screenwriting techniques they inherited from their theatrical and literary works.[37] Formally, Shanghai cinema in the 1920s therefore emphasizes the integrity of the stage, the two-dimensionality of a stage representation, the use of diffused lighting that emulates a "naturalistic" stage light, the allowance of seeing an actor enter and exit the frame fully, exaggerated performances and narratives that are structured not by means of a story's cause-and-effect chain, but by the flow of entrances and exits of the characters in a series of loosely connected acts. In other words, these critics and makers worked under the semicolonial conditions of Shanghai by maintaining the cinema as a form of entertainment and cultivation of *quwei,* but in so doing, they also constructed a certain national character in their imagination, and in the production of film forms and modes of representation to express it.[38]

To put matters crudely, Zhong implies that Bazin's preoccupation with the photographic image as the basis of his ontology can be seen as a form of *xiao youchan jieji quwei* (petite bourgeois cultivation) that is completely blind to the historical materialist conditions of the Shanghai audience in the 1920s. Yet by the same token, the shadow play theory overlooks the importance of the photographic image because the cinema to these writers is nothing more than a narrational device for the purpose of entertainment. Zhong's underlying assumption is that Bazinian ontology, like any other body of knowledge, is subject to its historical conditions and limits. Likewise, the Shanghai version of ontology based on the play-drama is also bound by its own sociohistorical edges.

Nonetheless, the political motto of the late 1970s and early 1980s was *chongchu Yazhou; zouxiang shijie* (dashing out of Asia; marching towards the World). Zhong Dafeng and his colleague Chen Xihe aspired to elevate the shadow play theory from a historically conditioned view of cinema ontology to a philosophical system that could potentially compete with Bazinian ontology. Chen chose to approach it through a close reading of Hou Yao's 1926 book *Yingxi juben zuofa* [Methods of writing a shadow play]. In the early 1920s, Hou wrote screenplays for the Changcheng (Great Wall) Film Company, a production company formed by a group of Chinese students returning from New York City.[39] When Hou wrote his book in 1925, he was a contracted director in the Hong Kong–based China Sun Film Company and a professor at his alma mater, the Southeast University in Nanking.[40] *Methods* is thus intended as a screenwriting manual, but Hou devotes the first chapter to a discussion of the relationship between the cinema, drama, and life, thus inspiring Chen and later film scholars to reconstruct a system of ontological thinking.

In his short preface, Hou writes, "I advocate the principle of regarding the screenplay as the core of cinema. I believe that the only way to produce a good play is to have a good script. The shadow play is a kind of play. A script of the electric shadows is the soul of the electric shadows." In response to this statement, Chen argues, "the author clearly sees the 'play' as the essence of the 'shadow play.' In other words, the electric shadows—i.e. cinema as an objective system—is built structurally and functionally upon the foundation of the 'play.' " Hence, for Chen, Hou's argument "departs from the 'play' as cinema's ontological and epistemological basis." In this sense, Chen argues that the " '*ying*' [shadow or image] is a method by which the 'play' can be brought to the point of completion." To push his idea further, Chen observes that Hou discusses the different aspects of *mise-en-scène* in the cinema in the order of "plot, explication, dialogue, expressions" and eventually "composition and scenery."[41] In fact, Hou suggests that a director's choice of scenery must either "harmonize" with the character and her or his action or establish certain spatial and atmospheric connections between scenes.[42] On aesthetics and forms, Hou believes that the function of a play is to "harmonize" and "aestheticize" life, and goes so far as to suggest what subject matters are best represented and avoided for these purposes.[43] Chen thus argues that while Euro-American film theory connects aesthetics with forms, Hou associates aesthetics with representation and *rensheng* (life).

The term *rensheng* is a precarious concept in the context of Hou's *Methods,* an idea that I shall elaborate further in chapter 3. In one register, the term can simply be understood as a life process, that is, an act of life as it unfolds in time. In this sense, Hou could claim that in the theater, an act of play is best considered an act of life as it unfolds in the world as a stage.[44] However, the term *rensheng*, together with others such as Representation and Spirit—written in English and specifically capitalized as they would have been written in a philosophical essay—suggest that Hou might have in mind references from German philosophers, including Immanuel Kant (1724–1804), Johann Gottlieb Fichte (1762–1814), G. W. F. Hegel (1770–1831), Arthur Schopenhauer (1788–1860), and Friedrich Nietzsche (1844–1900).[45] German philosophical works were translated and circulated among Chinese intellectuals around the May Fourth Movement (1919), though it is unclear which philosopher Hou had in mind when he employed these terms. In general, however, *rensheng* can be understood in this context as "life-itself." During the life-process as it is experienced on a day-to-day basis, life is not palpable for the sentient body or perceiving subject. Yet life is instantiated as the life-process. Hence, when Hou talks about the power of the shadow play to harmonize and aestheticize life, he probably had in mind the idea that art has the power to inform and make palpable life so that the beholder could regard it and come to terms with it as an aesthetic experience. Chen therefore argues that the Chinese view of cinema ontology is a holistic philosophical system that regards *meixue* (aesthetics) as a *rensheng de taidu* (attitude of life). Therefore, the cinema—as a form of play-drama—cultivates such an attitude of life not through the mediation of film forms, but through an attempt to represent and elevate the quality and aesthetics of life.[46]

Based on this observation, Chen proposes the following:

> From the ontological perspective, the Chinese people see the "play" as the basis of the cinema, whereas the Westerners [Bazin and his followers] see the "shadow" [image] as the cinematic foundation. For the Chinese people, the "shadow" is simply a method by which the drama can be brought to its completion, whereas for the Westerners, the "play" is a concrete state of the "shadow." The Chinese people are preoccupied by ideas such as *xiju xing* (theatricality) and *wenxue xing* (literariness), whereas the Westerners are preoccupied by the difference between the long shot and montage. . . . [In short,] in China, the cinema is being studied as a totality seen from a direct objective view; in the West, the cinema is analyzed by means of abstraction and subjective observation.[47]

In their attempt to construct a Chinese ontology, Zhong Dafeng and Chen Xihe therefore presupposed and maintained a clear-cut East-versus-West dichotomy, which is symptomatic of the sociopolitical mindset during the mid-1980s: to assert Chinese originality and specificity as an alternative to the Euro-American West. On the one hand, by setting out to find cultural differences in theoretical thinking about film, Chen conveniently omits any discussions that may allow us to connect Hou's ideas with Bazinian ontology. Thus in the name of establishing a dialogue between Bazinian ontology and Hou's, Chen in fact starts from the assumption that the two schools of thinking are fundamentally different, deactivating any potential to allow negotiable elements to emerge. On the other hand, as Lagesse aptly points out, Chen's understanding of Euro-American theory is based on Henderson's presumed dichotomy between the Bazinian long shot and Eisensteinian montage, a view that reduces both theories to the level of film forms and aesthetics.[48] It is on the basis of this presumed dichotomy that Chen and Zhong both came up with their own rehistoricization of Chinese cinematic styles and film forms. The curious point is this: in their original writings, Hou Yao and Gu Kenfu both arrive at a proto-Bazinian notion of ontology, arguing that film forms are contingent upon the way reality is approached.

Approaching Reality

In this sense, Chen and Zhong's attempt to reconstruct a Chinese cinema ontology represents a missed opportunity to establish a productive dialogue between Bazinian ontology and the early film thinking in Shanghai. Hou's *Methods* was written as a screenwriting manual, and of course his primary objective in the book is to underline the importance of the screenplay and narrative structure in the creation of an entertaining, artful, and educational film. Yet, if we want to tease out the rather rarified discussion of cinema aesthetics, representation, and life in the first chapter of *Methods,* and compare it with a remarkably similar one in the writings of Hou's predecessor Gu Kenfu, we cannot simply take what these writers discuss on the textual surface as theoretical statements about ontology. Rather, we need to deduce what kind of cinema ontology is implied when they negotiate these problems.

Film criticism of this kind in the 1920s in fact responded to a political crisis. It was often written with a political agenda in mind: to rectify the misrepresentation of Chinese characters, society, and culture in Hollywood and European films, productions that were often referred to as the *ru Hua pia* (humiliation film; literally, films that humiliate the Chinese nation). In 1921, for example, Gu Kenfu started a new film magazine called the *Yingxi zazhi* [*Motion Picture Review*]. In his "Fakanci" [Inaugurating preface], Gu argues that the ultimate objectives of initiating a debate in the magazine were to "prevent hazardous films from being circulated" (i.e. representations of sexuality) and to "fight for the human dignity of the Chinese people in cinema."[49] Hence, by understanding the cinema as a tool that draws the spectators near reality and allows them to reflect upon their own moral conditions, Chinese filmmakers could improve the aesthetic quality of their productions, which would eventually be used as a tool to inculcate the Euro-American audience with the reality of Chinese life. Similarly, in *Methods,* Hou Yao argues that by identifying the proper sensuous excitements that could help cinematic spectators harmonize their conflicting desires, the cinema could aestheticize life by entertaining and elevating the human spirit.[50] In so doing, these film images would serve as a tool to rectify unfavorable representations of Chinese characters.[51]

In this light, both Gu and Hou had a common objective: to represent the life of the Chinese people truthfully, first in the Shanghai productions, then in Hollywood cinema. Underneath the seeming preoccupation with drama, narrative structure, and screenwriting techniques, they share an underlying assumption that the cinema is apprehended by spectators as a form of reality, and as a result, is taken as a piece of evidence that contributes to an audience's knowledge about a political community and its culture. Neither Gu nor Hou was formally trained as a rhetorician, however, so the question of what they mean by reality, and how such a reality forms a relationship with the spectators, leaves much room for further debate.

Nevertheless, Hou Yao's theorization of the relationship between the cinema and theater can be traced back to Gu's preface. At first glance, it does seem that Gu considers the shadow play a kind of play, drama, or theater. In the opening paragraph, he argues:

> The moment we enter the theater and watch a tragedy being performed, tears will come out from most of us. If the play performed is a comedy, we will all laugh heartily. What is the reason? The reason is that a well-performed play can touch its spectators, *ru shen ru qi jing* (as though their bodies have entered the scene itself).[52]

By starting from an analysis of the spectators' affects in the theater, Gu appears to hold the assumption that the cinema is a form of theater. Yet, the core of the argument in this opening paragraph is not the theater itself, but the reason why such affects are produced by watching someone perform a dramatic action. Hence, the key to understanding what Gu wants to argue is his last sentence: "as though their bodies have entered the scene itself."[53] In other words, in front of the performance, the entire bodies of these spectators apprehend a state of consciousness, an idea that seems to be not entirely far from Bazinian ontology, with the exception of the use of the word *ru* (as though). What Gu suggests here is therefore a distance between the state of consciousness one apprehends in lived reality, and the state of consciousness one arrests in front of a performance.

Notice that in Gu's analysis, he has carefully constructed a schema of how the readers should understand the word *xi* (play, drama, theater, or performance):

> *juchang* (theater) *banyan* (performance) of a *beiju/xiju* (tragedy/comedy; i.e. the dramatic text) *qing* (affects)

In other words, the theater is an architectural or institutional apparatus in which a performance (of a dramatic text or human action) affects the spectators, as though they had apprehended a state of consciousness. Hence, the ontological link that Gu wishes to explore is not the dramatic text itself, but the relation between the performance, the affects, and the state of consciousness. In this sense, unlike Chen and Zhong's version of Chinese ontology, Gu's ontological essay (if we call it that) gives less emphasis to the dramatic forms and structure than to the reason such consciousness can be apprehended.[54]

In the following paragraph, Gu further narrows down his focus:

> Play-drama is an entertainment. When one is entertained, one is easily affected. It is because at the moment of being entertained, one surrenders everything in the world and pays attention to only the object that entertains. [In such a condition] one does not have *guannian* (concept, presupposition, or point of view) to analyze one's *xin* (heart or psychological state).[55]

What Gu suggests is that in the process of being entertained, the spectators have given up the state of consciousness they have grasped outside the performance, and instead take what is being performed and the affects it produces in their bodies as their own consciousness. For Gu, in the theater, the spectators are not preoccupied with conceptualizing what they see, sense, read, and feel (for example, as a dramatic text or an aesthetic experience), but as an affective state that excludes reasoning and interpretation.

With this in mind, Gu then argues that human beings have a determination to improve the means by which this state is achieved. If one maps out the development of different theatrical and dramatic forms around the world, one can see an evolutionary trend of moving towards a state of *bizhen* (approaching reality). For Gu, in older theatrical forms the performer knows her or himself as a performer, and likewise, the spectators know themselves as spectators. However, in more advanced theatrical forms, such as the cinema:

> The performer forgets her or himself as a "performer," and instead believes her or himself as the "person in the dramatic action" by having the same emotions the character has. Meanwhile, the spectator also treats her or himself as the "person in the dramatic action." Like being in the dramatic action itself, the spectator can be in an affective state a thousand times more powerful than in the older theatrical forms.[56]

Gu argues that in human history, theatrical innovations were made possible by means of technological improvements, literary ameliorations, and scientific progress. However, the shadow play surpasses all other traditional forms by means of mechanical reproduction. Because of that, it saves the money, time, effort, and cost of restaging the same play over and over again. It also preserves a performance that can put large numbers and even generations of spectators into the same affective state.[57]

Scholars of Chinese art and literature can rightly point out that the term *bizhen* has been a subject of debate among artists, writers, and critics for centuries. I do not intend to trace Gu's use of this term along the lines of Chinese art criticism, primarily because Gu probably took this term from a more vernacular perspective. We can, however, learn something from the historical debate itself. As Wen C. Fong suggests, the term *bizhen,* despite its multiple interpretations, never quite assumes the European meaning of "mimesis." For Fong, *bizhen* in the context of Chinese art criticism does not necessarily imply a proximity between the appearance of the painted image and the reality it represents; rather, it refers to an affective state that the painting is capable of producing in the sensorium of the beholders, one that either recalls their affective state when they apprehended the image-consciousness in their lived reality before, or inserts such affective state into them as though they had been there.[58]

With this in mind, we can begin to locate an intersection between Gu's notion of cinema and Bazin's—that they both suggest a delicate distance between the image-consciousness, as it is apprehended as an affective state, and the reality into which such image is capable of drawing the spectators. As Andrew and Elsaesser point out, after the publication of "Ontologie de l'image photographique" ["The Ontology of the Photographic Image," 1945], Bazin has often been accused of naïvely and simplistically believing that the cinematographic image is reality, or at least, a window that opens into a reality that is in fact an ideologically inflected construction.[59] Yet, when examined more closely, Bazin's writings carefully configure the relationship between the cinematographic image and reality as an aporia, very often—as Serge Daney would claim—with "mathematical" precision.[60]

Andrew, based on his careful examination of the notes and marginalia in Bazin's copy of Jean-Paul Sartre's *Imaginaire* [*The Imaginary*, 1940], which Bazin might have purchased shortly after the book's publication, argues that Bazin's formulation of cinema ontology is based on Sartre's notion of the relationship between the photograph and the image-consciousness.[61] In the second chapter of *The Imaginary*, Sartre discusses how he came to apprehend the image of his friend Pierre, based on a photograph of Pierre. For Sartre, the "photo, taken in itself, is a *thing*." Nonetheless, the photograph is merely an analogon; it "lacks life: it gives perfectly the external characteristics of Pierre's face; it does not capture his expression." Here, as in Hou's *Methods,* life is best understood as life-itself; but to add to this, Sartre, based on the thoughts of Henri Bergson, sees life as being instantiated and made palpable as the life-process unfolds in time. Despite being a chemical and mechanical trace of Pierre, life seems to be absent from the photograph; such absence generates in the perceiving subject an intention to apprehend the image of Pierre, one that corresponds to the subject's perception of the living Pierre, or, the Pierre that exists in time. Sartre argues that such intentionality to generate a mental image (of Pierre) is so powerful that the materiality of the photograph is often overlooked. For the perceiving subject, what she or he sees is indeed Pierre himself.[62]

As Andrew argues, Bazin does not completely agree that in the cinema, this process of image-apprehension is a mental one. It is because what the photographic image preserves is not merely a lifeless analogon, or an index (one of the most popular ways by which Bazin is understood) that refers to a living object. Rather, it embalms a passage of time, a moment of transformation from life, which immanates from the photographed object, to the very instant prior to the advent of death—understood as the moment when the camera shutter is triggered and the trace of a life that is no longer is registered.[63] Yet, such transformation is not to be understood as a passage of linear time, but a measurement between life in its living state and the instant of its cessation—and with it, the cessation of time—that the camera's trigger calls forth. In this sense, what the cinematographic image envelops is a threshold between life and death, one that opens a measurement in depth between linear time and the very concept of Time (*durée*) by making palpable the potentiality of both its cessation and its coming into being. In fact, by making Time palpable as it is being represented in time, reality, which is actually absent from the photographic image, immanates from the image and is apprehended by the spectators in its totality and immediacy: as here and now. What is at stake in Bazin's ontology is therefore neither photographic indexicality nor mimesis, but the temporality that is made palpable by the trace of reality the photographic image registers in the process of mechanical reproduction.

But the role mechanical reproduction plays in the encapsulation of reality is a debatable question. As I mentioned earlier, Gu and Hou acknowledge that mechanical reproduction is a technology that makes it convenient, economical, and scientifically precise to preserve a performance, disseminate it to a large audience, and preserve it for future generations. Yet, neither photographic indexicality nor mimesis is configured as the conceptual basis of their understanding of approaching reality. For Gu, mechanical reproduction preserves the potentiality of a performance that would put future spectators into the same affective state. But the focus of Gu's argument is not on the photographic image as an index, but the performance itself. In his argument, the performance imitates reality and a powerful imitation (as a performance) allows the spectators to get close to, or approach, reality. The way Gu defines a successful performance is unique. If the European notion of mimesis is commonly (mis)-understood as a form of suspension of disbelief, Gu's notion of *bizhen* is based on a suspension of knowledge, that is, the knowledge that the performer is only a performer and the spectator is only a spectator. The character is therefore a vehicle that conveys the actor's response to the affective state in a real (dramatic) situation—i.e. the emotions—to the dramatic action, which produces the same affective state among the audience. Yet, no matter how close—or in fact, how far—the representation is in relation to the appearance of the reality it seeks to represent, a successful performance can always allow the spectators to suspend their knowledge and succumb to their belief through their affective state. In other words, mechanical reproduction is indeed a necessary condition in the constitution of the shadow play, but it is not in itself an entry point into reality. What it does is preserve and convey a powerful performance that can put the spectators into a shared affective state, as though their sentient bodies have lived it.

In comparison, in *Methods,* Hou delves more deeply into the notion of life. He argues:

> Life is best understood as a series of performances. It performs those phenomena such as happiness and sadness, union and separation, life, death, and illness, strength and weakness, fullness and emptiness, lost and found, rise and fall. Seeing a life as a drama, a drama is like a life itself.[64]

As this point suggests, by seeing drama as a "miniature of life," the spectators can use a play to critique, adjust, and aestheticize life. Nonetheless, Hou Yao is not referring to the performance's mimetic power to imitate a life-process, but to a performance that makes *rensheng de xianxiang* (the phenomena of life) palpable. For Hou, the shadow play goes one step further than the staged theater because the photographic image does not imitate; it captures life and replays it, so that the spectators could approach reality. As Hou puts it, "while other theatrical forms use the stage as a stage, the shadow play uses the universe as the stage." In this respect, when Hou talks about the play-drama as the core of cinema, he has in mind not an imitation of a life-process; rather, he believes that life can be preserved and re-presented as a palpable image, by which the spectators can grasp what he calls the "human Spirit."[65]

The salient fact here is that the cinema reveals to its spectators what gives life, or what Giorgio Agamben would call a "spark of life," that would otherwise be concealed from the eyes and sentient bodies of the spectators without the aid of the photographic medium.[66] In this light, Bazin, Gu, and Hou arrive at an intersection in their respective processes of wrestling with the intricate relationship between the photographic image, the life-process it preserves, and the reality—i.e. life as it unfolds in time—that is made palpable in the process of image-apprehension. Yet, to push this one step further, Gu Kenfu and Hou Yao's fascination with such an ontological problem was a response to their concern about the dignity of Chinese life that seemed to be lacking in Hollywood's image of China and its people. For Gu and Hou, the problem with Hollywood's representation of Chinese characters and culture did not necessarily lie in these films' failure to imitate the appearance of Chinese life, but in the absence of life as represented in these photographic images. Their concern is whether cinematographic representation can be improved in such a way that both the Shanghai and Euro-American audiences could be put into a common affective state. In this sense, common affective states could allow these two audiences, film industries, and communities to work through what they perceive as a cultural difference, that is, as beings that share in them a life that immanates from their day-to-day existence.

The Temporal Dimension

My reading of Gu and Chen may help to establish a dialogue with one frequently-problematized dimension of Bazianin ontology—Bazin's seeming reliance on the mechanical reproduction and indexicality of the photographic image. In fact, if one reads Bazin this way, one easily perceives the crisis brought about by the digital image as a problem primarily based on the potential or actual absence of a human being or physical object to which the image refers.[67] In addition, the capability of the digital technology to offer a nonhuman perspective on spatial relationships (images that are too big or too small, too high or too low) problematizes our understanding of the anthropocentric notion of cinema—or at least, classical Hollywood cinema.[68] Nonetheless, as Elsaesser argues, Bazin never once referred to photographic indexicality; rather, he treats photography and its capability of preserving and re-producing the "imprint" of a physical object or being as a way to open up a new way of thinking about time—a problem most famously phrased by Bazin as "change mummified."[69]

What is at stake in Bazin's idea, then, is how the cinematographic image preserves time and reactivates it. What is captured in a photographic image, I want to stress, is not a state of being but a process of becoming—and with it, a passage of time—what Sartre calls an image's retentionality. The screening process, meanwhile, reactivates not only a state of being, but also a process of becoming in the past (that is, a passage of time that is no longer) that is re-enacted as the present that opens up new possibilities in the future—what Sartre calls the image's protentionality.[70] The photographic image captures and replays the passage from being in time to nothingness, and from time to the instant immediately before the cessation of time. Along these very lines, in his essay "Death Every Afternoon" (1958), Bazin's thoughts about the film *La course de taureaux* [*Bull Fight,* Myriam Borsoutsky and Pierre Braunberger, 1951], a documentary in which a scene captures a real death, inspire him to think further about the question of cinematographic time. He writes:

> [M]usical time is immediately and by definition aesthetic time, whereas the cinema only attains and constructs its aesthetic time based on lived time, Bergsoninan "*durée,*" which is in essence irreversible and qualitative. The reality that cinema reproduces at will and organizes is the same worldly reality of which we are a part, the sensible continuum out of which the celluloid makes a mold both spatial and temporal. I cannot repeat a single moment of my life, but cinema can repeat any one of these moments

indefinitely before my eyes. If it is true that for consciousness no moment is equal to any other, there is one on which this fundamental difference converges, and that is the moment of death. For every creature, death is the unique in moment par excellence. The qualitative time of life [*durée*] is retroactively defined in relation to it. It marks the frontier between the duration of consciousness and the objective time of things.[71]

In more recent European film theory, the temporal dimension was further explored by Gilles Deleuze and Giorgio Agamben. For Deleuze, the classical cinematographic image (the movement image) is apprehended as movement unfolds in time—making the spectators conscious of their own process of becoming as chronometric time unfolds itself.[72] Yet, such image-consciousness is also apprehended as an affect (affection image), and in this affective process, time is crystalized into a potentiality (crystal image) that folds back to the past and projects into the future.[73] More recently, Agamben introduced the notion of the *kairos* (the time it takes for time to end) into the discussion. *Kairos* is a concept of time mentioned in Paul's Letter to the Romans, which describes the moment Saul was being called (vocated) by the voice of the Messiah (from the end of time, or from a nonstate where time no longer exists), and is then returned to the earthly world to continue his secular vocations, as though he had never been called in the first place. Agamben argues that in ancient and medieval Judaic theology, the period of Paul's life during which he continues to fulfill his earthly obligations as though nothing had happened is in fact understood as a form of *kairos,* for when Saul is called by the voice, time ends. In other words, there is no such thing as an afterward after the end of time, only a conceptual measurement—that is, the time it takes for time to end. For Agamben, this is not a form of chronometric time that unfolds linearly, but a measurement in depth, a distance between the chronometric and the abyss where time—along with consciousness itself—ceases to exist.[74] What *kairos* configures is a potentiality that envelops time and its cessation in a state of indistinction—or in fact, more properly speaking, a nonstate, that is always ready, but yet to be actualized through a schismatic process.

Gu Kenfu does not go as far into the philosophical depth of time as those formulations proposed by Deleuze and Agamben. But when he discusses the benefits of mechanical reproduction in cinema, he argues:

When a famous actor dies, a play [more specifically, a performance] is normally considered a *juexiang* (literally, the last sound, but can also be

> understood as a reflection or a voice from the end [of time]). Yet, a film never dies. If one preserves it well, it will reenact this performance in clarity for decades.[75]

Gu probably did not have a complex philosophical reason to make such a statement. But from the perspective of the debates in film theory today, the performance of a dead performer would inevitably disappear into the depth of time, a memory that would only be reflected (from the end of time) through literary records or word of mouth. Then, we might also say that every performance in itself is a *juexiang*. After all, no performer can ever repeat or reenact the same performance in time. What the cinema can do is simply snatch a performance from the flow of time (a vocation) and preserve it for the purpose of future reenactments. Being encapsulated in the process of image-apprehension, for Gu, is an affective state that oscillates between an excitement for life and a nostalgia for death, that is, for life as a potentiality.

In a very similar manner, Hou argues:

> The shadow play not only has a *pupian xing* [capability or quality of being shared and distributed among a large audience] but also a *yongjiuxing* [temporal permanence]. A valuable film can be preserved for over a hundred years, in order that people from different historical periods could appreciate the art of those actors who performed in the past, the great [political] thoughts of the [film] author, and the delicately designed scenario.[76]

When Hou wrote this, he was most likely envisioning the cinema as an archive of remarkable performances. But again, read retroactively and retrospectively from the perspective of our understanding of cinematic time today, what Hou hints at is that the cinematographic image, as a trace of time, encapsulates not only a performance that deserves to be appreciated for generations to come, but also those political thoughts and artistic designs that instantiate a life that is no longer. As the cinema reenacts this life as though it were here and now, those great thoughts and creativity continue to live and give life to future generations.

Has the digital image put such a concept of time into a state of crisis? The current state of debate has a tendency to swing between two poles: an unequivocal yes or no. No, because commercially released feature films and many independent or amateur filmmakers still generally follow a certain expectation in perspectives, styles, narrational devices, and aesthetics, which emulate the mode of perception—and as a result, the affective state—that we are used to seeing in the photographic image.[77] Yes, because the digital camera no longer preserves an imprint of the physical object through optical perception; rather, its microchip analyzes and records the thermal energy emanated from light, which is then scrambled and stored as digital data. In this sense, each time the camera itself or a computer program shows the user an image, the process is no longer one of reactivating an indexical trace, but of recomposing the image by means of informational analysis. In addition, what seems to the user to be a simple process of touching up, animating, or transforming an existing photographic trace is in fact interfaced by the computer as an emulation of its analogue predecessor. What the computer does is recompose each image with the available information.[78] If we use a metaphor to make this technical process more understandable, the digital production process is analogous to storing the DNA of an individual, and the filmmaker repeatedly reconstructs the image of the human body or object in the editing and recomposing process. Likewise, what the spectators see is analogous to an avatar of the actor.

What I want to say here is not that the digital image has fundamentally changed our perception of time. It opens up a dimension in the way we think about time—not only in the cinema, but also in our lived reality—in the first place. Does an avatar constructed out of the stored information of the thermal energy of a person assume the same subjectivity and identity as the body from which the DNA was drawn? Does the dramatic action of this avatar really render a reactivation of an action preserved from the past, or is it a different one in a different time? Does the information that is stored into a hard drive, ignorant of the human perception of space-time (unless it is interfaced via the computer) have the capability of reenacting any form of space-time? Is the digital image simply a lifeless-timeless recomposition (not even a simulacrum)? Or does it activate a new spatiotemporal flow each time the image is recomposed in relation to our chronometric sense of time?

Let us look at another example. In his 2009 book *Wired for War*, P. W. Singer points out an interesting phenomenon. In recent years, he reports, the U.S. military has begun sending robots to carry out dangerous missions in Iraq and Afghanistan. In missions like these, a military officer sits in a control room in an office building in the United States and carries out a bombing or assassination by monitoring a digitally simulated image on screen. With this, Singer argues, war becomes a nine-to-five job. On the one hand, the whole point of this technology is to minimize not only injuries and death to U.S. personnel, but also the trauma associated with carrying out brutal killings. These soldiers can go home comfortably to play with their children and have dinner with their spouses without any sense of shame or guilt. On the other hand, their superiors often need to remind them that they are not playing a video game; in reality they are carrying out a serious mission that has an undeniable human dimension. Singer points out the incongruity between the soldiers' perception of a space-time that is carefully distantiated from their own—a suspension of the knowledge that the digitally rendered killing is really happening and an underlying belief that they are seeing a parallel universe—and a real-time connection between the computer button they press in their office and the life that is taken in that parallel universe. Singer argues that these soldiers are indeed traumatized by the moral implications of their actions, not only by their acts of killing, but also by the absence of the human affects that would normally accompany them.[79]

As we can see, then, the spatial-temporal dislocation between a recomposed image and the physical reality to which it is supposed to refer (via an interface that convinces us of their mutual referentiality) does have a profound impact on the way we understand how affects and image-consciousness are interrelated. Yet I want to emphasize that the digital image does not necessarily signal an ontological shift from its analogue predecessor; rather, it reminds us that Bazinian ontology—and the Shanghai critics' discussion of cinema ontology—are both based on a very particular concept of space-time, and in turn, on an underlying presumption about the direct correlation between action and affect that requires reconsideration and reconfiguration. I will address these questions further in the conclusion of this book.

Conclusion

To conclude this discussion, I want to return to a problem that opened this chapter: the presumed epistemic distance between China and the West. Chen Xihe and Zhong Dafeng's work between 1985 and 1986 overemphasized the cultural, linguistic, and epistemological specificities of Shanghai film criticism in the 1920s. They responded to a sociopolitical crisis of the mid-1980s: the perception that China, in order to assert its sociocultural integrity during its transition into a market economy that was largely modeled on the Euro-American mode of capitalism, had to insist that China was different from the World. Such imaginary incommensurability inspired these two film scholars to search for an epistemological space that could be reconstructed as a system of thought unique to the history of Chinese cinema, yet universalizable as an alternative to Bazinian ontology. However, in an attempt to claim that the Shanghai film critics and makers in the 1920s employed a critical lanague fundamentally different from that of the West, Chen and Zhong had inadvertently excluded any common ground between China and Euro-America. As a result, a cross-cultural dialogue was effectively shut down.

At the same time, I would not travel to the other pole of the argument by saying that Bazinian ontology and the ontological view implied by the writings of Hou Yao and Gu Kenfu are fundamentally the same. Rather, they both try to work through an aporia: the intricate relationship between the cinematographic image and reality. What fascinates these thinkers—in the case of Bazin, directly, and in the case of Gu and Hou, in a more subtle register—is the potentiality that is encapsulated in the process of mechanical reproduction, that is, the very potentiality of capturing a passage of time immediately before it ceases to proceed (or exist), i.e. the very transformation from being to nothingness, and of reactivating this moment as a spark of life that changes from nothingness to being. Such delicate distance makes Time palpable in its totality and immediacy, and the distance itself is cinema's approach to reality. What the digital image opens up are in fact the multiple gaps and inconsistencies in the process of human apprehension and perception, and with these gaps, the suggestion that there are more possibilities and variations, more potentialities on one's way to reality, than the photographic version of cinema ontology activates. In our approaches to reality, time may not be conceived of as having a beginning and an end, or as something that can be activated or deactivated; we might want to think about time afresh with concepts such as transposition, transference, reflection, inflection, inversion, reversion, shuffling, recomposition, counterpoint, and resequencing. Indeed, if the photographic image was once considered able to mummify time, we may want to reconsider it now as *time undead.* In this sense, the undead image revisits us from a nonstate in which time is suspended or irrelevant and we are at once obsessed by the lure of its vampiric eternity and the fear of its disappearance, a parallel universe that we have yet to find a vocabulary to analyze.

2 CINEMA OF THOUGHT

Directed Consciousness in Chinese Marxist Film Theory

IN THE 1930S, the version of approaching reality proposed by Gu Kenfu and Hou Yao was seriously challenged by a group of filmmakers and critics who began to employ Marxist vocabulary to reexamine both Chinese and Hollywood cinemas. For these emerging "left-wing" critics, films and their criticisms from the previous generation were not only shaped by the semicolonial conditions of Shanghai, but also engaged in the perpetuation and active construction of a political consciousness, that only capitalism, imperialism, and feudalism could continue to guarantee their spectators' material pleasure and political survival.[1] More importantly, these new critics believed that the film itself also has a consciousness: it thinks, feels, and actively instills its thoughts, feelings and perception of reality in the sentient bodies of its viewers. As intellectuals who became aware of the semicolonial inflection of their collective consciousness, these Marxist critics argued that they had a social obligation to reveal in their works the political reality that actively defined and informed their spectators' sensoria and the cinematographic experience they had enjoyed all along.

This politicized notion of approaching reality emerged in the Shanghai film magazines and newspapers in the spring of 1930, in response to the Japanese Kwantung Army's military invasions of Manchuria on September 18, 1931, and of Shanghai on January 28. The debate was eventually merged into a more widespread discourse on the *guofang dianying* (national defense cinema) by the summer of 1935, as further political confrontations between the Chinese and Japanese armed forces took place in Manchuria.[2] After 1949, many historians believed that Marxist film criticism in the 1930s determined the plots, tropes, narrational devices, and stylistic traits of the left-wing Shanghai cinema during that decade, a view that has been increasingly contested in recent years.[3] However, even though the actual impact of this Marxist discourse is debatable, it left an indelible mark on the sociocultural imagination of Chinese cinema and media for years to come.

Yet, when Marxist film theory first appeared between 1930 and 1932, it was dismissively labeled by screenwriter Huang Jiamo (1916–2004) as the *yingxing dianying* (hard film theory) or *yishi lun* (theory of consciousness), that is, a formulaic critique on the political correctness of a film's consciousness, with no regard for cinema as an aesthetic experience.[4] For Huang, Liu Na'ou (1905–40), and Mu Shiying (avant-garde literary writer and screenwriter, 1912–40), or even for Marxist film critic Wang Chenwu (1911–38), these "left-wing" intellectuals subscribed to a rather naïve notion of Marxism, largely based on their misreading, mistranslating, and misconstruing of Russian and Japanese texts in a fragmented and unsystematic manner.[5] In the following intervention, I demonstrate that Marxist film theory in Shanghai was far from a mishap of careless translation and guileless misunderstanding of Marxist theories and film criticisms from Europe, the Soviet Union, and Japan. Rather, it is best understood as a complex set of philosophical and conceptual inventions, and an intricate cross-cultural dialogue between the modes of Soviet, Japanese, and Chinese Marxism. Based on the Leninist notion of directed consciousness, these Marxist cultural producers, I argue, not only reformulated approaching reality and cinematographic temporality in political terms, but also addressed how the cinema, as a sociopolitical apparatus, embodies its own consciousness. With it, the cinema has the political agency to redefine the consciousness of its spectators by revealing the work that goes into the construction of their belief in the ontological consistency of life under capitalism, imperialism, and feudalism.

Historical Background: Film as an Educational Tool

Marxist film criticism, although it was always associated with the Chinese Communist Party (CCP), emerged out of a public belief that the cinema is a *jiaoyu gongju* (educational tool), an idea that was initially proposed and institutionalized by the Guomindang (Kuomintang [KMT] or Nationalist Party). In 1924, the newly reorganized KMT headquarters in Guangzhou (Canton) established the Zhongyang xuanchuan bu (Central Ministry of Propaganda or CMP), which devised a plan of nationalizing Chinese cinema as a propaganda machine. In 1926, the CMP moved to Nanking, as the KMT took over the control of the coastal provinces and established its central government there.[6] Between 1925 and 1929, the KMT invited an advisor from L'Unione Cinematografica Educativa (LUCE) from Italy to advise its ideologues on how to establish a similar institution to oversee the writing, production, distribution, and censorship of films.[7] In 1930, the Neizheng bu (Ministry of Interior) and Jiaoyu bu (Ministry of Education) formed the Guomin dianying jiancha weiyuan hui (National Film Censorship Committee or NFCC). Between 1930 and 1933, the CMP was reorganized into a semi-independent organization: the Zhongyang xuanchuan weiyuan hui (Central Committee of Propaganda or CCoP). The CCoP administered three areas in the film industry: (1) policy making via the Zhongguo jiaoyu dianying xiehui (National Educational Cinematographic Society of China or NECSC); (2) film censorship by incorporating the NFCC (renamed in 1933 as the Zhongyang dianying jiancha weiyuan hui [Central Film Censorship Committee or CFCC]) into its organization; (3) production of newsreels, educational films, and dramatic features through the Zhongyang dianying gu (Central Film Branch or CFB).[8]

In the private sector, KMT's centralization plan was facilitated by the synergy between Li Minwei (Lay Ming-wei, 1893–1953), the owner of the Hong Kong-based China Sun Motion Picture Co., and Luo Mingyou (Lo Ming-yau, 1901–67), the Beijing (Peking)-based national theater-chain owner, who at the time also acquired the Huabei (Hwapeh or North China) Film Company and the Great China Lilium (Da Zhonghua baihe) Film Company.[9] The result was a merger of all these companies into the Lianhua dianying gongsi, known officially in English as the United Photoplay Service (UPS), which was financed initially by bankers and politicians who occupied high positions in the KMT administration.[10] The company was registered with the Hong Kong government on October 25, 1930, but operated from both Shanghai and Hong Kong as a conglomerate of four studios: the China Sun (Minxin) Shanghai Studio (Studio 1; combined with Studio 3 as Studio 1 in 1934), the China Sun Hong Kong Studio (Hong Kong Studio; renamed Studio 3 in 1934), the Great China Lilium Studio (Studio 2), and the Lehua (Lo Hwa) Studio (Studio 3).[11] By 1934, it became the second most productive film company in Shanghai, after its rival the Star (Mingxing) Film Company.[12]

Nonetheless, how the cinema could be instrumentalized as a form of public education and what kind of message it should convey were points of debate. These two questions became politically urgent after the Japanese invasions between 1931 and 1932.[13] In response, filmmakers across the board formed the Chinese Association of Film Culture or CAFC. Many of its key committee members, including Tian Han (1898–1968), Xia Yan (1900–95), and Yang Hansheng (1902–93), were leading participants of the Zhongguo zuoyi xijujia lianmeng (Chinese League of Left-Wing Dramatists or CLLD).[14] Those CAFC and CLLD filmmakers who worked for the UPS produced and directed a number of socially conscious and commercially successful films, which were recognized and promoted by the CMP and NECSC as educational features.

The idea that the KMT authorities would sanction those films produced and directed by the left-wing dramatists may sound baffling at first. However, one may argue that some of the early Marxist thoughts on the cinema and sociopolitical revolutions were largely built upon the existing ideological infrastructure laid down by the KMT, under the guidance of ideologue Chen Gongbo (Ch'en Kung-po, 1892–1946). Ch'en was a key party member who supported KMT's Wuhan faction and its leader Wang Jingwei (Wang Ching-wei, 1883–1944), who, during the 1920s, was sympathetic to CCP's cause. Ch'en was initially attracted to Marxism, yet he found that the economic conditions in China were too fragmented for the Euro-American mode of capitalism to emerge—a precondition for the inception of the kind of class consciousness necessary for a socialist revolution. For Ch'en, capitalism in Shanghai and other trading ports was an imperialist imposition made possible by the semicolonial conditions there, which was in turn supported by the quasi-feudal economic infrastructure in the rural areas. Ch'en therefore argued that what China needed was, first and foremost, a social, economic, and political agency in order that a national consciousness could take form. He therefore proposed to reconstruct the Chinese nation as a collective production machine called a corporation, where individual biological (or one can say biopolitical) lives (as opposed to citizens) could be trained and turned into *guomin* (nationals), who would submit themselves to the nation as a unified political body. Despite the uneasy relationship between him and KMT's commander-in-chief Jiang Jieshi (Chiang Kai-shek, 1887–1975), Ch'en's idea was adopted by the KMT and put into practice by Chen Lifu (Li-fu Ch'en, 1900–2001), who would later on become the head of the NECSC.[15]

The adoption of Ch'en Kung-po's idea led to the launching of a nationwide sociocultural movement towards the end of the 1920s called the Xin shenghuo yundong (New Life Movement). The principle of the New Life Movement was to encourage individual lives to submit themselves to a series of state-sanctioned disciplines (*li*, rituals; *yi*, responsibilities; *lian*, frugality; and *chi*, shame). Such disciplines were supposed to regulate the sense-certainty and moral integrity of these individuals by instilling in their sensoria a consciousness that they were parts of the nation as a corporation (details of the New Life Movement will be discussed in chapter 3).[16] The New Life Movement gave rise to a new form of femininity: the *xin nüxing* (new women). For Chiang, the new women, as members of the industrially productive and biologically reproductive force, were supposed to be modern, sexually attractive, but morally pure.[17]

With the emergence of the new women, most UPS productions represent women as innocent country girls who are forced to migrate to the city. Then, in the city, they are corrupted by modernity and urbanity: they become sex workers, for example, or indulge themselves in capitalistic pleasures. After they have taken control of their roles as modern women, they become aware of their lack of frugality and shame. To redeem themselves, they either sacrifice themselves as revolutionary martyrs, all-encompassing mothers, or self-debasing wives, or return to the bucolic countryside in peace. In other words, these women, once having grasped a modern consciousness, go through the ritual of sacrificing themselves by fulfilling their socially designated political and biological responsibilities. Scholars of Chinese cinema have discussed this trope since the 1990s, and Zhang Zhen calls it "the modern girl versus the country girl." Based on Miriam Hansen's observation, Zhang argues that Shanghai cinema in the 1930s employs such a trope to negotiate the spectators' contesting opinions, experiences, affects, and ethical values associated with the shocks and pleasures of modernity, especially those excitations, moral dilemmas, uncertainties, and anxieties that were perceived as crises of femininity—or in fact, masculinity.[18]

Nevertheless, UPS' productions were considered not thorough enough for the Marxist intellectuals because the UPS, following NECSC's notion that the cinema is an educational tool, tried to use films to illustrate a new way of life as imagined by the urban bourgeoisie and rural landowners. In so doing, these films reinforced the political infrastructure and power of KMT's ruling classes by convincing viewers that imaginary solutions could be found within the established political system. Meanwhile, the left-wing film critics and makers saw the cinema as a social production that was part and parcel of the daily life-process of the viewers. For them, the cinematographic image is indeed apprehended by the spectators as a consciousness, and in this sense could approach a reality where these moviegoers would begin to become aware of the way capitalism, imperialism, and feudalism had molded their consciousness. A socially conscious cinema could therefore return these spectators to their life-process with a newly acquired awareness, and with it, they could eventually reach a state of *rengzhi* (understanding) and implement social changes.

Such a Marxist vocabulary was first introduced in 1930. That year, the *Mengya yuekan* [Seeding monthly], a journal in Shanghai that features essays on Marxist sociopolitical, economic, and cultural theories, published Lu Xun's (1881–1936) translation of Iwasaki Akira's (1903–81) article "Xiandai dianying yu youchan jieji" ["Modern Cinema and the Bourgeoisie"]. Iwasaki's essay not only introduced to the Shanghai intellectuals the language of Marxist cultural criticism from Japan, but also, through Lu Xun's commentaries, reconfigured key concepts in response to the semicolonial conditions in Shanghai. After the Japanese invasions, Marxist film writings began to appear in the *Shen Bao* [*Shun Pao* or *Shanghai News*], and screenwriter (and later on, director) Shen Xiling (1904–40) published one of the first film magazines devoted to Marxist film criticism, *Dianying yishu* [Film art]. Eventually, in 1932, in the process of converting itself to a sound-film studio and competing with its business rivals, the Star Film Company went through a financial crisis.[19] In view of the success of the socially conscious films made by the UPS, the studio executives of Star, Zheng Zhengqiu (1889–1935) and Zhang Shichuan (1890–1954), hired Tian Han, Xia Yan, and Yang Hansheng as screenwriters in hopes of producing their own version of socially progressive films.[20] They also published the *Star Monthly*, with the goal of assuming a leading position in advocating the most cutting-edge political thoughts in the industry. Indeed, it was in this magazine that the most significant part of the debate on Marxist film thinking took place.

Iwasaki Akira in Shanghai

A central idea in the Marxist film debate in the 1930s is *yishi*. This term is properly translated as consciousness, though it actually signifies a liminal space between awareness and consciousness in one's process of political awakening. In 1935, Mu Shiying commented dismissively:

> One might say that early Marxist criticism is a kind of criticism centered on an examination and discussion of consciousness. This was the time before the CLLD invaded the film industry. During this period, members of the

> CLLD were trying hard to infiltrate into the cinematic circle. On the one hand, they wanted to find a way to connect with those actors who migrated from the stage to the silver screen; on the other hand, they used the power of film criticism to demand from the film producers a progressive consciousness. They did not want any art; they only needed a political path and order. They saw the cinema as a very useful tool for propaganda. Instead of seeing their film criticism as a form of aesthetic critique, one might as well see it as a judgment on the [consciousness of the] screenplay. Their critical essays follow one formula: consciousness is equivalent to Marxism. For them, a film with a correct consciousness—rather than one that is aesthetically rich—is considered a distinguished production. Their critical standard is consciousness.[21]

Nonetheless, how one should understand *yishi* is a highly problematic matter. Historically, the term reached the Shanghai audience through a pluralistic semantic field, as a result of a series of translations between the Russian, Japanese, and Chinese languages. To a certain degree, the very term "*yishi*/consciousness" can be understood as what Lydia Liu would call a super-sign, a signifying unit constructed by throwing together two different semantic fields that were formerly unrelated to each other. The resulting super-sign often conveys a different set of meanings and implications than those generated from their linguistic sources. In our case, the new signifying unit *yishi*/consciousness suggests something that cannot be understood as entirely synonymous with—though close enough to—the Euro-American notion of consciousness.[22]

The construction of the super-sign *yishi*/consciousness in film criticism can be traced back to Lu Xun's translation of Iwasaki's "Modern Cinema and the Bourgeoisie."[23] Iwasaki's article is originally titled "Senden • sendō shudan toshite no eiga" [Propaganda: film as a tool for incitation, 1928], published initially in the Marxist magazine *Shinkō geijutsu* [Burgeoning arts], which was then included in his book *Eiga to shihon shugi* [Cinema and capitalism, 1930].[24] In the early 1920s, Iwasaki was a supporter of the shinkankakuha (new sensationist) writers and their Jun'eigageki undo (pure film movement), who advocated cinema as an independent visual art form that requires no verbal explanation from the *benshi* narrator. He then became a founding member and chair of the Nihon Puroretaria Eiga Dōmei (Proletarian Film League of Japan or Purokino), a Marxist filmmaking and theoretical movement that was disbanded by the Japanese government with the Peace Preservation Law in 1925.[25] It is in this article that the translating process between *yishi, ishiki* (the Japanese pronunciation of the characters for *yishi*) and consciousness offers a new set of interlinguistic definitions.

Iwasaki wrote his article in response to the accusation made by the rising militarist government in Japan that the Purokino filmmakers were propagating and inciting their followers to socialist beliefs. In his article, Iwasaki argues that Hollywood and Japanese cinemas had been historically conditioned as instruments of mass propagation of bourgeois consciousness.[26] They did so, however, not by preaching bourgeois values and ideas to their spectators. Rather, they produced mass entertainment that aroused bourgeois desires for wealth, sex, individual freedom, and submission to the state, nation, and religion. When these spectators became used to the idea that the pursuit and fulfillment of these desires were pleasurable, they demanded more films from their industries. In so doing, they inadvertently ensured that the production machine that promulgated these pleasures and the overall bourgeois social relationships that supported it would continue to thrive.[27]

For Iwasaki, the term *senden eiga* (*xuanchuan dianing* or propaganda film) is often used as a label to describe those educational documentaries that were exhibited free of charge in public assembly halls or school auditoria, such as the Purokino films. For the spectators, the fact that these films were available for free made transparent the *mokuteki ishiki* (*mudi yishi* or directed consciousness) of these films. Meanwhile, a commercially released tragedy about an aging mother who loses her only son in the war would only be seen as an entertainment that served no political purpose. Unlike the educational documentaries, these films were shown in regular movie theaters with admission fees. For Iwasaki, these viewers were not aware that they were "incited by a delicately directed piece of propaganda" precisely because "they exchanged for it with money."[28] Therefore, for Iwasaki, a film critic's task is:

> To identify and make visible those minute and hidden *mokuteki* (*mudi,* aim or directedness) of all kinds of films produced today. Sometimes, it may be too far for us to talk about a "directed consciousness." Some films only have a *keikō* (*qingxiang* or tendency) towards a certain *shumi* (*quwei* or taste). But such tendency towards a certain taste still has an important propagandist value.[29]

In his translation, Lu Xun grafted a term unquestionably from Japanese to Chinese: *mokuteki ishiki* (*mudi yishi* or directed consciousness).

Iwasaki inherited this term from a theoretical discussion on proletarian literature in Japan by Aono Suekichi in the magazine *Bungei sensen* [Frontline of art and literature] between 1926 and 1927.[30] The term has its root in Lenin's pamphlet *Shto delat'?* [*What Is to Be Done?*, written 1901, published 1902]. In this essay, Lenin argues that the working-class movements that emerged in St. Petersburg between 1895 and 1896 were made possible by a "spontaneous" form of class consciousness, a nebulous awareness of the existing social relations that defined these workers' political existence.[31] However, for Lenin, such spontaneous consciousness is only in its "*embryonic form*."[32] He argues that in their revolts:

> The[se] workers were losing their age-long faith in the permanence of the system which oppressed them and began . . . I shall not say to understand, but to sense the necessity for collective resistance, definitely abandoning their slavish submission to the authorities. But this was, nevertheless, more in the nature of outbursts of desperation and vengeance than of struggle. . . . Taken by themselves, these strikes . . . marked the awakening antagonisms between workers and employers; but the workers, were not, and could not be, conscious of the irreconcilable antagonism of their interests to the whole of the modern political and social system.[33]

Following Lenin's argument, Aono Suekichi, in his article "Shizen seichō to mokuteki ishiki" [Naturally generated and directed consciousness], argues that when the workers and farmers become aware of the set of social relations that generate their "dissatisfaction, anger, and frustration," such consciousness is only a form of *shizen seichō*, that is, consciousness generated by nature, a vague awareness that is driven by their common affectivity, which produces a sensation that remains to be explained and rationalized.[34] Aono suggests that intellectuals, writers, and critics need to "organize, manage, systematize, and critique" such naturally generated consciousness and reformulate it into a form of directed consciousness, a kind of intellectual understanding of the set of sociopolitical relationships and historical conditions that inform their day-to-day life-process.[35] In so doing, they can *chūnyū* (*zhuru* or instill) a more disciplined political modality in the lives of these workers.

In the context of the Peace Preservation Law, Iwasaki tried to find a language to critique state authority on the one hand, and justify turning cinema into an educational tool on the other. In his article, Iwasaki analyzes the different popular Hollywood genres as propaganda for American capitalist values. He then argues that these films might have been perceived as entertainment, though they in effect *kanshi* (*jianshi* or put under surveillance) and *seiyaku* (*jushu* or control) public affectivity not by acts of law, but by the very "capitalist production methods" of the films and the "bourgeois governance" by means of censorship.[36] In this light, Iwasaki suggests that *ishiki* (consciousness) has a modality, that is, a design that manifests itself through the state's power to survey and control public affectivity and opinions.

The Leninist turn embedded in Iwasaki's use of the word *ishiki* allows Lu Xun to pursue this problem further in terms of Shanghai's semi-colonial conditions. In fact, when the super-sign *ishiki*/consciousness is thrown together with the word *yishi*, two levels of complication arise. The first is a linguistic one. The word *yishi* is generally understood as an intermediary mode between sensory apprehension and full understanding. In this sense, an individual who *yishi* something has a certain schema in her or his mind and a sensation in her or his body, but she or he cannot fully articulate what the object is. Politically, it means that individuals become aware of, but without cognizing, a certain underlying principle that informs their day-to-day existence and social relations. Such indefinite social awakening will become rational knowledge only after the individual has received proper education. In this case, the term *yishi* corresponds to Lenin's understanding of spontaneous consciousness and Aono's naturally generated consciousness. In fact, Marxist writers in the 1930s employed the term *yishi* as a verb to indicate the meaning "to become aware of," and as a noun to signify "consciousness," thus creating a sliding scale between awareness and consciousness in its usage.

The second complication is a sociopolitical one. Lu Xun complains that Iwasaki has completely overlooked one problem: under the semi-colonial conditions of Shanghai, consciousness is a prosthesis grafted onto an individual's sentient body not only by the bourgeoisie, but by the imperialists during the process of colonization. In his translator's notes on Iwasaki's article, Lu Xun claims that he was initially inspired to translate Iwasaki's work by the film advertisements he saw in the Shanghai newspapers:

> On each Shanghai newspaper, there are always two large pages of film advertisements. One after another, they claim exaggeratedly that these [Hollywood] films were made with casts of over ten thousand actors and budgets of more than millions of dollars. They are [supposed to be] never-seen-before blockbusters. They are seductive, romantic, fragrant, erotic, fleshly,

> humorous, amorous, and passionate. These films feature strong, adventurous, brave, and chivalrous warriors [who fight against] gods and demons.[37]

For Lu Xun, Iwasaki has identified the bourgeois consciousness of these cinematic spectacles. But as exports with an imperialist ambition, these Hollywood productions had an additional impact on the Chinese spectators: they incited their desire to consume capitalist pleasures that were fundamentally unattainable by them as the subalterns. Lu Xun argues that the "fleshly" images of the Hollywood productions only made the colonized male spectators feel "helpless—ashamed of their filthiness," and by extension, impotence. And in order to overcome that sense of impotence, they would "hire White Russian sex workers" in order to prove to somebody that they could physically consume the sexual pleasures represented on screen.[38] In this light, these Hollywood films in fact generated displeasure, shame, and a sense of failure among the Chinese spectators. Such displeasure countered the very belief that these films were supposed to be entertainment. In the eyes of these viewers, if these films failed to entertain, the problem lay not with the films, but with their own sense of emasculation. Hence, in Shanghai, Hollywood cinema had the power to compel the colonized individuals to internalize, misrecognize, and perform with a sense of shame and failure as though these feelings were entirely innate in their sense-certainty.

It is tempting to read that Lu Xun is blaming only the colonizers for such emasculating images. But he asks further: without subscribing to the imperialist consciousness in the first place, would these Chinese male viewers ever feel any sexual incompetence and the need to overcome it under somebody's gaze? In other words, by proving to themselves that they could enjoy the sexual pleasures represented by these Hollywood films, these men somehow believed that they were proving to the colonizers that they were equal. In this light, Hollywood cinema instilled a directed consciousness in a Shanghai male spectator in the following manner: "It is because my colonizer's consciousness is mine, and by reconfiguring my consciousness, my colonizer's will inevitably change. It is also because my consciousness is always under the gaze of my colonizer's, and in order to convince myself that I am not impotent, I need to first convince my colonizer that I can enjoy not only his pleasure, but my displeasure, which is in fact inscribed in the cinematic experience as a form of universal entertainment. In short, as a man—that is, in the universal sense of it—I shall enjoy my impotence!"

Lu Xun further elaborates this by citing an incident reported in the *Shanghai News* on December 19, 1929.[39] According to this article, Douglas Fairbanks (1883–1939) refused to interact with the Chinese film industry during his visit to China. A week later, however, he entrusted the Japanese studio executives to the arrangement of his itinerary in Japan, which was regarded by the Shanghai film industry as a humiliation. In addition to this, film critics were also deeply offended by the representation of a Mongolian prince in a film Fairbanks produced, *The Thief of Bagdad* (Raoul Walsh, United Artists, 1924). In the literary version of the story in *One Thousand and One Nights,* the Mongolian prince is supposed to climb up to the moon and wed a princess. In the film, however, the prince falls from the ladder to heaven in order that the white character Ahmed (Fairbanks) can wed the Arabic princess. As a result, the Shanghai dianying gonghui (Shanghai Film Union) published a letter to Fairbanks urging him to use his future productions to "guide all the people in the world to love and respect each other" and to understand the kindness and sophistication of the people in China, a "nation with four thousand years of civilization."[40] In response, Lu Xun writes:

> This shows exactly the spirit of the people of an ancient empire that is being colonized, an idea with which only those who reside in a foreign concession can come up. Because these people are colonized to submission, they see themselves as being useless. They can only beg their colonizer—with sincere humility—to tell the world about them. Nonetheless, since these people have "four thousand years of civilization," their request for Fairbanks to communicate that to the world is also a form of pride. Such a mixture of pride and humility is the characteristics of the people of a fallen ancient empire.[41]

The Shanghai Film Union published this letter to prove to itself that it could demand that Fairbanks change his consciousness, in much the same way the Chinese male film-viewers attempted to bolster their self-esteem by sleeping with white Russian sex workers. And in so doing, the Union somehow believed that it had proven to Fairbanks that it had a consciousness of its own. In other words, the subaltern's consciousness is constantly under the gaze of the colonizer's, and it is grafted onto the subaltern's body not as a form of sense-certainty, but as a form of sense-uncertainty, something that requires constant reassurance and supervision from the colonizer.[42]

Shen Xiling: Film and Its Consciousness

When film critics like Shen Xiling and Wang Chenwu began to employ the vocabulary outlined in Iwasaki's "Modern Cinema and the Bourgeoisie" in their writings after the Kwantung Army's invasion of Shanghai in 1932, Liu Na'ou criticized them, calling the left-wing film critics' view a *neirong pianzhong zhuyi,* that is, a principle that overemphasizes a film's *neirong* (contents), as opposed to its *xingshi* (forms) and image.[43] In fact, Huang Jiamo and Mu Shiying complained that the hard film theory overlooks the relationship between the cinematographic image and *xianshi* (reality, a compound word composed of *xian* [present] and *shi* [concreteness]—or present in its concreteness), and the state of absorption when the image draws the spectator into the reality it *miaoxie* (describes).[44] In other words, for these critics, left-wing intellectuals only offer a naive critique of a film's narrative and representation; they completely ignore the delicate distance between the cinematographic image and reality, which maintains the ontological consistency of the cinematographic experience.

When examined more closely, however, this line of Marxist discussion on cinema scrutinizes not simply the narrative and representation of individual films, but the way the spectators apprehend the cinematographic image as a consciousness, and eventually misconstrue it as their reality. Understood retrospectively and retroactively, the mode of Marxist film criticism from Shanghai during this period resonates with the theory of the cinematic apparatus, proposed in France by Jean-Louis Baudry, Jean-Luc Comolli, and Jean-Paul Narboni in the early 1970s, which examines the relationship between the cinematographic *appareil* (apparatus, i.e. a mechanical apparatus), which also serves as a sociocultural institution that interpellates individual spectators as political subjects, and the *dispositif* (ideological apparatus), that is, the structure of knowledge that informs the constitution of the mechanical apparatus and puts into action a process of intersubjective interactions.[45] In other words, the discourses of capitalism, imperialism, and feudalism constituted a structure of knowledge that convinced the Shanghai spectators in the 1930s to apprehend the cinematographic image (e.g. of Hollywood) as a here and now that gave them a sense-(un)certainty, one that the mechanical apparatus itself constantly reaffirms, in the name of the colonizer, as the only mode of biological and political existence that can guarantee their survival and pleasure. What cinema does effectively is conceal the distance between the image-consciousness and the actual sociopolitical relationships that produce and inform it.

In this sense, Marxist film critics in the early 1930s reconfigured and revised approaching reality as a political concept. In 1932, Shen Xiling wrote the article "Zhongguo dianying zhi weiji yu xin lujing" [The crisis and new path of Chinese cinema] in his magazine *Film Art.* At the time, he worked for the Tianyi (Unique) Studio and was developing his first new-women screenplay *Nüxing de nahan* [*Cry of Women,* 1933], which he would eventually bring to the Star Motion Picture Company for production. In his article, Shen writes:

> If art is an instrument for *biaoxian* [expressing, or showing and revealing] the *zhenxiang* [truth, or real appearance] of human feelings, rationality, and will, it should become a body through which the reality of the social conditions (that is, its danger and safety) and the people's emotions (that is, their sorrow and happiness) should factually manifest themselves. Therefore, art must be a reflection of a specific society at a specific time. A work of art that does not reflect the specific society that produces it is not a real piece of art.
>
> However, art is not simply a mirror that reflects the society. We can see clearly that in our society, when its productivity increases and when its objective political consciousness becomes its own handcuffs, a new social force would arise. This kind of internal dialectics in our social development must be reflected upon our cultural movement. This kind of new social force, at the time when the cultural movement emerges, will inevitably facilitate our positive social transformations through its dialectical exchanges. . . . [Hence,] art has its own social mission, and the same can be said about the cinema.[46]

In this passage, Shen Xiling proposes a series of ways by which the cinema could be understood; but the series itself could also be seen as steps by which the cinematographic image approaches reality. In the very beginning, Shen argues that the cinema could be regarded as an instrument that *biaoxian* (shows and reveals) the *zhenxiang* (real appearance) of "human feelings, rationality, and will." The two terms that he uses, *biaoxian* and *zhenxiang,* are precarious ones. At first glance, they could mean "to express the truth." Yet *biaoxian,* composed of two monosyllabic words *biao* (to show) and *xian* (to reveal), conveys rather the sense of making visible or palpable something that would otherwise be concealed by the ideological apparatus. Meanwhile, *zhenxiang* never quite means the same thing as the Euro-American concept of truth; rather, it signifies real or actualized phenomena, precisely those that produce "human feelings, rationality and will."[47] As an instrument that makes palpable what the sentient bodies feel, think and desire, the cinematographic image is indeed best understood as a "body" with a consciousness, where the "reality of the social conditions . . . and the people's emotions . . . should factually manifest themselves."[48]

In one register, therefore, Shen Xiling argues that the cinematographic image is a "reflection of a specific society at a specific time," that is, it gives the spectators a mirror image of the sociopolitical and historical conditions that inform their consciousness. Yet in another register, the cinematographic image does not merely reflect; as a consciousness, it is an instantiation of the existing sociopolitical relationships, and in fact, the very "internal dialectics" that constitute and push forward these relationships in a historical process. Shen's understanding of the cinematographic image has two implications. First, contrary to the accusations made by Huang Jiamo, Liu Na'ou, and Mu Shiying, Shen does not regard a cinematographic image as a piece of rhetoric; it could neither inculcate the spectators directly with political ideas, nor reconfigure their political consciousness by directly intervening with the real sociopolitical relationships that inform it. Nonetheless, as an aesthetic experience, it can draw the spectators closer to reality by making palpable the sociopolitical conditions that actively shape their sense-(un)certainty. Furthermore, as an embodiment of the collective consciousness, the cinema instantiates the internal dialectics that set into motion the historical process of these discursive intersections.

Shen Xiling, not unlike Gu Kenfu and Hou Yao before him (see chapter 1), did not believe that the camera, by means of its mechanical reproduction, could somehow access the truth, either as defined by Lenin as the objective reality that is independent of human sense-perception, or by Marx and Engels as an Idea that cannot be fully grasped, but can be approached by understanding the distance between it and the reality one senses and perceives.[49] This in fact marks a difference—at least at first glance—between Shen Xiling's theory and those proposed by two of his Soviet predecessors in the 1920s, Dziga Vertov (1896–1954) and Sergei Eisenstein (1898–1948). Vertov and Eisenstein based their theories of montage on the assumption that the camera captures reality as the basic creative material, and that by juxtaposing pieces of reality against each other, the images and their interstices produce a sensual shock in the spectators' sentient bodies. For Vertov, it is in those interstices that the spectators come to grasp the objective truth, what Vertov calls "life caught unawares."[50] Shen Xiling, however, was fascinated with the works of Vsevolod Pudovkin (1893–1953), whose film *Potomok Chingiskhana* [*Storm Over Asia*, 1928] was shown in Shanghai in the beginning of 1932, and became the top box-office hit of that year.[51]

What attracted Shen to Pudovkin's writing, as opposed to those of Vertov and Eisenstein, is Pudovkin's conceptualization of the cinematographic image not as a construction of individual shots of mechanically reproduced reality, but as an overall "scenario," an idea that corresponds to Gu Kenfu and Hou Yao's notion that the performance as a whole constitutes the cinematographic experience. For Pudovkin, this cinematographic whole is broken down—in the process of editing—into sequences, scenes, and shots that are structurally related to the overall scenario, and each shot "directs the attention of the spectator to [a] detail which is, at the moment, important to the course of the action."[52] Yet, while most films—especially Hollywood films—construct a set of structural relationships that convey dramatic continuity, editing can likewise control "the 'psychological guidance' of the spectator by directing their attention to conceptual relations" such as contrast, parallelism, symbolism, simultaneity, and leitmotif (reiteration of theme).[53] In this sense, for Shen, the cinematographic image can redirect the spectator's attention to those structural relations that are usually concealed by the capitalist *dispositif.* In other words, the cinematographic image cannot reveal the truth; rather, it helps expose the "work" that informs the way the spectators apprehend it as a consciousness.

As Mu Shiying observed, however, a peculiar philosophical problem arises in Shen's discussion; individual films are divided into two categories: those with a consciousness and those without. In this light, Mu writes that for Shen, consciousness becomes synonymous with Marxism, that is, a film that has a consciousness is understood as one that conveys a Marxist political message.[54] Nonetheless, what Shen suggests is that every film has a consciousness, and a film that is aware of its own consciousness makes palpable those social relationships that inform the reality it approaches. Meanwhile, a film that remains unaware of its consciousness conceals this intricate distance between the cinematographic image and reality by masking the historical process that fabricates the seeming totality and immediacy of its bourgeois worldview. It is in this light that a film sees, smells, feels, thinks, and acts; in short, it exercises an active agency in grafting its own consciousness onto the spectators' bodies as prostheses.

Redirecting Consciousness: The *Star Monthly*

Based on Shen Xiling's idea of cinematographic consciousness, producers, screenwriters, and filmmakers at the Star Motion Picture Co. launched a critical debate on how progressive filmmakers in Shanghai could actively reveal the consciousness of Chinese cinema and its spectators. In the first issue of the *Star Monthly*, Star's executive Zheng Zhengqiu published his article "Ruhe zoushang qianjin zhi lu?" [How to follow a progressive path?, 1933]. In his abstract, Zheng wrote:

> From changing ourselves in accordance with the changes of our [social] environment to transforming our environment itself, I was inspired to cry out the slogan "*Sanfan zhuyi*" [Three-anti's principle: anti-capitalism, anti-imperialism, and anti-feudalism]. Stop being obsessed with your pursuit of beauty [on the Hollywood screen]. Let's oppose the self-conflicting phenomenon of "double censorship." Let's unite our allies together and drive our enemies out [of our nation]![55]

Zheng Zhengqiu's declaration may sound mechanical and naïve at first, and has been seen since the time of its publication as the manifesto of the Chinese left-wing film movement.[56] Far from being simplistic, however, his statement changes the underlying assumption of the humiliation-film criticism in the 1920s by suggesting that Chinese filmmakers could actively make palpable the directedness of the modality of consciousness embodied by Hollywood cinema, instead of waiting for the American producers to change their opinions. Second, in line with Iwasaki's argument, Zheng suggests that cinema's potential to transform actual social relations remained unfulfilled in the 1930s for two reasons: (1) that the viewers had been directed under the imperialist gaze to pursue capitalist pleasures, ones that were in fact unattainable by the Shanghai spectators; (2) that the cinema was being censored actively by the CFCC and the foreign consulates (in their respective concessions, as a form of extraterritorial power) on the one hand, and passively by the bourgeois mode of production and governance on the other; both of which put public affectivity and opinions under surveillance. In fact,

Zheng calls state and foreign censorships *qianjin de zhangwai* (obstacles against progression).[57]

However, the real obstacle against progression, for Zheng, was the interlocked relationship between capitalism, imperialism, and feudalism, an idea that he had in fact borrowed from the writings of Ch'en Kung-po. For most Marxist writers of the time, the impact of capitalism and imperialism on Chinese cinema and culture was relatively obvious; however, the significance of the feudal infrastructure in the rural areas in the process of industrialization, colonization, and modernization in the urban centers had been grossly overlooked.[58] Historians today tend to regard the term anti-feudalism as an overly encompassing term that emerged around the 1890s. By that time, feudalism had long ceased to be the economic mode in China. But despite what Marx predicted, its disappearance was not followed by the emergence of capitalism. Rather, although land was traded as a commodity, it was still accumulated and acted as a political sphere of influence as in a feudal economy. However, capitalist cities such as Shanghai and Canton depended on a steady supply of human and natural resources from the countryside, which in turn relied on the status quo of the feudal economy in the rural areas. Immediately after the May Fourth Period (1919–21), feudalism was a label that both intellectuals and popular writers would attach to this semifeudal and quasi-capitalistic state, and the term gradually came to be used to describe anything "premodern."[59] In his declaration, Zheng argues that capitalism and imperialism made their way into urban China, but they could not flourish without the feudal social relations in the country that facilitated its propagation and dissemination.[60]

In response to Zheng's call for a critique of feudalism, Wang Chenwu, in his "Zhongguo dianying zhi lu" [The road of Chinese cinema, 1933], argues that the cinema had been historically conditioned as a commodity, which concealed its directed consciousness under capitalism.[61] In the beginning of his essay, Wang discusses Iwasaki's thesis in the first chapter of his book *Cinema and Capitalism*, "Shihon shugi eiga hatsutatsu shi" [History of the development of capitalist cinema], part of which was translated in the second issue of the *Star Monthly*.[62] Here, Wang points out that capitalist filmmakers have made a mistake by identifying cinema as a *shinkō geijutsu* (*xinxing yishu* or burgeoning art). In his view, since 1905, American cinema had led the world to develop the cinematic institution into a form of "commerce, corporation, and a profitable capitalist commodity," not art.[63] He quotes Iwasaki:

> The film business has already gone through the era of monopolization. Many small production companies have been consolidated into big film studios. Since the emergence of the sound film, some studios have been further consolidated in order to put into practice the capitalist [ambition] to conquer [the world] by means of capital centralization.[64]

Nevertheless, for Wang, capitalism was not the core of the problem with the Chinese film industry (unlike that of Japan). Wang saw that the Chinese economy was under the control of the Euro-American and Japanese imperialists, who wished to turn China into a market for their products and a supplier of raw materials for their industries. They extended their power into the rural area by using the *fengjian canyu* (remnants of feudalism) as their infrastructure. Wang believed that the cinema was one of the few industries that had yet to be completely controlled by the imperialists, because it had a "cultural and linguistic dimension, and Euro-American products were by no means perfect substitutes for domestic productions." In addition, Hollywood studios had to rely on Chinese distributors to release their films in China. In this sense, although the Chinese bourgeoisie had been "held hostage by the imperialists and the remnants of feudalism," the situation was not entirely irreversible.[65]

Both Zheng and Wang, in their respective ways, felt the urgent need to activate cinema's potential to reveal the interlocking relationship between capitalism, imperialism, and feudalism. Zheng did not believe that filmmakers could do this without reclaiming the means of production and reorganizing the consciousness of the cultural producers and the films they produced. To this end, progressive filmmakers could not possibly rely on a state organization like the CCoP; rather, Zheng wished to mobilize all those cultural producers and audiences who had become aware of the directedness of their consciousness as the *dazhong* (masses). But in order to produce such masses, filmmakers had to seek opportunities to instill a *dazhong yishi* (mass consciousness) in the viewers in public spaces outside the bourgeois-controlled movie theaters and in intellectual forums such as film magazines and newspapers, that is, by actively constructing new social spaces and institutions that could *jieru* (intervene or mediate) or even *jianduan* (interrupt) the bourgeois governance.[66]

On this note, Zheng's business partner Zhang Shichuan argues in his article "Chuanshengtong li" [From the loudspeaker, 1933] that the construction of an anti-capitalist, anti-imperialist and anti-feudal cinema required mass professionalization. In light of the Nanking government's notion that the cinema was a tool of education, mass professionalization involved teaching the existing directors, technicians, and actors that their job was to serve the masses. It also involved training members of the masses as actors, directors, and technicians so that the means of production could be handed to them. Zhang Shichuan believed that left-wing filmmakers should collaborate with each other and come up with a more effective means of storytelling, that is, an alternative narrative system to the Hollywood paradigm, one that would allow the cinema to embody a new kind of consciousness.[67]

Here, the pluralistic meaning of the super-sign *yishi*/consciousness is crucial in that the members of the masses would have yet to apprehend a reconfigured mode of consciousness in cinema; rather, they would simply become aware of a set of social relationships that informed their consciousness. In other words, mass cinema does not offer a solution; instead, it merely intervenes with the spectators' consciousness by making palpable the ideological work that defines it. In this sense, the intricate distance between the cinematographic image and reality would be opened up, and its disconcealment would instantiate a potentiality from which new configurations of consciousness could be produced.

Furthermore, Zhang Shichuan suggests that producing a cinematographic image that can reconfigure the delicate distance between image and reality, even under the control of filmmakers who are determined to serve the masses, is a matter of how the actual scenario as a whole is structured. This problem was exemplified by the socially conscious films produced by the UPS that featured the *xin nüxing* (new women). In his article "Dianying zuiyan—bianxiang de dianying shi ping" [A critique on cinema—or, a criticism on contemporary cinema, 1933], Zheng Boqi (under the pseudonym Xi Naifang, 1895–1979) criticizes the trope of the "modern girl versus country girl." While he acknowledges that UPS productions were intended to be politically progressive, he faults "the method and attitude by which they resolve their main themes." Because the male screenwriters who wrote these films had no vested interest in the futures of the women they portrayed, he argues, they did not feel the need to posit these women in the sociopolitical reality that produced the problems they had to negotiate. Rather, they were treated simply as vehicles who could convey and mediate the screenwriters' anxieties about masculinity. Zheng Boqi argues that in order to change this, screenwriters and other film workers had to realize that they were engaged in a profession that could reconfigure the spectator's consciousness by making visible its directedness.[68] In his view, what Shanghai cinema needed were not women who embodied male anxieties, but women who could call the spectators into a state of awareness of the very sociopolitical relations that marginalized them.

In addition to recognizing the social impact of their works, he believed screenwriters should also reconfigure the classical Hollywood notion of plot development and resolution, in order to avoid providing imaginary solutions to real social problems that required political actions. For Zheng Boqi, classical Hollywood cinema offered three forms of resolution: coincidence, escape, and transformation. Zheng argues that transformation is often symptomatic of the screenwriter's own sympathy with the protagonist.

> The [male] screenwriter loves his [female] protagonist so dearly that he wishes to live in the totality of her consciousness. He wants to sympathize with the protagonist as much as possible. If impossible, however, the screenwriter should not force her to transform her character. Don't transform a character for the sake of giving [the narrative] a transformation . . . such an attitude is only a result of the screenwriter's narcissism.[69]

By letting characters live in the political consciousness that produces them, the screenwriter can create a form of "social exposé." Such social exposé can inspire the "progressive spectators to feel the pain of the social injustice and internal conflicts of their reality," and the non-progressive ones to discern the consciousness that has thus far disguised the unjust social relations. Zheng Boqi further argues that UPS' films may appear to take the form of the social exposé, but they all provide the *xiao shimin* (petite urbanite[70]) protagonists and spectators a hint of hope by the end. For him, such a narrational strategy was based on the assumption that viewers would never cease to enjoy the forms of pleasure that were socially conditioned to be unattainable to them (the hope itself), a strategy identical to that of the Hollywood films.[71]

Similarly, Wang Chenwu observes that in 1933 the UPS produced a number of *fan fengjian dianying* (anti-feudal films) that were, in fact, produced out of the consciousness of the *xiao youchan jieji* (petite bourgeoisie, of which the petite urbanites were a part) under the guidance of the KMT. The KMT, like the CCP, was promoting their own version of anti-feudalism. Yet the KMT ideologues, following the ideas proposed by Ch'en Kung-po, believed that feudalism should be attacked not by raising moviegoers' political awareness of the semicolonial conditions in which they lived, but by teaching them that they were part of the nation's productive force. In the KMT anti-feudal films, the imaginary solution[72] could be found within the existing social structure (not by questioning and reconfiguring it), or by sacrificing one's life so that the nation as a collective production force could be preserved. Therefore for Wang, these films continued to instill the political consciousness of imperialism-feudalism-capitalism into the sentient bodies of their spectators, thus convincing them that the established sociopolitical system was the only way to guarantee their political stability. For Wang, the fact that the KMT ideologues and the UPS considered the cinema to be an educational tool showed that they did not intend to "posit Chinese cinema in the masses, for the masses did not need to be educated; they educated."[73]

Likewise, in his essay "Lun Zhongguo dianying wenhua yundong" [On the film cultural movement, 1933], A Ying (1900–77, written under the pseudonym Feng Wu) openly criticizes three of UPS's anti-feudal productions. They are: (1) *Sange modeng nüxing* [*Three Modern Women,* Bu Wancang, 1933], a film about a director who tries to represent the struggle of three urban women, who eventually find peace in the country; (2) *Chengshi zhi ye* [*Night in the City,* Fey Mou, 1933], a film about a young woman who fights against the exploitation of her landlord in Shanghai and eventually returns to the country with her fellow workers; and (3) *Tianming* [*Daybreak,* Sun Yu, 1933], a story about a country girl who goes to Shanghai and is coerced to become a sex worker. She finally redeems herself by sacrificing herself for the KMT revolution. In addition, A Ying criticizes a Star production written by Xia Yan, *Kuangliu* [*Raging Torrent,* Cheng Bugao, 1933], a film about a group of peasants who unite against local landlords trying to make money out of the suffering caused by the flood along the Yangtze River.[74]

For A Ying, these four films have successfully turned away from *lian'ai yu pijiu* (love and beer), that is, the kind of capitalist pleasures that are often represented on screen but were unattainable by the masses. However, they all share a common motto, *hui dao nongcun qu* (return to the country), as though all the social problems in the city would be automatically resolved in the country:

> The representation of the country in these films is based on empty constructions out of a Euro-American-styled imagination, not subject matters that are derived from the reality in China. The way they romanticize the

country is to represent at most those struggles that are barely motivated by the peasants themselves.[75]

Historically, these films were produced as "answers" to CCoP and NECSC suggestions that a stronger emphasis be put on the representation of rural China in Shanghai cinema.[76] For A Ying, the way these films romanticize the country still embodies the capitalist and imperialist consciousness: that the country is pitted against the city as a space untainted by urban modernity. In fact, by representing peasants who unite not because they have become aware of the social relations they want to change, but because of an external need, a film like *Raging Torrent* has not done enough to heighten the spectators' sociopolitical awareness.[77]

For A Ying, left-wing directors had the responsibility not only to represent reality, but also help approach the *shijian benzhi de yuanyin* (the reasons behind the essence of the events, best understood as the social relations underlying such events). A Ying complains that although these four directors were aware that the petite urbanites were "struggling and moaning" under oppressive social conditions, they seemed to be ignorant of the fact that these "urban problems" were symptomatic of the *nongcun pochan* (rural bankruptcy) caused by agricultural imports from Euro-American countries replacing domestically produced products in the urban Chinese market.[78] Meanwhile, warlords and local landowners who governed the rural areas continued to raise taxes to compensate for their military expenses and collapsing economy, thus triggering large-scale rural-to-urban migration, rapid urbanization, and all the associated social problems in the city.[79] A Ying did not believe that filmmakers would find a satisfying answer to the urban problem by simply examining the traditional Marxist notion of class conflicts when the conflicts they observed were sustained by a feudal infrastructure that supported KMT's policy. Instead he believed that the left-wing filmmakers should not simply represent the quotidian reality but reveal the intricate relationships among capitalism, imperialism, and feudalism.[80]

In order to achieve these goals, A Ying makes three suggestions. First, filmmakers should strengthen the cinematic cultural movement not only by means of the centralized efforts of the CAFC, but also by organizing directors, technicians, and actors into discussion and activist groups, which would then train the new generation of cultural producers. This point echoes Zheng Zhengqiu and Wang Chenwu's proposal for the masses to seize the means of production. Second, filmmakers should fight for complete freedom in thoughts and speech, demanding not only the removal of all forms of censorship administered by the CFCC and foreign consulates, but also a critical review of the way individual thoughts had been monitored and limited by the capitalist, imperialist, and feudal modes of governance. This point corresponds to Zheng Zhengqiu's schema of the feudalistic *dispositif.* Third, A Ying urges critics to attack imperialism and leisurism. He further exhorts them to avoid their tendency to believe that film criticism is limited to a binary view of form-versus-content and instead realize that both form and content are in fact manifestations of their *jieceng xing* (class nature). Hence, the only way the cinema can be effectively evaluated is to question the class nature of its own consciousness.[81]

Cinema of Thought

The inseparability of forms and contents is a point many Marxist film critics would reiterate. For these thinkers, forms and contents are instantiations of a film's consciousness, thus implying that the cinema can be considered as a sentient body that thinks and generates political actions. The idea that forms and contents are one, in the context of the Shanghai Marxist film debate, goes back to Pudovkin, as the overall scenario of a film is best understood not as an abstract narrative that unfolds separately from the narrational process, but as the way various narrational devices are put together in order to direct the spectators' attention to a detail or a set of structural connections (e.g. causal relationships and spatiotemporal relationships) privileged by their capitalist consciousness.[82]

Unfortunately, in the debate I outlined above, not much attention was paid to experimentation with film forms. However, in both Marxist and non-Marxist film magazines, the montage theories of Pudovkin and Léon Moussinac (1890–1964) were both translated and discussed.[83] As Jessica Ka Yee Chan argues, Chinese filmmakers during the 1930s selectively adopted the Soviet montage as their principle of narrative and rhetorical constructions.[84] Oddly enough, however, while the opponents of the Marxist film theorists—the *ruanxing dianying* (soft film) theorists like Huang Jiamo, Liu Na'ou, and Mu Shiying—discuss film forms substantially in their writings (discussed in chapter 3), the hard film writers almost conformed to the stereotype that they were only interested in a film's contents and consciousness. In fact, it was not until 1935 that director Zheng Junli (1911–69), a CLLD member who worked for the UPS, proposed a possible idea. In his essay "Zai lun yanji" [Again, on the techniques of performance], Zheng Junli summarizes an idea of Pudovkin:

> The creative material of a director [for Pudovkin] does not consist of living human beings, real sceneries, or actual installations, but simply a description: a combination of a number of discontinuous pieces of film, which, in accordance with the director's intention, would be extended, condensed, transformed, and arbitrarily reordered. . . . The director uses a unique sequence that he discovers out of an arbitrary process of combination, puts together these pieces of film . . . for the purpose of creating a cinematographic space and time. . . . From the director's perspective, the actors' performance within the three dimensions of the frame . . . is simply a way to create a new fourth dimension.[85]

Zheng Juni therefore suggests that formal intervention can reconfigure the spectators' sense of temporality. In so doing, Zheng argues, these viewers would begin to grasp a structural difference between their day-to-day sense of temporality and its arbitrary representation in the cinema; this would allow them to *gongzuo* (work through) their consciousness by uncovering relationships between matters of which they are unaware when time is experienced in a linear manner. In short, a film generates—or even constitutes—a thought by means of providing a temporal shock.

Historically, Marxist film theorists from the Soviet Union and Western Europe proposed the idea that by actively intervening with the formal elements codified to maintain the integrity, continuity, and self-coherence of the spectator's sense-perception, a film can generate a thought that puts into question the hegemonic ideological apparatus. For example, Jean-Louis Baudry ponders this question in his essay "Effets idéologiques produits par l'appareil de base" ["Ideological Effects of the Basic Cinematographic Apparatus," 1970]. For Baudry, the cinematographic image as a work carefully conceals the transformation between "objective reality" and the finished product, i.e. its being apprehended as human consciousness. The mechanical apparatus, including the camera lens, the film stock, and the screen, is itself a product of the social relations and ideological discourses informed by the structure of knowledge ever since the Enlightenment (e.g. discourses on modernity, individuality, and political subjectivity) For Baudry, the apparatus posits the spectator as a transcendental subject who has the illusion of being omniscient in the diegesis. Technically, the film image is constructed by means of editing to secure such a transcendental position for the spectator; it posits the spectator as a viewing subject who constantly looks at and knows what happens in a narrative from a privileged position. It in fact does so by assimilating the way a spectator would put a series of presentations together in order to get to know the actual material object "out there." [86] In order to support his theory, Baudry cites Husserl:

> "[A]spects," sometimes of "proximity," sometimes of "distance," in variable modes of "here" and "there," as opposed to an absolute here (which is located—for me—in "my own body' which appears to me at the same time), the consciousness of which, though it remains *unperceived,* always accompanies them. . . . Each "aspect" which the mind grasps, for example, this cube here in the sphere of proximity, is revealed in turn as a unity synthesized from a multiplicity of corresponding modes of presentation. The nearby object may present itself as the same, but under one or another "aspect." There may be variation of visual perspective, but also of "tactile," "acoustic" phenomena, or of other "modes of presentation" as we can observe in directing our attention in the proper direction.[87]

From this citation, Baudry argues that continuity in film is not part and parcel of "objective reality" independent of human perception. Rather, it is supplied by the viewing subject as a form of sense-perception as it puts together various presentations into a synthesized unity. But the very desire to assemble the "fragmented body into a unity" is not natural to the subject. Instead, it comes from the Renaissance ideology that tells the spectator to construct the "transcendentality of the self" and to make her or himself the "giver of unifying meaning" to a series of presentations. In other words, the cinema gives the spectator the impression that it substitutes for her or his sensory organs. But it does so by erasing its own "instrumentation," that is, by hiding both its mechanical apparatus (the very techniques and technology that create the spectator's illusion of transcendentality) and its ideological apparatus: that is, the ideology that informs the spectator's desire to give all the presentations a sense of unity.[88]

In "Le Dispositif: approches métapsychologiques de l'impression de réalité" ["The Apparatus: Metapsychological Approaches of the Impression of Reality," 1975], Baudry goes further by arguing that the "cinematographic apparatus is unique in that *it offers the subject perceptions 'of a reality' whose status seems similar to that of representations experienced as perception.*" It is because "cinema" functions like a dream, in which "representations are taken as reality in the absence of perception."[89] Yet, unlike a dream, the cinematographic apparatus perceives on behalf of the spectator but hides its own work. In this sense, as Zheng Junli, Shen Xiling, and other Shanghai Marxist film theorists suggest, the film work actively senses, perceives, and thinks for the spectators, and the spectators apprehend the cinematographic image as though they were in a dream, that is, without any actual sensory perceptions. Meanwhile, the cinematographic apparatus recalls memories of their sensory-motor stimuli and convinces them to approach these memory-images as reality.

In 1939, film critic Fan Yufei proposed a similar idea:

> The eye is the most sensitive sensory organ of a human being. Therefore, the kind of *zhijue* [intuition] produced by vision provides the easiest and quickest way for the spectator to arrive at a state of understanding.
>
> Intuitions can be divided into external and internal ones. Meanwhile, the process by which an external intuition is stimulated and leaves an impression [on one's sensorium] can be divided into primary and secondary. Primary intuition is a sensation a body produces in accordance with [in response to] the original shape and form of an external object. Yet the impression the brain registers has already passed through the psychological effects of the said individual. Hence, human intuition is always secondary. . . . And the impression registered in the human brain and body through painting and cinema is a form of secondary intuition.[90]

In other words, for Fan, what I have been calling "cinematographic sense-perception" is not really a form of perception; rather, it is a form of intuition, an inference that the brain draws out of a set of sensory-motor stimuli and processes through a set of psychological conditions. It occupies a liminal space between sensory awareness and understanding that is yet to be fully formed into a consciousness. Furthermore, Fan believes that in the cinema, the image projected on the screen directly impresses this intuition upon the human brain. Thus, in the cinema, the apparatus has already produced an inference—or, by implication, thought—for the spectators. Hence, for Fan, the cinema does not inculcate the spectators with political messages; it trains the brain to think the way the film thinks.

In more recent years, the idea that the cinema thinks is brought again to film scholars' attention by Jacques Aumont in his book *À quoi pensent les films?* [What do films think?, 1996]. Aumont's thesis is in fact based on Deleuze's notion of thought and the cinema, which can be traced back to the film theories of, coincidentally, Pudovkin and Eisenstein. Nevertheless, for Deleuze, Pudovkin's cinema of thought has a limitation: he merely focused on how the cinema could provoke a thought by producing a sensual shock. Yet, Eisenstein brought this idea further by identifying "opposition"—not simply in terms of what the film represents, but how the image produces it—as the source of "violence of the image."[91] To push this idea further, Deleuze argues that the film image, that is, the entire film as a consciousness, is a "*relationship with a whole which can only be thought in a higher awareness, the relationship with a thought which can only be shaped in the subconscious unfolding of images, the sensory-motor relationship between world and man, nature and thought.*" For Deleuze, this is the classical movement-image: a form of image that represents time indirectly as movement unfolds spatially, which is in turn sensed and perceived as measurements of time.[92]

But the movement-image as proposed by Eisenstein does not put fragments of movement and action into a logical chain of causes and effects; rather, it juxtaposes them "synthetically as the dynamic effect of images 'on the whole cortex.'" In other words, these fragments of movement-images do not build up the very matter that constitutes the image-consciousness; rather, it produces it, as they are "constructed like the great Spiral in accordance with the laws of dialectic." Each fragment produces a set of "harmonics" that make up the overall perception of the "dominant image," like the way a music listener would sense and be stimulated by a set of harmonics, but perceive only the musical tone they build up synthetically. The shock is therefore not simply a momentary experience of imagistic difference. Rather, it is a set of "suprasensory relations" that sends a "nervous vibration" that informs the spectators' "totally physiological sensation." It is such harmonic vibration that produces the very cortex that "gives rise to thought, the cinematographic I THINK: the whole as subject." It is from this cortex that a sentient body (of the film image) is concretely defined, as in "I see, I hear . . . I FEEL." It is a body, as Deleuze claims, which does not impose itself as an obstacle between the image and thought, but as the necessary container of thought.[93]

I do not want to suggest that the Shanghai film critics in the 1930s anticipated Deleuze. My comparison shows, however, that the Marxist theoretical preoccupation with consciousness generates this resonance between Eisenstein and Pudovkin, the Shanghai critics and their Soviet counterparts, and Deleuze and generations of Marxist film theorists who believe that the film as a body thinks and enacts a political thought. The precarious problem here is the liminality of the cinematographic image: the Shanghai intellectuals understood the cinematographic image as an intermediary state between awareness and consciousness (i.e. the super-sign *yishi*/consciousness), Baudry considered it as a sensory-motor memory without perception, and Fan Yufei regarded it as an intuition that has already been perceptually processed by the image and the human brain. In this light, the cinematographic body is a potentiality that is yet to be completely actualized.

In European theory, Pier Paolo Pasolini (1922–75) ponders this question in his essay "Il cinema di poesia" ["Cinema of Poetry," 1965]. Pasolini was fascinated with the way "deaf and dumb Neapolitans" communicate with each other by means of signs and gestures without having acquired verbal language, with its syntactic structure and grammatical rules.[94] From his observation, Pasolini argues:

> One can suppose . . . the existence of a *unique* system of signs by gestures as *unique* instrument of communication for man . . . : it is from such a hypothetical system of visual signs that language derives the foundation of its existence and the possibility of allowing the formation of a series of naturally communicative archetypes (Pasolini's emphasis).

This is what he calls the im-sign, which is the basic unit that makes up "*the world of memory and of dreams,*" an irrational form of "*linguistic instrument*" that "prefigures" and makes up the photographic image (Pasolini's emphasis). For Pasolini, the im-signs are "images of communication with oneself (and of only indirect communication with others, in the sense that the image which another person has of a thing about which I am speaking constitutes a common reference)."[95] In this sense, the im-sign is not in the order of human consciousness (as understood in European terms). Rather, it is a schema that an individual draws from her or his memory, as she or he recalls a mode of sense-perception from a past event and regenerates an affective state associated with it.

In *Cinéma 2, l'image-temps* [*Cinema 2: The Time-Image,* 1985], Deleuze compares the im-sign to the Bergsonian notion of the sensory-motor schema, or Bergson's *image moyenne* (mediating image). It is an image drawn from the body's sensory-motor memory of a similar sensation in the past, and is therefore associated with a set of external stimuli and the object that produces them. Therefore, it can be understood as "an image which is almost matter in that it still allows itself to be seen, and almost mind in that it no longer allows itself to be touched."[96] As David Rodowick comments, "Deleuze sees in Bergson's definition an exact description of the cinematographic image." Not only that, Bergson argues that these sensory-motor schemas reproduce human perception by means of synthesis. It produces a kind of "*attentive* perception" that is projected "outside ourselves," actively "created" as an image "identical with, or similar to, the object on which it comes to mold itself."[97] In other words, the cinematographic image is indeed a *yishi*/consciousness that occupies a time between a memory reproduction and a full perception, a process in which the human body comes to awareness of the reality that it is about to approach.

Reconfigured in Bergsonian and Deleuzian terms, *yishi* (become aware of) implies a process of recalling and synthesizing a set of sensory-motor schemata. These schemata reactivate sensorial stimuli generated in the past (again, the Sartrean concept of retentionality), and project into the future what the human body senses as the present in all its concreteness (Sartre's protentionality). Deleuze, in *Cinema 2,* defines this as a crystal-image. He argues:

> What constitutes the crystal-image is the most fundamental operation of time: since the past is constituted not after the present that it was but at the same time, time has to split itself in two at each moment as present and past, which differ from each other in nature, or, what amounts to the same thing, it has to split the present in two heterogeneous directions, one of which is launched towards the future while the other falls into the past.[98]

For Bergson, the intermediary state between memory recall and perception—the sensory-motor schema—can be understood as "what may happen in reality," a potentiality that crystalizes a pure memory that is about to be actualized as perception. As Rodowick argues, the "direct presentation of time is fundamentally paradoxical. Because time passes, and cannot do otherwise, the present will coexist with the past that it will be, and the past will be indiscernible from the present it has been."[99] For Deleuze, the "crystal-image was not time"; rather, it is the "perpetual foundation of time, non-chronological time, Cronos and not Chronos," that is, time undead.[100]

To *yishi* something is therefore to dwell in a nonstate in which time is no longer measured against the end of time. At first glance, this Bergsonian-Deleuzian notion of time is far away from the political problems that the Marxist film theorists in Shanghai tried to discuss. But if one begins to translate this concept in political terms, one might discover a *mise-en-abîme* in the Shanghai Marxist notion of what a socially conscious cinema can potentially do. Recently, Giorgio Agamben observes a structural affinity between the Judaic understanding of the *kairos,* i.e. the time it takes for time to end (see chapter 1), and Marx's understanding of the term *Klasse* (class). Agamben argues that Marx, in his writing, clarifies that a class is not the same as an estate; the latter is produced out of the set of social relations that make up the historical process of feudalism. A class, however, is formed as a result of a temporal intervention, such as a speech, pamphlet, or social discussion, that acts as an external calling or vocation that interrupts the temporal certainty of a historical process, which an individual has taken all along as her or his consciousness. In fact, such a temporal interruption calls the individual to the end of history, a moment at which all the existing social relations and conditions would come to an end. When such an individual returns to her or his daily life-process, she or he is living the time it takes for history to end—all that remains, for this individual, is a conceptual measurement between the historical process that continues to unfold in time, and the end of history at which a new form of temporality and political existence would be engendered.[101] For Agamben, the community of individuals that is being called is a *Klasse,* an idea akin to Zheng Zhengqiu and Wang Chenwu's notion of the masses. In this sense, approaching reality, understood in Marxist terms, can be regarded as a form of political *kairos,* a temporal measurement that is in fact configured as a potentiality for further sociopolitical actions.

New Chinese cinema should, as Zheng Boqi argues:

> [p]ut into display in front of the audience, in all its nakedness, the reality of the conflicting irrationalities, in order that it would sense deeply the necessity of social changes, which would in turn motivate them to find their own ways out [of the established sociopolitical relationships.][102]

In fact, Deleuze himself notes, the crystal-image instantiates the "powerful, non-organic Life which grips the world."[103] In other words, what the spectators become aware of is a spark of life that is emancipated from the process of history, one that is freed from the sociopolitical contingencies that shape the consciousness of their life-process. It is the measurement of this Life that manifests itself in the crystal-image and the time it takes for the sociopolitically contingent life-process to end, which returns the cinematic spectators to a political *kairos*—the time it takes for the historical process of capitalism, imperialism, and feudalism to end.

Conclusion

The Marxist film debate between 1930 and 1935 was not founded upon a naive understanding of Marxism or a set of mistranslations. Rather, it was produced out of a sea of thoughts deposited by an assemblage of inter- and intracultural dialogues where their discursive topos was delicately repositioned in keeping with Shanghai's semicolonial conditions. Understood as a form of political *kairos,* the Marxist film theories in the 1930s in fact share the assumption of their predecessors in the 1920s that the cinematographic image approaches reality. On both theoretical and practical levels, Marxist criticism maintains adamantly that consciousness is always politically inflected. In this sense, what the cinematographic image does is draw the spectators to a point where not only are the existing social relationships revealed, but a potential end of history can be measured.

These Marxist thinkers employed the term *miaoxie xianshi* or *xieshi,* often translated as "describing reality," but best understood in this context as a process of approaching reality via a film's overall scenario. The cinematographic image—with all its epistemic edges and limitations defined by the ideological apparatus itself—is capable of approaching reality as part of the directed consciousness of the spectators. But in so doing, the cinematographic image reveals the directedness of its own consciousness and calls the viewers to a state where capitalism, imperialism, and feudalism are potentially in-operative (not yet operative and in the process of becoming operative). In this sense, a film does not represent or reveal real sociopolitical conditions in which the spectators live; it simply describes and constructs an illusion of reality informed by the hegemonic ideology. Yet by making visible the ideological work that conceals the spectators' reality, progressive cinema enables the spectators to approach a potentiality from which a new form of life and reality is revealed, and hopefully realized.

3 SOFT FILM THEORY

Life in All Its Presence and Concreteness

WHAT IS LIFE? This question emerges in the two discourses on cinematographic reality I have examined thus far: Hou Yao and Gu Kenfu's discussion on approaching reality in the 1920s, and the Marxist film critics' debate on cinema's directed consciousness in the 1930s. Both debates, via their respective trails, converge on one idea: that the spectator, once called into the temporal distance between the day-to-day sense of chronometric time and a nonstate in which time is about to become inoperative. In this nonstate, life in all its presence and concreteness will manifest itself. Yet, this life, which is made palpable and approachable by the cinematographic image, has yet to be rigorously defined in the critical conversations I have outlined in the previous chapters. Likewise, how life reveals itself in the cinematographic experience is a process that has, until this point, remained unexplored.

A critical debate that came close to defining this life emerged in 1933, when avant-garde fiction writer and art critic Liu Na'ou (1905–40) and screenwriter Huang Jiamo (1916–2004) launched a "counterattack" on Marxist film criticism in their magazine *Xiandai dianying* [*Modern Screen*]. In his article "Yingxing yingpian yu ruanxing yingpian" [Hard film and soft film, 1933], Huang mocks the Marxist film theory for being reducible to a theory of consciousness and a set of *geming kouhao* (revolutionary slogans). He goes so far as to call those films produced and directed by members of the Chinese League of Left-Wing Dramatists (CLLD) *jiangjin guo* (starched, as in starched shirts) that completely ignore film forms, aesthetics, and spectatorial pleasure. For Huang, the sole concern of the Marxist film theorists was to turn the cinema into an educational tool, which, ironically, was an idea first promoted by the KMT and its ideologues. Huang believed that Shanghai cinema needed a kind of *ruanxing dianying* (soft film), a cinematographic image that would allow the beholder to *xinshang xianshi rensheng de fengmei* (appreciate the richness and beauty of life in all its presence and concreteness).[1] As a reaction against the Marxist film theory as a *neirong pianzhong zhuyi* (principle of overemphasizing film contents), Liu Na'ou suggests that Shanghai filmmakers should learn how to manipulate film forms so their viewers could immerse themselves in the film as an aesthetic experience.[2]

This soft-film position could be considered a redevelopment of Hou Yao and Gu Kenfu's thesis on approaching reality in the 1920s, which assumed that the relationship between the cinematographic image the spectator apprehends and the reality it approaches is encapsulated in an aesthetic experience. However, the soft-film theorists employed a critical language that is best understood as another pluralistic semantic field constructed out of decades of cross-cultural translations and reinventions of concepts in aesthetics, life, and cinema from France, Germany, and China. Although the actual soft-film debate—that is, the portion I am going to discuss in this chapter—is relatively short-lived (1933–34), it remained popular in Shanghai throughout the rest of the 1930s. For example, after *Modern Screen,* Liu and Huang were joined by Mu Shiying (1912–40), Yao Sufeng (1906–74), Ma Guoliang (1908–2011), and Yan Ciping (dates unknown) in the *Qingqing* [*Chin Chin*] magazine, *Lianyou* [*Good Companion*] magazine, *Linglong* [*Ling Lung*] magazine, and *Lianhua huabao* [UPS pictorial], where they continued to discuss the cinema in terms of aesthetics and sensorial stimulations.[3] Arguably, their ideas even informed a mode of cosmopolitan Marxism experimented with by the young filmmakers in the Diantong (Denton) Studio, including Yuan Muzhi (1909–78), Nie'er (George Njal, pseudonym of Nie Shouxin, 1912–35), and Situ Huimin (1910–87). The Denton group believed that by mediating the exciting sensations, sexual stimulations, and political angst sensed by their viewers, the cinema could foster an active creative life among them, and renegotiate their relationships with modernity.[4]

The soft film theory, unfortunately, acquired a negative reputation among Marxist film scholars after 1949, which held sway until Zhang Zhen reexamined the theory in her book *The Amorous History of the Silver Screen* (2006).[5] Prior to that, in the *Zhongguo dianying fazhan shi* [History of the development of Chinese cinema, 1953], Cheng Jihua, Li Shaobai, and Xing Zuwen dismissed the soft film theory as an apolitical petite bourgeois taste, and for them, the soft-film theorists were disinterested in treating the cinema as an education tool for inculcating the spectators with progressive political ideas. This was partially because many soft-film theorists were affiliated not with the CCP (Chinese Communist Party), but with the KMT, the UPS, the Zhongguo minzhu tongmeng (China Democratic League, a political party established in 1941, which was made up of left-wing intellectuals, but not necessarily Communist sympathizers), or even the Nanking collaborationist faction of the KMT (1940–45) under the leadership of Wang Ching-wei (1883–1944).[6] Yet a closer examination of their critical works shows that these soft-film theorists did not envision the cinema simply as a petite bourgeois entertainment. Rather, in conformation to the KMT film policy and like their Marxist counterparts (discussed in chapter 2), soft-film theorists believed that the cinema was an educational tool, and for them, the spectators were best educated via an aesthetic process of immersion.[7]

The political environment within which the soft film theory gained momentum was a complex one. In 1930s China, cultural producers and policymakers held three interrelated notions of life: (1) *rensheng* (human life), understood as a force of life as a whole; (2) *shengtai* (life form), understood as an organic and biological life that evolves in time; (3) *minsheng* (national life), debated and understood as a collection of political lives that partake of a shared life process (the day-to-day praxis of life) and national consciousness.[8] These notions of life, I argue, serve as a cross-cultural semantic field that attracted those Shanghai intellectuals who considered cinema an aesthetic experience from which these three kinds of life would be reconfigured and negotiated. In the following intervention, I explore the various strata of cross-cultural, interlinguistic, and multiphilosophical deposits that constructed this pluralistic field. I undertake this task by first contextualizing the soft film theory in the intellectual debate on life between the 1890s and the 1930s. With such a discursive framework in mind, I analyze the discussion between Liu Na'ou and Huang Jiamo and find out how they understood the cinema as an aesthetic experience. From Liu and Huang's critical ideas, I shall reach a definition of life (in the cinema) by reconfiguring and repurposing the soft film theory via a philosophical framework that forms these two writers' common underlying assumption: Immanuel Kant's aesthetics and its reinvention, through Buddhism, by late-Qing, early-Republican philologist Wang Guowei (1877–1927). Finally, in the conclusion, I put this definition of life in a retroactive and retrospective dialogue with Gilles Deleuze's definition of life in its pure immanence.

Life: An Intellectual Debate

The intellectual and political environments from which the soft film theory emerged were multifaceted. In "Life as Form: How Biomimesis Encountered Buddhism in Lu Xun" (2009), Lydia Liu conducted a mapping of the intellectual discussion on life around the turn of the twentieth century. In her article, Liu repurposes a term proposed by Lothar Ledderose in his book *Ten Thousand Things* (1998): biomimesis. For Ledderose, the "fundamental differences between the Western tradition and the Chinese tradition lie in the fact that the former has tried to make things *look* like creations of nature (i.e., appearance), whereas the latter imitates the *principles* of nature (i.e., essence), which turns out to be a modular system with quantitative dimension."[9] For Liu, "Ledderose reverses the ethnocentric priority of imitative acts by bifurcating the West and China along the imaginary line between mimesis and biomimesis, but the difficulty is that biomimesis presumes a theory of life that originated in European evolutionary biology."[10] In this sense, what Ledderose calls biomimesis is not a fundamentally Chinese imagination; rather, it was a product of the simultaneous arrival of European literary realism and evolutionary theories (both social and biological) by the late nineteenth century, which persuaded those Chinese intellectuals who were well versed in Buddhism and Confucianism to reconsider the Chinese notions of *ren* and *rensheng* in conversation with the European notions of human and human life.[11]

This process of reconfiguring the definitions of *ren*/human and *rensheng*/human life as two super-signs has political, literary, and cultural dimensions. In terms of politics, scholars including Benjamin Schwartz, Hoyt Tillman, Susan Brownell, and Liu Dong have discussed how social Darwinism became popular among late-Qing and early-Republican scholars including Yan Fu (1854–1921), Kang Youwei (1858–1927), and Liang Qichao (1873–1929).[12] Yan Fu translated utilitarian and social Darwinist texts from English literature, most memorably the *Tianyan lun* [Discussion on natural evolution, 1896–98], a translation of "Evolution and Ethics" (1893) by Thomas Huxley (1825–95); *Qunji quanjie lun* [On the boundaries between social and individual rights, 1903], a translation of *On Liberty* (1869) by John Stuart Mill (1806–73); *Qunxue yiyan* [On the study of the collective, 1903], a translation of *Principles of Sociology* (1864) by Herbert Spencer (1820–1903).[13] In his commentaries, Yan Fu is fascinated with how *ji* (self or individual life) and *qun* (collective or political life) is shaped by *tian ze* (natural selection) on the one hand, and a process of artificial selection based on human desires on the other.[14] The former depends on an individual's biological strength or a collective's social and military strength, whereas the latter is regulated by ethics. For Yan, natural selection is a relentless process operated in accordance with the principle of *homo homini lupus* (a man is a wolf to his fellow man). For him, absolute *ziyou* (individual liberty or will of the self) would render *minzhu* (democracy or collective determination) dysfunctional, whereas absolute democracy would eventually limit individual freedom. Nevertheless, Yan believes that with ethics, "A wolf . . . having been tamed, can be used to herd sheep."[15] In other words, evolutionary theory has to work hand-in-hand with political ethics in order to attain a balance between freedom and democracy.

For Schwartz, Yan Fu's reading of Huxley and other European evolutionists had the effect of grafting social Darwinism onto the ethical framework of Confucianism.[16] Nonetheless, for Liu Dong, Yan did more than simply translate social Darwinism in Confucian terms; rather, understanding evolutionary concepts in translation requires an active rewriting of the ontological framework in the Chinese language itself.[17] In this case, the word *tian* (often translated as heaven), for example, is thrown together with the word "nature" as a super-sign, thus transforming it from a signifier of a cosmological concept (as in Confucianism, Buddhism, and Taoism) in which *ren* subsists through a process of negotiation, to an environmental concept against which human beings must strive to conquer.[18] Likewise, *ren*, which was understood as having a codependent relationship with *tian*, is now considered (as argued by Lu Xun's brother Zhou Zuoren, 1885–1967) "the human species, as it has progressively evolved from the animal kingdom," which struggles against nature.[19] And for Yan Fu, *ren*/human is distinguished from *lang* (wolf) or animal because of the individual's ability to regulate her or his desires by means of ethics. Interestingly, *ren*/human, a biological and organic unit, is understood in Yan's translation also as a form of political subjectivity: *ji* (self) and *qun* (collective). Thus, a semiotic assemblage is formed, in which *zoë* (biological life) and *bios* (political life) are intricately linked in terms of *tian*/*ren* and *qun*/*ji*.[20]

Yan Fu's reading of Huxley, for Lydia Liu, is in itself symptomatic of a fascination among the late-Qing and early-Republican scholars with reconciling the evolutionary concept of *shengtai* (life form), an organic life (be that vegetative or animal) that was seeded, germinated, gestated, given birth, and posited among other life-forms in a competitive and relentless evolutionary process, and *rensheng* (human life), which gives the concept of "life as form" an ethical grounding and "critical consciousness." Lydia Liu argues that such an attempt to redefine life as form gave rise to the concept of biomimesis, that is, the idea of using literary realism as a "technology" not necessarily to describe life in its reality or truthfulness, but to "grapple with the problem of 'life as form'" by fictionalizing it, aestheticizing it, improving it, exposing its potential horror, and giving it a sense of ethical coherence—functions that were once performed by religion or mythology. Lydia Liu found numerous examples of Republican literary works, including those works of fiction and translation done by Lu Xun, which can be understood as creative processes that would help his readers negotiate their "existential crisis."[21]

The kind of existential crisis that Lydia Liu identified was not only negotiated in literature, but also in philosophy and religion, and, as I will demonstrate, in the theoretical discourse on the cinema. One strand of thought was the reconfiguration of Buddhism by Lu Xun's mentor, philologist Zhang Taiyan (1868–1936), and by other Buddhist masters at the time, including Yuan Huanxian (1887–1966, mentor of Buddhist scholar Nan Huaijin or Nan Huai-chin, 1918–2012). Zhang Taiyan was known for rearticulating Yogācāra Buddhism, Huang-Lao Daoxue (the philosophy of *dao* of the Yellow Emperor and Laozi), Kantianism, and Hegelianism in each other's terms. Like Yan Fu, Kang Youwei, and Liang Qichao, Zhang Taiyan wrote with the intention of rethinking history as a way that Chinese life, in both biological and national terms, would live and compete for survival under a different ontological framework. For Zhang:

> *Qiwu* [putting things together on the same plane] is often discussed as *pingdeng* [equality]. But if we consider the meaning of *pingdeng* more carefully, it does not simply refer to seeing sentient [things or beings] as equal, regardless of their being better or worse. One must speak of *xiang* [appearance] without words, nominate appearance without name, and think of appearance without relating it to one's heart. After all, equality means: to put things together on the same plane.[22]

What Zhang Taiyan calls *qiwu* can be understood as an equalizing plane. On it, all *wu* (which is further divided into *qingjie*, or sentient beings, and *qijie*, or things that convey other things or beings) are equal in the sense that they all come from the same *qianzai xing*/potentiality from which *rensheng*/life is engendered or *zhuoxiang* (manifested as an appearance).[23] For Zhang, when one is capable of speaking of appearance without resorting to any discourse, understanding it without either reasoning or mythologizing, and letting it approach without holding onto it as an image or concept, one can begin to see how this transcendental plane cuts through all spatiotemporal planes that define one's existence. Towards the end of this chapter, I will demonstrate the proximity between Zhang's equalizing plane and Deleuze's idea of the transcendental plane or plane of immanence.

Zhang Taiyan's ideas fascinated a whole generation of Chinese intellectuals, including Chen Duxiu (1879–1942), Hu Shi (Hu Shih, 1891–1962), Guo Moruo (1892–1978), Lu Xun, and Zhou Zuoren, who attempted to understand the question What is life?[24] Yuan Huanxian, and later on Nan Huai-chin, came up with a molecular cosmology based on Chan (Zen) Buddhism. They believed that all things that are manifested came from the same set of molecules that make up the entire universe, and those universes beyond us. In this sense, life is best understood as a molecule that has the potential to manifest itself in a finite—but uncountable—number of appearances; but in the end, life is best understood as "*bu sheng, bu mie, bu zeng, bu jian*" (not engendering, not extinguishing, not augmenting itself, and not diminishing itself).[25] As Lydia Liu points out, many of the May Fourth figures debated the question of life via philosophy, biology, and literature, culminating in the *Kexue yu xuanxue* (Science and metaphysics) debate between 1923 and 1924. At the height of this debate, Zhang Junmai (Carsun Chang, 1886–1969) gave a lecture at Tsinghua University called "Rensheng guan" (*Weltsschauung* or views on life), adopting Henri Bergson's argument that the "*vital impetus*" for human survival is not simply a biological need, but creativity, a view of life that inspired many intellectuals—including those literati who would later on work in the film industry—that cultural productions, especially literature and cinema, were crucial in negotiating the dialectics between science and metaphysics, and the synthesis would bring forward the evolution of both individual and collective lives in China.[26]

The Chinese intellectual revision of evolutionary theories is crucial to the question of the self and subjectivity, a problem that was given an extra political twist by KMT's ideologue Ch'en Kung-po. In Ch'en's view, classical Marxism did not translate well to the semicolonial conditions of the Chinese economy. According to Marxist theory, in one register the economy of China had to go through large-scale industrialization before a social awareness that the working class and the middle classes were dialectically related could emerge. In another register, the semicolonial conditions in China had grafted capitalism onto the social structure and economy of the Chinese trading ports through imperialism, which in turn hindered the industrialization of the rural areas. In response to this dilemma, Ch'en came up with a theory that offered an alternative to the *laissez-faire* notion of capitalism practiced widely in the trading ports of China where state intervention was effectively absent. It also offered a way for sovereign authority to be constituted so that state power could be equally shared, but at the same time equally exercised upon, each member of the imagined political community: a political form of *qiwu*/equalizing plane.[27]

Ch'en proposed to configure the nation as a corporation—that is, a collective life. In this unified economic life, the nationals were not seen as citizens, but as producers and workers who pushed forward a grand industrial machine.[28] Ch'en's theory inspired the New Life Movement, which was summarized in a speech given on February 19, 1934, by Chiang Kai-shek and his wife Song Meiling (Soong May-ling, 1898–2003):

> What is this New Life Movement that we are advocating? Put it simply, what the movement does is militarize thoroughly the lives of all the nationals in our entire nation. This allows us to nurture courage, speed, and perseverance, especially a unified habit and instinct. This allows us to give up our lives to our nation![29]

In "The Cinema of Sun Yu" (2011), an article in which I discuss the New Life Movement in conjunction with the UPS, I have summarized Chiang's ideas regarding *minsheng*/national life as follows:

> For the purpose of enwrapping individual bodies into an imagined collective life, Chiang proposes the motto *li* (defined by Chiang as rite, courtesy, regulation, and responsibility), *yi* (responsibilities or appropriateness), *lian* (simplicity, frugality, and honesty) and *chi* (shame). These four moral categories, for Chiang, are interconnected as a cycle of self-regulation. For Chiang, *li* is referred to as synchronized and ritualized bodily movements. For him, these . . . movements are expressions of social positions, responsibilities, and relations, and these relations are instantiations of the nationals' proper social positions—that is, *yi*. The maintenance of these relations (again, *yi*) would be impossible without *lian*. . . . For Chiang, as a virtue, *lian* reminds the nationals that all they need is a down-to-earth, simple and economical way of life, i.e. the basic necessities required for maintaining their biological existence. For Chiang, such virtue . . . would check the

> nationals against their desires for material excesses, since these excesses should inspire them to feel *chi* (shame). In return, shame would allow the nationals to be conscious of their responsibilities and the need to regulate their [ritualized] actions within the framework of appropriateness . . . and honesty. . . . For Chiang, the result of fulfilling this cycle of self-management would be *shenghuo yishu hua* (aestheticization of life), that is, individual lives were to be collectively formalized (aestheticized), regulated, and managed as parts of a national life for the purpose of maximizing productivity and efficiency.[30]

The intellectual debate from which the soft film theory emerged therefore produces three interrelated concepts of life: *rensheng*/human life, *shengtai*/life form, and *minsheng*/national life. To use Lydia Liu's term, one may argue that the soft-film theorists understood the cinema as a biomimetic technology that negotiated the intricate relationships among these three kinds of life. The term in fact corresponds to the notion of approaching reality, especially for the soft-film theorists, in that the cinema does not imitate life; rather, it reveals life in an aesthetic experience, a process in which the beholder is immersed in the cinematographic image in its approach to reality. Such an aesthetic experience would also aestheticize life into a common-sensical (as in a shared sense of) *shenghuo jiezou*/life rhythm.

In addition to the already complex semantic field regarding life, the soft film theory was also informed by the Parisian debate on the *photogénie*: a form of beauty specific to the filmic medium and life. In 1921, Louis Delluc (1890–1923) compared *photogénie* to a state of affection as one beholds a mirage of a beautiful woman observing her reflection on the surface of a lake as she combs her long hair.[31] On the one hand, it seems like Delluc is referring to a pleasing sensation when the beholder sees the image of a beautiful woman, her contemplation of her own beautiful image, and the sensual gesture of her combing her long hair. On the other hand, by comparing the cinematographic image to the mirage and a reflection on a body of water, Delluc also emphasizes the immateriality and transience of the image. Such a mode of aesthetic appreciation is at once contemplative and distractive, concrete and ephemeral, pleasing and unsettling—in Kantian terms, both beautiful and sublime.[32] In a way, Delluc's notion of the *photogénie* is a state of indiscernibility between observation and reflection, contemplation and transience: life as it unfolds in time.

In 1926, Jean Epstein further elaborated the concept of the *photogénie* in his essay "La cinématographe vu de l'Etna" [The cinema seen from Etna; translation by Stuart Liebman]. The essay contains two anecdotes. In the first one, Epstein stands on top of Etna, where he witnesses a landscape of total annihilation:

> In front of one's eyes, every leaf on every tree passed through all the colors of autumn until, cracked, twisted, and scorched, they fell into the fiery blasts. And each naked, blackened tree held itself upright for but an instant during this scorching winter. There were no more birds, no insects at all. Like the roadway of a bridge when a heavy truck rolls across it, the earth, lined with thin crevices, was continually traversed by tremors. The lava collapsed with the noise of a million plates breaking at once. Pockets of gas burst, hissing as softly as snakes. The inferno's smell, an odor without scent, filled with tingling, acrid sensations, poisoned our lungs to their very depths. Under the sky, pallid and parched, death truly reigned.[33]

In the second anecdote, Epstein walks down a spiral staircase surrounded by mirrors in the hotel where he stays. As Epstein walks down, he sees multiple images of himself staring at him, making him feel naked and reduced to a state of nothingness:

> This immense spiral of stairs portended vertigo. . . . I descended surrounded by images of myself, by reflections, by images of my gestures, by cinematic projections. At every turn I was caught from another angle. There are as many different and independent positions between a profile and a three-quarter view as there are tears in an eye. Each of these images lived but an instant, no sooner caught sight of than lost from view, already something else. Only my memory could hold on to one of their infinite number, and by doing so, missed two out of every three. . . . I descended as if moving across the optical facets of an immense insect. The opposing angles of other images cut across and amputated each other; reductive and fragmentary, they humiliated me. For the moral effect of such a spectacle is what is so extraordinary. Every glance brings a baffling surprise that insults you. I had never been seen this way before and I regarded myself with horror. . . . I thought myself to be one way, and perceiving myself to be something else shattered all the vain notions I had acquired. Each of these mirrors presented me with a perverse view of myself, an inaccurate image of the hopes I had. These spectating mirrors forced me to see myself with their indifference, their truth. I seemed to be in a huge retina lacking a conscience, with

> no moral sense, and seven stories high. I saw myself stripped of my sustaining illusions, surprised, laid bare, uprooted unfeelingly and presented truthfully, exactly for what I was.[34]

In both anecdotes, it would be hard for the readers not to identify the *photogénie* as the cinematic sublime. In the first anecdote, Epstein comes face-to-face with the annihilation of all lives by a force engendered in the depth of the earth, the source of all terrestrial motions, and a zone where all matters melt and blend into a primordial soup. Yet it would be too easy for us to argue that Epstein is overtaken by death. Rather, what he senses seems to be a much larger "force of life" that annihilates, incorporates, and potentially regenerates individual lives. In the second anecdote, he is engulfed by a displeasing sensation when he sees himself "analyzed," multiplied, dissected, and reduced to a bare life in all its nakedness. At that very moment, Epstein does not see himself anymore. Rather, he is posited in a "huge retina lacking a conscience, with no moral sense," where he is "uprooted unfeelingly and presented truthfully." Here, Epstein is referring again to a force of life that reduces him to the eye—a sensory organ sans human subjectivity. Nonetheless, the process by which Epstein approaches this state of the sublime is by immersing himself in an aesthetic process of observation-reflection, i.e. a process in which the beholder not only observes the art object, but is also observed by the art object as her or his own reflection. In such an approach to reality, life manifests itself as a force where the distinction between subjectivity and objectivity is dissolved.

But what appears to be a purely aesthetic discussion could carry a covert political agenda. As Michael Cowan points out in a study of the Weimar era (1919–33) theoretical discussion of cinematographic rhythm (one of the favorite subjects of discussion among the soft-film theorists) the cinema was understood as a machine that impresses directly onto the human bodies a form of natural rhythm, thus allowing them to regain life from the mechanicity and seriality of modernity. Cowan is especially interested in *Das Wesen des Rhythmus* [The nature of rhythm, 1923], written by Ludwig Klages (1872–1956). He argues:

> For Klages, "rhythm" [*Rhythmus*] resided not in the succession of identical elements characteristic of mass production, but rather precisely in the *deviations* from mechanical succession. Visible in biological processes . . . and diurnal cycles . . . rhythm expressed the essence of life, while *Takt*

made visible the rational, ordering, and segmenting activity of the intellect (or "spirit"—*Geist*—in Klages's terminology).[35]

For Cowan, Klages' idea of rhythm directly informs the films made by Walter Ruttmann (1887–1941) and Hans Richter (1888–1976), which used to be thought of as "experimental films," but were in fact advertisements and educational films funded directly by the state or even Hollywood as celebrations of collectivity.[36] It also informed Kracauer's critique that modernity demythologizes life and reduces it to its primitive form: an abstract and mathematical component of the society's overall production.[37] In some ways, such abstraction, demythologization, and mathematization leave no room for the cinematic spectators to "make sense of" this unsettling sensation, and the one place they can look is in a melancholy and nostalgia for the loss of a higher and transcendent national or traditional value—a form of proto-fascism. As Standish Lawder argues, such thoughts also entered the theoretical debate of the *photogénie* in the 1920s.[38] The soft-film theorists would have been able to read the works of Klages and Kracauer through the translations and discussions made by the Kyōto-gakuha (Kyoto school) philosophers.[39] This line of film thinking both provided an effective critique on modernity and its dehumanizing impact, and, ironically, an incentive to subscribe to a proto-fascist notion of life as a manifestation of a collective sensibility.

The Soft Film Theory in *Modern Screen*

The intellectual background outlined above can be considered an assemblage of deposits that inform the soft film theory's understanding of the cinema and life. The soft film theory was officially inaugurated in *Modern Screen*. The magazine was edited by Huang Jiamo and Liu Na'ou between 1933 and 1934, and it featured articles written by UPS filmmakers including Sun Yu (1900–90) and Cai Chusheng (Tsai Chu-sang, 1906–68). As a result, it was sometimes regarded as a mouthpiece for the UPS and KMT's party machinery. Huang himself was often typecast as the quintessential soft-filmmaker, as a film he wrote, *Huashen guniang* [*Tomboy*, Fang Peilin, Yee Hwa, 1936], a screwball comedy about a young woman who cross-dresses as a young man in order to convince her grandfather that she is his grandson, is sometimes showcased as a petite bourgeois comedic indulgence.[40] Nevertheless, *Modern Screen* also featured a few Marxist critical writings in every issue, and it did not by any means represent a unified or coherent political position.[41]

From an industrial perspective, the UPS itself was far from a top-down political machine.[42] The four studio executives, Lo Ming-yau (1901–67; North China), Lay Ming-wei (1893–1953; China Sun), Lu Hanzhang (dates unknown; Great China Lilium), and Zhu Shilin (1899–1967; Chu Shih Ling, Lo Hwa), in fact made their own decisions in their respective studios, and expressed various degrees of support for KMT's plan of nationalization. Moreover, although the UPS started in 1930 with a strong financial profile backed by top KMT bureaucrats and bankers, the company was left to its own devices to balance its budgets. Hence, Lo and his cohorts still made business decisions based on their responsibilities to their investors, not national policy.[43] Even during the 1930s, some journalists argued that the UPS was more a personal project of Lo Ming-yau than a fully concerted political effort. Lo climbed KMT's political ladder by getting himself elected into the National Educational Cinematographic Society of China (NECSC), a position that allowed him to make the UPS the sole producer of educational newsreels for the KMT. Lo eventually became a representative of the NECSC both in Shanghai and abroad.[44] In this sense, the political positions of the UPS and *Modern Screen* were in fact highly ambivalent and pluralistic.

KMT's cinematic infrastructure did serve to produce a hegemonic critical vocabulary for filmmakers and critics across a wide spectrum of political opinions. In this light, the soft-film theorists did believe that the cinema, if configured and employed properly, could help promote social changes. In the inaugural article in *Modern Screen*, "*Xiandai dianying* yu Zhongguo dianyingjie" [*Modern Screen* and the Chinese film profession, 1933], Huang Jiamo establishes his argument by outlining his own comparative history of Chinese cinema and its Euro-American counterparts:

> In China, the film industry has been developed extensively enough to cover an expansive [geographical and economic] area. Movie theaters were opened in every metropolis and in every town. It was clear that the cinema had surpassed the theater in its [cultural] position, which deeply attracted this youthful Chinese nation. But what I described was made possible by the foundation of Euro-American cinema in the past twenty years. During this time period, our *guochan yingye* (national film industry) went through its first ten years of pioneering and had finally come to its maturity. Since the emergence of the sound film, a linguistic barrier has plagued the popularity of Western cinema in China. For the general spectators who are only equipped with Chinese ears, they can neither understand

> any Euro-American languages nor those day-to-day affairs and objects of the White race. Hence, they all turned to our *guochan dianying* (national cinema) and hoped that we would achieve success as early as possible.[45]

In this paragraph we get a glimpse of the key political assumptions of the soft film theory. Huang emphasizes the nation as the basic unit of productive life from the opening "In China." He points out that the cinema, as a cultural endeavor that has surpassed the theater, has "deeply attracted" not the youth of China, but the "youthful Chinese nation." He refers to the national film industry and national cinema, and underlines the notion of production, putting a specific stress on the film "industry" and its extensive coverage over "every metropolis" and "every town." In a sense, Huang's term *guochan yingye* (national film industry) can be more closely translated as national film-production industry. Likewise, *guochan dianying* (national cinema) can be more carefully translated as nationally produced cinema. By focusing on the Chinese nation as a youthful one that has spent the last ten years in pioneering a new film industry, Huang produces an affect of youthfulness, productivity, adventure, courage, and modernity, a political language adopted directly from the New Life Movement.

The common goal of this productive life, according to Huang, is to improve the aesthetic quality of the Shanghai film productions. In Huang's view, Euro-American cinema had the advantage of developing ten to twenty years ahead of Chinese cinema. He therefore believed the Shanghai filmmakers should grasp the moment of cinema's transition into sound as an opportunity to catch up to the aesthetic level of Euro-American films. What at first glance appears to be a simple argument, however, in fact reflects several interconnected political desires and fantasies. First, Huang posits the Chinese nation's productive life as designed, constructed, and measured against Euro-American life, implying an imagined difference between China and the Euro-American West and positioning China as a proto-organic living entity that will compete against the World with its creative impetus. Second, Huang assumes that Euro-American cinema has been successful during the silent era, presumably losing its audience with the advent of sound. In this sense, Huang implicitly subscribes to an argument that silent cinema had been developed into a form of art universal to all human beings. Hence, on the one hand Huang argues that the task of the Shanghai filmmakers is to produce films that "represent the colors and characteristics of China."[46]

On the other hand, such homegrown artistic sensibility should be elevated to a point of universality—an art form that could be exported to Europe and the United States as a universal aesthetic experience.

When the soft-film theorists discuss aesthetics, they are therefore not simply talking about individual taste. Rather, they are looking for an aesthetic judgment that takes place prior to the beholder's apprehension of her or his relationship with the art object as a consciousness, a state where the distinction between collectivity and self has yet to be defined. Such an aesthetic judgment: (1) allows human life to manifest itself on an equalizing plane, as proposed by the work of Zhang Taiyan; (2) permits the spectators' sentient bodies to be synchronized to the cinematographic rhythm and its molecular structure, an idea corresponding to the molecular cosmology of Yuan Huanxian and the theories of bodily rhythm proposed by Klages; (3) produces a sensation that is universalizable to all humans, thus convincing these spectators that they all share a common political life.

Nonetheless, an underlying *problèmatique* in the soft film theory, not unlike its French counterpart, is its peculiar uncertainty about the definition of cinematic beauty. In fact many of the soft-film theoretical texts navigate in a zone of indiscernibility between beauty and the sublime, life and death. In this light, the sensation of life these theoretical thoughts explore is a pleasing yet unsettling one, where the beholder comes face-to-face with life not in its mimetic form, but in its biomimetic one: that is, a mode of life that has yet to be instantiated in appearance, but serves as an underlying force and principle of all life-forms. It is neither dead nor alive, good nor evil, being nor becoming, but a potentiality that can either trigger a life process in all possible dimensions or fold back to its own cessation. In other words, the mode of life that the cinematographic image dis-conceals is life on an equalizing plane, and the reality it approaches is this very plane that cuts across human existence.

In the second issue of *Modern Screen,* Liu coined an aesthetic term: *écranesque,*[47] a variation on some of the French critical terms circulated between 1918 and 1942, most notably *photogénie* and *cinégraphique.* Liu's first article in *Modern Screen,* "Écranesque" is a protofuturist analysis of the cinematic effect that both acknowledges the immanence of modern life and attempts to transcend it to a higher form of productive life. In the opening of the article, he echoes the words of Ricciotto Canudo (1877–1923), who proposed that the cinema be considered the "Seventh Art," one that sums up and puts an end to all aesthetic experiences.[48] Liu responds: "Cinema: It is a *yundong de yishu* (art in motion) produced when artistic sensation and scientific rationality are blended together." He goes on, "Like building a general stronghold of rationalism that can fundamentally materialize mechanical civilization, the cinema is the most characteristic representation of the society of mechanical civilization."[49] These two introductory statements may, at first glance, read like a straightforward celebration of cinema's mechanical reproduction, mechanical culture, and material modernity. What Liu is interested in, however, is the "artistic sensation" specific to the age of mechanical culture. The implicit idea, which he probably borrowed from Kracauer, is that the mechanical age has rationally condensed human beings into bare components in a larger productive life.[50] In this sense, the cinema addresses this new sensation as it relates to the spectators' day-to-day anxiety about the depreciation of human life. But here, Liu seems to suggest that the larger production machine—or the nation—can ultimately transcend this unsettling experience into a unified collective one. And the way this sense of collective life can be created is, as suggested by Klages, to turn cinema into an "art in motion," one that puts into synchronous motion the natural rhythm of the sentient bodies and, as suggested by Bergson, the creative productivity that propels human evolution.

It is based on such an idea that Liu defines the term "*cinégraphique*" as a form of beauty that is "non-literary, non-dramatic, and non-painterly." Hence, *cinégraphique* is rooted in "the organic interaction between the non-stopping flow of the motion of the image and sound." Therefore, what constitutes the cinema is not the image as an optical effect, but the way movement, as an audiovisual counterpoint and an instantiation of *jiezou* (rhythm), unfolds in this aesthetic experience. To this, Liu comments, "The real impact of sound does not come from its synchronization with the image. Rather, it depends on how well it brings out the *neimian de yiyi* (what immanates from within [the cinema])."[51] Here, Liu implies that cinematic sensation mirrors the way the spectators' senses are stimulated by the mechanical age, that is, by a counterpoint of mechanical rhythms of the various production machines, modes of transportation, mass media, snap shots, sound bites, and the actual flow of the human bodies on the street. But more important, the cinema juxtaposes these mechanical, mathematical, and serial rhythms into a harmonious rhythm of life, which puts all things onto an equalizing plane.

Liu Na'ou's argument centers on cinematic rhythm, which can be interpreted in two different ways. In one sense, Liu simply means a film's formal rhythm. In his essay "Dianying jiezou jianlun" [On film rhythm, 1933], Liu attributes this way of thinking to two French formalist writers: René Clair (1898–1981) and Léon Moussinac (1890–1964).[52] Clair was a member of the Dada and surrealist movements. For him, "formal manipulations including optical effects, tilted framing, juxtapositions of shapes and lines between shots, and manipulations of shot durations in an edited sequence [are] techniques that would defamiliarize the spectators' normalized perceptions of reality, and unleash repressed desires and drives from the unconscious as a way to cope with the fragmented, distracting, or even traumatic experience of modernity."[53] Meanwhile, Moussinac studied the theory of Sergei Eisenstein (1898–1948), and suggested that these formal manipulations "would offer sensual shocks to the spectators' normalized perceptions, which would inspire them to rethink the way political reality has been presented in other social discourses."[54]

Liu goes on to suggest that there is another level of rhythm in a piece of art. As Moussinac argues:

> If the cinema, as a plastic art of space, derives part of its beauty from the *arrangement* and *form* of the individual images, one must not forget that, as an art of time (since the parts of the whole are successive), it derives the complement of its beauty from the *expression* of the image.[55]

Liu Na'ou calls this *nei de jiezou* (inner rhythm), a kind of rhythm not accountable by the mathematical or formal components of a film, but immanent in the overall cinematic sensation of the spectator's body, and expressed through the cinematic body as a rhythm of life. For Liu, even though inner rhythm is more abstract, it is intrinsic to the human body, comparable to a body's response to a piece of music as it involuntarily swings to its rhythm. In this sense, the concepts of biological life and human life are intricately connected through Klages' understanding of natural rhythm with a life rhythm.

Nonetheless, while life rhythm is inborn, formal or outer rhythm requires more specialized training in order to understand its rational beauty. Liu argues that Chinese filmmakers must learn to instrumentalize this inner rhythm in order to communicate political ideas effectively. Liu agrees with his Marxist counterparts that the capitalists have turned this rhythm into a "sleeping pill" and a "spiritual ambrosia" for the petite urbanites (e.g. by making melodramas or gods-and-demons films), reducing it to "sentimentalism, irrationalism, trendiness, leisurely taste of the intelligentsia, romanticism, and imagination."[56] Yet, for Liu, the solution is not to take away the sleeping pill itself and "turn cinema into the Grand Gobi Desert." Rather, Chinese filmmakers should relearn how to grasp this rhythm as an affective and effective tool to generate a "common sensation" among members of the masses. In other words, educating the masses cannot be done rhetorically, but must be done as a kind of *jiaohua* (inculcation through immersion) by carefully synchronizing individual rhythms to a common natural rhythm.[57]

In "On Film Rhythm" Liu Na'ou identifies cinematic "common sensation" as a form of expression, that is, something that is immanent in the film image, and is crystalized as a film form. Zhang Zhen argues that Liu's obstinate insistence upon theorizing film form, despite the fact that he seems to be more interested in the deeper level of spectatorial sensation, is attributable to the popular belief among many Shanghai art critics that forms and contents are fundamentally separate.[58] In fact, in "Zhongguo dianying miaoxie de shendu wenti" (On the depth of representation in Chinese cinema), published in the third issue of *Modern Screen,* Liu elaborates on the relationship between film forms and representation based precisely on this presupposition. He argues, "In a work of art, its 'how it represents' is often more important than 'what it represents.'" Aside from those films that represent situations of absurdity, for Liu the cinema often portrays a fairly mundane experience. Yet, it still manages to attract spectators because the "author" uses her or his specific methods to represent a mundane experience with an analytical sensibility. In fact, the author's ability to analyze a mundane event and elevate it to a level of interest allows the audience to "determine whether a film is art or not."[59]

Liu argues that a film's author uses *dongzuo* (action) as a means of representation by turning action into *anshi* (implied meaning).[60] In one register, Liu simply regards cinematic acting as a form of pantomime, which indicates, instead of portraying fully, a dramatic action. In another register, Liu uses the term *anshi xing* (implicitness) to suggest that in the cinema, the image is first apprehended as is, but is read by the spectators within the overall narrative structure as a readable sign (in the semiological sense).[61] Liu's argument resembles European structuralist film theory in the 1960s, which interpreted the cinema as a form of language. For the structuralists, the image, captured directly as reality, is read as a sign or discourse (i.e., as a structure of signs) by the viewers. In such terms, what Liu Na'ou describes is the process of an image being converted to a sign. "For Liu, action is a common language of all human beings; hence, cinematic implicitness, by definition, trespasses national and class boundaries."[62] In addition to the narrative level, the cinema also provides the film author a set of mechanical narrational tools, i.e. camerawork, optical effects, and editing.

Implicitness, however, may also have a third meaning on the level of film forms. Liu argues that Chinese filmmakers failed to use any of the narrational tools in the cinema effectively. He points out that in an average Chinese silent film (in 1933, most Shanghai productions were silent), 40 percent of the screen time is taken up by "titles" (intertitles that communicate the general settings), of which 35 percent are "sub-titles" (intertitles that explicate further what the scenes are about) and 5 percent are "spoken titles" (intertitles that convey dialogues). An additional 40 percent of the screen time is taken up by "busts," that is, close-ups or medium close-ups that provide visual references to the text in the titles, not as part of the film's narrative. Then, 15 percent of the screen time is devoted to actual dramatic scenes and 5 percent to optical effects. Liu argues that in this scenario, 80 percent of the screen time is in fact literary, whereas only 20 percent is cinematographic. By comparison, in *Sunrise* (Fox, 1927), F. W. Murnau uses only 5 percent of his screen time for his "subsidiary titles" (nondialogue intertitles), and the ratio of dramatic scenes to intertitles is 18:1. Hence, Liu argues that Chinese cinema has a "penchant for overemphasizing a film's contents," especially in preaching to the audience ideas on "society, class, and consciousness."[63] In sum, Liu believes that whatever political content filmmakers wish to represent is best expressed not in verbal language, but in the form of cinematic implicitness.

But is cinematic implicitness simply a question of using the proper forms to convey a film's contents? Liu himself did not offer a very straightforward answer to this question. However, a more productive way to read his theoretic solution is to reconnect his formalist theory to his notion of the cinematic inner rhythm. In some sense, what he calls cinematic implicitness is best understood not simply as an implied meaning produced as part of the process of turning the image into a discourse. Rather, it refers to a way by which the cinema could produce a formal rhythm, which would be perceived by a spectator's sentient body as a natural rhythm. From such a process of rhythmic synchronization, a common sensation would manifest itself, a sensation produced as a result of the spectators' approaching an equalizing plane.

This idea is explored by Liu Na'ou in "Guanyu zuozhe de taidu" [About the author's attitude], which is the most philosophically engaged piece of writing Liu has ever produced on the cinema. Liu coins a term *mei de guanzhao taidu* (attitude of aesthetic observation-reflection), an attitude that allows the film author to turn life in all its presence and concreteness into an artistic expression, which in turn becomes a creative impetus that furthers the evolution of life.

> The attitude of aesthetic observation-reflection is a quest for grasping the objective fact by infiltrating oneself into the contents, in order that one stays within a silent [state of] observation-reflection; this is a special kind of attitude that allows the author and the observed to become one.[64]

In this sense, Liu believes that the film author should immerse her or himself in life in all its presence and concreteness. But in order to do so, these authors cannot simply grasp such reality as a piece of raw material. Rather, they need to blend their role as an observer with the object's role as a reflection of their act of observation. Liu's idea not only inherits the assemblage of intellectual thoughts I have discussed, but also echoes the way Arthur Schopenhauer (1788–1860)—whose work Liu Na'ou could read in its Japanese translation—regards the process of an aesthetic experience as one in which the subject surrenders its will to that of the object. In other words, by surrendering one's subjectivity completely in the act of observation, one is entirely absorbed into the state of existence of the other. In this sense, the self and the other are reflections of each other, so that one is the representation of the other. In so doing, the relationship and difference between these two positions are effectively suspended.[65]

Up until this point, Liu has regarded the cinematic experience as a sensorial response to modernity and the internal rhythm of life. However, once the question of authorship is introduced into Liu's discussion, such a sensation becomes a quality that can be abstracted and learned by the filmmaker, who can in turn authorize and manipulate it as a creative ingredient. In "About the Author's Attitude," Liu theorizes about the attitude of the author in preparation for her or his act of creation—even though an author is, first and foremost, a spectator. Initially, Liu remains within the register of immanence, suggesting that the author and the object she or he observes should become one. Yet, Liu furthers his idea by suggesting that such a state of oneness can be aestheticized and abstracted as a form of beauty, a sensation that can then be mechanically reproduced in the author's act of creation and production. In this sense, beauty becomes a transcendental (i.e., a concept that has been understood by the author a priori), if not altogether transcendent (i.e., a supersensible quality that lies beyond human knowledge), value.

I want to make this rhetorical shift even clearer by comparing Liu's idea with Bazin's notion of the film image as the *objet lui-même* (object-itself) liberated from its *contingence temporelle* (temporal contingency).[66] "By grasping the object-itself of the observed, for Bazin, the camera is no longer a perceiving subject of the things represented; rather, it merely lets the object *be* in cinema."[67] Yet, by staying in the register of the camera's mechanical objectivity, Bazin has carefully evaded the role of the author. In the heated debate of the *politiques des auteurs,* Bazin generally likes the idea of cinematic authorship. Yet, in some senses it stands in opposition to the very idea that the camera mechanically observes and that the *réalisateur* (director or someone who realizes the image, as opposed to the theatrical *metteur en scène,* or someone who puts a scene together) is supposed to let reality be realized through the camera's *objectif* (lens).[68] For Bazin, therefore, the cinematic effect is immanent in the objective reality itself, whereas for Liu Na'ou, cinematic beauty was increasingly treated as a value independent of any cinematic experience. Yet, cinematic beauty, for Liu, indeed takes place in a preindividuated nonstate between the subject and the object, and the role of the author is to use cinematographic forms and rhythm to take the spectators (back) to this nonstate of preindividuation.[69] Hence, for Liu, such a transcendental experience can be understood as an experience that has taken place before the distinction between the subject and the object is delineated, something that is in fact immanent in life. As Deleuze argues, the purely transcendental is, curiously, pure immanence.[70]

While Liu's writing manifests this transcendental turn (though it is in fact an expression of immanence), Huang Jiamo stays on a more immanent level. In "Hard Film and Soft Film," the very article that gives the theory its name, Huang begins his discussion with a definition of the cinema we have already seen in the writings of Gu Kenfu and Hou Yao: the cinema is a "beautiful crystallization of integrating various forms of art and sciences, which, after all, is a form of play-drama." Because of this, Huang argues that the cinema is, by definition, a soft medium: "Cinema is ice cream for the eye, a sofa for the spirit." Huang argues that the Chinese producers, by advocating the cinema as an educational tool, had turned cinema into a starched shirt.[71] The idea that the cinema should offer visual pleasure and spiritual comfort had been accepted by the international market as a standard, and in this sense, the hard-film theorists and those producers who supported them steered Chinese cinema away from such a standard, and consequently, its international marketability.

After that, Huang responds to Liu Na'ou's philosophical musing:

> Today, we need . . . soft and *touming* [transparent] films. These films are made up of the *shengming de benzhi* [original quality of life or life-in-itself], which is always only capable of being given to us by drama. These are elevated and admirable films that make the masses feel pleased and welcomed. These films are the portraits of life in all its presence and concreteness. They enable their spectators to appreciate the wealth of life in all its presence and concreteness. Upon seeing these films, the spectators will become interested, of their own volition, in the rich sensations of life's presence and concreteness.[72]

Here, the word *touming* (transparent[cy]) can be read in two registers. In one register, it refers to the materiality of the celluloid film, that is, film as a transparent and soft surface that records, reflects and allows the spectators to observe the life form that is registered upon it.[73] In this sense, cinematic beauty, for Huang, immanates from not only the very materiality of the celluloid film, but also the image its transparent surface reveals. In a deeper register, it corresponds to Liu's idea of the "aesthetic attitude of observation-reflection." For Huang, the transparency of the soft film puts the spectators in direct contact with drama, which in turn represents not only *rensheng de xiezhao* (representation and reflection of life), but also the original quality of life or life-in-itself. The original quality is the very quality that allows the spectators to apprehend human life as being actualized with multiple appearances, yet all these manifestations are, in the cinematographic image, condensed and crystalized in this direct sensorial contact with the rhythm of life.

Therefore, between the theories of Liu Na'ou and Huang Jiamo there is a subtle point of convergence. Liu believes in the cinema's power to present an object liberated from subjectivity via the filmmaker's aesthetic attitude of observation-reflection, while Huang Jiamo believes that the cinematographic image allows the spectator to see through its surface and apprehend the inner quality of life. The former suggests that the beholder transcends her or his own subjectivity, while the latter suggests that life-itself immanates from the image in the process of viewing. For Liu, in cinema, a being can be liberated from the confines of a subject–object relationship. In this state of liberation, the spectator is completely drawn not only to the image itself, but also to the passage of time it instantiates, thus enabling the spectator to approach life-itself in its presence. This is comparable to Heidegger's notion of Dasein: there-being (often translated in Chinese as *cizai*, here-being or the hereness of being). Dasein is the very hereness or presentness that is not sensible, but is instantiated in all life-forms in time. For Liu Na'ou, the hereness of being is disconcealed to the spectator as the cinematographic image allows her or him to become one with the object. Meanwhile, for Huang, the transparency of the image allows the subject to realize that she or he is part of the image as an equalizing plane, from which immanates life in all its immediacy: the hereness of existence from which life acquires its form or appearance, a (non)state similar to the one described by Liu. Liu's transcendental theory and Huang's immanent one can therefore be understood as two paths leading to the same point.

Life and Cinema: Immanuel Kant and Wang Guowei

This point of convergence between Liu Na'ou and Huang Jiamo marks a zone of indiscernibility about art and life, with which European and Chinese philosophers and aestheticians all wrestle. In this zone of indiscernibility, one can identify a set of semiological relationships (hereby expressed as super-signs): *mei*/beauty and *chonggao* or *zhuangyi*/sublime; *qun*/collective and *ji*/self; *rensheng*/life and *shengtai*/biological life; *shengtai*/biological life and *minsheng*/national life; *neizai*/immanence and *xianyan*/transcendence. To a certain degree, the intersection between Liu and Huang is symptomatic of the very aporia embedded in the theorization of the cinema as an aesthetic experience. Therefore, in order to locate the *mise-en-abîme* of the soft-film debate, and to repurpose it as a systematized line of thinking in dialogue with both European and Chinese aesthetics, we must rethink this set of semiological differences in the context of two philosophers: Immanuel Kant, whose aesthetics inform all the major strands of film theory I have discussed in this chapter, and Wang Guowei, the scholar who translated and reconfigured Kant's ideas in Buddhist terms, all of which collectively form the presuppositions about cinematographic beauty among the soft-film theorists.

The zone of indiscernibility I have identified in the writings of Liu and Huang was in fact questioned by Kant in his "Analytik des Schönen" ["Analytic of the Beautiful," 1790]. In the end, Kant acknowledges that it was impossible for him to immediately work out what seemed to be a logical inconsistency. In his essay, Kant emphasizes that the beautiful is: (1) not a value inherent in the art object itself; (2) not an idea posited somewhere outside human knowledge (not transcendent); (3) not a value within human knowledge upon which we can ground our aesthetic judgment (not transcendental). For him, aesthetic judgment comes entirely from a pleasing sensation that the body generates as it beholds the art object. "The judgment of taste is therefore not a cognitive judgment," Kant argues, "hence not a logical one, but is rather aesthetic, by which is understood one whose determining ground *cannot* be *other than subjective*."[74] This is indeed the *point de départ* in Liu's definition of "observation-reflection," that the process of one's immersion in cinematographic beauty begins with one's subjective observation, and with the cinematographic image serving as a reflection of one's subjectivity.

The interesting point here is that Kant chose to write, "*cannot* be *other than subjective*," instead of, "can only be subjective." What is left unsaid is a hint of indiscernibility and indetermination. Here, Kant clarifies that beauty, as a bodily sensation, does not come from human cognition. In this sense, one does not know that something is beautiful based on any preconception of beauty. Yet, this brings to the beholder a sense of gratification unto itself, not a satisfaction with an end or purpose in mind. Hence, Kant argues, "*Beauty* is the form of the purposiveness of an object, insofar as it is perceived in it *without representation of an end*."[75] Again, this presupposition informs the soft-film argument regarding the cinema as an educational tool: that the aesthetic satisfaction of the spectators should come not from the fulfillment of a political purpose, but from allowing the spectators to immerse themselves in a common sensation, from which a sense of collectivity would inevitably emerge.

However, this process of feeling and satisfying may not be truly subjective. What complicates Kant's phrase "*cannot* be *other than subjective*" is the fact that sensation is not part of human consciousness; rather, it informs it. In other words, aesthetic judgment takes place before the beholder apprehends the art object in relation to her or his body as a consciousness, and cannot be subjective in the strictest sense of the word. It is because such a sensation is generated within the body before subjectivity is reconstituted and reaffirmed by the viewing experience. In fact, it even takes place before the division between the subject and the object is delineated. What is at stake in Liu's term "observation-reflection" is the reciprocity between the subject and the object: as the beholder observes a piece of art as an object, such a piece of art also serves as a reflection of the subject, which reflects the beholder as an object. The aesthetic experience is therefore one in which the beholder and the image she or he beholds enters a state of preindividuation, a state where consciousness of the difference between the self and the other is inoperative. In a similar manner, for Huang, the transparency of the cinematographic image signifies the potentiality of the beholder's entering the image as one—and by extension, the unity of substance between the beholder and the image, organic rhythm and universal rhythm.

Yet, what Kant wants to capture—but was limited by his own language (hence, the phrase "*cannot* be *other than subjective*" in its obscurity)—is the very sensation when the beholder first encounters the art object before identifying what it is and how she or he would relate to it. For example, when I see a painting and find my senses pleased by my contact with it, I can say that it is agreeable, or even beautiful, but all of these would take place before I consciously identify what is represented in the painting, its forms and composition, its author, and my subjectival position in relation to this piece of art. By Kant's logic, I could not call a painting beautiful if I knew a priori what I was supposed to expect. Therefore, if someone brings me to an exhibition of Rembrandt's work, and I have already predetermined that all of Rembrandt's paintings are beautiful, the gratification of my being pleased by all the paintings in the exhibition is a satisfaction with an end represented: it satisfies my desire to see these objects that have already been judged by other people and myself as beautiful.

An interesting difference between Bazinian ontology and Kantian aesthetics is that if I base my understanding of the cinema upon the former, I would first apprehend the image as a form of consciousness. Then, my full cognition of such consciousness, that is, when I begin to read the image as a sign, would impart to me a sensation. For example, when I see a medium close-up of Marlene Dietrich facing the camera under one single flattering light in a train compartment in *Shanghai Express* (Josef von Sternberg, Paramount, 1932; see Figure 1), I apprehend this as an image of Dietrich-cum-Shanghai Lily, and read it immediately and syntactically as "Here is Dietrich/Shanghai Lily contemplating her own unrequited love, the violation of her companion, and the ostracized position she occupies as a sex worker among a group of uptight and misogynistic colonialists." It is out of this syntactical relationship that my body generates a complex structure of viewing pleasures: my scopophilic pleasure, my pleasure at being omniscient in the fictional world in which I posit myself, my admiration of Dietrich's beauty, my empathy with Shanghai Lily as a person who occupies a socially liminal and marginal position.

However, Kantian aesthetics acknowledges a step before our apprehension of such consciousness. In other words, the very sight of Dietrich/

Shanghai Lily in this aesthetic form, which I did not expect to see, triggers my body to generate a pleasing sensation, mixed with an overwhelming sensation that I cannot name immediately (what Kant would call the sublime). Then, I apprehend it as an image-consciousness and begin to read it as a sign within the film's syntagma. More important, my body generates this mixture of pleasing and overwhelming sensations precisely at a moment when Dietrich/Shanghai Lily and I are in a state of oneness—that is, I cannot help but be completely immersed in the represented world as mine, a state of observation-reflection that posits me in life in all its presence and concreteness. Following this argument, for Liu and Huang, consciousness is temporarily suspended in the cinema as an aesthetic experience.

Yet, what bothers Kant is: how can a private bodily sensation be universalized, i.e. transferred from individual biological bodies to a collective? He concludes that one must presuppose that our bodies share a certain "common sense," that is, a common process of producing the same feeling when a living body encounters the same experience. But there is no way to verify that: I cannot possibly ask everyone in the world whether they would agree with my judgment. Hence, an aesthetic experience that I find pleasing can be treated by me only as an example of how other living bodies could potentially feel or should feel.[76] It is important to note that beauty is universalizable precisely because it is a bodily experience, a biological reaction to which I can anticipate a certain agreement among other biological lives. It is on the level of life form, not of subjectivity, that universalization is conceivable.

This idea in fact does not sit well within Kant's overall belief in transcendence. In his discussion of teleology, Kant argues:

> Now we have in the world only a single sort of beings whose causality is teleological, i.e., aimed at ends and yet at the same time so constituted that the law in accordance with which they have to determine ends is represented by themselves as unconditioned and independent of natural conditions but yet as necessary in itself. The being of this sort is the human being, though considered as noumenon [thing-in-itself]: the only natural being in which we can nevertheless cognize, on the basis of its own constitution, a supersensible faculty (*freedom*) and even the law of the causality together with the object that it can set for itself as the highest end (the highest good in the world).[77]

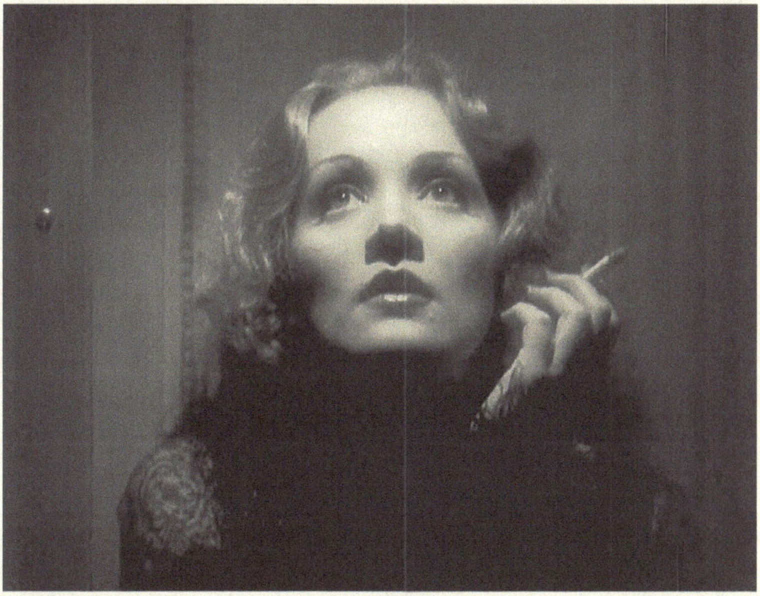

Figure 1. Marlene Dietrich as Shanghai Lily in *Shanghai Express* (Josef von Sternberg, Paramount, 1932): from a Bazinian perspective, the image is apprehended by the spectators as an image-consciousness; from a Kantian perspective, before the image is apprehended as consciousness, it first triggers a mixture of pleasing and overwhelming sensation.

Here, Kant connects the human sensation of beauty to the supersensible faculty of freedom. In plain language, real freedom, that is, freedom from all natural or social conditions, causality, and design, belongs to the noumenon, and thus is not nameable, graspable, or knowable by the human mind. Nevertheless, Kant believes that human being is the one kind of being that is capable of sensing it. It is because human beings, unlike all other beings in the world, are both situated within the set of natural conditions and outside it. They have the capability of exercising their own desires and determinations somewhat independent of the overall design of the world. Such liminality of humanity between nature and what lies beyond it allows human beings to access what would otherwise be supersensible. In this light, the pleasing sensation that we call beauty is a form of pleasure when one senses one's own freedom, or one's relationship with life-in-itself. Hence, when Kant wrote that beauty "cannot be other than subjective," what he means is that *it cannot possibly be subjective, but we cannot think of it otherwise.* In this sense, the cinema, which makes what is supposed to be supersensible palpable or tangible—that is, life-in-itself—is indeed a biomimetic technology par excellence.

The Kantian notion of freedom, when translated by Wang Guowei in the early twentieth century, was filtered through Buddhism and Bergsonianism. For Wang, an aesthetic experience has a temporal dimension: in addition to beauty and the sublime, there exists another *xingzhi* (essence, quality, or nature) called *guya.* The term *guya* is often understood as a form of elegance arising from the aging of an artistic object, similar to the European concept of patina. Yet, the word *ya* can in fact mean an interesting sensation that is capable of absorbing a beholder into a state of *wangwo* (forgetting myself). Meanwhile, the word *gu* does not necessarily mean old or old-age; it can also mean a passage of time passed (as in *huaigu*—remembrance of time passed). In other words, the term *guya* can be understood as forgetting oneself in time, a concept akin to two ideas that we have seen before: *juexiang* (reflection from the depth of time) and *kairos* (the time it takes for time to end), two notions that characterize the cinematographic approach to reality.

In a discussion of *guya,* Wang writes:

> The nature and quality of *guya* are different from those of *youmei* [beauty] and *hongzhuang* [sublime]. But *guya* only exists in art, not in nature. One's ability to judge something as *guya* is different from one's ability to judge something as beautiful or sublime. The latter is intrinsic to life, while the former is a result of training. One's aesthetic judgment on an object's beauty or sublimity depends on an inborn sensation; such a judgment is both common to all and can be accepted as a human predicate. This is why Kant, in his discussion on aesthetic judgment, talks about a predictable common sensation. However, what people consider *guya* is in fact a judgment based on their perspective today. Objects from the past are not necessarily more *ya* (elegant) than those objects produced today. For example, readers today regard those coarsely written literary works in the past as *guya.* From the perspectives of their contemporary readers, they could be nothing special.[78]

Here, Wang Guowei proposes an alternative form of aesthetic judgment that can be acquired and inculcated in a nationalized education program. Yet, from the perspective of the cinema's approach to reality, Wang's *guya* may be considered a form of aesthetic experience in which one loses oneself in a passage of time preserved in the continuous temporal existence of an art object. In other words, the art object exists in chronometric time, and cannot be conceived otherwise; yet, it also preserves a passage of time undead when an artist brought it into its existence.

In this sense, *guya* is neither a pleasing nor an overwhelming sensation; rather, it is a nonstate of losing oneself or surrendering one's subjectivity in time. Wang describes an aesthetic experience as a process with three *jingjie* (stages), from *zhiguan* (direct observation) to *mojian* (sudden reflection), the very mapping that Liu Na'ou uses—either consciously or incidentally. The term *jingjie* comes from Buddhism. It is usually referred to as the different stages on one's path towards *wudao* (enlightenment).[79] Meanwhile, the term *wudao* is in fact composed of two words: *wu* (getting, grasping, or sensing, as opposed to understanding) and *dao* (often understood as principle, but more properly referred to as an imaginary origin of all appearances, which is in fact a nonstate in which the distinction between appearance and nothingness is dissolved).[80] When one passes from one *jingjie* to another, one begins to grasp the nothingness upon which all appearances are grounded, until at one point, even the difference between appearance and nothingness is *wu*'ed. When one hangs on to appearances, one is in a state of *zhuoxiang* (living in appearance), and when one tries to shed the idea of appearance, one is in a state of *bu zhuoxiang* (not living in appearance)—which is, after all, a way to hold on to the idea of appearance. The ultimate *jingjie* is therefore *zhuoxiang, ji bu zhuoxiang*: living in appearance *as not* living in appearance, that is, the difference between living in appearance and not living in appearance becomes inoperative.[81]

For Wang Guowei, an aesthetic experience mirrors this process towards *wu*. In his explication, he cites three lines of poems as allegories. For him, the first *jingjie* is best illustrated thusly:

> Last night, under the westerly breeze, the once verdant trees shed off their foliage.
> I climbed up to the top of a tall building;
> I saw every path leading to the end of the world.[82]

At this stage, the beholder apprehends—in its totality and immediacy—an image. In this *jingjie*, the beholder observes this image directly as a subject observing an object. In cinematographic terms, this *jingjie* is comparable to the idea that the cinematographic image is apprehended by the spectator as an image-consciousness, a here and now that seems to offer the spectator an objective reality. The second stage is then described:

> The garb and belt are both getting loose;
> [The beholder] is emaciated in search for her or his love object.[83]

This stage is comparable to the aesthetic experience of *guya*. Here, the beholder is captivated by a fascination with a passage of time, passed, preserved, and returned within its chronometric passage of temporal existence. Finally, Wang depicts the third stage:

> Having searched for it for hundreds and thousands of lifetimes,
> The beholder turns her or his head around [to reflect],
> And *that person* [whom the beholder has been searching for] is now under a light,
> Standing next to a gate.[84]

Here, the beholder realizes that what she or he has been searching for is not elsewhere or another object or person; rather, the object or person is here and now. In fact, if we read "that person is now under a light" as the beholder's own shadow, which she or he finds at the moment when she or he turns her or his head around to reflect, what the beholder arrives at is a reflection of her or himself.

If an aesthetic experience is analogous to the process of *wudao*, the three poems could be connected together into three parallel processes: living in appearance, not living in appearance, living in appearance *as not* living in appearance; *wo* (me), *wuwo* (forgetting me), *wo ji wuwo* (me *as not* me).[85] Wang's reformulation of Kantian aesthetics in Buddhist terms, is applicable to the cinema in several ways. First, the cinema, after all, is about appearance. Wang Guowei's notion, unlike Zhang Taiyan's idea of the equalizing plane or Kant's idea of beauty and the sublime, does not suggest that the spectator is supposed to enter a state of formlessness. Rather, the spectator would arrive at a state in which the difference between living in appearance and not living in appearance is, at least temporarily, suspended. Second, the Buddhist notion proposed by Wang does not suggest that an aesthetic experience must come out of contemplation; instead, the Buddhist vocabulary employs terms such as searching, living, reliving, etc. Each line of poetry Wang uses indicates a passage of time-passed, thus implying that the path to *wudao* is an ongoing negotiation of one's life or temporality in relationship with the passage of time-passed, preserved in the art object on the one hand, and on the other in a larger cosmological temporality: a change in season, in bodily appearance, or in life.

But then, what is at stake in Wang Guowei's notion of aesthetics is that this process of *wudao* is a cyclical one. In the *Vajracchedikā Prajñāpāramitā Sūtra* (more commonly known as *The Diamond Sutra,* translated into Chinese circa 401 as the *Jingang jing* by Kumārajīva, 344–413), whenever the Buddha is asked what life is, his answer is always a simple one: *rushi* (like/is or the way it is) or *rushi wo wen* (like/is what I sense or the way I sense).[86] These two answers retain the indiscernibility between like and is, thus suggesting that the process of becoming and being, potentiality and actuality are being mapped onto the same equalizing plane. The three lines used by Wang Guowei to describe an aesthetic experience begin with an aboveboard image of the sensible (all paths leading to the end of the world) and end with finding *it,* albeit after lifetimes of searching and cultivation, in one's own sensible image (the person or shadow under the light). In this sense, Wang's concept encapsulates the very aporia that the notion of approaching reality has been negotiating: the immediacy and totality of the cinematographic image, and the reality it approaches. In the process of observation-reflection, therefore, the spectator is not supposed to find anything more perfect, more beautiful, more sublime, or more transcendent than what would be called reality; rather, reality is/is like the way it is, or is/is like the way I sense. In the cinema, reality is not identical with the image—and in fact, for Bazin, it is absent—but reality is not anything in excess of or lesser than the image itself, and what the image does is to make such distance present *as not* present.

Conclusion: Speaking to Deleuze

In this chapter, I recontextualized the soft film theory in a semantically pluralistic and cross-cultural environment, a discourse ranging from the 1890s to the 1930s in which the question of life in its three forms—human life, biological life, and political life—was actively negotiated. I also examined the soft film theory itself and reconfigured it through the philosophical frameworks of both Immanuel Kant and Wang Guowei. The soft film theory, therefore, can be reunderstood as a cross-cultural semantic field, based on a presupposition that the cinema is an aesthetic experience—or as Lydia Liu argues, a biomimetic technology—in which these three kinds of life would be reconfigured and negotiated.

Seen this way, the soft film theory can offer us a point of intersection between the Shanghai filmmakers' thinking on approaching reality and

Deleuze's ideas about cinema and life. Deleuze's notion of life can in fact be traced back to Spinoza's notion of pure immanence. Recently, Agamben conducted an exegesis of Deleuze's idea of immanence based on Deleuze's last published essay, "L'immanence : une vie . . ." ["Immanence: A Life . . ."].

For Spinoza, the universe is one single substance, which is God in itself. Each life is a substance that participates in the universal substance, which tries every possible means to subsist in it (an idea corresponding to what Aristotle would call the nutritive life). Not only that, each life desires (wills) to subsist in the universal substance itself. In this sense, each individual life immanates within the universal substance and every desire is immanent within the universe.[87] For Deleuze:

> The concept of univocal Being is perfectly determinate, as what is predicated in one and the same sense of substance in itself, and of modes that are in something else. . . . Thus it is the idea of immanent cause that takes over, in Spinoza, from univocity, freeing it from the indifference and neutrality to which it had been confined by the theory of a divine creation. And it is in immanence that univocity finds its distinctly Spinozist formulation: God is said to be the cause of all things *in the very sense (eo sensu)* that he is said to be cause of himself.[88]

To say that desire immanates from a univocal desire does not mean that desire is universal. Rather, what Deleuze suggests is that each individuated desire is in itself immanent. It is not connected in any sense to a universal ideal. Instead, It is immanent in itself as an idea of desire. Agamben points out that according to Deleuze's idea of immanence, the agent of an action is also its patient. Agamben uses as an example proposed by Spinoza, that in Ladino (the language of the Sephardi Jews), "'to stroll' or 'to take a walk' is expressed by the verb *pasearse* ('to walk oneself,' which in modern Spanish is instead expressed as *pasear* or *dar un paseo*)." What such a reflexive active verb conveys is that the agent of walking is in her or himself the patient: I walk myself; I take myself for a walk.[89]

Therefore, in Spinoza's philosophical system, "action" is referred to as the effort or "striving" (*conatus*) to subsist, which is in itself a manifestation of a life's desire to survive in the larger universal substance—and by extension, the self-subsistence of the universal substance. In this sense, the agent of desire (*vis immanentiae*) is the patient of desire, as in: I desire my desire to strive for my self-subsistence. For Agamben, "The movement of *conatus* thus coincides with that of Spinoza's immanent cause, in which agent and patient cannot be told apart. And since *conatus* is identical to the Being of the thing, to desire to persevere in one's own Being is to desire one's own desire, to constitute oneself as desiring. *In* conatus, *desire and Being thus coincide without residue.*" In this light, for Deleuze, "life" is therefore defined as absolute *conatus*. It is neither completely alive nor completely dead, but is the very process of becoming (or extinguishing), indetermination and virtuality (defined by Deleuze as yet to be actualized). For Deleuze, "life" as absolute immanence—that is, life that is contingent only upon itself—is beatitude.[90]

But for Agamben, Deleuze's notion of "life," or, defined more precisely in Agamben's own term, "bare life," stands in almost direct contradiction to Foucault's. For Foucault, by reducing human beings to their state of animality, i.e. to the state of "bare lives," they subject themselves to the power of the state to manage or execute them directly.[91] Yet, what Foucault identifies in *Histoire de la sexualité* (*History of Sexuality*, 1976) is precisely the human penchant to look for a "deeper" transcendental authority. Keep in mind that Foucault's historical reference was the French Revolution, a moment when human beings released themselves from their previously prescribed social bonds and tried to actualize what they believed to be their universal humanity, that is, their commonality as bare lives. But what the revolutionaries had failed to do was precisely to let life be in its virtual state. Rather, by institutionalizing universal humanity into a form of state power, universal humanity became a transcendental value and was mythologized as a transcendent authority in the age of democracy. It is in this sense that life, biological life, and political life are intricately connected—what Foucault called biopolitics.[92]

The pleasing sensation that one's body generates when one comes face-to-face with an object of art is the pleasure of desiring one's own desire, that is, the pleasure of desiring to be one with the object that imparts to the beholder such a pleasing sensation, but not yet having such desire actualized. Also pleasing is the sensation of sharing such a sensation with all other lives that might have the same sensation. However, such a sensation is not grounded in some supersensible freedom; rather, it is immanent in life. In other words, it is tempting for the beholder to attribute the cause of such pleasure to a higher authority or national cause, but such a desire is in fact part and parcel of the movement of immanence itself, a desire that would feel gratifying only as long as it remains virtual.

In *Cinema 1* and *Cinema 2,* Deleuze never uses the term immanence, but the concept of immanence is in fact embedded in the time-image, from which immanates time in its virtuality. In his chapter "The Crystal Image," for example, Deleuze talks about a kind of film in which the present image is surrounded by a world, one in which a character's—or in fact, a film's—recollections always bring the spectator back to the present and vice versa. What one has is therefore a short-circuit between the actual image and the virtual image, that is, an image of pure potentiality: "like a double or a reflection." He continues:

> In Bergsonian terms, the real object is reflected in a mirror-image as in the virtual object which, from its side and simultaneously, envelops or reflects the real: there is "coalescence" between the two. There is a formation of an image with two sides, actual *and* virtual. It is as if an image in a mirror, a photo, or a postcard came to life, assumed independence, and passed into the actual, even if this meant that the actual image returned into the mirror and resumed its place in the postcard or photo, following a double movement of liberation and capture . . . running behind each other and referring back to each other around a point of indiscernibility.[93]

The crystal image is in fact an image where observation and reflection are being put on the same plane. To a certain degree, the cinematographic image, by capturing an image from the past and re-presenting it in the present as reality that unfolds itself here and now, is a mirror image that reflects itself unto itself. It is where the actual and the virtual, the past and the present coalesce in a zone of indiscernibility. What generates the pleasing (or overwhelming) sensation inside a spectator's body is precisely the intimacy of such coalescing between the self and the other, the past and the present, the private and the common. Being enveloped in this cinematic experience is therefore the perpetual state of suspension of one's desire—the pleasing sensation of desiring one's own desire. In fact, the crystal image is the very image where the distance between the cinematographic image and the reality it approaches is crystalized in a state of observation-reflection, from which life manifests itself as a *hereness.*

4 FEY MOU

The Presence of an Absence

No book on Chinese film criticism before 1949 can be considered complete without a serious discussion on the theory of Fei Mu (Fey Mou, 1906–51). Fey was born in Shanghai in a *shuxiang shijia* (a family filled with fragrance of books) in 1906, and moved with his parents to Beijing (Peking) when he was ten years old. His family cultivated in him a strong sense of Confucian social order, ethical values, and personal responsibility, while his French-language schooling nurtured in him an equally tenacious attraction to creative freedom, aesthetic sensation, and human rationality. In 1930, he joined the North China Film Company in Peking as a screenwriter. Then, with the incorporation of North China into the UPS, Fey went back to his "hometown" Shanghai with the new film conglomerate, where he directed a number of *xin nüxing* (new women) films, *Chengshi zhi ye* [*Night in the City,* 1933], *Rensheng* [*Life,* 1934], and *Xiangxue hai* [*Sea of Fragrant Snow,* 1934].[1] In 1940, he met producers Jin Xinmin and Tong Lian, and they set up the Minhua (Min Hwa) Film Company, where he directed the epic *Kongfuzi* [*Confucius* or *Master Kung*], which took almost a year to finish with a budget of ¥160,000. The film was shown in Shanghai's Jincheng (Lyric) Theater between December 19 and 31 and Jindu (Golden Palace) between January 12 and 18; it was considered a box-office flop.[2] After the Japanese invaded the foreign concessions of Shanghai on December 8, 1941 (areas known between 1937 and 1941 as the *Gudao* or Solitary Island), Fey became a stage director.[3] After the Sino-Japanese War (1937–45), in 1946, Fey Mou joined the Wenhua (Wen Hwa) Film Studio headed by former UPS executive Wu Xingzai (1904–79).[4] Wu needed a low-budget soft film that could be screened between the studio's blockbusters. As a result, Fey directed *Xiaocheng zhi chun* [*Spring in a Small Town*]. The film was a box-office success, but was immediately criticized by the Marxist film critics as a soft film and by the soft-film theorists as a "boring" film with "no technique."[5] The political criticism worried him enough that after the Liberation Army took over Shanghai in May 1949, Fey moved to Hong Kong in fear of possible counter-revolutionary charges.[6]

Fey Mou did not begin to fascinate film scholars until the mid-1980s, when *Spring in a Small Town,* shelved in the China Film Archive for over thirty years, was screened again in Beijing. At that time, film historians not only in China, but also in Europe and North America, believed that Shanghai cinema in the 1930s and 1940s was fundamentally politicized and pro-Communist. *Spring in a Small Town,* however, does not pretend to be anything other than a story about the unrequited love between a young doctor, Zhang Zhichen (Li Wei), and his former lover Zhou Yuwen (Wei Wei)—now the wife of his best friend, Dai Liyan (Shi Yu). The film was shot and edited in a lyrical—or as it was more popularly known, poetic—style with a series of long takes, elegant camera movements, and deep staging.[7] The film aroused a tantalizing desire among cinema scholars to open a comparative dialogue between Fey's style and post–WWII European modes of poetic realism such as Italian neorealism. In an engaging comparative analysis of the film with David Lean's *Brief Encounter* (Cineguild, 1945), Susan Daruvala argues that *Spring in a Small Town* negotiates the conflicting values between a Confucian sense of duty and personal desire, but it does so in the context of a patriarchy that was deeply traumatized by foreign invasions, economic crises, and rapid regendering of social roles and spaces, crises that were experienced transnationally and transculturally during and after WWII. For Daruvala, the fact that both Fey and Lean employed homologous stylistic devices to convey two highly similar plots shows how "poetic realism" (in itself an arbitrary term) emerged in response to this historical moment.[8]

In 2001, the long-considered lost print of *Confucius* was donated by an anonymous patron to the Hong Kong Film Archive (HKFA), and was restored by the HKFA and the Italian company L'Immagine Ritrovata in 2008. In the film, Fey presents the life of Confucius largely in accordance with the *Shiji* (*Records of the Grand Historian,* written between 109 and 91 BCE by Sima Qian [c. 145 or 135–86 BCE]). Rather than a continuous narrative of Confucius' life as a chain of causes and effects, the film offers the spectators selective moments from Confucius' teaching and contemplation before or after he makes certain important decisions. Stylistically, Fey reconfigures highly theatricalized staging through his painstaking graphic design, framing, and composition, thus creating a visual style that oscillates between theatricality and reality, staging and nature, graphical complexity and pictorial simplicity. Wong Ain-ling and Sam Ho compare Fey Mou's framing with the aesthetics of Danish director Carl Theodor Dreyer (1889–1968), whose most famous work is *La passion de Jeanne d'Arc* [*The Passion of Joan of Arc*] (1928). For Wong, while Dreyer lets the "unadorned face of the title damsel [Joan of Arc] fil[l] the entire 1.33:1 frame, confronting the viewer with an extraordinary power that strikes the soul," Fey "painted his canvas of 1.16:1 Movietone with austere mise-en-scene and graceful composition, portraying Confucius' perseverance and sorrowful dignity against worldly dictates."[9] Ho argues that the compositions of both Fey and Dreyer are based on the principle of avoiding anything that is unnecessary, while letting the concrete reality manifest itself by means of graphic abstraction.[10] The subject matter of the film and the unique aesthetics persuaded scholars including Carolyn FitzGerald and Koo Siu-sun to explore the Confucian influence in Fey Mou's aesthetics.[11]

Comparisons between Fey Mou's work and its European counterparts, and the temptation to ground his aesthetics in Confucianism, can be both productive and risky. In order to avoid (mis)-translating Fey's aesthetics in Western terms on the one hand, and committing cultural essentialism on the other, most of these scholars frame their arguments within the larger context of postwar social sensibility or the Republican discourse on art and aesthetics. For example, Daruvala avoids falling into an East-West dichotomy by tracing Fey's cinematic style to a postwar and post-traumatic sensibility that emerged within the various urban communities around the world.[12] Meanwhile, FitzGerald posits Fey's Confucian aesthetics within the larger context of a postwar *yuan* (desolation) where victory was felt as a form of defeat.[13] Meanwhile, Ho and Koo believe that Fey Mou's Confucian aesthetic is a result of a more general social and intellectual *qianyi mohua* (formation, transformation, and assimilation in a hidden and silent manner), something that incidentally manifests itself through Fey's stylistic and creative choices.[14]

This subtle but fundamental social and intellectual shift during the 1940s led filmmakers around the world to reconsider the question of what cinema is for themselves and their viewers. For Bazin, for instance, Italian neorealism represents a qualitative change in the way filmmakers negotiate cinematographic reality and cinematic art that abstracts and symbolizes reality as aesthetic devices. Such a trend was made possible by the liminal position of cinema between reality and art.[15] Bazin argues that the photographic image preserves a piece of time in the filmed subject's existence. But in the cinema, the spectator apprehends this piece of time—which is by definition absent—as though it were present. Cinematographic reality is therefore after all an illusion; it opens up all kinds of aesthetic devices to turn the cinema into an art by manipulating the spectators' relationship with time.[16] For Deleuze, in postwar European cinema, cinematographic time is no longer represented as a series of chronometric moments laid out in space as movement. Rather, postwar cinema has been increasingly interested in allowing the spectators to apprehend time in its absolute immanence: the *durée* that is in itself a potentiality that makes present the sensation of time, which would normally be concealed in movement.[17]

At stake in this line of debate is the idea that many cinemas around the world in the 1940s make present an absence. In this sense, the imperfection of the cinematographic image—or in other words, the very distance between the cinematographic image and reality—allows filmmakers to manipulate the liminal position between art and reality. In the following intervention, I focus primarily on Fey Mou as a theorist, and use examples from his films to illustrate his theoretical notions. I argue that Fey, like most of his European counterparts, explores the intricate distance between the cinematographic image and reality as a creative tool that makes present the very potentiality of time, desire, and life. In his writings, Fey comes up with two terms that he casually explores but rigorously puts into practice: *xuanxiang* (suspension-imagination) and *kongqi* (air, but more commonly translated as atmosphere).[18] More important, however, Fey locates the ontological basis of the cinema not necessarily in time, but in the Confucian concept of *ren*. *Ren* is often translated as benevolence, which is understood as the highest ethical principle in social and political relations.[19] However, *ren* can also be understood as being human, that is, an ontological order that is instantiated in all human relationships. *Ren* is in fact best regarded as neither good nor evil; rather, it measures the difference between these two imaginary poles and serves as a regulating force in order that nothing is excessively good or excessively evil—either of which is believed to be self-destructive.[20] In this light, the cinema can be understood indeed as a biomimetic process of negotiation, where human relationships, and by extension, political relationships, could be transformed and regulated in a covert and quiet manner.

Formalism and Ontology

The idea of suspension-imagination first appears in Fey Mou's article "'Daoxu fa' yu 'xuanxiang' zuoyong" ["Inverse narration" and the functions of "suspension-imagination," 1934], in which he discusses the narrative forms of his film *Sea of Fragrant Snow.* Meanwhile, the term air was first mentioned in the same year in his article "Lue tan 'kongqi'" [Let's talk about "air" briefly]. In both articles, however, Fey considers inverse narration as a *xushi fa* (narrational device), and suspension-imagination and air as *xushi gongyong* (narrational functions).[21] Hence, in some sense, it looks like Fey employs terms that would be by now associated with Russian formalism, or, in terms of cinema studies, the neoformalist arguments of David Bordwell and Kristin Thompson.[22] Nevertheless, formalism and cinema ontology, according to Bordwell and Thompson, are supposed to be mutually exclusive lines of investigation, whereas Fey, I argue, uses formalism as an entry point into his discussion on cinema ontology. An adjudication on these two lines of thinking would therefore be useful in understanding how cinematic forms, which are supposed to be aesthetic tools, can be mobilized to open up questions of time, desire, and life.

When neoformalism emerged in the United States in the 1980s, Thompson, and to a lesser extent, Bordwell, adamantly opposed the "grand theories" written between the 1940s and the 1970s, including Bazinian ontology. As a result, the followers of Bordwell and Thompson have a tendency to pit their theories against any attempt to impose an all-encompassing notion of what cinema is, which, for Thompson, has the effect of "reducing the complexity of film" to a "top-down" and one-size-fits-all philosophical model.[23] Thompson accused film analysts in the 1970s of proposing an analytical method, and then choosing a film to analyze that would illustrate it. Thus the film would simply confirm that the analyst's assumptions have been right all along. She borrows from Russian formalism a set of terms to analyze how literary writers, and by extension, filmmakers, use narrational devices to construct their plots or syuzhets. In the cinema, filmmakers also deploy a set of technical or stylistic devices, including camerawork, editing, framing, lighting, sound, and composition, for the purpose of putting the syuzhet together (hence, the term *mise-en-scène*). These devices and functions are creative tools that human beings have developed in accordance with their cognitive functions, though how they are composed paradigmatically can differ from one culture to another, or in fact, from one film to another.[24]

However, the syuzhet only represents the formal building blocks of the process of narration. For Bordwell and Thompson, the other set of building blocks is provided by the human brain in the form of the schemata or prototypes that our brains draw from everyday perceptions, which allow us to quickly determine what types of characters we are seeing, where the story is set, and how scenes and segments are connected causally, temporally, and spatially. With these schemata, the human brain can put together the syuzhet into a coherent narrative, the fabula. Through the workings of many individual films over the years, these schemata form a paradigm that both conventionalizes and challenges the existing conventions of how the narrative film is constructed and understood.[25]

Bordwell and Thompson's readers in 1985 would have been sensitive to their reference to Christian Metz's essay "À propos de l'impression de réalité au cinéma" ["On the Impression of Reality in the Cinema"], published in 1968 in his *Essais sur la signification au cinéma* [*Film Language: A Semiotics of the Cinema,* trans. 1974]. In it, Metz considers a way to reconfigure Bazinian ontology by transposing cinematographic reality from the register of human consciousness to that of human language:

> One of the most important of the many problems in film theory is that of the *impression of reality* experienced by the spectator. Films give us the feeling that we are witnessing an almost real spectacle—to a much greater extent, as Albert Laffay has noted, than does a novel, a play, or a figurative painting. Films release a mechanism of affective and perceptual *participation* in the spectator (one is almost never totally bored by a movie). They spontaneously appeal to his sense of belief—never, of course, entirely, but more intensely than do the other arts, and occasionally films are, even in the absolute, very convincing. They speak to us with the accents of true evidence, using the argument that "It is so." With ease they make the kind of statements a linguist would call fully assertive and which, moreover, are usually taken at face value. There is a filmic mode which is the mode of presence, and to a great extent it is *believable.*[26]

In other words, viewers believe they are apprehending the cinematographic image as reality because the image speaks assertively to them in a way that claims what it says is self-evident. Yet this mode of linguistic address is precisely what makes a strict comparison between the cinema and human language extremely difficult. For it to become self-evident, the addressee cannot possibly break down the syntagmatic structure of the utterance (in this case, the cinematographic image or syntagma) into smaller formal units. In other words, no matter what kinds of paradigmatic combination and reshuffling the film or filmmaker does formally, the utterance or image addresses the viewer in its entirety.[27] The film *The Big Heat* (Fritz Lang, Columbia, 1953), for example, opens with a close-up of a gun. This is not perceived as a composition of discrete formal elements such as lines, shapes, shades of light, camera distance, or camera angle. Rather, it is grasped for what it is: "This is a gun." The image is an utterance that does not address the viewer; rather, it addresses itself as a piece of self-evident truth.[28]

In some sense, as opposed to what some scholars in the 1970s believed, Metz's semiotic approach to the cinema does not depart entirely from Bazinian ontology. In fact, his idea, much like Bazin's, is indebted to the discussion of the photographic image by Sartre. What Metz tries to say is that the cinematographic image is still received—as opposed to apprehended—in its totality and immediacy, and the image approaches reality by claiming itself as is. Metz's notion, at least at this stage, corresponds to Roland Barthes's later idea that the photographic image is a "signifier without a signified." It is because the photographic image as a signifier does not signify reality or a piece of narrative information. Rather, it signifies its own self-evidentiality.[29] Later on, in *Le Signifiant imaginaire* [*The Imaginary Signifier,* 1975], Metz, based on this idea, developed his famous formulation that the photographic image signifies via the presence of the photographed object's absence:

> In order to understand the fiction film, I must both "take myself" for the character (= an imaginary procedure) so that he benefits, by analogical projection, from all the schemata of intelligibility that I have within me, and not take myself for him (= the return to the real) so that the fiction can be established as such (= as symbolic): this is seeming-real. Similarly, in order to understand the film (at all), I must perceive the photographed object as absent, its photograph as present, and the presence of this absence as signifying. The imaginary of the cinema presupposes the symbolic, for the spectator must first of all have known the primordial mirror. But as the latter instituted the ego very largely in the imaginary, the second mirror of the screen, a symbolic apparatus, itself in turn depends on reflection and lack. However, it is not fantasy, a "purely" symbolic imaginary site, for the absence of the object and the codes of that absence are really produced in it by the *physis* of an equipment: the cinema is a body (a corpus for the semiologist), a fetish that can be loved.[30]

In other words, for Metz, the cinematographic image does not really signify. Rather, it is an apparatus, a body that allows the spectator's imaginary to signify itself, via the symbolic order that was first constituted when the spectator was subjectivized in front of the mirror, and then reinstituted as the subject is re-interpellated by the ideological apparatus, that is, the structure of knowledge that informs the constitution of the mechanical apparatus and puts into action a process of intersubjective interactions (see chapter 2). In other words, such apparatus allows the subject to rehearse its own constitution and reaffirm its self-evidentiality. The way the cinema achieves this is by effacing its own mechanical or material presence (e.g. the subject erases the presence of the apparatus) and inviting the subject to project her or his own ego onto the screen as the hero. Yet, the hero is not identical to the ego; rather, as a mirror image, it is projected as the imaginary Other, one that authorizes the subject to take the cinematographic image as a symbolic order that corroborates the subject's imaginary integrity and self-evidentiality. In so doing, the cinema as an overall apparatus is configured as a fetish, a body that can be loved, as its image coalesces with or approaches—but not completely reveals—the Real that is in fact unliveable and insensible.

As a response to Metz's linguistic and psychoanalytical methods, Bordwell and Thompson assert that: (1) film is an art; hence, every form, including reality, is utilized by the filmmaker as a narrational device; (2) although film has a "communicativeness," its primary function is not to communicate; it is to please or entertain the viewers as an aesthetic experience; (3) therefore, film as a piece of art does not address its viewers as addressees; instead, its constructed syuzhet enables the spectators to actively construct the fabula; (4) in this sense, the spectators do not submit themselves to an imaginary apparatus; instead, their cognitive functions allow them to engage themselves, question, reconstruct, and rethink the believability, reliability, coherence, and comprehensibility of the narrative and the mode of narration in a specific filmic experience.[31]

By considering cinematographic reality as a narrational device, Bordwell and Thompson in effect regard Bazinian ontology as one mode of narration that dominated Hollywood and European cinemas between 1926 and 1960. Strategically, what Bordwell and Thompson argue is that by regarding cinema as an art, the broader question of ontology can be left to the aesthetes. Ultimately, though, they end up treating cinema as *poeisis* (producing).[32] In this sense, Bordwell and Thompson do have a version of cinema ontology: it is the very process of producing. As

Agamben argues, the idea of *poeisis* is not limited to the process of producing something (e.g. a piece of art); rather, it refers to the larger context of life producing itself, of which the production of art and its aesthetic evaluation are componential.[33] Hence, for Bordwell and Thompson, stylistic analysis is a study of the very life-process of producing that is engaged during the course of constructing the film as a work or praxis.

It is in this light that one can fully understand the position of Fey Mou in the overall discourse on cinema ontology. It is true that Fey's theoretical focus is on those narrational devices and functions that he tries to put into practice, but that does not mean it has nothing to do with cinema ontology. Rather, Fey's interest in poetics is deeply entrenched in his fascination with the cinema as a process of producing that approaches time, desire, and life via its liminal position between art and reality.

Suspension-Imagination

For Fey Mou, a filmmaker can manipulate a set of narrational devices or formal elements not only for the purpose of telling a story, but also for approaching time, desire, and life in the form of a spectator's suspension-imagination. The term suspension-imagination may sound esoteric at first. In the beginning of his essay " 'Inverse Narration' and the Functions of 'Suspension-Imagination,' " Fey writes:

> During the early stage of the principal photography of *Sea of Fragrant Snow*, I had intended to photograph and produce such a simple *gushi* (story) by means of a device called NARRATIVE [in English] (commonly translated as *xu jie fa* [narrative-splicing], though I believe that it should be translated as *xushi fenmu fa* [narration by means of breaking a narrative down into film segments]—a bit more troublesome, but in fact closer to what it really means). Nonetheless, because I lacked the "courage" to do so, half way through the production, I fell back to the form of *dao xu fa* (inverse narration).[34]

The complexities of how screenwriting terms were translated in the 1930s (a task we, as film historians, still need to address) can make this passage highly confusing. However, Fey Mou's terms, I propose, can be broken down through a careful semiological reading of this passage.

The print of *Sea of Fragrant Snow* has been lost. However, the synopsis of the story is still available for us. A young woman, Ruan Lingyu (played by Ruan herself), is engaged to a young man, Gao Zhanfei (played by Gao himself), by her widowed mother. However, her uncle tries to force her to marry a local banker, Fei Boqing. Ruan seeks refuge in a convent, and her uncle eventually allows her to marry Gao. Their marital life, however, is plagued by the heavy taxation levied by the local warlord. When the news about the KMT's Northern Expedition (1926–28) reaches the village, the local warlord appoints Gao as a tax collector. But Gao refuses to pay his taxes and is beaten up by the local hoodlums. Gao then leaves his wife and his son (Li Keng). On his way to the city, he meets some KMT revolutionaries, who persuade him to join the Northern Expedition. At home, Ruan's mother passes away and her son is seriously ill. Ruan promises the Bodhisattva that she would be willing to become a nun the day her husband returns and her son recovers from his illness. Eventually she does become a num. After a year, however, her son climbs over the mountains in order to visit her, and she cannot help but embrace him in a sea of snow fragranced by plum blossoms.[35]

This synopsis is the story itself, which Fey Mou puts in contrast with the film's narrative, that is, the way the story is being narrated. This in itself is a common divide in many narratological theories. But an important question then arises: how does he distinguish the difference between "narrative-splicing" and "narration by means of breaking a narrative down into film segments"? The former describes a process of putting together discrete dramatic scenes into a causally, temporally, and spatially coherent narrative. In Bordwell and Thompson's terms, this would be the cognitive process by which the spectators mobilize their schemata to construct their own fabulae. Meanwhile, when Fey talks about "narration by means of breaking a narrative down into film segments," he seems to be talking about what Bordwell and Thompson refer to as a film's syuzhet, i.e. the screenwriter's or director's process of breaking down a story into scenes that can guide the spectators to come up with their own fabulae. Like Bordwell and Thompson, Fey conceives of an opposition between the spectator's process of narrative fabrication and the screenwriter's task of narrative construction.

It is important to note that in Metzian terms, such an opposition in fact takes place within the viewing subject's psyche, and the process of subjectival reconstitution is in fact dependent on these two seemingly opposite forces: segmentation and recohesion. For Metz, film spectators do not simply put seemingly discrete film sequences together into an imaginary unity by means of splicing them together. Rather, the spectator subconsciously segments what appears to be an imaginary whole into self-evident assertive utterances called syntagmas. In this sense, the spectator's ego requires a constant reslicing and resuturing of these syntagmas together into an imaginarily seamless unity, which confirms and rehearses the imaginarily self-evident coherence of the spectator's subjectivity. Hence, for Metz, both "breaking down" and "splicing" work together in the spectatorial process as an apparatus that reconstitutes the viewing subject's imaginary sense of self-coherence.[36]

However, in his own criticism of *Sea*, especially in his explanation of why the device "inverse narration" might have caused a problem in his film, Fey Mou seems to suggest a third way of understanding cinema's approach to reality via a narrational process. The term inverse narration was coined during the Republican period in textbook discussions of literary poetics. In literary studies, it is often conveniently translated as the flashback. Nevertheless, inverse narration offers a slightly different set of emphases than the term flashback does. Inverse narration is usually defined as an A-B-A' structure: (A) a narrator (either a first- or third-person) introduces the story by informing the reader of the protagonist's current physical and psychological state (narrational present); (B) the story itself is then framed as the narrator's reminiscence (narrative past), with a moral or critical stance communicated both in her or his *cuo ci* (paradigmatic choice) and *xing wen* (syntagmatic structure), and in direct expressions of (self-)criticism or regrets; (A') a brief return to the narrational present. From a temporal perspective, inverse narration is identical to a flashback, both in its rearrangement of the chronological order of events during the course of narration, and in its foregrounding of the narrational present as a framing device.[37] Nevertheless, the Republican notion of inverse narration emphasizes the aspect of self-criticism and sense of morality underlying the process of narration. In fact, the narrator constantly maintains (via her or his choices of words and direct expressions, or at times, a voiceover) a critical and epistemic distance from the reader by placing the best words to achieve this narrational function (paradigmatic choice) and by syntactically foregrounding the narrator's sense of regrets. In fact, inverse narration is always pitted in textbooks against the *shunxu fa* (narration in accordance with the chronological order of the events), which is supposed to reduce, if not completely efface, the presence of the narrator and her or his critical stance.[38] In this light, the term inverse narration also suggests that the resulting narrative not only refers to a series of dramatic events that the narrator claims to remember, but also to the process of the narration turning inversely to itself as the locus of its literary action—or simply put, the piece of narration refers not to an imaginary fictional world; rather, it refers to itself as a piece of narration.

In the second paragraph of his essay, Fey Mou criticizes the technique of inverse narration as a dramaturgical—as opposed to cinematographic—device that encourages the spectators to connect discrete dramatic points into a coherent piece of narration. It draws attention to the process of narration itself, instead of giving the spectators the *pingdan* (flat and flavorless, but often understood as simple) reality of life. Up to this point, it sounds like Fey believes that the narrational artifacts should efface themselves for the purpose of producing an illusion of reality. Yet, Fey is actually interested in how the cinema could narrate not by strategically putting together seemingly discrete scenes that would persuade the spectators to concatenate them causally, temporally, and spatially, but by evading precisely what the dramatists would consider strategically important points, and by letting the life-process itself unfold in its utmost simplicity. For Fey, the dramaturgical mode of inverse narration destroys a fundamental cinematographic property: the narrational function of suspension-imagination.[39] In this light, Fey advocates a process of narration that is not based on narrative segmentation and recohesion; rather, by presenting segments of time or pieces of life in a way that would discourage any temptation to recohere them causally, temporally, and spatially, imagination—as opposed to perception—emerges.

In "'Inverse Narration,'" Fey Mou uses examples from *Sea of Fragrant Snow* to illustrate his ideas. For example, in *Sea,* the film withholds the precise knowledge of how Ruan Lingyu becomes a nun and how she returns to the secular sphere. For Fey, even though the spectators are asked to "fill in the blanks" with their inferences, these gaps do not invoke what he would call suspension-imagination. Rather, Fey argues that in the scene in which Ruan's son is critically ill, Fey deliberately indicates from the beginning that he will not die.[40] He wants to draw the spectators' attention not to the drama of the scene but to the reality of the life-process or life-situation that unfolds on the screen in all its simplicity.

At first glance, Fey's example seems to be a self-defeating one: by allowing the spectators to be in a life-process in all its flatness and flavorlessness, what more can they imagine? To understand his argument, it is necessary to go back to how the term suspension-imagination is understood both through its translation from Japanese and as a philosophical term. In Japanese, the term *keisō* signifies an amorous thought, a form of romantic or erotic feeling in the absence of the object of desire. This term can be used, for example, when a young couple has been engaged, but remains divided and separated until the wedding. In this sense, the separation arouses the young person's amorous feeling for the object of desire while the potentiality of its consummation remains temporarily suspended. Hence, a love letter is also called a *keisōbun,* a letter of suspension-imagination. In the absence of both the object of desire and the possibility of consummating an erotic relationship in the foreseeable future, the lover constructs her or his own object of desire and an erotic scenario out of its suspended actualization. In this sense, the *keisōbun* is not actually a letter written from one person to another, but from one person's desiring position to an object of desire she or he constructs. It is best understood as a letter that addresses itself, that is, an utterance that addresses the very process of desiring, or a desire of one's own desire.

In the various exegeses of Buddhist scriptures, the term *xuanxiang* is often understood as an unsubstantiated imagination. From the perspective of theological or philosophical reasoning, any kind of logically unsound or unsupported statement can be regarded as *xuanxiang.* However, any object that is considered not substantial or immanent can also be classified as *xuanxiang.* For example, the idea of an anthropomorphic God that transcends the substantial universe is understood in Buddhist philosophy as a form of *xuanxiang.* Alternatively, the all-too-common belief in a transcendent notion of nothingness is also a form of *xuanxiang,* for nothingness and its potential of becoming something are both immanent unto itself.[41]

In this sense, there are two interrelated ways to understand what Fey Mou may mean by suspension-imagination, and Fey does not adhere completely to either the Japanese or the Buddhist understanding of the word. On one level, in the example Fey offers—the scene in which Ruan's son is critically ill—life is reproduced in front of the spectator in all its immanence. What I mean is that life, like sensation, manifests itself in all processes of life but is ironically absent—one cannot sense life even though life makes all senses sensible. Likewise, time in itself is absent, but is made sensible when it unfolds as chronometric time; meanwhile, desire is also absent until an object of desire and the act of desiring make palpable the sensation of desire. Fey's narrational strategy is not designed to encourage the spectators to come up with any form of causal connection between dramatic elements. Yet, ironically, in this state of absolute immanence, the spectators would begin to see how the mundane reality of life is in fact a trace of time, life, and desire. As a result, time, life, and desire—as variations of potentiality—emerge and manifest as an imagination, a virtual image that is in the process of informing.

Air: *Spring in a Small Town*

In his writing, Fey Mou does not explain further how a virtual image emerges in the viewing process. Hence, one way to tease out this process is to analyze a scene from *Spring in a Small Town*, a story about a young doctor, Zhang Zhichen, and his former lover, Zhou Yuwen, who is now the wife of his best friend, Dai Liyan. This film is widely understood as a story about unrequited love, and the internal conflict between desire and duty within all the three main characters. While these narrative points can be inferred from the film's narrational process, the actual sense of unfulfilled desire is best understood as a form of suspension-imagination. By showing scene after scene of the quotidian life in all its simplicity and flavorlessness, the film asks the spectators to observe and be engaged in this almost stagnant and aimless life-process, impregnated with an air of unfulfilled desire.

For example, in the first evening of Zhichen's arrival, Zhichen, Liyan, Yuwen, and Liyan's young sister Daixiu (Zhang Hongmei) are all gathered together in Liyan's bedroom. Daixiu, who has developed a crush on Zhichen, performs a song she learned in school, which is about the unrequited love of a Cossack for a young woman named Maria. The scene opens with a long shot of the room (Figure 2). Yuwen, framed in a medium-shot distance, stands on the left of frame and pours out a dose of medication for Liyan. Meanwhile, in the middle ground, Zhichen sits on the right of frame with his back against us, looking up towards Daixiu in the background. Shortly after the shot begins, Daixiu, who stands in the middle of the frame in a three-quarter-shot distance, but entirely out of focus, begins singing her song. From a narrative perspective, the composition of the shot allows the spectators to focus on the emotional distance that Yuwen maintains in order to appear to be detached from Zhichen. But by having Zhichen turn his back to us, the shot conveys an air of longing between Yuwen and Zhichen by showing how Zhichen performs his obligation—as a guest of the house and an old friend of the family—to listen to Daixiu's childish performance. This air of longing is then subtly confirmed on the narrative level as Zhichen turns his head around and steals a glance at Yuwen (Figure 3). None of the actors

Figures 2–14, pages 123–31.

In *Spring in a Small Town* (Fey Mou, Wen Hwa Film Studio, 1946), desire and its frustration are made tangible by means of narrative inferences, semiological structuring, suspended imagination, cinematographic desolation, and last but not least, a negotiation between *ren* and *qing*.

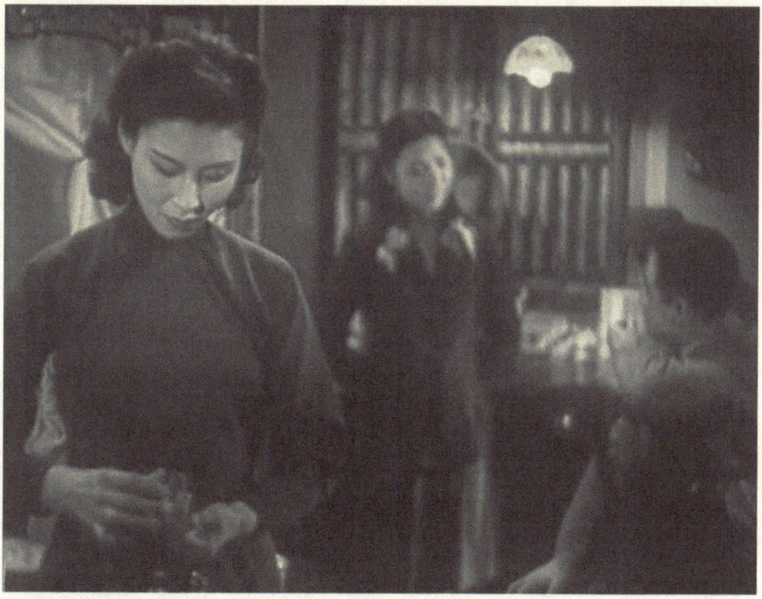

Figure 2.

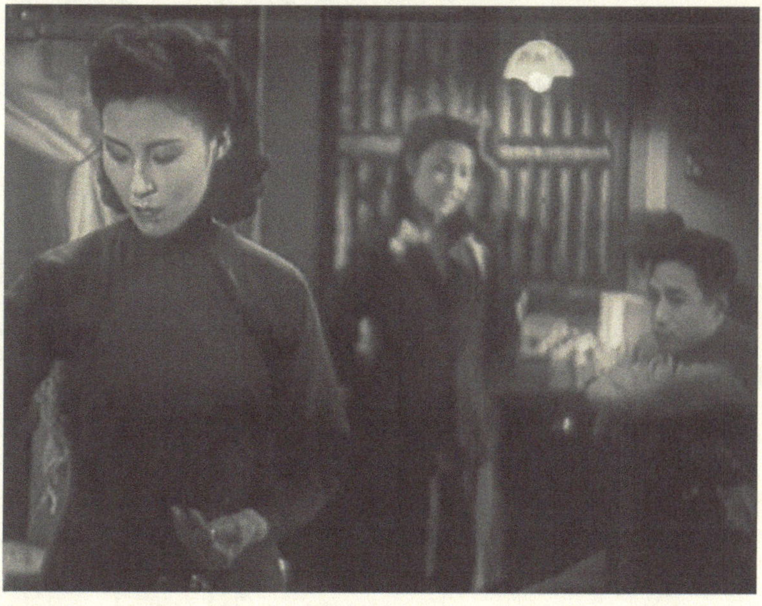

Figure 3.

emote or deliberately exhibit their longing within the shot. In fact, without any dramatic announcement, Yuwen picks up a cup off screen and turns around nonchalantly, which motivates the camera to pan and dolly slightly to the left. As it does, the camera reveals Liyan sitting in front of his bed, while Yuwen offers the cup and the medicine to him in a three-quarter-shot distance (Figure 4). Here, her gesture of offering almost takes on a symbolic meaning, as she seems to be handing all her sexual longings, and by extension, her sacrifices, to her sick husband. In the overall narrative of the film, this gesture also serves as a foreshadowing of Liyan's attempted suicide by means of an overdose: a symbolic attempt to imbibe Yuwen's unfulfilled desires and sacrifices and redeem himself by killing his body, together with her longings and sufferings.

As Daixiu sings offscreen, the spectators see Liyan taking a few pills from Yuwen's hands. He then longingly looks up at Yuwen (Figure 5). Yuwen quickly hands Liyan the cup and turns away from him gracefully, as though she had failed to understand her husband's desire (Figure 6). After Liyan has finished drinking from the cup, he hands it back to her. Yuwen, with the same grace and appearance of insouciance, walks towards the camera in order to put the cup down onto the desk in the foreground of the frame (Figure 7). As Yuwen walks towards the camera, Liyan's eyes follow her body longingly. Yet, instead of turning Yuwen into Liyan's object of desire, her performance of sexual detachment towards her husband, to the extent that she continues to perform (or lie), as she turns towards the camera (and by extension, the spectators), configures her gesture as a denial of the male gaze. After she has put down the cup, Yuwen takes a couple of steps towards the right of frame, which motivates the camera to follow her. She turns her back against the spectators and sits down in the foreground, suggesting that she looks directly at Zhichen, who has been watching her amorously (Figure 8). Their intimate look is then quickly broken by a subtle gesture as Yuwen wipes her face, and then by Daixiu leaning forward towards Zhichen as she tries to regain his attention (Figure 9).

In response, Zhichen claps his hands a few times and then turns his back to Daixiu again. After that, he looks absentmindedly at a space between him and Yuwen. The camera, unmotivated by any narrative element, dollies along a curve to the right and pans slightly towards the left, thus revealing Liyan with a satisfied look on his face (Figure 10). The camera then pans left. Before it stops, however, Liyan gets up and compels the camera to pan back to the right as he walks towards Zhichen

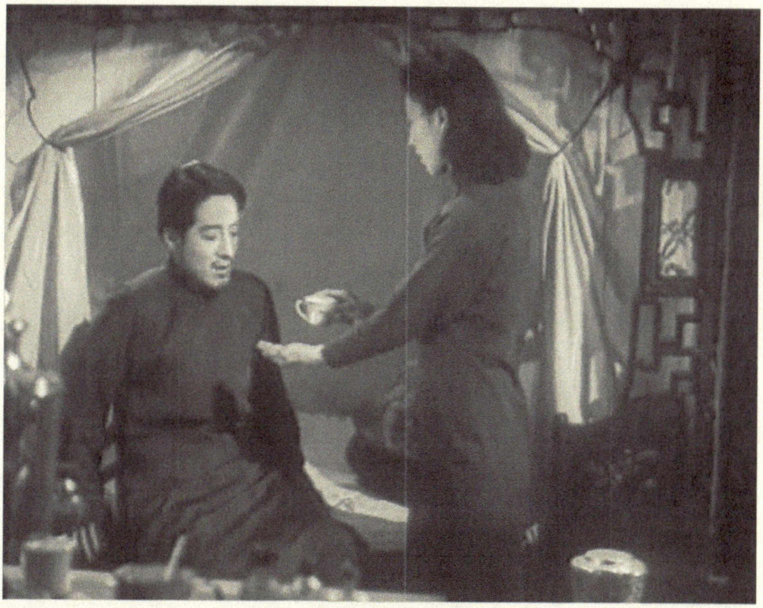

Figure 4.

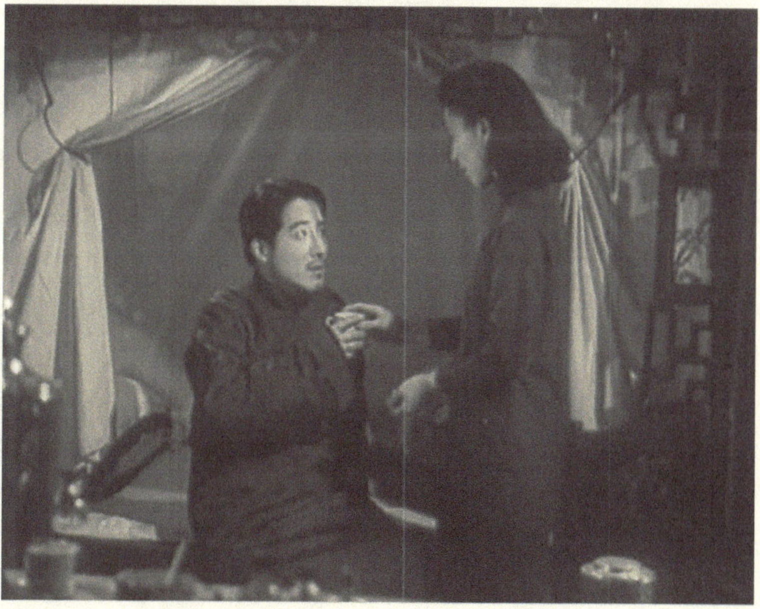

Figure 5.

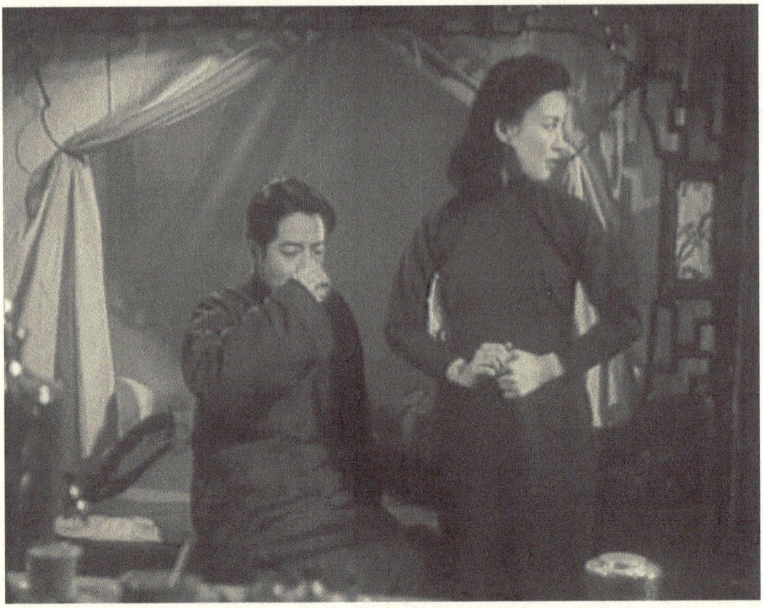
Figure 6.

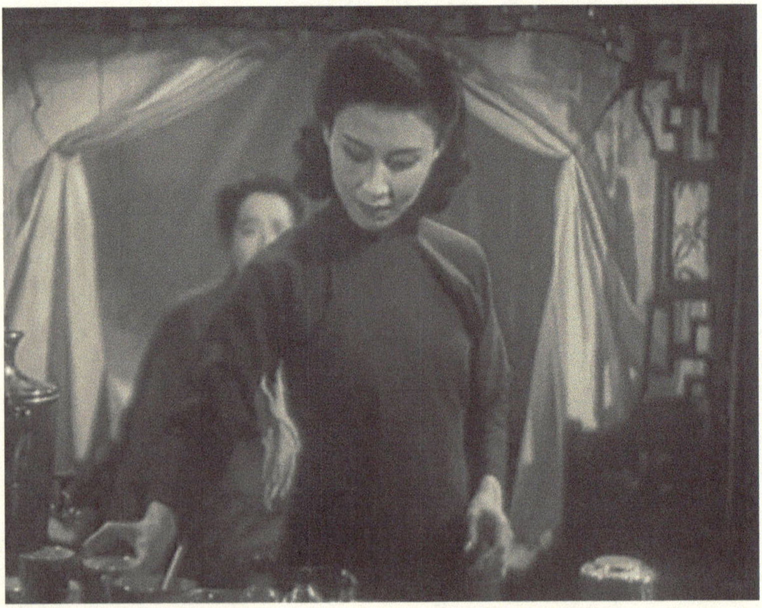
Figure 7.

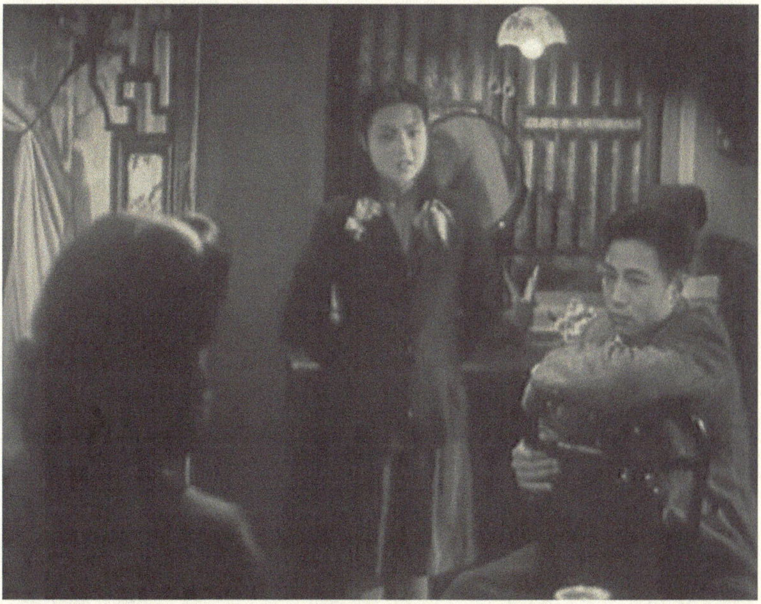

Figure 8.

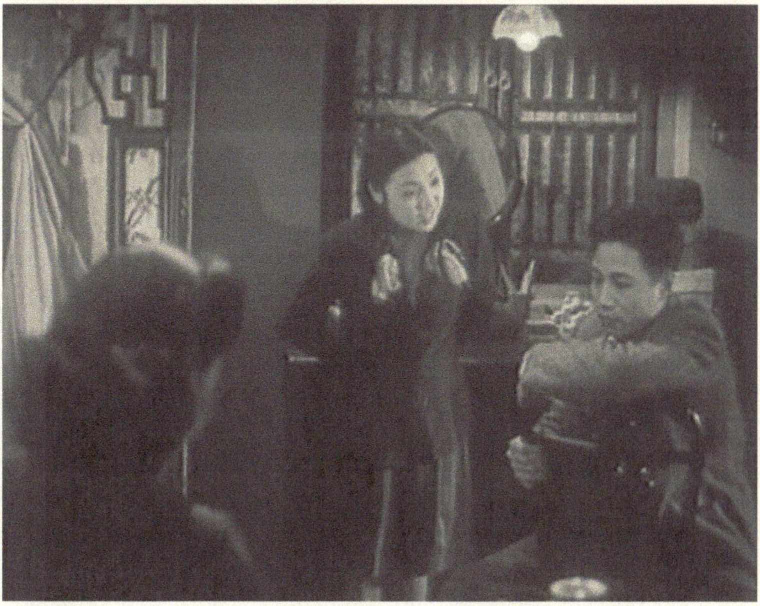

Figure 9.

(Figure 11). The camera then stops as Liyan arrives at the side of Zhichen. As Zhichen looks up to greet Liyan, Liyan pats Zhichen on his shoulder (Figure 12). As Liyan and Zhichen begin to exchange friendly gestures, the camera quickly pans to the left. Yuwen stands up and walks towards the bed (Figure 13). As she starts making the bed, the camera once again pans back quickly to Daixiu, Liyan, and Zhichen, where Daixiu finishes her song (Figure 14).

This scene in fact works in four different registers (and later on, I will demonstrate that there is a fifth register as well). First, as Bordwell and Thompson argue, the spectators are invited to make inferences about the causal relationship among these characters. Bordwell would probably see the scene as an example of "*light-writing* . . . tracing the texture of the world onto the sensitized filmstrip. . . . [The] word *trace,* derived from *tractus,* a track or course, . . . implies both carving a path (as the filmmaker does) and following another's path, as we do in watching the film—or in studying the image traces."[42] In this sense, Fey's camera traces the characters' desires, longings that are not overtly expressed by any of their actions but are made clear by their subtle glances, bodily gestures, and even their deliberate acts of impassivity, thus persuading the spectators to follow this continuous trace of desire from one action to another, or from one relationship to another. Following Bordwell's argument, this picture is made a whole precisely by the camera's fluidity in carving out this trace of desire that permits the spectators to form a cognitive picture capable of producing a cross-cultural understanding.

In the second register, the scene establishes a constellation of signs that can be read semiologically. I have already pointed out the configuration of the pills and pill-feeding as signs of Yuwen's transference of her longing and sacrifices to Liyan through his act of imbibing and receiving: a transference that will be sublimated or redeemed towards the end of the film through Liyan's attempted suicide (i.e. by over-imbibing those pills and killing his body as an embodiment of her sufferings). This set of signs, so carefully planted, developed, and performed on the left side of the chamber, is juxtaposed against Daixiu's unstoppable singing on the right of frame: her constant emitting of words that express, perform, and put on display her desire for Zhichen, which Zhichen refuses to decode, decipher, absorb, or appreciate. In a way, Daixiu's infatuation with Zhichen is a symbolic transference of Liyan and Zhichen's infatuation with Yuwen; but while the former is expressive, the latter is reserved and unsaid. In

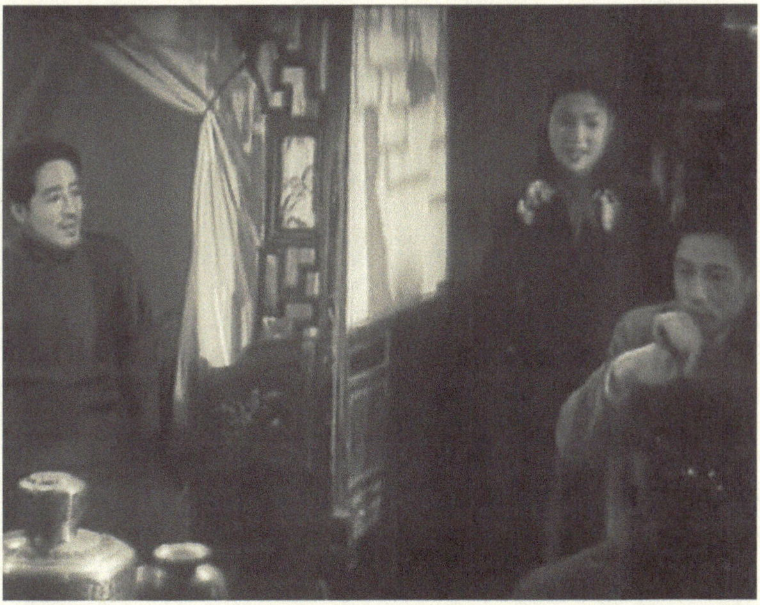

Figure 10.

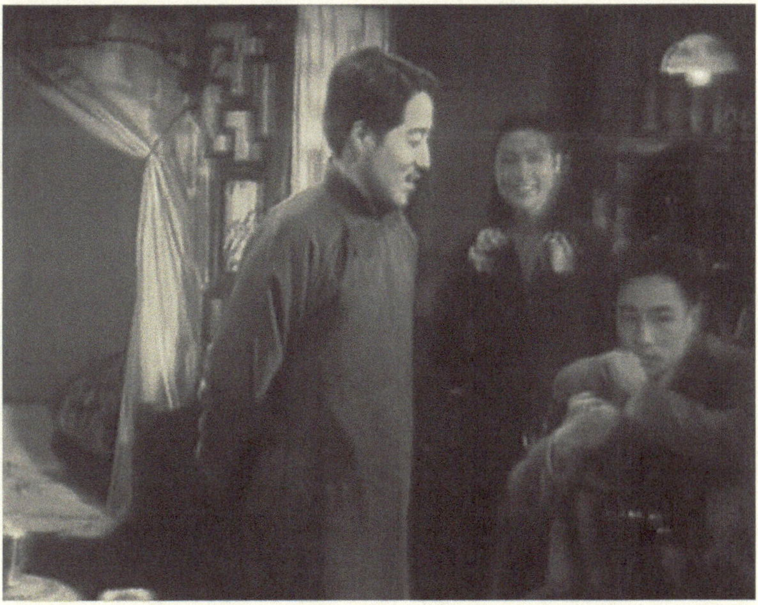

Figure 11.

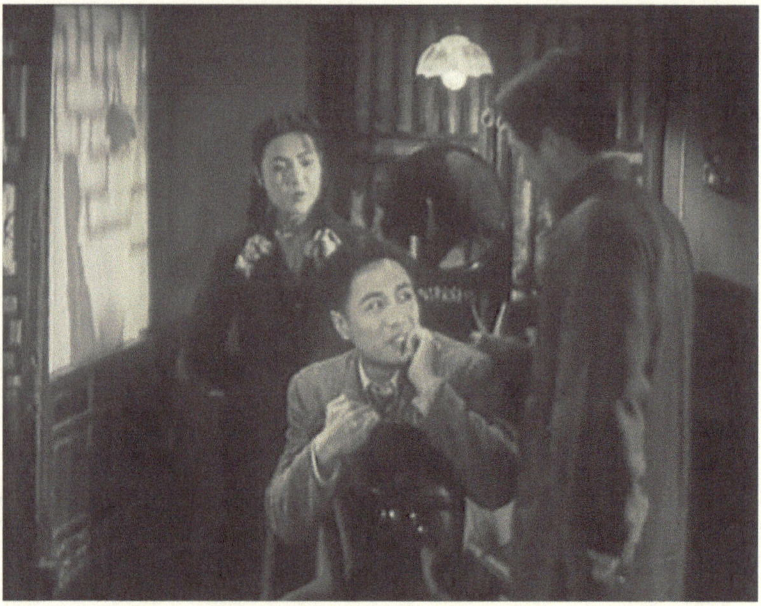

Figure 12.

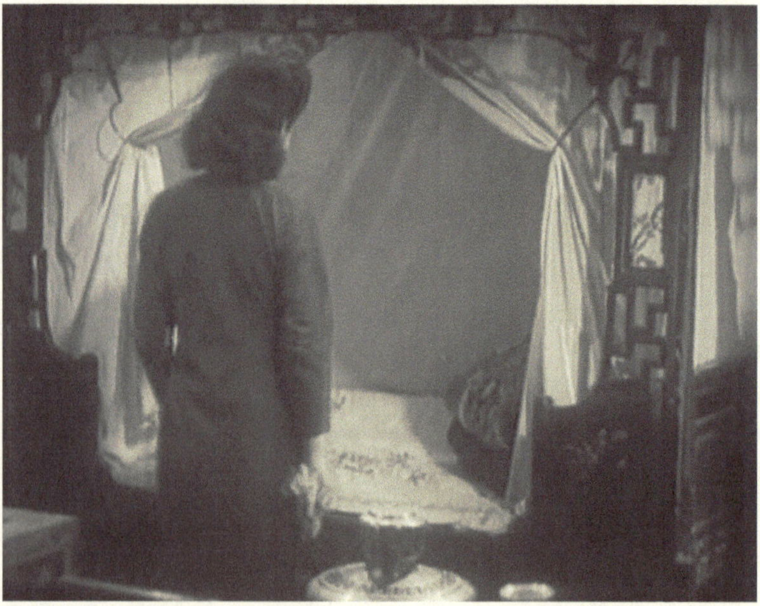

Figure 13.

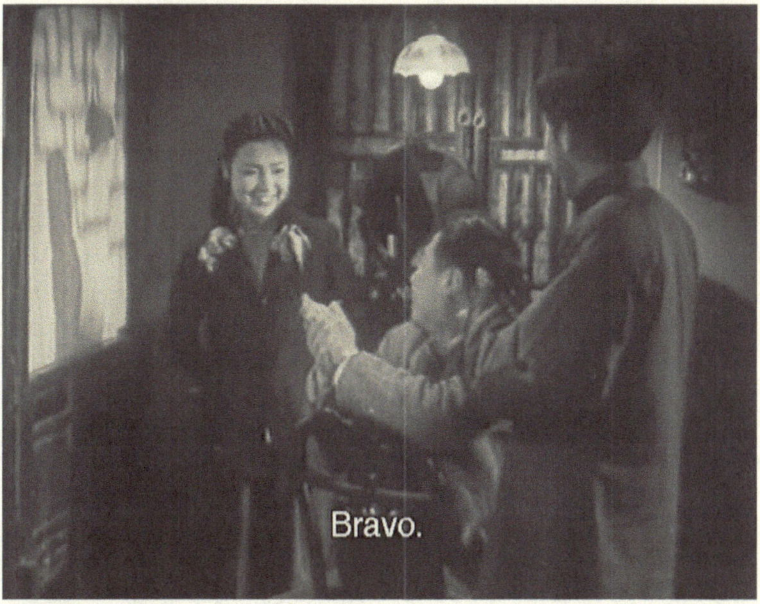

Figure 14.

this regard, Daixiu's song even articulates Zhichen's unexpressed love on a manifest level. Nonetheless, while Liyan's love for Yuwen will be sublimated through his attempted suicide, Daixiu's enchantment will be first tarnished by her realization of the unrequited love between Yuwen and Zhichen, and then by Liyan's attempted suicide. In this sense, one trajectory depicted in the film is Daixiu's education, and this process of education is prefigured in the choice of her song: one about unrequited love that she has just learned in school, but will not fully understand until the end of the film.

Meanwhile, Daixiu and Liyan's yearning to look and make connections are contrasted by Zhichen and Yuwen's inability to do so openly. In a larger context, Liyan's sickness and impotence (signified by the pills) are contrasted by Zhichen's health and potency (signified by his amorous relationship with Yuwen, his sexual and fatherly appeal to Daixiu, and his profession as a medical doctor). Interestingly, Yuwen is the only person who is constantly mobile in the beginning and middle of this scene, thus suggesting her seeming sexual agency and mobility, something that she expresses throughout the first half of the film. Yet, for the same reason, she is also the person who has no place to settle, and when she finally sits down, Liyan becomes mobile, and what he does is to go to his friend and pat him on his shoulder. This act both consummates a homosocial (or even homoerotic) relationship between Liyan and Zhichen, thus turning Yuwen into a commodity of exchange between them, and transfers Yuwen's unrequited love to the love between these two men.

In the third register, the scene can also be understood as a suspension-imagination. Daixiu's song helps the spectators be absorbed in a state of "boredom" or flavorlessness, in which these characters simply continue with their life-process. Yet, it is when time no longer progresses, but is instead crystalized in this state of flavorlessness that the characters' desire from the past, Daixiu's desire in the present, and the potential of their fulfillment if and only if someone takes a dramatic action are all invoked as a suspension-imagination. In fact, out of such desire that obstinately refuses to actualize itself, the spectators are engaged in the imagination, or virtual image, of a desire that seems to stand outside of the self and the substantiatedness of the universe. Nonetheless, what the spectators experience is not really a transcendent form of desire. Instead, it is a desire that folds back to itself, a desire for desire that lingers in the air in all its immanence. In 2014, the British Film Institute (BFI) screened the restored print of *Spring in a Small Town,* and for the first time Daixiu's singing is subtitled, thus revealing the Russian lyrics about the unrequited love of a young Cossack for a woman named Maria. Thus desire is fully embedded in the lyrics; yet for many years, for those spectators who did not know Russian, the love message that the song conveys was hidden. Stimulated purely by the sound of the lyrics, the audience, knowing nothing about the love message, could nonetheless feel the desire that was concealed within the lyrics, as though it rose into the air as a form of suspension-imagination.

Desire in this scene is inferred not only from the narrative action or from the causal relationship that the characters suggest. It lingers in the air by means of its absence. The idea might sound esoteric and nonsensical at first, but it is something that Fey Mou cares a lot about in his writing. In his essay "Let's Talk about 'Air' Briefly" the term *kongqi* (air) is often translated and understood as atmosphere or ambience. In fact, in his overall discussion, Fey never quite defines what he means by *kongqi.* His primary concern is how a filmmaker can manipulate cinematic forms for the purpose of producing *kongqi:*

> I believe that there are four ways to create an "air" within a drama: (1) by means of cinematography itself; (2) by means of the photographed object itself; (3) by means of indirect manipulation; (4) by means of sound editing.
>
> The eye of a camera is often more technical than the human eye. Because of this, we can use the camera to produce different kinds of optical effects. The camera angle can change in accordance with the tonality of the dramatic beat. In fact, the camera lens' sensitivity to light can also change in accordance with the changes in mood within a scene.
>
> If we combine photography with other cinematographic techniques, we will see many variations. In location shooting, we need to find a beautiful object in nature; but the actual effects that we see in the image are determined by the camera's perspective, the time of the shooting, and sunlight. On the sound stage, the air depends on production design; hence, the set designer is crucial in the production. Creating "air" in this case relies on the matching and juxtaposition between lines and light. The set designer therefore needs to understand the subject matter of the screenplay down to the level of the environment of each scene. She or he needs to avoid any unnecessary object to be included in the photograph, but must have the sense of emphasizing the crucial elements on the set. By collaborating with the camera crew, she or he can contribute to the overall effects of the film.[43]

A casual reading may tell us that cinematic "air" is interchangeable with "atmosphere," and in a sense, the two terms can be understood as two sides of the same coin. The term atmosphere, which would have been written in Chinese as *fenwei* (ambience), is considered a formal or narrational device, whereas cinematic air is regarded as a substance that the cinematic spectator, quite literally, inhales and exhales in the cinematographic image.

In literary poetics, the word *kongqi* is often used doubly as a metaphor and a literal description. For example, when a narrator claims that she or he could feel a *bingleng de kongqi* (an icy cold air), the phrase is supposed to impart to the reader a bodily sensation, but at the same time, it metaphorically refers to such mental states as solitude, brutality, cruelty, or sorrow. In other words, the *kongqi* in space or time denotes a bodily sensation that crystalizes the presence of an affect that is in fact absent. Meanwhile, the term *fenwei* describes an overall ambience that gives out this *kongqi*, or in cinematic terms, a composition of an assemblage of formal devices that are schematically fabricated into a bodily sensation.

With this in mind, Fey Mou wrote: "I feel that a film's air can also be indirectly manipulated. By this I mean that we can use the dramatic events and objects around the main theme in order to foreground the subject matter."[44] This in some ways sums up what Fey has in mind in terms of producing the proper cinematic air. For him, a filmmaker's task is not to break down the dramatic action into scenes in accordance with its relationship with the main theme. Rather, the main theme is made present by means of its absence: it is being teased out as the film traces everything and everybody around it. What Fey would prefer to do is put together dramatic events and objects around the main theme so that the absence of the main theme would be crystalized as an air that lingers in the cinematographic image.

This is a crucial concept when put back into the narrative of *Spring in a Small Town*. The film's main theme is in fact the unfulfilled desire of every character in the film: Liyan's desire to consummate his desire with his wife, which is restrained by his sickness and impotence; Zhichen's desire to consummate his desire for his best friend's wife or his ex-lover, which is checked by his moral integrity; Yuwen's desire to make open her desire for Zhichen, which is discouraged by Zhichen's unwillingness to do so and her moral responsibility as Liyan's wife; and Daixiu's desire to be Zhichen's object of desire, which is frustrated by Zhichen's unresponsiveness. In other words, the film image crystallizes desire that is yet to be actualized, and to a certain extent, the human decision not to desire despite each individual's desire to do so. In other words, what the cinematographic image captures is the potentiality of desire—a desire that folds back to itself. In fact, what the film invokes in the audience's mind is a profound desire for desire itself, the very amorous feeling for an absented object or *keisō*. In this sense, what the film makes present is the absence of desire in its actual form, and the presence of desire's absence is precisely crystallized in the cinematographic air, a bodily sensation of a substance that is not really there.

This question of desire can in fact help the spectators access the fourth register of this scene. As Daruvala and FitzGerald point out, one remarkable feature of *Spring in a Small Town* is the use of Yuwen's voiceover as we see her walking on top of the ruins of a city wall in a long shot and in a number of images throughout the film where she pauses in contemplation. According to the suture theory, developed in the 1970s and 1980s, Yuwen's disembodied voice addresses an empty space outside the film's imaginary (a coherent diegesis or an unbroken illusion of reality), which is translated to the cinematic experience in the theater as the spectatorial space. In so doing, her voice may make the spectators aware of their position as viewing subjects, thus taking them out of the film's diegesis (or in psychoanalytical terms, imaginary coherence). In classical Hollywood cinema, this temporary break in the film's and the spectators' imaginary can be restored by suturing her voice to a reaction shot, e.g. a close-up shot of Yuwen to allow the spectators to infer that her voiceover addresses herself, or to a shot of Zhichen to indicate that her voiceover addresses him.[45] Yet in *Spring*, Yuwen's voice stays in the imaginary empty field without being sutured to any reaction shot, as though it were a *juexiang* (voice reflected from the abyss of time; see chapter 1). In fact, what unfolds in the film image is what Deleuze would call the interstices between causes and effects, i.e. the very imaginary field that is often eclipsed, ignored, and sutured in a classical Hollywood film. FitzGerald calls her voice an expression of *yuan* (desolation), which, according to Zhang Ailing (Eileen Chang, 1920–95), is a sense of someone in a state of emotional liminality: between alienation and familiarity, sadness and happiness, and entrapment and liberation. In fact, this sense of desolation is supposed to be desolate because of a person's inability or lack of incentive to take action to actualize one pole over the other.

Daruvala and FitzGerald trace this sense of desolation back to a form of thirteenth-century poetry, the *guiyuan shi* (boudoir [desolation] poetry). Both of them cite Grace Fong's pristine analysis and observation:

> Frequent transposition between reality (actual experience) and the illusory experience of dream and reverie, vision and flashback is a pronounced feature of these love poems. As the development, or movement, of the poem is primarily guided by memory, emotional association, and sense perception, rather than any apparent logic, time sequence is often disrupted and spatial viewpoint shifted without any clear demarcation: the poem moves backwards and forwards between reminiscence and description, between past and present.[46]

For me, Fong has identified precisely the intricate relationship between Fey Mou's cinematographic image and the reality it approaches. To a certain degree, in *Spring*, Fey indeed resorts to the poetics of inverse narration. Yet, the voiceover, which initially seems to suggest a dream, reverie, vision, or flashback, is not systematically sutured to Yuwen's expressed pursuit of her desire. Rather, her voice remains a disembodied one, even when her body is shown in the film, as part of a flavorless display of reality. The dissociation between her voice as it tries to transfer what the spectators apprehend as an image-consciousness to her memory (or fantasy) and the spectators' sense perception that what is displayed is a consciousness instantiated in the present, and cannot be conceived otherwise, opens a distance between a time-passed (constantly claimed and reclaimed by Yuwen's voice)—where desire has already been rendered unrequited—and a time that continues to unfold in movement—where desire obstinately refuses to be actualized, yet can potentially do so. Desolation is therefore crystalized in this voice that measures a desire that continuously folds back to itself; it becomes a crystal image where "reminiscence and description . . . past and present" coalesce.

Theater and Painting: Presence of an Absence

In 1942, Fey Mou tried to tackle the question of suspension-imagination once more in his article "Guanyu jiuju dianyinghua de wenti" [On the question of cinematizing the old theater]. Wang Ching-wei's (1883–1944) KMT government (1940–45)—which was under the control of the Japanese military occupation—had issued a call to cinematize the Peking opera in an effort to preserve it as a *guocui* (national treasure). Film would be utilized as a medium to preserve the performances of the existing Peking opera stars (a policy that Mei Lanfang, 1894–1961, had famously resisted). In addition, Chinese cinema could potentially turn the Peking opera into a cinematic genre, in the same way MGM had transformed the Broadway musical into a cinematic form. Needless to say, the suggestion was considered a reactionary one.[47] Hence, Fey's article was in some ways written with a tone of sarcasm. Yet, within that tone, he did raise some serious questions about what the cinema can potentially do as it compares itself to the Chinese theater and painting, a discussion I wish to compare with a similar one—Bazin's theorization of the relationship between the cinema and theater—for the purpose of understanding further the way these two film thinkers understood the intricate distance between the cinematographic image and reality, and the liminal position of the cinema between art and reality.

Policymakers at the time Fey Mou was writing simply used the slogan "*ban shang yinmu*" (move [the Peking opera] onto the silver screen). In so doing, however, Fey believed that filmmakers would simply theatricalize the cinema, instead of cinematizing the Peking opera. Hence, Fey argues:

> The Chinese theater—that is, the purely artistic theater, which is by no means limited to the Jingchao pai [Peking imperial school]— is highly similar to the Chinese painting. The Chinese painting paints an idea. It is often understood as an art form whose mobile thought is extremely difficult to grasp, and its subtle theme is posited outside its language and figure. What it paints is not a description of life, yet the impression it gives is real and concrete. Such painting embodies the subjective in the objective. The beholder apprehends the painting in all its clarity by seizing its spirit, yet its forms change after a minute of contemplation. At first glance, the beholder may see a piece of paper filled with smoke and clouds; other times, the beholder may discern a few light strokes from the overall composition, which convey the spirit and tonality of a mountain, a body of water, a flower or a bird—all without caring how it approaches reality.[48]

The idea that the Chinese painting relies more on abstraction and formalization than on mimesis is in fact an arguable point, something that I will discuss further in the following chapter. What interests me here is not how Fey analyzes his imaginary Chinese painting, but how he uses his analysis as a way to convey his theory of filmmaking. The key sentence in this entire passage is: "It is often understood as an art form whose mobile thought is extremely difficult to grasp, and its subtle theme is posited outside its language and figure." In other words, for Fey, a film's theme is not supposed to be conveyed either linguistically or figuratively by the image. Rather, the image invokes the presence of an absented thought or imagination (*xuanxiang*) that lingers and moves in the air. Fey believes that a film does not need to imitate life in forms; rather, life can be apprehended by means of an impression. In this sense, formal elements are composed not for the purpose of giving the beholder a clear idea of what the artist tries to convey. Instead, they are put onto the screen in a way that can allow the spectator, through a process of contemplation (hence, Fey's preference for the long take), to discern a few important strokes that can approach life in all its presence and concreteness.

In this light, what appears at first to be a formalistic discussion of the cinema is in fact a discussion on cinematographic realism. On this note, Fey continues:

> The singing, dialogue, action, and methods of dramatic expression in the Chinese theater are all included in highly formularized music and choreography. Its actors are not "realistic and concrete" figures. In order to enjoy the interest and flavor of the Chinese theater, the audience must understand

> the *shenghua* (trans-figuring or evaporating) function of the artistic forms in the old theater. Yet such task can only be achieved in a state of absolute obscurity.[49]

What Fey Mou means by the "trans-figuring" function is that the theme and the reality of life in the Chinese theater are not *con-figured* in the highly formalized performance itself; rather, the abstract artistic forms, which obscure the life and action they are supposed to imitate, do nothing beyond referring to themselves as an aesthetic experience. Yet such an experience allows the actual theme to evaporate and linger in the air—beyond the linguistic and figurative representation—or a *xuanxiang* that would otherwise be repressed by any mimetic mode of representation.

For Fey, these highly abstract, obscure, and seemingly unrealistic forms "demand the audience to cognize them as real people, that is, people who live in the present and concrete reality. In other words, the spectators are asked to apprehend a sensation of concreteness and reality from irreal [neither real nor unreal] people and drama." This can only be done when "the mind of the spectator and the art of the performers can achieve a mutual understanding, spiritual blending, and a same wavelength." But for Fey, the difficulty that the filmmakers need to overcome is that the cinema "expresses itself by means of its absolute reality."[50] In other words, the reality of the cinematographic image refers not to anything beyond itself. Rather, it refers to itself in all its immanence, and it leaves no room for graphical abstraction. The question then becomes, how can the cinema trans-figure when the basic substance of the cinematographic image is reality, and cannot be conceived otherwise?

This is a question pondered over by Bazin in his theorization of the relationship between the theater and cinema. For Bazin, the photographic image is characterized by the presence of the object being represented. In part two of "Théâtre et cinéma" ("Theater and Cinema," 1951), Bazin writes:

> Presence, naturally, is defined in terms of time and space. "To be in the presence of someone" is to recognize him as existing contemporaneously with us and to note that he comes within the actual range of our senses.... The photograph proceeds by means of the lens to the taking of a veritable luminous impression in light—to a mold. As such it carries with it more than mere resemblance, namely a kind of identity.... But photography is a feeble technique in the sense that its instantaneity compels it to capture

> time only piecemeal. The cinema does something strangely paradoxical. It makes a molding of the object as it exists in time and, furthermore, makes an imprint of the duration of the object.[51]

Here, Bazin offers one of the most overt references to what some film scholars would call photographic indexicality. Nonetheless, he does so only to complicate it by introducing the temporal dimension of the photographic image. For Bazin, the photographic image does not simply make present an object that the camera has once captured as an identical mold. Rather, it preserves the duration of time from the past, and re-presents this piece of time as though it were contemporaneous with us—presence. With this temporal dimension, Bazin argues, "[I]t is no longer as certain as it was that there is no middle stage between presence and absence. It is likewise at the ontological level that the effectiveness of the cinema has its source."[52]

What Bazin underlines here is that the ontology of the photographic image is not an unquestionable reality in all its presence. Instead, the cinematographic image occupies the threshold between presence and absence. With this in mind, Bazin argues that identification in the theater is an intellectual process. In it, the spectator is aware of the actual presence of the actor on stage—and vice versa—and hence, the spectator must "intervene actively" in a process of transposing such an actual presence to an imaginary world that is absent (i.e. a diegesis). In the cinema, however, the film requires the spectator's "passive adhesion" to the presence of an absented world, i.e. an imaginary hero who is not here and now; but is out there to pursue his own desire. However, as the cinema reactivates a passage of time-passed (the time when the image of the hero was molded not only as himself, but also as a trace of time), it approaches a cinematographic here and now that comes close to reality. For Bazin, such temporal immediacy not only makes present what is absent, but also allows the spectators to project their desire onto the very desire the hero pursues.[53]

What Bazin had in mind was the European realist theater that emerged in the late nineteenth century. At first glance, what Fey Mou argues almost seems to be the opposite. For Fey, the Chinese theater, by means of its abstraction and formalization, obscures the immediate presence of the actor. This facilitates the spectator to contemplate upon the irreality of the forms and conjure up her or his own imaginary reality. Yet, the absolute immanence of the cinematographic image makes it difficult for the filmmakers to adopt such a strategy of narration. However, the point that Fey makes is not the incommensurability between the Chinese theater and cinema. Rather, he suggests that both the Chinese theater and cinema are capable of enabling the spectator to come up with her or his own suspension-imagination. The apparent opposition between the irreal in the Chinese theater and the real in the cinema is in fact misleading. For Fey, what the spectator tends to identify as an immediate presence in the cinema in fact signifies the absence of an imaginary world in which desire folds back to itself—as itself. What the spectators take as the here and now in the cinema is, after all, the irreal. Meanwhile, for Bazin, the cinematographic image is not reality; rather, it occupies the threshold between reality and art, proximity and distance.

I have repeatedly used the phrase "the presence of an absence" to discuss Fey Mou's notion of cinema. What is being configured in this threshold or distance is potentiality. In "On Potentiality" (1999), Agamben defines potentiality in reference to Aristotle's *De anima:*

> As to why there is no sensation of the senses themselves. Why is it that, in the absence of external objects, the senses do not give any sensation, although they contain fire, earth, water, and the other elements of which there is sensation? This happens because sensibility is not actual but only potential. This is why it does not give sensation, just as the combustible does not burn by itself, without a principle of combustion; otherwise it would burn itself and would not need any actual fire.[54]

What is important here is that our senses do not give us any sensation of themselves. This does not mean that our senses do not exist. Rather, they exist in absentia, or as a potential that is not actualized. Once a body is in contact with a substance, our senses actualize themselves; they make present their absence.

The theories of Bazin, Metz, and Fey Mou are all based on this underlying assumption, though with slightly different approaches. For Bazin, "the presence of an absence" manifests itself in the photographic trace. In this sense, the cinematographic image preserves not only an imprint of a person, but also the duration of this person's existence. When the spectator sees the image of this person, such existence is not actualized in the cinematic presence, yet the image makes present such an absence. Later on, Deleuze would develop this idea in his theorization of the time-image. When Deleuze considers postwar European cinema as a form of time-image, what he means is that such an image makes present the absence of time. In many ways, time, like the human senses, does not activate a sensation until we sense its finitude. When Deleuze argues that narratives that suggest the virtuality of time, nonchronometric time, disjointed time, multiple dimensions of the same duration, imaginary time, and so on, the sense of time that has been concealed by the presence of movement is now revealed to us, not as a sensation contingent upon movement, but as an imagination or *xuanxiang* that emerges out of the interstices of the film images.[55]

Nonetheless, Bazin also suggested an intellectual-psychological dimension of the presence of absence in cinema, one that is related to the spectatorial process of identification. For him, the presence of the hero is an imaginary one. In this sense, the cinematic spectator, as opposed to the theatrical one, no longer needs to imagine her or his own imaginary world in order to negotiate her or his desire. As Christian Metz argues, the cinematographic image becomes a signifier that signifies the imaginary, articulated via the symbolic order in such a way that it carefully conceals the real. In this light, the spectator simply appropriates the imaginary produced by the apparatus and cathects her or his own desire to that of the hero—and ideologically, to the *dispositif* the hero instantiates.[56]

Fey Mou's theory, in some ways, synthesizes these two lines of thinking. In a sense, Fey finds that photographic reality can potentially hinder the spectator's imagination. For him, classical narrational conventions, adopted mostly from the European realist theater, simply encourage the spectator to take the cinematographic absence unquestionably as presence. In such classical dramaturgy, desire is inferred by the spectators as they fabricate causal and temporal relationships between scenes and dramatic actions. In this case, desire is in fact concealed in the image and is re-posited in the spectator's body as the locus of her or his imaginary. What interests Fey is the way the Chinese theater abstracts and formalizes reality until reality itself is completely obscured. Such a formal strategy allows the spectator to come to sense the existence of reality as an absence. In the cinema, however, Fey abstracts reality, ironically, by laying out reality in its most mundane manner, and in a way that would discourage the spectator from making any direct causal connection between scenes. As a result, chronometric and causal relations are no longer present (or dominant) in his work, and what the film shows are those interstices between dramatic causes and effects. The pure banality of life, however, makes present what is usually concealed in the classical dramatic action: desire in all its presence.

Fey Mou: Towards a Confucian Film Theory

While desire is the featured theme of *Spring in a Small Town*, it is arguably not the ultimate goal that Fey Mou's film tries to reach. For many film scholars, the thematic core of Fey's cinema is the Confucian notion of *ren*. Within the larger Confucian ontological schema, *yu* (desire) is only one component. The Confucian understanding of *yu* can be traced back to the *Laozi* (arguably written around the sixth century BCE) and its supplements. In these classical texts, *yu* is in fact best understood as an idea similar to the Spinozian notion of *conatus*, that is, a will to subsist in an overall cosmological order, which is in itself sustained and driven forward by a universal *yu*. When *yu* is lacking, an individual and its relationship with other individuals within the universe lacks the drive to move forward in time; but when *yu* becomes *yin* (excessive), it turns itself into a self-destructive force.[57]

In the *Laozi* and its various supplements, this principle is often illustrated in political terms. For example, when a political community's desire to survive becomes too excessive, it strives to conquer other political communities and appropriate their resources. This upsets the overall power structure among communities, and by extension, the order of the world. The excessive desire of a political community or individual eventually persuades other political communities or individuals to unite and restore the overall political order of the earth.[58] This notion of checks and balances informs the Confucian notion of *zhongyong* (middle ground), the idea that the best way for an individual to survive and bring her or his desire to its full potential is to stay in the middle ground between excessiveness and deprivation.[59]

However, desire can also be understood as a form of *qing*, a term that is often used in the various Confucian classics to designate ideas including affection, emotion, desire, love, amorous feelings, the sensible, human nature, or understanding. *Qing* itself does not give out any sensation; it nonetheless informs all sensations—or in fact, the relationships among all sensible things. For example, the way I define my relationship with a cup of tea is that the cup of tea gives me a sensation of warmth and comfort. Hence, my relationship with this cup of tea is engendered from a form of *qing* actualized as I drink it. Or, for instance, the way I define my relationship with my father is a set of sensations such a relationship inspires in me: awe, admiration, intimacy, frustration, and love. But for Confucius, what stops any of these *qing* from being excessive or deprived—for example from loving my father so much that I begin to desire him romantically, or from hating my father so much that I would perform patricide—is a set of *li* (rites). Rites, as defined by the *Li ji* [Book of rites, written during the Warring States period (circa 481, 475, or 403–221 BCE), edited and revised mainly from the first century BCE to the second century CE], are ceremonies, or simply social behaviors, that not only express, but also impart to the sentient bodies of those who perform them, the distance and boundaries that one must observe in order that *qing* may not become excessive or deprived.[60] Furthermore, *li* is after all a means to regulate *qing* by making palpable the sense of *ren*. *Ren* is usually understood as benevolence or unconditional love. However, for Confucius, unconditional love is the *xing* (nature or original quality) of being human, or life-in-itself. Hence, being *ren* also means being human.

In the previous four registers of reading the scene we have looked at from *Spring in a Small Town*, I have argued that desire—understood as a form of *qing*—is instantiated by the camera's trace, the scene's semiological structure, its suspension-imagination, and its sense of desolation and time. In other words, the scene as a world that the spectators inhabit is made sensible by *qing*. In this light, *qing* engenders all the actions—or more accurately, the image traced in light by the camera—and all the relationships that the film image invites the spectators to negotiate. However, such *qing* is always checked by *li* from being excessively expressed. From this set of Confucian ideas, one can open up a fifth register of reading this scene. FitzGerald notes that Fey Mou instructed Wei Wei to embody the Confucian notions of *fa hu qing zhi hu li* ([all things] are engendered from *qing*, but are checked by *li*).[61] Sam Ho argues that Fey's work adopts the Confucian aesthetics of *le er bu yin, ai er bu shang* (expresses joy without being licentious [excessive] and sadness without morbidity).[62] So, for example, Yuwen's actions and her fluid movement in the world she inhabits are both engendered by her *qing* and checked by her observation of *li*, and the same could be said about Zhichen's ambivalent and somewhat awkward ocular and physical positions. Likewise, Daixiu's almost unbridled expression of her *qing* is checked by Zhichen's *li*. Meanwhile, Liyan not only checks his *qing* by *li*, but also subtly intervenes everybody's *qing* by walking up to Zhichen and patting his shoulder, thus both reaffirming their *qing* as friends and checking the *qing* that hangs in the air by the *li* between friends.

To what extent Fey Mou could be considered a Confucian filmmaker or theorist, however, is debatable. With the exception of two essays that he wrote about his film *Confucius,* Fey rarely appeals to Confucianism directly as a source of his inspiration. Even then, Fey does not really theorize the cinema in either of these two essays. Instead, in line with the argument proposed by Sam Ho, I see Confucianism as one of the many strands of thought that made up the complex semantic field in which the Shanghai intellectuals in the 1930s and 1940s wrestled with their ideas on the cinema.[63] In general, one may argue that traces of Confucian thoughts could be found in Fey's *xingshi guan* (view of [cinematic] forms), *rensheng guan* (view of life), and *zhengzhi guan* (view of politics).

The idea that Fey Mou's view of cinematic form is informed by Confucianism was proposed by Wong Ain-ling. Wong argues that Fey had always been fascinated with theatricality and stylized performance, but his deeper fascination was to transpose the stylistic performances on a theatrical stage to the larger cosmological view of the world as stage, which, through the lens of the camera, can be transfigured as a "pure cinema."[64] For example, the film *Confucius* begins with a rite performed by the army of the state of Qi (1046–221 BCE) in preparation for its invasion of the state of Lu (1042–249 BCE), where Confucius lived and would become prime minister. This opening sequence takes place on a sacrificial alter that is shaped as a European-styled theatrical stage with three steps leading up to the altar proper, and the camera is positioned at the front, observing the rite from a spectator's point of view. On this altar, the soldiers are all lined up from left to right, with the priest on the left of frame and the sacrificial cauldron in the middle. As one shot fades into another, the camera obstinately observes the altar and the rite itself from this frontal view, thus keeping the viewers behind the imaginary fourth wall. Yet Wong argues that the sequence's theatricality is constantly broken. For example, as two soldiers carrying a wild boar walk up the steps, they enter from the bottom corner of the left of frame to the cauldron at the center, thus cutting the horizontal line in the background of the frame diagonally. Likewise, as the soldiers march and "dance" with their drums, the lines in the foreground and those in the background always move in opposite directions. For Wong, although these graphical contrasts could be achieved by means of staging in a theater, they are consciously condensed, highlighted, and made "shocking" by the camera's frame, and foregrounded by montage. By transforming the theatrical stage to pure cinema in this scene, the sacrificial rite also serves as a preparation for the audience's ritual of entering the cinema by regulating their bodily rhythm to that of the historical events, an idea comparable to Klages' notion of natural rhythm.[65]

In fact, Wong Ain-ling cites other examples to further argue that Fey Mou's pure cinema instantiates the late-Ming version of Confucianism, one that was combined with Taoism by reconfiguring the Confucian notion of political order as a sense of universal order: *tian* (heaven), *di* (earth), and *ren* (human). In the first scene in which Confucius preaches, he and his three disciples Tse Loo (Zhang Yi), Yen Huei (Sima Yingcai), and Tse Kung (Pei Chong) stand on a slope in accordance with their ranks. Fey Mou uses three spotlights to highlight the three characters, and the result is a highly theatricalized arrangement of the figures as if on a stage (Figure 15). However, Fey Mou uses a crane to gradually move the camera up the slope, while high-contrast and depth-of-field photography suggests an extension of the frame into a deeper world, thus implying that the "stage" in the foreground is part and parcel of a larger cosmological notion of heaven-earth-and-human.[66] To extend Wong's argument, this type of framing and staging is in fact repeated and transferred from the opening sequence of the pre-battle sacrifice to the alter on which Tse Loo performs his rite of archery, and the stage on which Confucius preaches, also known as the Xingtan or Apricot Altar.

In addition, Wong argues that such a cosmological view is interiorized in the scene where Confucius decides to resign from his post as the prime minister of the state of Lu, abandon his home, and travel to the neighboring states in order to persuade their heads of state to exercise *ren* as an ethical value (Figure 16). In this scene, Confucius (human) is positioned on the left of frame within a room with no décor other than a *guqin* (zither) in the middle. A rectangular window is open on the wall at the back, from which Confucius and the spectators behind him could see the world beyond (heaven). The *guqin* is put on the ground (earth), which graphically resonates with the *guqin* music in the soundtrack. The music of the *guqin* is often understood as a means of regulating the perturbed relationship between heaven, earth, and human; in the film, such a relationship is disturbed by the political turmoil of the Warring States. Similarly, after Confucius visited the supposedly lurid Nan Tse (Murong Wan'er), who actually disturbs (sexually) and upsets (morally) Tse Loo, Confucius is seen resting under a tree (Figure 17). The action of this scene simply involves Confucius asking Tse Loo, who is initially positioned in the frame's background, to come up and see him. Yet, the framing allows

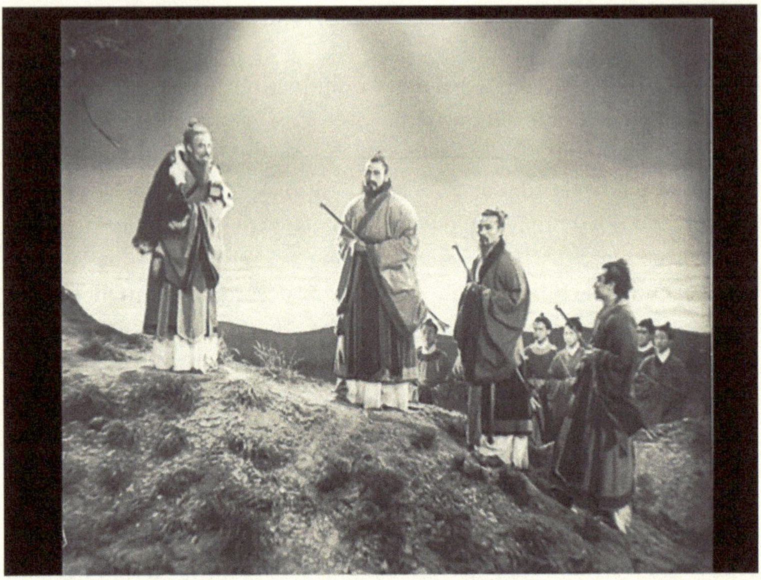

Figure 15. *Confucius* (Min Hwa Film Company, 1940), Tse Loo (Zhang Yi), Yen Huei (Sima Yingcai), and Tse Kung (Pei Chong) stand on a slope in accordance with their ranks, embodying the cosmological notion of heaven-earth-and-human.

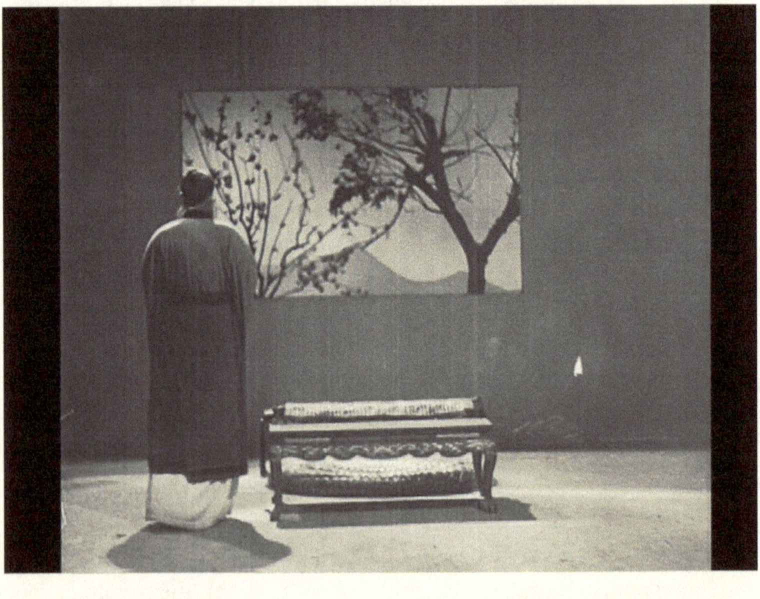

Figure 16. In *Confucius*, Confucius abandons his home and travels to the neighboring states in order to persuade their heads of state to exercise *ren* as an ethical value. The composition of this shot illustrates how *ren* regulates the perturbed relationship between heaven, earth, and human.

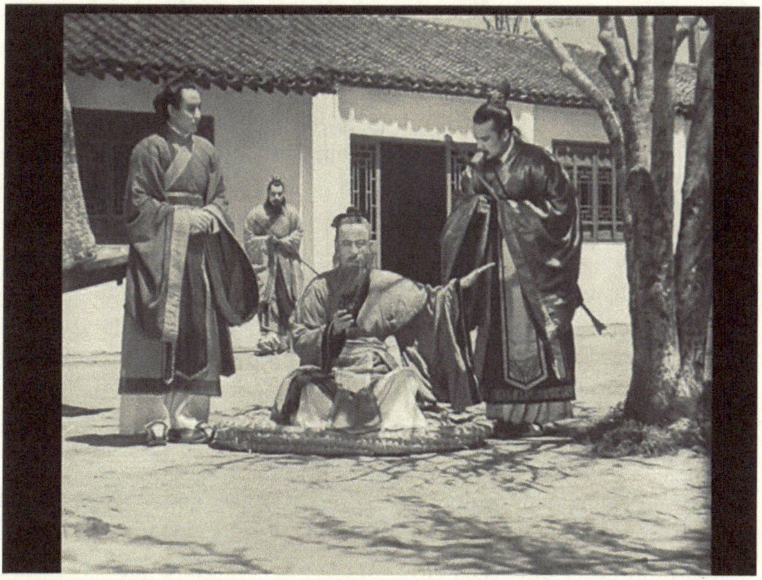

Figure 17. In *Confucius*, after Confucius visits the supposedly lurid Nan Tse (Murong Wan'er), who disturbs (sexually) and upsets (morally) Tse Loo, Confucius is seen resting under a tree. In the shot, Tse Loo walks from the back of the frame to the right of frame, thus symbolizing his personal path of reconciling his disturbed sexuality and personal morality with Confucius as the cosmological mediator.

the spectators to focus not on the action, but on the semicircular movement of Tse Loo, who walks from the back of the frame to the right of frame, thus symbolizing his personal path of reconciling his disturbed sexuality and personal morality with Confucius as the cosmological mediator.

The stylistic argument is in fact further developed by Koo Siu-sun, who argues that Fey Mou considers the cinema a form of *wenti* (literary form). However, the term *wenti,* for Koo, can mean *wenyi zaiti* (a body that conveys culture and art). In this sense, Koo, based on Fey's notion of cinematographic air, argues that Fey's "film writing" aims at a *jingjie,* a stage towards *wudao* (grasping *dao,* more popularly understood as enlightenment, an idea I introduced when I discussed the aesthetics of Wang Guowei in chapter 3) of *huanjing tonghua* (environmental assimilation). The idea is that Fey eliminates or "eclipses" all unnecessary objects in the frame and allows the camera angle, light, and composition to merge the human characters and the environment into a unified body. According to

Koo, what is at stake in this unified body (or assimilated environment) is neither a narrative point nor a dramatic action, but an air that impresses *dao* upon the spectators. In the scene in which Confucius decides to tender his resignation, Fey "seamlessly applies Western modern art's concept of space treatment," which is repeated and "answered" by the scene in which Confucius mourns the death of Yen Huei (Figure 18). In a reverse framing (in this case, Confucius is seen from the "world beyond" to the interior of his house), Confucius wails, "*Tian sang yu! Tian sang yu!*" (Heaven is destroying me! Heaven is destroying me!). Koo argues that the character "seems to be breaking out of a 'variation' of a square frame of an abstract painting."[67] Or, the character is engendered by his *qing*, but is restricted by the window as an instantiation of *li*. But in this case, Confucius' *qing* is unified to the world outside precisely via this rectangular window.

Sam Ho, meanwhile, argues further that Confucianism can be found in Fey Mou's work not only in terms of style or his abstract sense of cosmology, but also in his view of life and aesthetics. Ho argues that what characterizes Fey's cinema is the Confucian notion of *wenzhi binbin*, understood by Ho as an art work's equal emphasis on *wen* (*xingshi* or form) and *zhi* (*neirong* or contents). In the larger Confucian view, *wen* can be understood as *li*, the rites that carry out a sense of human order, and *zhi* can be understood as *ren*. In the *Lunyu* (*Analects*, written during the Warring States period and revised during the Han dynasty, around 206 BCE–220 CE), *ren* is supposed to be "*xing yu shi, li yu li, cheng yu yue*" (stimulated by poetry, established by rites, and made complete or conveyed by music). It also states that "*shi, keyi xing, keyi guan, keyi qun, keyi yuan, ni zhi shi fu, yuan zhi shi jun*" (poetry can stimulate a subject matter, can observe one's environment, can regulate the relationships between people, can express personal or collective desolation, can be used to serve one's father, or can be used to serve one's ruler). In this sense, Ho uses Tan Jiazhe's notion of four *jingjie* (stages) or *xinjing* (stages of heart) in music appreciation: *xiru* (approaching integration and harmony), *cunru* (approaching purity), *jiaoru* (approaching clarity), and *yiru* (approaching a continuation between one's interior and exterior, being and nonbeing).[68]

Sam Ho comes close to formulating an ontological view of approaching reality by deducing a film theory from Fey Mou's *Confucius*, one that is close to Wang Guowei's notion of aesthetics: living in appearance, not living in appearance, living in appearance *as not* living in appearance;

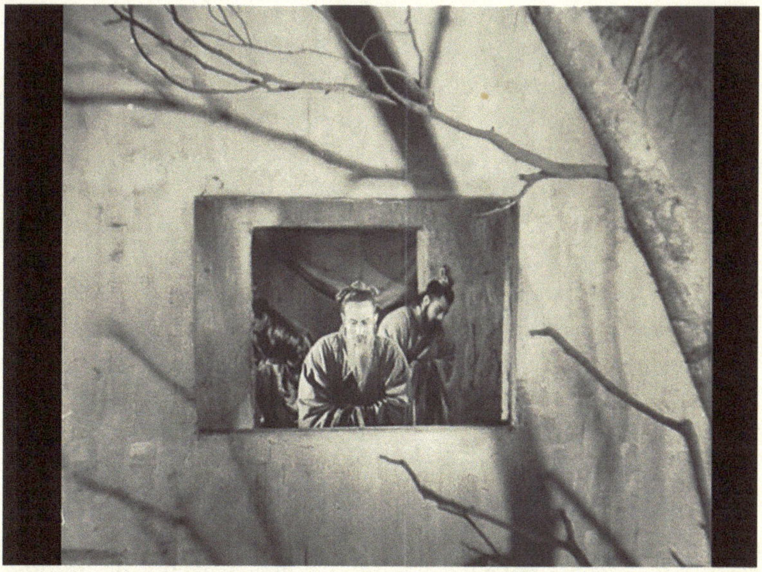

Figure 18. In *Confucius*, Confucius mourns the death of Yen Huei: "Heaven is destroying me! Heaven is destroying me!" The modernist composition of this shot unifies the characters, objects, and their *qing* into an assimilated environment, thus allowing its air to impress *dao* upon the spectators.

wo (me), *wuwo* (forgetting me), *wo ji wuwo* (me *as not* me). Wang's idea is eventually summed up in Tan's notion of *yiru* (approaching a continuation between one's interior and exterior, being and nonbeing). And the state to which *yiru* approaches is *ren*. In the beginning of the *Analects*, Confucius wrote:

> *Junzi wu ben, ben li er dao sheng; xiao di ye zhe, wei ren zhi ben yu.*[69]
>
> A scholar works on [cultivates; puts into practice] one's *ben* [ontological basis]; once such a basis is established, *dao* emerges; the filial relationships between people are [in fact] the basis [of all sensible things], which is called *ren*.

The word *dao* can be traced back again to the *Laozi*. The exact definition of *dao* is a highly debatable one, and in fact, if *dao* can be properly defined, according to the *Laozi*, it is no longer *dao* itself.[70] For my current purpose, *dao* can be considered a cosmological potentiality from which good and evil, life and death, being and nonbeing are engendered; it is, in some ways, an equalizing plane that cuts across all forms of existence.

If *dao* is this formless potentiality that is in itself absent, but manifested in all sensible things as presence, *ren* is the instantiation of a cosmological order it engenders. But in Confucianism, *ren* is not something highly abstract or even cosmological; rather it simply means being human, a common quality or sensation shared by all humans. The writer and editors of the *Laozi* supplements argue that *ren* is a measurement that regulates human relationships: a mediating threshold between being human and not being human, being with other humans and not being with other humans, being good and being evil, and in fact, being art and being reality. It is not a *wu* (thing), but a *zhunsheng* or *shenggui* (measurement) that makes sensible the difference between two things or two values. It is something that is absent, but is made present by one's actualizing it in the process of mediating human relationships in order that *yin* (excesses) can be checked by *li*.[71] In this sense, the cinema can be understood as a *zhunsheng* (measurement) where *ren* could manifest itself and regulate the *xin* (hearts) of its spectators; it makes the very difference that defines human relationships palpable: be that desire, time, or being human. It is in this sense that the cinema can be understood as a biomimetic machine that mediates the various desires in order that *ren* can emerge and be approached.

Conclusion

Fey Mou's film theory can be understood as having an ontological dimension and an ethical dimension, both of which are intricately linked to the cinema's approach to reality. For Bazin, the imperfection of cinematographic reality allows filmmakers to manipulate the liminal position between art and reality, thus producing new approaches to reality. For Fey Mou, such imperfection permits filmmakers to manipulate film forms and narrational devices so the cinematographic image no longer invites the spectators to make causal, spatial, and temporal associations between scenes or images. Instead, the film puts on display mundane day-to-day life in its flatness, boredom, and flavorlessness, or what Deleuze would call the interstices between causes and effects. However, when the spectators encounter such seemingly uneventful and unremarkable reality, the frustrated, unfulfilled, unacknowledged, or unexplored desire somehow becomes tangible as a suspension-imagination, which hangs in the air for the spectators to inhale. It is therefore in the threshold between art and reality, film forms and contents, that desire or *qing* emerges in its absolute immanence, which engenders all things and relationships in the sensible world we inhabit.

Fey Mou's view of cinema responded to the wartime and postwar political desolation of Shanghai, as Ho and FitzGerald point out, and was partially informed by KMT policy that saw the cinema as an educational tool. Yet Fey did not use the cinema as a means to turn individual biological lives into political instruments; rather, he wished to use cinema's ability to make present an absence to reveal the Confucian idea of being human—neither simply as "humanity" as it would be understood in European terms, nor as the highest ethical value, as though it were something noble or transcendental. Rather, *ren,* or being human, is best understood as a measurement that adjudicates on human relationships. It is absent, but is instantiated in the very human order—or even the order of all sensible things—which has the effect of restraining human desire from becoming excessive and thus damaging or hurtful to the larger human order.

In his essay "Confucius and His Time," Fey writes, "To save the world, it is important to rectify the hearts of the people first; to practice a policy of benevolence [*ren*] one will need 'good men politics.'" Later he adds, "A coup, or a war, can transform a country and its social system overnight. But it was 'benevolence' [*ren*] Confucius was preaching; it is, after all, a form of edification and moral education and a virtue that cannot be attained in one leap. This is where his vision coincided with that of Christ."[72] Fey indeed opens *Confucius* with three still images, the Buddha, Christ, and Confucius, thus suggesting that these three thinkers and religious figures are mutually comparable. To a certain degree, even though Fey did not intend to conform to KMT's notion of biopolitics, Confucianism, configured as a principle of middle ground, is compared both in his writing and in the opening of the film itself as being analogous to Christianity, and could be interpreted as a form of sociopolitical conservatism.

However, in the midst of the Sino-Japanese War and in its aftermath, Confucianism, understood as a form of political conservatism, may not be the ultimate solution that Fey Mou had in mind. In fact, if *Confucius* represents the apex of Fey's Confucian idealism, *Spring in a Small Town* could be understood as an expression of his desolation and frustration with a social condition in which Confucianism had already failed. In *Spring,* Zhichen ultimately leaves Yuwen, Liyan, and Daixiu, supposedly as a gesture of *chengren* (to accomplish *ren*), not necessarily as a gesture of defeat or surrender, but as a way to carry his desire to a larger world where it can potentially engender further relationships. However, what hope could one possibly conjure up as the spectators, at the end of the film, watch the sexually frustrated "family" (Yuwen, Liyan, and Daixiu) sending Zhichen off to the ruins of the war, and implicitly, an ongoing civil war (1945–49)? Meanwhile, as Li Ling observes, the film *Confucius* ends with the character Confucius dying (indicated, not actually shown) in an archery garden called Jueshuangpu, which was converted during the Republican period into a cinema.[73] In this sense, the film allegorically embalms the death of Confucius as a cinematographic image in a space that is now a cinema. In one register, the film can be understood romantically as a preservation of Confucius and his teaching as a *juexiang*, a voice reflected from the abyss of time. However, in another register, in the political turmoil and uncertainty of the foreign concessions back in 1940, the image could also be read as a symbolic fall of Confucianism as a form of sociopolitical conservatism. The endings of both films can be understood as expressions of a frustration of frustration, that is, a point at which the desire to live or the desire to love is so frustrated that even frustration itself is rendered inoperative.[74] But perhaps it is out of this ultimate frustration of frustration that a new mode of life emerges, in which one desires *as not* desires.

5 CINEMA OF IDEATION, CINEMA OF PLAY

The Early Cantonese Sound Film

CONSOLIDATING AND MAPPING OUT the theoretical discourse on the Hong Kong Cantonese sound films produced between 1930 and 1949 can be a thorny task. One set of difficulties is related to the cinema's overt theatricality. Since its emergence in 1930, the Hong Kong Cantonese sound film was considered a *zhengyou* (*zangjau*) of the Yueju (Jyutkek or Cantonese theater). The term *zangjau* means companions who are so intimate that they are not afraid to offer straightforward advice to one another. Yet, it also indicates that the two art forms were regarded as *tongchu yichuang* (*tungceot jatcoeng* or coming out of the same school).[1] At first glance, this idea seems to support what Chen Xihe and Zhong Dafeng would call an ontology based on the play-drama. Nonetheless, such a concept of companionship was formulated by theater and film practitioners between the 1930s and 1940s as a means to explore their shared mode of approaching reality. Another set of hurdles is related to the Cantonese cinema's abstruse relationship with the Shanghai-Nanjing (Nanking) notion of national cinema. While most Shanghai filmmakers and critics believed that Chinese national cinema should embody the consciousness of the nation-state as a unified production machine, the Cantonese filmmakers believed that the cinema approaches the reality of Chinese life through a pluralistic assemblage of historical, linguistic, cultural, and political deposits.

On a conceptual level, these two strands of thought can be approached via a set of terms that has underlined art and literary criticisms in China since the Tang (618–907) dynasty, and were invoked by the critics and historians of the Cantonese theater and cinema: *xieshi* (*sesat*), a term I have translated as describing reality; and *xieyi* (*seji*), often translated as "sketching thoughts," but perhaps best understood as sketching ideation, i.e. sketching an idea in its process of informing.[2] By referring to these two categories, I do not imply that Chinese art and literary criticism has stayed the same since the seventh century; rather, I simply suggest that these two terms, as they were repurposed between the 1930s and 1940s as critical signposts of the Cantonese theater-cinema, may help us push further the idea of approaching reality.

In the following intervention, I argue that the early Cantonese sound film is best understood as a cinema of ideation, that is, it sketches an outline of life that invokes an affective state, which in turn invites the spectators to engage themselves in the process of ideation. On the ontological level, the Cantonese sound film inherits the Cantonese theater's notion of sketching thoughts in its approach to reality. On the sociopolitical level, the Cantonese filmmakers believed that while the Shanghai filmmakers were preoccupied by the task of describing reality, the Cantonese directors were more interested in sketching ideation so their spectators would appreciate not a fictional representation of life, but life itself as it is instantiated in a network of human relationships. They did this not by elevating the cinema as an aesthetic experience that engages the spectators in a deep contemplation about the meaning of life, but by putting life, its ontological and political existence, at play.

The Cantonese Sound Film: A Historical Overview

In order to understand the critical and theoretical discourses on the early Cantonese sound films, one must understand the historical development of the Cantonese cinema, its intricate relationship with the theater, and the political debate such a relationship generated. The companionship between Cantonese theater and cinema can be traced back to 1906, when a group of Chinese students in Tokyo established the Haruyanagisha (Chunliushe). These students included Li Shutong (1880–1942), Zeng Xiaoju (1873–1936), and Ouyang Yuqian (1889–1962). They advocated the use of two modern technologies, *guangxue* (light) and *dianxue* (electricity)—two elements that were believed to be the basis of cinema—to stage European-style plays, which would allow the spectators to "approach an 'illusion of life' by means of mimesis." The resulting *shingeki* (*xinju* or new theater) was often used by these students as a vehicle to promote anti-Manchu revolutionary thoughts.[3] In the Guangdong (Kwangtung) region, the new theater attracted actors who were trained in the Cantonese theater, including Ouyang Yuqian, Chen Feinong (Chan

Fei-nung, 1899–1984), and Mai Xiaoxia (Mak Siu-ha, d. 1941), to establish theater groups including the Youtianying (Jautinjing, or Shadows of heavenly comedians) and Linluohuanjing (Lamlowaanging, or Dazzling displays of illusions).[4] In fact, the names of these groups, with their use of words such as *jing* (shadows), *lamlo* (dazzling displays), and *waanging* (illusions), allude to the cinematic effects that these plays were supposed to achieve.

In Shanghai, however, new theater became the dominant mode of cinema, and remained so into the early 1930s. In the Canton-Hong Kong region, the new-theater performers delivered their lines by singing and reciting, as they usually did in the Cantonese play, thus effectively converting the new theater to a new form of Cantonese theater. Yet the new theater and other "modern" elements did not simply disappear into the Cantonese play. Rather, the Cantonese play itself was modified with the introduction of these new elements.[5] For example, the young playwrights and performers employed the pantomimic style of acting from the American silent films, most notably the slapstick comedies. Such a new acting style was supposed to bring into the Cantonese theater the lure of the *xinqi* (*sankei* or new and strange) from the cinema.[6] Beyond singing and acting, these young artists also found a certain similarity between the structure of a cinematic experience and that of the Cantonese play. As Charles Musser argues, early showmen and exhibitionists often strung together a number of shorts, known in the Guangzhou (Canton)-Hong Kong region as *ben* (*bun* or reel), thematically into a rough narrative order.[7] Similarly, a Cantonese *zhengben xi* (*zingbun hei* or feature play) is made up of a number of *bun* (acts). These acts are arranged, as in the early cinema, in a thematic order, though the function of each act is to feature the vocal talent of a *hangdang* (*hongdong* or role).[8]

By 1907 the new theater had been absorbed into the Cantonese theater. During the 1910s and 1920s, the Cantonese theater and cinema evolved hand-in-hand both formally and industrially. Arguably, the earliest (silent) motion pictures being shot in Hong Kong (though copyrighted in the United States) *Wapan shenyuan* [*Ngaapun sanjyun*, or Vindicated by the earthenware basin, not datable], *Tou shaoya* [*Tau siungaap*, or Stealing a roast duck, Li Minwei or Lay Min-wai, Yaxiya or Asia Film and Theatre Company, 1909], and *Zhuangzi shi qi* [*Zongzi si cai*, or Zhuangzi tests his wife, Lay Man-wai, Huamei or China-America Film Company, 1913]—were filmed versions of these cinematic plays.[9] When the feature film became popular during this period, Mak Siu-ha, Ouyang Yuqian, and Chan Fei-nung (and into the 1920s and 1930s, Xue Juexian [Sit Kok-sin, 1904–56] and Ma Sizeng [Ma Si-tsang, 1900–64]) adapted Hollywood feature films and slapstick comedies as Cantonese cinematic plays.[10]

Industrially, all *ling* (singers or stage performers) and playwrights were managed by their guild, Bahe huiguan (Baatwo wuigwun, Chinese Artists Association or CAA). These *ling* would be formed into troupes and assigned to the different *xiyuan* (*heijyun* or theaters) in Canton and Hong Kong. But top-billing stars would often stay in the major theaters such as the Astor Theatre (opened in Midlevel Sheung Wan in 1890 and Yau Ma Tei in 1902), the Tai Ping Theatre (opened in Shek Tong Tsui in 1904), the New Theatre (opened in Kau Yue Fong in 1909), and the Ko Sing Theatre (opened in Sheung Wan in 1928). A star system soon developed during this period, with the theaters functioning like Hollywood film studios: they maintained the image and marketability of the stars, commissioned plays tailored to their talents, and later on, produced silent short films that could be screened with live orchestral accompaniment between bookings or as promotional materials. In time, these theaters also came to double as movie palaces.[11] In the Canton-Hong Kong region, the term for watching a motion picture is still the same as for watching a Cantonese play: *taihei,* and the term *heijyun* refers to both stage and movie theaters.

Industrialized filmmaking began in Hong Kong in 1922 with the establishment of China Sun (Minxin), the official documentary unit of the KMT. China Sun made mostly newsreels, but they produced one silent feature film: *Yanzhi* [*Jinzi* or Rouge, Guan Wenqing or Kwan Man-ching, 1924, released in 1925], which was based on the new Cantonese theater format. Despite the film's box-office success, its HK$9,000 budget was only partially recovered (HK$6,000), which effectively bankrupted the not-yet fully formed feature-film unit of China Sun. Political events also intervened to slow the growth of the Hong Kong film industry. In Shanghai on May 30, 1925, anti-imperialist protestors were massacred by British police forces. In response, the Canton-Hong Kong strike was carried on from June 1925 to October 1926. In Hong Kong, the colonial administration under Governor Reginald Edward Stubbs (1876–1947, in office 1919–25) retaliated by banning all entertainment activities in Hong Kong, effective until the end of 1926. As a result, filmmakers, actors, and technicians sought work in Shanghai and Canton instead.

Cantonese film production recovered around 1929 and 1930, and the *fangyan dianying* (*fongjin dingjing* or dialect sound film) emerged around

1930 in Hong Kong, Canton, and Xiamen (Amoy).[12] By that year, the major movie theaters that showed Hollywood films—Central Theater (Yuesxiu or Yuet Sau, Canton), Lee Theatre (Causeway Bay, Hong Kong), Astor Theatre (Yau Ma Tei, Kowloon), and Queen's Theatre (Central, Hong Kong)—were all equipped with Warner Bros.' Western Electric sound-on-film system. In December 1930, with the sweeping box-office success of *All Quiet on the Western Front* (Lewis Milestone, Universal, 1930) and Lianhua's (UPS) release of its first sound feature, the musical *Genü Hongmudan* [*The Sing-Song Girl Red Peony,* Zhang Shichuan], these major movie theaters declared in their gazettes the end of the silent era.[13] Local filmmakers responded to the demand for Cantonese sound features. Between 1931 and 1933, Studio 3 of the UPS (a.k.a. the Hong Kong Studio) produced four films in a style closer to the mode of narration and aesthetic standard of classical Hollywood.[14]

In 1933, Li Minwei's (Lay Ming-wai, 1893–1953) brother Li Beihai (1889–1955) and Beihai's apprentice Tang Xingtu (Tong Sing-to, dates unknown) opened the studio Zhonghua (Chung Wah) Sound and Silent Movies Production Company and produced the Cantonese-theater sound film *Shazai dongfang* [*Sozai dungfong* or The idiot's wedding night, Li Beihai, 1933], featuring the Cantonese theater comedians Liao Mengjue (Liu Mung-kok, dates unknown) and Huang Peiying (Wong Pui-ying, dates unknown). Between 1933 and 1934, Chung Wah produced a series of Cantonese sound films featuring theater actors, including *Liangxin* [*Loengsam,* or *Conscience,* Mak Siu-ha, 1933] and *Boxing* [*Bokhang,* or *Tragedy of Love,* Li Beihai, 1934].[15] These films marked the beginning of the full-fledged fusion of the Cantonese theater and cinema. In the production process, for example, a Cantonese play was conceived both as a stage play and a screenplay. The stage play usually contained more musical numbers than the screenplay, whereas the screenplay contained more dialogue scenes. A troupe was responsible for providing performances on the stage and the screen, and for producing a recording of the show's music. Very often, the troupes toured around Southeast Asia or traveled to New York City and San Francisco to promote an upcoming film release of a play by offering a stage revue or giving concerts that would promote record sales.[16] These Cantonese play-films were advertised in newspapers and film magazines as *hei* (plays) that could be enjoyed in three different media.

This conflation of the theater and cinema in the Canton-Hong Kong region was looked down upon by the Shanghai filmmakers and critics in the 1930s as a sign of premodernity, cultural poverty, and national disunity, since by the 1930s, filmmakers and critics in Shanghai had begun to see the cinema not as a form of *xiju* (play-theater), but as an art form and institution with its own specificities. The Shanghai filmmakers also believed that the cinema should represent only modern subjects, and local theaters and operas were seen as premodern or even primitive art forms. Between the late 1920s and the early 1930s, Mandarin was increasingly promoted as a national language, and in 1932, the Guoyu tuixing weiyuanhui (National Language Committee) decided to set Beijing (Peking) Mandarin (as opposed to Cantonese) as the *guoyu* (national language), allegedly by one vote.[17] Mandarin was generally spoken and understood north of the Yangtze River and in the Shanghai-Suzhou (Soochow) areas, whereas Cantonese was more popularly used in Kwangtung, Guangxi (Kwangsi), Hong Kong, Macau, and the Chinese diasporic communities in Southeast Asia, North America, and Europe, which covered far more urban centers than the Mandarin-speaking regions. Since national-language education was not carried out until 1932, Mandarin films could not be understood by the audience in the Cantonese-speaking regions, and vice versa. The two regions also had very different local customs, cultural sensibilities, and senses of in-group loyalty. This language issue was not a problem during the silent period, since written Chinese in both its classical and vernacular forms has been standardized for centuries. However, with the advent of sound, audiences began to demand films made in their local dialects, so if the Shanghai studios made films only in Mandarin, they stood to lose their markets not only in the south, but also overseas.

To compound the problem, as early as 1930, the Central Committee of Propaganda (CCoP), in anticipation of the advent of sound, decreed that all sound productions be made in Mandarin.[18] Meanwhile, since the late 1920s the KMT film authorities had banned all films from being subtitled, a measure originally designed to discourage viewers from watching Hollywood films.[19] As a result, film producers could not make Mandarin films more marketable in the south by subtitling them. The NECSC suggested that studios produce a sound version in Mandarin for release in Shanghai, Peking, and other urban centers in the north, while silent prints with intertitles would be struck for distribution in the Cantonese-speaking regions.[20] The Shanghai studio executives, however, considered this proposal costly and impractical.[21] As a result, other major studios, including Mingxing (Star) and Yihua (Yee Hwa), tried to emulate the UPS by setting up studios in Canton or Hong Kong, where they could make Cantonese-language films.[22]

To complicate matters, the Kwangtung region was a semiautonomous province governed by the Canton faction of the KMT under the leadership of Hu Hanmin (1879–1936), known at the time as the Xinan zhengfu (Sainaam zingfu or the Southwest Government). Meanwhile, Hong Kong was a British colony. Hence, the CCoP and NECSC had very little influence over the production and distribution policies in the Canton-Hong Kong region.[23] In addition, conducting business as *waijiang ren* (*ngoigong jan* or people who came from outside Kwangtung) in the Canton-Hong Kong region in the 1930s was difficult in many respects. Until 1933, the Chinese Artists Association (CAA) guild oversaw all the contracts and business transactions among theater artists, owners, and managers, and between 1932 and 1933, under the leadership of Sit Kok-sin, theater artists began to form their own theater troupes and enter into contracts with theater managers on freelance bases.[24] Under the influence of CAA, business interests and spheres of financial power were largely divided among different *shetuan* (*setyun* or societies), which ranged from financial groups built upon regional clans to what one may now call the *sanhehui* (*saamhapwui* or triads), which, as Teemu Ruskola argues, were best seen as investment groups with limited liabilities.[25] In fact, there was no reason Chinese-Americans in San Francisco could not make their own Cantonese sound features for North American distribution. In 1935, Zhao Shushen (Chiu Shu-sun, 1904–87), under the encouragement of UPS film executive Luo Mingyou (Lo Ming-yau, 1900–67), registered his San-Francisco-based film company Daguan (Grandview) in Hong Kong for producing and distributing Cantonese films for the Chinese-American audience, a project originally conceived of as the Haiwai Lianhua (Overseas UPS).[26] As a result, the Shanghai filmmakers began to see the Cantonese sound film as a serious threat to their domestic and overseas markets.

While the Shanghai filmmakers were waiting for a solution, Shao Zuiweng (Runje Shaw, 1896–1975), one of the Shaw Brothers who owned the Tianyi (Unique) Studio in Shanghai, signed a contract with the young Cantonese stage star Sit Kok-sin, and established the Nanyang (South Sea) Film Studio in Hong Kong. Sit adapted an American comedy, *The Grand Duchess and the Waiter* (Malcolm St. Clair, Paramount, 1926), to a Cantonese theater production and film: *Bai Jinlong* [*Baak Gam-lung* or *White Golden Dragon*, 1934]. The film was a box-office success both in Shanghai and the Canton-Hong Kong region, which created bitter indignation among the Shanghai studio executives against Shaw.[27] In retaliation, the UPS and Star began to launch sound-film productions in Mandarin.[28] They also encouraged journalists and educators in Shanghai to criticize the South Sea films as being *caozhi lanzao* (*couzai laamzou* or roughly produced and hastily made).[29] In fact, the Shanghai filmmakers even tried to sabotage the production of the sequel to *White Golden Dragon* between 1934 and 1935 by hiring triad members to set fire to the printing room of South Sea's Pak Tai Street Studio.[30] But despite the attacks, fifty production companies and film studios sprang up on Pak Tai Street. These included Sit Kok-sin's Nanyue (South China), Ma Si-tsang's Quanqiu (Globe), Chiu Shu-sun's Grandview, Runje Shaw's South Sea, and Lu Gen's Fenghuang (Phoenix).[31]

The business acrimony between the Shanghai and Hong Kong filmmakers was gradually politicized based on one crucial factor: as a dialect cinema, the Cantonese film remained theatrical (as a sign of provincialism) and *lisu* (*leizuk* or vulgar). The Shanghai filmmakers argued that the use of the Cantonese language in sound films was an obstacle to the modernization of Chinese cinema. Between 1930 and 1936, a series of intellectual debates and an intense competition ensued between the Shanghai filmmakers and their Cantonese counterparts, followed by a serious attempt by the Nanking government, which wanted to unify the Chinese language by promoting Mandarin as the standard, and the Shanghai film industry, which tried to reclaim its lost territories, to ban Cantonese film production in the Canton-Hong Kong region. The NFCC (National Film Censorship Committee), reorganized in 1933 into the CFCC (Central Film Censorship Committee) with Luo Gang (1901–77) as its director, had reiterated that Chinese cinema should speak only Mandarin, and issued a ban, not on all dialect cinemas, but only Cantonese cinema. However, CFCC's intervention could not fully materialize until the death of Hu Hanmin in May 1935, when the CFCC declared that it would implement the ban.[32] Seeing the imminent threat, in December 1936, over three hundred Cantonese filmmakers, businesspeople, journalists, and educators convened in the Jinlong (Kam Lung or Golden Dragon) Restaurant in Hong Kong. They sent a telegram to Nanking to demand a postponement of the ban to July 1937.[33] The demand was at first neglected. Then, in May 1937, the CFCC sent a delegation to Canton to prepare for the implementation of the ban. In response, the Cantonese producers formed the Huanjiu Yuepian lianhe xiehui (Waangau Jyutpin lyunhap hipwui or United Association for Rescuing the Cantonese

Cinema), and sent a delegation to Shanghai and Nanking to demand yet another postponement.[34]

As a response to the delegation's demand, Minister of Central Propaganda Shao Lizi (Shao Li-tzu, 1882–1967), under pressure from his party's senior, Canton mayor Zeng Yangfu (1898–1969), agreed to a three-year postponement, on condition that the Cantonese production companies and studios submit their films to the CFCC for censorship. In answer, the Cantonese filmmakers demanded that the CFCC set up an office in Canton, with a further extension of the transitional period to six years. The CFCC accepted the first suggestion, but not the second, and within a few weeks, Luo Gang proposed a new licensing policy, by which only production companies with studio facilities would be licensed and allowed to submit films to the CFCC. This effectively disqualified most of the Hong Kong Cantonese production companies. As a result, the United Association refused to send their films to the CFCC, and when the war broke out in July in the Mainland, the CFCC's Canton-Hong Kong offices soon became defunct.[35]

The dialect problem, together with its cultural overtones, became a permanent fixture in the theoretical debate on Cantonese cinema during and after the Sino-Japanese War (1937–45). After the Battle of Shanghai (August 13–November 26, 1937), Grandview called for a united front among the Cantonese filmmakers and produced the patriotic film *Zuihou guantou* [*Zeoihau gwaantau* or *At This Critical Juncture,* 1938] directed by Zhu Qingxian (Chuk Ching-yin, dates unknown), Tang Xiaodan (Tong Hiu-dan, 1910–2012), Chen Pi (Chan Pei, d. 1966), and Lu Dun (Lo Duen, 1911–2000).[36] The film examines how different college students in Canton responded to the invasion in Northern China and Shanghai.[37] The film was shot in Sit Kok-sin's South China studios, and starred Sit, Ma Si-tsang, Tan Lanqing (Tam Lan-hing, 1908–1981), Wu Chufan (Ng Cho-fan, 1911–1993), and Lo Duen.[38] The idea of mobilizing a regional cinema for a national cause between 1937 and 1938 was called the *Yuepian zhengming yundong* (*Jyutpin zingming wandung* or Rectification of the Cantonese film movement) or *Yuepian qingjie yundong* (*Jyutpin cinggit wandung* or Cantonese film cleansing movement).[39] But the movement was short-lived, as Hong Kong soon became a center of production for the gods-and-demons films, the Mandarin folklore films, and historical epics.[40] By the end of 1937, Cai Chusheng (Tsai Chu-sang, 1906–68) proposed a form of filmmaking called the Huanan guofang dianying (Waanaam gwokfong dinjing or South China national defense cinema).[41] Tsai's works during the

Sino-Japanese War, including *Gudao tiantang* [*Gwudou tintong* or *Orphan Island Paradise,* Dadi or Tai Tei Film Company, 1939] and *Qiancheng wanli* [*Cincing maanlei* or *Ten Thousand Li Ahead,* Xinsheng or San Sang Film Company, 1941] feature a mixed Shanghai and Hong Kong crew and cast. His primary interest was to represent the economic frustration and patriotic sentiment of the Shanghai émigrés, who came from a diverse linguistic, cultural, and economic background.

The effect of the Cantonese film cleansing movement and the South China national defense cinema was an emerging separation between those actors and filmmakers who were trained primarily in the Cantonese theater and those who were trained in the new theater. Between 1952 and 1953, actor and producer Ng Cho-fan started the *Lingxing fenjia* (*Lingsing fangaa* or Separation between stage and screen actors movement). Yet, despite such growing differences between the two spheres, the Cantonese theater remained a companion of the Cantonese cinema until the early 1960s, and because of that, its Mandarin counterpart continued to typecast it as an inferior popular entertainment.[42] In other words, any attempt to theorize the Cantonese cinema cannot overlook its theatrical debt and the idée fixe about its status as a dialect cinema.

Mak Siu-ha: On Ideation and Musicality

Mak Siu-ha's *Guangdong xiju shi lue* [*Gwongdung heikek siloek* or Brief history of the Cantonese theater], written during the early years of the Sino-Japanese War and published in Hong Kong in 1940, is still regarded by theater and film historians as the first critical investigation into the history and theory of the Cantonese theater, and to a certain degree, cinema. Although it is arguable whether Mak's study was indeed the first, it does form the basis of subsequent art historical studies, including Ouyang Yuqian's "Shitan Yueju" [Let's try talking about the Cantonese theater, 1956], Chan Fei-nung's *Yueju liushi nian* [*Jyutkek luksap nin* or Sixty years in the Cantonese theater, transcribed from Chan's oral description in the early 1980s, published in 2007], Chan Sau-yan's *Shengong Yueju zai Xianggang* [*Sangung Jyutkek zoi Hoenggong* or The sacred Cantonese theater in Hong Kong, 2008], and Lai Kin's *Xianggang Yueju xulun* [*Hoenggong Jyutkek zeoileon* or Discourse on the Hong Kong Cantonese theater, 2010]. Therefore, I wish to begin my theoretical discussion with Mak's account as a way to understand how artists and historians theorize the Cantonese theater and cinema, and to retrospectively and retroactively reframe the critical discourse on the Cantonese cinema in the 1930s and 1940s.

When Mak Siu-ha wrote *Brief History* in the years leading up to 1940, he had one political agenda in mind: to prove not only that the Cantonese theater was a legitimate national art form, but also that it was the culmination of Chinese culture in the modern era. In his introduction, Mak argues that both the bureaucratic and academic historians during the imperial period had grossly overlooked studies of the Cantonese theater, for they all "habitually despised the play-drama as a form of *xiaodao* [*siudou* or minor vehicle]." Meanwhile, intellectuals liked the fact that the Cantonese theater could "sketch one's ideation, express *qing* [*cing*], transform social trends, and change local customs." Nevertheless, these writers were hardly trained in the art and practice of the theater itself, and they were unable to produce any professional criticisms.[43] For Mak Siu-ha, not only was the Cantonese theater stigmatized as being "minor," its historical association with revolutionary movements also generated an uneasy relationship between the imperial government and its guild. In 1648, for example, the governor of Guangdong, Li Chengdong (d. 1649), was inspired by the Ming-styled costume worn by stage performers to rebel against the Qing Empire (1644–1911). Later, in 1854, in response to the Taiping Rebellion (1850–64), Li Wenmao (dates unknown) from the theatrical guild of the time, Qionghua huiguan (Kingfaa wuigwun), led a troupe of Cantonese performers to fight against the Qing Empire.[44]

Mak Siu-ha's opening remarks emphasized that the Cantonese theater had been, since the transition between the Ming and Qing, placed in a geopolitically, culturally, and artistically marginal position, an attitude adopted by the KMT authorities as well. But despite such marginalization, the Cantonese theater not only inherited the same theatrical traditions that made up the Jingju (Peking opera), but also actively appropriated new elements from the Euro-American theater and cinema, thus making it a locus for cultural components, social values, and political thoughts from different time periods and geographical spaces to be pluralistically deposited and renegotiated.

For the purpose of legitimizing the Cantonese theater, Mak Siu-ha's study can be categorized in two dimensions: *jianbie* (*gaambit*, identifying a system of differences or ontologizing) and *suoyuan* (*sokjyun* or searching for the origin). Mak argues that the ontological basis of the Cantonese theater-cinema is not describing reality; instead, it approaches reality by means of sketching ideation. In *Brief History*, Mak writes:

> The essence of describing reality is to experience life. The essence of sketching ideation is to approach life in the form of *xiangzheng* [*zoengzing*, often translated as symbolization or representation, but perhaps more closely as biomimesis].
>
> Like the sciences, describing reality gives the spectators a pleasing and refreshing sensation. Like philosophy, sketching ideation generates a rich flavor that lingers [on one's palate] as an aftertaste.
>
> Describing reality is a way to observe the "conflicting and hypocritical" cruelty in our social life from a vernacular perspective; sketching ideation is a way to penetrate into the "tyranny and violence" of our self-conflicting social values in order to reach the end of it.
>
> Describing reality is a way to use "material civilization" and "scientific experience" to alleviate the suffering of the human kind; sketching ideation is a way to use "mental reconstruction" and "spiritual triumph" to emancipate the human soul.[45]

For Mak, the Cantonese performers use "beautiful and skillful poses and signs to express the profound and delicate *cing* of the spectators," which requires not realistic description, but "economic and concise [performative] methods to achieve a dramatic effect."[46]

The differentiation between describing reality and sketching ideation can be traced back to art and literary criticism in the Tang dynasty. In art criticism, describing reality is achieved by means of the *gongbi* (meticulous strokes). In one register, a painting that describes reality would allow the beholder to approach reality in all its concreteness. But in another register, the *gongbi* style would also invite the beholder to admire the skillfulness of the way the artist plans and executes her or his design.[47] In poetry, the style of describing reality is often seen as a means by which the poet flaunts her or his mastery over such skills as paradigmatic inversion, reversion, displacement and substitution, rhyming, symmetry, and tonal fluidity.[48] In other words, describing reality corresponds less to the European idea of realism than formalism. Meanwhile, the style of sketching ideation was often regarded as a *Liuchao yifeng* (legacy from the Six Dynasties, circa 220–589), a style that defies conventional forms in favor of *haoqing* (broadness and openness in its expression of *qing*), *yixiang* (ideation in its suggestion and overall atmosphere), *zhi* (personal will), and *qi* (continuity in rhythm and breathing).[49]

Sketching ideation, however, does not mean that the art form has no material basis in reality or narration. Mak Siu-ha's claim would in fact trouble Ouyang Yuqian, who wrote about the history and form of the Cantonese theater under the rubrics of Marxist art criticism. For Ouyang, the notion of sketching ideation is best illustrated by a Tang-dynasty form of staged ballad, *ta yao niang.* The *ta yao niang* literally means a dance of a lady rocking back and forth while divulging her sufferings. The art form had a legendary origin traced back to the state of Northern Qi (550–77), in which a beautiful woman was known to be abused by her hideous husband. The ballad is supposed to be performed by an actor (who plays the role of the husband) and a female impersonator (who plays the role of the wife), who would walk along the stage while singing. The actress is supposed to sing about her sufferings, while the husband would "answer" her by arguing against her or hitting her. Ouyang argues that sketching ideation in this case means that the art form "uses a basic *qiangdiao* (vocal style) to sketch a simple and straightforward narrative. In other words, sketching ideation, for Ouyang, should be considered a way to approach reality, and the art form functions not simply as a spectacle or vocal attraction, but also as a mode of narration.[50]

Mak Siu-ha's notion of sketching ideation in the Cantonese theater, and later on, cinema, can be attributed to its historical basis in music. In *Brief History,* Mak draws a genealogy of the Cantonese theater (one that has been disputed by Ouyang Yuqian and other theater historians). For Mak, the Cantonese theater-cinema has its historical origin in the *yue* (music) and *ge* (song) from the reign of the legendary Yellow Emperor (2698–2598 BCE). This music-song tradition was, for Mak, institutionalized around the Qin (221–06 BCE) and Han (206 BCE–220 CE) dynasties as the *yuefu* (lyrical poetry). After a series of generic and stylistic variations, the music-song became the *Jin yuanben* (brothel repertoire of the Great Jin, 1115–1234). The brothel repertoire was then transformed into the *haiyan qiang* (sea-salt style) of the Zhejiang region around the Yuan dynasty. One of its seven variations, the Geyang *qiang* (Geyang style), would later on be developed into the *luantan* (miscellaneous style) during the reign of the Ming Emperor Chongzhen (1627–44). It was from the miscellaneous style that the *bangzi* (*bongzi*) and *sipi-erhuang* (*saipei-jiwong*) were developed during the reign of the Xianfeng Emperor (1850–61), which would then become the Peking opera in the north and the Cantonese theater in the south.[51]

In his discussion, Mak argues that the term *ling* came from the reign of the legendary Emperor Yao (c. 2356–2255 BCE) as a name for someone who sings in a sacrificial ceremony. For Mak, the visual and narrative aspects of the Cantonese theater were later additions to the musical form. According to his account, the visual dimension of the Cantonese theater came from the *wu* (dance, witchcraft, or martial arts) during the reign of the legendary Emperor Yao, while the narrative dimension came from the *huaji* (comedy) during the reign of the Emperor Shun (circa twenty-third to twenty-second centuries BCE). The dance became the *jiaodixi* (wrestling) during the Qin dynasty, which, together with the comedy, would become one of the *baixi* (hundred plays) during the Three Kingdoms (220–280 CE). The hundred plays would then be transformed into the *canjunxi* (military revue) during the Chen dynasty (557–89), which would then evolve during the Tang dynasty (618–907) into the *chuanqi* (narration of extraordinary acts, usually those of female warriors; it is now often seen by film historians as the origin of the *wuxia* or martial arts films) and the *hesheng* (musical, often with erotic subject matters and cross-dressing performances). For Mak, the narration of extraordinary acts and the musical would later on become the *zaju* (miscellaneous play) during the Song and Yuan dynasties, and would become the Kunqu, whose forms became the physical, visual, and narrational dimensions of the Cantonese theater-cinema.[52]

For Mak Siu-ha, the Cantonese cinema is best understood as a new form of Cantonese theater. In fact, he dated the formalization of both the Peking opera and the Cantonese theater as late as 1909, the very year the Cantonese theater had fully absorbed the new theater into its form and structure, and the short film *Stealing a Roast Duck* was released in Hong Kong. It is indeed tempting to argue that Mak's genealogy can be used to corroborate the shadow play theory. But curiously, for Mak, the *kuailüxi* (puppet theater) from the Xia dynasty (circa 2070–1600 BCE) and the shadow play (dated and located by Mak to the state of Later Zhou, 951–60) were excluded altogether from the genealogy of the Cantonese theater-cinema.[53] The crucial point here, once again, is that for Mak, the Cantonese play is best understood not as a primarily visual and narrative form; rather, it was principally developed out of an auditory tradition, which approaches reality not by means of describing it, but by sketching ideation.

Mak Siu-ha's notion of ideation and musicality has been widely accepted as a general theory of the Cantonese theater (e.g. both Chan Fei-nung and Lai Kin define the Cantonese theater as a school of vocal styles), although its applicability and consistency have been challenged by other theater artists and historians.[54] Ouyang Yuqian argues that Mak based his musicality claim on the assumption that the Cantonese theater came from the Hanxi (Hakka theater), a form of moral play performed in local religious ceremonies in the Hakka regions of Guangdong, which employs primarily the Zhongzhou yin (Central Plain pronunciation, closer to modern Mandarin than Cantonese). However, Ouyang believes that the two major vocal styles, *bongzi* and *jiwong*, were more likely introduced by the *waijiang ban* (*ngoigong baan* or itinerant troupes from the north), which performed these tunes in the Kunqu, and later on, the Peking opera.[55] The Kunqu certainly has a choreographic dimension, whereas the Peking opera is known for its acrobatic agility; both forms continued to influence the performing style of the Cantonese theater artists into the twenty-first century. In addition, in the early twentieth century, with the introduction of the concept of mimesis from the new theater and Hollywood cinema, the Cantonese theater also evolved from the use of the *yizhuo eryi* (*jatcoek jiji*, or one table, two chairs) as the only stage props to realistic stage designs. Hence, Ouyang argues that while the Cantonese theater may still be defined as an auditory art, its staging and narration are not always subservient to its musical performance.[56]

Meanwhile, Chan Sau-yan, in his studies of the *shengongxi* (*sangunghei* or plays devoted as virtues to the deities), argues that neither visuality nor musicality is to be considered as the basis of the Cantonese theater. Rather, for Chan, the Cantonese theater is grounded in its ceremonial function. The *sangunghei* are not subgenres of the Cantonese theater; instead, they refer to the Cantonese plays as they are performed as parts of a religious ceremony. For example, when a troupe performs a play on a newly built stage, it must perform the one-act play *Ji Baihu* [*Zai Baakfu* or Offering for the White Tiger]. *Offering*, for Chan, is a rite in which the deity of wealth, Zhao Gongming (Chiu Kungming), feeds the White Tiger. In the play, Chiu Kungming is played by two actors: one embodies his divine form and the other his human form, thus suggesting that the performance itself serves as a threshold between the human and the divine. Meanwhile, the White Tiger is the incarnation of a five-hundred-year-old tiger, which is also the name of a star that symbolizes ill fate. The dramatic action involves an elaborate set of *zouwei* (*zauwai* or choreographed steps) that circulate around the stage, which ritualize the myth of Chiu offering the White Tiger a piece of raw pork as a sacrifice. In the entire ritual, neither the performers nor the stagehands could utter a word. If anyone produces a sound, unexpected ill fates may interrupt the performance of the secular plays that follow. For Chan Sau-yan,

Offering, among a number of plays that would be performed regularly (a.k.a. *lixi* or *laihei*, that is, set pieces) in the opening night of a run, is best understood as neither primarily musical nor visual, but ritualistic.[57]

However, while some ritualistic dimensions of the Cantonese theater did enter the sphere of screen practice, the musical and ideational aspects of the Cantonese theater, I argue, became the basis of the early Cantonese sound film. In this sense, the Cantonese sound film approaches reality in a way different from its Shanghai and Hollywood counterparts. It engages the spectators in a primarily musical or auditory experience, and it draws the spectators into reality not by means of describing it, but by means of ideation.

Cinema of Ideation: Sit Kok-sin and His View of Life

The musicality and ideationality of the Cantonese theater-cinema defines the narrational style and structure of the early Cantonese sound film, which approaches reality in a way different from those the spectators experienced in Shanghai and Hollywood cinemas. Unfortunately, for many years, the formal "peculiarities" of the Cantonese cinema were seen as signs of its primitivism and vulgarity. In 1978, Hong Kong film critic Lin Niantong (Lam Nin-tung, 1944–90) summarized the Cantonese style of narration, which was developed in the 1930s but continued to dominate the Cantonese sound film into the 1950s, as follows:

1. The extensive use of the long shot and medium long shot to preserve the integrity of the dramatic space; and the absence of any shot-reverse-shots (cutting back and forth between one character and another) in dialogue scenes;
2. The use of deep-focus composition to create dramatic tension between characters within a unified dramatic space;
3. The use of diffused lighting for domestic scenes versus the use of high-contrast lighting in scenes that portray crimes and sexuality, although continuity is often overlooked in favor of dramatic effects;
4. The use of asides to convey moments of dramatic decisions;
5. A narrative structure that is not based on a cause-and-effect chain triggered by a character's want and obstacles; rather, the film is constructed as a series of chronological events, each being caused by the larger sociopolitical conditions that leave the characters with no political agency to change the situation;

6. Editing is rarely motivated by a dramatic action; rather, the integrity of a performance, with a beginning and an end, is often carefully preserved in a long take instead of tailored (by means of editing) for the sake of maintaining continuity.[58]

The Shanghai filmmakers in the 1930s and 1940s, and most Hong Kong film critics between the 1960s and 1980s, genuinely believed that the early Cantonese sound filmmakers had failed to master the cinematic language of Hollywood.[59] Yet, such a primitive-cinema argument overlooks two major problems. First, the early Hong Kong filmmakers were well versed in Hollywood cinema, and it would be absurd to imagine that they had no knowledge of the Hollywood style of narration. Second, historically many Cantonese producers, directors, and actors had experience working in the Shanghai industry and the new theater. Hence, historians are often puzzled by the fact that these early cultural workers seemed to adopt a non-Hollywood mode of narration whenever they made their films for a Hong Kong Cantonese audience.[60] But if one takes into account the musicality and ideationality of the Cantonese theater, some of these ostensibly incomprehensible stylistic choices can in fact be explained.

Understanding the Cantonese theater-cinema requires some basic knowledge of its music theory. The backbone of the Cantonese theater, and later on, the Cantonese sound cinema, is not its *wenben* (*manbun* or literary script), but its *yueben* (*ngokbun* or score). In fact, most Cantonese plays and films do not have scripts, but are instead composed of *paichang* (*paaichoeng* or programming).[61] The Cantonese theater is often compared to the Italian opera. However, since the second half of the eighteenth century, European operas have been considered self-contained and unified works with original music composed for them. The music of a Cantonese play, however, is made up of a number of standardized but highly variable tunes, which could be roughly grouped into three categories: the *jiwong*, *saipei*, and *bongzi*. The *jiwong*, sung and played in the key of G, is usually employed to convey tragic and melancholic effects. It consists of six variations (original, slow, fast-slow, recitative, sighing, and the *erliu* [*jilau*] or triple time), and each variation produces further subvariations. Each sub-variation consists of a *shangju* (*soenggeoi* or lead) and a *xiaju* (*haageoi* or answer). When the *jiwong* is modulated to the key of D—known as the *fanxian* (*faansin*)—it is mobilized to convey a sense of longing and frustration. What in the Cantonese theater is called the *saipei* actually comes from the *siping diao* of the Peking opera, sung in the key of C. It is often used in passages of flirtation and male bravado. What the Cantonese theater artists call the *bongzi* is in fact the *xipi* in the Peking opera. The *bongzi* is usually sung in the key of F, which usually conveys straightforward ideas. It has nine variations (original, slow, fast-slow, moderately slow, moderate, recitative, sighing, moderately fast, and moderate *faansin*), and each has its own sub-variations (with leads and answers). In addition, since the nineteenth century, local Cantonese songs, recitations, and *xiaodiao* (*siudiu* or melodies) would be added into the mix.[62]

In the musical notation of an operatic score, the playwright is responsible for setting words to the variations and sub-variations of the *bongzi* and *jiwong*. The way these musical variations are arranged would inform the performers' choreography, staging, and acrobatic tricks, and the film directors' staging, composition, and editing points. Very often, standardized variations are notated only by their names. Note-by-note notations are only required when the variation is entirely new, or after the 1930s, when the playwright introduces a newly composed tune. The musical notation, called the *heche pu* (*hoce pou* or sol-re score, named after a *solfège* system developed in the theater) indicates the framework of the tune, the *ban-yan* (*baan-ngaan* or accented beat and secondary accented beat; e.g. the first and third beat of what would be equivalent to the European 4/4 time), a suggested mapping of the lyrics, and an indicated style of ornamentation.[63] How the performer will interpret it and how the director will put it on screen depends on the *qing* or *cing* it is supposed to generate. In short, the principle of the Cantonese theater can be understood as *you qiang sheng qing* (*yau hong sang cing* or let *cing* be engendered from the music).[64]

In a performance, the singers produce further variations by means of improvisation. Improvisations are often based on historical conventions, though they are usually tailored to the voices of the individual singers, and each singer has a unique style. For example, some singers are known for starting a tune with an upbeat ornamentation, others are known for their imperfect cadences. Words are sometimes placed from note to note, but can also be sparsely placed in a tune. As a result, the singer must provide sound substitutes that could extend the phonetic ending of a word. For example, after singing the word *jan* (human), a performer may need to extend the sound over a complex passage of ornamented music. In this case, the "n" sound, which is considerably monotonous, can be extended by using a variety of sounds that can fit the musical flow. For example, one can sing "*jan—n—i—ji—ejyu—e—ei—je—ja—a—e—i—n.*" Certain performers are known for the way they manipulate these fillers. For example, Ma Si-tsang had a penchant for breaking up these fillers, usually in a *faansin* passage, into a sobbing series of "*e,*" sung in an inflected raspy voice, which communicates a *cing* known as *qiliang* (*cailoeng* or sorrow and cold).[65] In some Cantonese sound films, the camera would stay on the performer during these passages specifically for the purpose of letting the spectators behold the process of improvisation. In others, this would be an opportunity for the director to cut to a reaction shot or a montage of images that would fit the *cing* that the song evokes.

The principle of *yau hong sang cing* is in fact crucial to understanding the narrational style of the Cantonese cinema. If the objective of the Cantonese theater is to allow the music to engender *cing,* the cinematographic image should preserve the integrity of the musical performance. As film historian Po Fung argues, the early Cantonese sound films seem to "distrust" any mimetic mode of narration.[66] In *Nanguo zimeihua* [*Naamgwok zimuifaa* or *Twin Sisters of the South,* Li Bin or Lai Ban, Hu Dieying or Wu Tip-ying Film Company, 1939], a *xi zhong xi* (*hei zung hei* or play within a play) appears in the beginning of the film, where one of the twin sisters, Tai-tip (Hu Dieying or Wu Tip-ying), performs on stage with a very minimal set. Throughout this one-act play, Tai-tip faces the camera and sings, in a medium shot, directly to the audience, both in the theater and in the movie theater where the film is projected. Her singing is only momentarily interrupted by a highly choreographed parade of performers around the stage, conveyed in a long shot. At this point, the orchestra repeats—specifically without any variation—one percussive interlude until the performers finish their parade. After that, in a medium shot again, Tai-tip resumes her presentational singing.

Likewise, in the beginning of *Cihen mianmian wu jueqi* [*Cihan minmin moujyutkei* or *Everlasting Regret,* Lo Duen, Daqun Film Company, 1948], a female singer performs a prelude in a three-quarter shot, which has no relationship with the narrative proper that follows. Likewise, in *Huang Feihong zhengzhuan shangji zhi bianfeng miezhu* [*Wong Fei-hung zingzyun soengzaap zi binfung mitzuk* or *The True Story of Wong Fei-hung, Part 1,* Hu Peng or Wu Pang, Yongyao Film Company, 1949], for example, a *nanyin* (*naamjam*) sequence performed by the artist Chao Feifei (circa 1900s–60s) is featured towards the end of the second-third of the film, which bears no relationship whatsoever with the rest of the narrative. In a similar manner, *Huang Feihong zhengzhuan xiaji zhi huoshao Bawangzhuang* [*Wong Fei-hung zingzyun haazaap zi fosiu Baawongzong* or *The True Story of Wong Fei-hung, Part 2,* Wu Pang, Yongyao Film Company, 1949] features a *niangshi* (*noengsi* or lady master), a blind female performer who possesses a rich baritone voice and is accompanied by the *yangqin* (hammered dulcimer).[67]

In a Cantonese theater performance, the *zhengbenxi* (*zingbunhei* or feature play), usually performed after one or a series of set pieces, is best understood not as a self-contained and unified event driven by a single dramatic action. Rather, it is a show with eighteen variety acts (*bun*), each derived from a one-act play from the Kunqu opera or the Peking opera. Although each act presents a dramatic unit, performers and playwrights consider each of them as a showcase of a voice. Most performers believe that by the Qing dynasty, troupes followed programming called the *jianghu shiba ben* (*gongwu sapbaat bun* or eighteen acts circulated in the world of rivers and lakes). Mak Siu-ha and Ouyang Yuqian argue that the programming should be called *da paichang shiba ben* (*daai paaicoeng sapbaat bun* or eighteen acts in a grand program).[68] Such a program mainly suggests to the playwright the order in which the vocal skills of each type of performer, known as the *hongdong,* would be featured. The standard *hongdong* includes the *wenwu sheng* (*manmou sang* or main male character, who can either play a literary or martial role), *xiaosheng* (*siusang* or versatile male actor who can play multiple leading or supporting roles), *zhengyin huadan* (*zingjan faadaan* or main female character), *erbang huadan* (*jibong faadaan* or supporting female character), *chousheng* (*causang* or unattractive roles) and *wusheng* (*mousang* or martial character).[69]

Yet, this is not to say that the structure of the Cantonese theater is purely formal and presentational. Rather, each act is supposed to put the spectators, by means of the performer's highly skillful singing, into a form of *cing,* which would either recall an affective state analogous to the dramatic situation or prosthetically insert such a state into the spectators' sensoria. This is exactly what Gu Kenfu in the 1920s would call approaching reality. Each *chang* (*coeng,* scene or act) is considered a *hei* in itself, and each *hei* plays out a register of *rensheng* (*jansang* or life). In some ways, as Mak Siu-ha argues, since life is by no means a chain of causes and effects, there is no reason why a play should be understood as an internally consistent unit.[70] Rather, each act of life performs a set of human relationships, and each set of human relationships is in fact engendered by an overall *cing*. In other words, a play, via its vocal performance, approaches reality by putting the spectators into a state of affection that emulates the way human beings respond to various life events. And it is by being immersed in *cing* that the principle of life is biomimetically imprinted in the minds of the spectators as an appearance.

This notion of cinematographic (bio)mimesis even found its way into the theoretical discussion of new-theater director and filmmaker Lo Duen. In "Lun biaoyan yishu" ["Leon biujin ngaiseot" or On the art of performance], Lo argues:

> A work of art is produced through two parallel creative processes—these two processes infinitely intersect and conflate with each other. They are best understood as a "relationship": one of them is art's inner expression, or in other words, its process of conceptualization; the other one is its outer expression, its process of formalization.[71]

For Lo Duen, the art of performance is a process of conceptualizing and formalizing a sense of reality. Yet, the key to approaching such reality is not "mimesis," rather, the actor must hypothesize her or himself as having an "alternative life, one that is created, imagined, and believed by her or himself." And it is from the *linggan* (*linggam* or genius) of such an alternative life that the *linghun* (*lingwan* or soul) of life would manifest itself in the action the actor carries out on stage.[72]

The formal and ontological aspects of the Cantonese theater-cinema can be further illustrated by the works and writings of Sit Kok-sin. Sit was born in Longjiang (Lung Kong), a township in the County of Shunde (Shuntak, now part of Foshan or Fatshan). His father was a *xiucai* (junior scholar) in the Academy. After a brief career in the imperial bureaucracy in Anhui (Anhwei), Sit's father settled down as a farmer in Hong Kong and became the language instructor of E. R. Hallifax, the Secretariat for Chinese Affairs, but passed away when Kok-sin was still an infant. Sit's mother sent her son to St. Paul's College, an English-language school from which he graduated at the age of eighteen. After that, Sit worked in a factory that processed cowhide. After a brief period of working on the production floor, Sit was promoted, based on his English-language skills, to the role of secretary. It was at this time that Sit was involved in performing in the new theater. In 1919, Sit, in response to the May Fourth Movement, opened a *pingmin jinhua xuexiao* (*pingman zeonfaa hokhaau* or civil evolutionary school) in the then low-income district of Sheung Wan. At school, he taught and promoted the use of the vernacular language as a legitimate means of education. Sit then spent two years in Shanghai learning the Peking opera, where he was encouraged to divert his interests in the theater to the Cantonese play. In 1934, before he put into production *White Golden Dragon,* he established his independent production company Fei Fei and produced the film *Langdie* [*Longdip* or *Butterflies of the Waves,* 1934], which was shot silent with sound dubbed and synchronized in postproduction.[73]

Like understanding the Cantonese theater itself, understanding the art of Sit Kok-sin must begin with a study of his music. For Chan Fei-nung, Sit's performance is "natural, delicate, and withdrawn to an aftertaste (i.e. not translatable into language)"—in other words, describing ideation more than describing reality. Meanwhile, for Chan, Sit pays attention to the linguistic articulation in his singing, and he maintains his linguistic clarity by eliminating any *zhuyu ci* (*zojyu ci* or assists), that is, additional words that the performers often like to add in order to provide an additional syllable to a sentence, which usually have no meaning.[74] For example, instead of saying *kui hai ngo loupo* (she is my wife), most Cantonese theater artists would insert assists into the sentence in order to make their singing easier: e.g. *kui hai ngo ge lou-ya-po.* With seven intonations, assists, which usually consist of sounds that would not change in meaning as their intonations slightly change and are paradigmatically interchangeable, can usually fit into a complex melodic passage with multiple ornaments. But by relying on the use of assists, the singer can obscure the poetry itself and vernacularize the lyrics. Hence, instead of using assists, Sit tends to *wenzi qiuqiang* (*manzi kauhong* or ask the word to beg the music).[75] In other words, his ornamentation is tailored in accordance not only with the syntagmatic structure of the lyrics, but also the intonations and accents of the original words.

Musically, Sit also invented the *erhuang erliu changju* (*jiwong jilau choenggeoi* or extended long syntaxes in triple time): starting a passage with a pair of three-worded, four-worded, or five worded phrases; followed by a number of seven-word sentences with minimal ornamentations; closing with a highly ornamented pair of four-worded phrases. The *jiwong jilau choenggeoi* breaks the rhythmic expectation of the seven-word phrases and is in fact an imitation of the Tang dynasty's *guti shi* (Six-dynasty style). The *guti shi* is known for its liberal use of forms, intonations, syntagmatic structure, and paradigmatic variations for expressive purposes and sketching thoughts.[76] In addition, Sit also prefers using the *kuhou* (*fuhau* or bitter tone) in his variations.[77] The *fuhau* is in the key of *yifan* (*jyutfaan*). In European music theory, the *jyutfaan* key is not really a key; it merely means that two semitones (*mi-fa; ti-do*) are added to the key of C. By singing a variation in *fuhau,* Sit lowers some pentatonic steps by a minor or major second. For example, instead of singing:

1 = C

3/4 2 5 3 5 3 2 1

Sit would prefer singing:

3/4 2 4 3 4 3 2 1

By inserting half steps between notes (in the example above, the minor-second interval between *mi* and *fa*), Sit gives the melody a more somber quality, and the resulting melody also matches the half-step intonations of the words. Furthermore, he often deliberately limits himself to the range of a *pinghou* (*pinghau* or baritone), thus avoiding any melodic peaks in passages that are supposed to convey sorrow and nostalgia. Last but not least, instead of ornamenting a passage by adhering steadfastly to a mode of variation, Sit keeps a tight control of his melodic rhythm in accordance with the *cing* he wishes to create. He names this formal technique *fangxin* (*fongsam* or imitation of the heart), as opposed to mimesis (imitation of the natural appearance of things).[78]

All of these formal elements are attempts to take the Cantonese theater out of its formalistic framework in order to achieve a state of simplicity and clarity that will make *cing* tangible to the audience. These formal elements can be considered musical manipulations that are created for the purpose of disconcealing what Chan Fei-nung calls the "aftertaste," that is, a quality that is not nameable or even present, but its absence is precisely made present by these formal manipulations. And what is being made present is the process of ideation. For Sit, therefore, these musical forms exist to make concrete an affective state that is not reducible to any linguistic unit, a way of approaching reality that sketches an idea in its process of informing.

Sit Kok-sin's biomimetic view of art is not limited to his music; it also informs his acting and narrative construction. In his autobiography, published in 1949 in the *Yilin* [*Ngailam* or *Art Lane*] magazine, Sit claims that he chose to become a *siusang* in the Cantonese theater because Chinese cinema, unlike Hollywood, "lacks any *siusang*."[79] What he means is a male actor who does not necessarily receive top billing, but precisely because of that, he is required to be completely versatile in playing a wide range of roles. However, in the film industry, the salary of a *siusang* cannot match that of a romantic lead. And even if a person wishes to become a *siusang*, film executives would usually want to nurture him into a romantic lead with a narrow range of performances for the purpose of protecting his public image. Sit argues that what he likes about being a *siusang* is that "the costume a *siusang* wears represents his individual personality and identity, and all the relationships he has in a film's narrative." In other words, for Sit, a *siusang* embodies all the relationships among all the characters around him, and it is through him that life manifests itself as a network of human relationships, which produce a set of *cing*. For Sit Kok-sin, the classical Hollywood film is best understood not as a chain of causes and effects, but as a network of human relationships interconnected via the personality and identity of the *siusang*.[80]

Sit Kok-sin in fact made a similar point in the "Zixu" ["Zizeoi" or Self-introduction, 1930] in his anthology of collected essays *Juexian ji* [*Goksin zaap* or The collected essays of Sit Kok-sin]. In his essay, Sit wrote:

> Over the years, [the Cantonese theater] is a point of convergence of the essences of the theaters from the north and the south. It also culminates the music of China and the West in its composition. Each play has a [political] objective, and each character—once played by the actor—must actualize her or his *gexing* (*gosing* or individual personality) to its very end. In the end, the Cantonese theater speaks the truth of the revolution.[81]

What Sit Kok-sin means by "individual personality" is not an individual who stands aloof from the rest of the political community. Rather, an individual personality is produced by a network of human relationships, and it conveys the political aspiration—and at times, the obstacle to that aspiration—of the community. For him, therefore, the *siusang* often instantiates all the contesting values within a social condition, which the revolutionary movement needs to address or negotiate. In fact, the Cantonese theater embodies the point of convergence between conflicting values from the Chinese north and south, and the different aesthetics from Euro-America and China. In this sense, the Cantonese theater and the Cantonese sound film are sites where these competing elements are actively negotiated, a process that produces the various character relationships that represent a variety of individual personalities, identities, and struggles within this larger political landscape. With this in mind, Sit argues that the Cantonese theater and the Cantonese sound film are "minor vehicles" that could "change the customs and habits of a society." And because of that, they should be cultivated seriously as an educational tool. For him, the Cantonese theater, being a point of convergence for different cultural practices and discourses, can potentially be the *shijie gonggong zhi xiju* (*saigaai gunggung zi heikek* or common theater of the world), one that represents the "human evolutionary process" in action.[82]

In "Zhuyan he daoyan *Xu Bai Jinlong* de houhua" ["Zyujin wo doujin *San Baak Gamlung* dik hauwaa" or After playing the lead in and directing *White Golden Dragon: A Sequel,* 1937], Sit Kok-sin elaborates the idea of the *siusang* even further. For Sit, a screen actor does not lead a "playful life, nor does he simply perform the experience and process of his natural life." Rather, the player "injects the minds of all kinds of lives into himself and turns them into appearances on his face." He continues, "the body and mind of an actor is not free." Rather, he "embodies the life-process of hundreds and thousands of people." In fact, this is the "bitterness and frustration of the player; the difficulty of being a player." Yet, for a director, the task is to "give his actors a set of instruments to achieve this, and to turn them into skillful instruments."[83] For Sit, a screen actor's subjectivity and agency are completely imprisoned in the acting process, in order that she or he can embody "all kinds of life and turn them into appearances." She or he is nothing more than an instrument in a set of dramatized human relationships. Yet, in so doing, what the actor activates—by taking up all lives in one body—is life itself in all its presence and concreteness. The actor and her or his cinematographic image is, therefore, a site that embodies a potentiality, from which all *cing* are engendered.

It is unfortunate that *White Golden Dragon* is no longer extant. In 1947, however, Sit Kok-sin remade his signature play into *Xin Bai Jinglong* [*San Baak Gamlung* or *New White Golden Dragon,* Yang Gongliang or Yeung Kung-leung, Great China Film Company]. The story of *White Golden Dragon* is about a wealthy Chinese-American gentleman, White Golden Dragon (Sit), who encounters a beautiful lady, Chueng Yuk-neung (played by Zheng Mengxia or Cheng Mang-ha in the 1947 version), on his way back from San Francisco. They meet again at a New Year costume ball, where they bicker and fall in love behind their masks in the back yard. But Yuk-neung obstinately refuses to confess her love. So in order to get close to Yuk-neung, White Golden Dragon decides to masquerade as a waiter in the hotel where Yuk-neung stays, with the help of his servant Ho Sui (Yi Qiushui or Yi Chau-sui, 1904–55). But when he learns that

Yuk-neung's father Po-wa (Lin Kunshan or Lam Kwun-shan, d. 1964) is at the verge of filing bankruptcy and is eager to marry his daughter to a rich man, White Golden Dragon dresses up as a rich man and presents himself to Po-wa as an investor, though ironically, White Golden Dragon himself is a rich man, thus the film suggests that presenting oneself as oneself is also a form of performance or self-masquerade. Meanwhile, Po-wa is involved in a con. Towards the end of the film, the con artists capture Yuk-neung, Po-wa, White Golden Dragon, and Ho Sui. But in the denouement, White Golden Dragon turns the situation around and captures the con artists and the love of Yuk-neung.

The fact that this is a remake, however, does not guarantee that the film is based on the narrational structure and style of the 1934 *White Golden Dragon.* In fact, in the production of *White Golden Dragon: A Sequel* (which was shot between 1934 and 1935 but not released until 1937 because of the multiple fires), Sit Kok-sin got into an argument with Runje Shaw on the set. Shaw complained that Sit, in the shooting of the scene "Huayuan xiangma" ["Faajyun soengmaa" or Arguing with each other in the garden], improvised too radically for the camera to follow. As a result, Shaw complained, Sit had wasted an excessive amount of raw footage. Sit retorted that this was the way any self-respecting Cantonese theater artist would work. For Sit, although the sequel follows the same programming as the original film, the same *bun* requires a completely new musical rendition, which engenders a different set of *cing.* Such a new rendition, however, should be spontaneously improvised based on the very *cing* that he, as the *siusang,* embodies.[84]

This bit of journalistic gossip tells a lot about how Sit Kok-sin worked creatively. Although Sit had a screenplay, the screenplay functioned simply as what the Cantonese theater artists would call a *tigang* (*taigong* or cue sheet). The 1947 remake, as an adaptation of an American film, follows more or less a chain of causes and effects. Nevertheless, individual sequences are assembled not in accordance with a strict observation of dramatic motivation. Rather, each scene provides a certain setting for a dramatic situation to be played out or a condition for the actors to interact and make visible their interrelationships. In fact, the overall narrative can be understood as a series of acts informed by the changing dynamic of the human relationships, and the *cing* that these relationships engender. No single protagonist drives the narrative with her or his want; rather, the narrational agency lies in the very *cing* and its process of transformation.

The narrational style of *New White Golden Dragon* in fact matches the stylistic summary offered by Lam Nin-tung. In each dramatic scene, the film favors the use of the long shot and three-quarter shots. Conversations are mostly conducted without resorting to any shot-reverse-shots. Rather, they are often filmed from a relatively frontal position by the camera, which captures the entire dialogue in a three-quarter shot. When the characters change positions in a room, the film also avoids using cuts. Rather, it privileges camera pans or dollies in order to maintain the spatiotemporal unity of the scene. Lam Nin-tung argues that such filming techniques allow the personal or social dialectics of the actual life-process that the film seeks to critique be presented in its entirety.[85]

The Garden sequence in fact illustrates how Sit Kok-sin's formal decisions were determined by the way the music generates *cing,* and how composition and editing help convey this *cing* and the dialectical relationships between White Golden Dragon and Yuk-neung. This musical number opens with a long shot of Yuk-neung looking up to the sky as she stands behind the handrail of an open corridor. The camera pans left to follow an unsuccessful suitor and to reveal the entrance of White Golden Dragon in his masquerade. The camera, however, pans left quickly as White Golden Dragon settles down on the right side of Yuk-neung (Figure 19). White Golden Dragon tries to chat up Yuk-neung. As Yuk-neung turns her head to the left in order to ignore White Golden Dragon, the film inserts a long shot of a group of people in the party chamber, which breaks up the theatrical continuity of the scene and prolongs our desire to find out what happens in the garden. The film then cuts back to the garden with a medium shot of the lovers from a frontal position (Figure 20). In this shot, White Golden Dragon asks why Yuk-neung turned down his dance invitation a while ago. Yuk-neung simply answers, "*Mou sowai*" (Who cares?). She repeats it three times. By the third time she repeats it, instead of cutting to a reaction shot, the film cuts to a three-quarter shot of the couple filmed from their right side, where White Golden Dragon begins by reciting a four-word couplet (each with an assist "zau," here the assist is permitted since it is a recitative): "*Nei zau mou sowai, ngo zau yau so jan*" (You said "You don't care," I say "I've reasons to care"). The orchestra plays a lead-in, and White Golden Dragon walks to the other side of Yuk-neung and holds her arm (Figure 21).

By not dissecting this dramatic beat into a series of shot-reverse-shots (as in Hollywood cinema), but instead showing long-to-medium two-shots of the scene from three different angles, the editing draws

Figures 19–26, pages 180–85.

The "Huayuan xiangma" ["Faajyun soengmaa" or Arguing with each other in the garden] number in *Xin Bai Jinglong* [*San Baak Gamlung* or *New White Golden Dragon*, Yueng Kung-leung, Great China Film Company]: the staging, camerawork, and editing are designed to preserve the integrity of the musicality and playfulness of the performance, in order that appearances of life can be put at play through the role of Sit Kok-sin as a *siusang*.

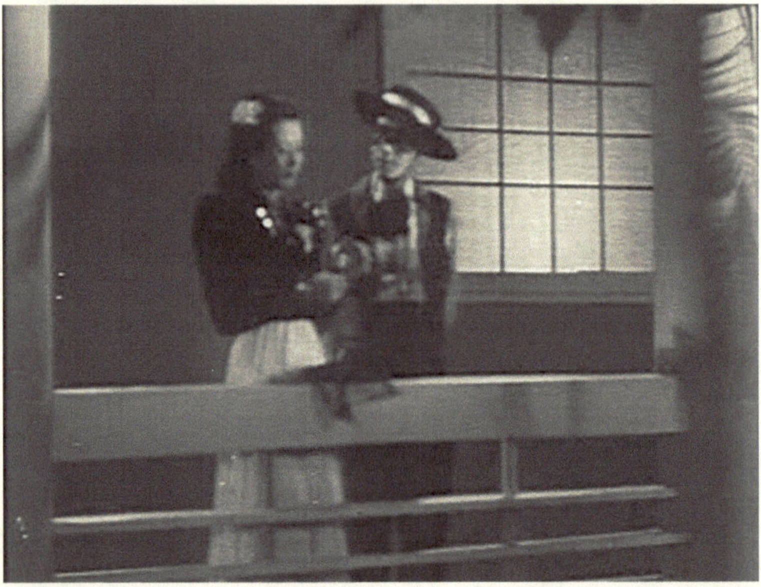

Figure 19.

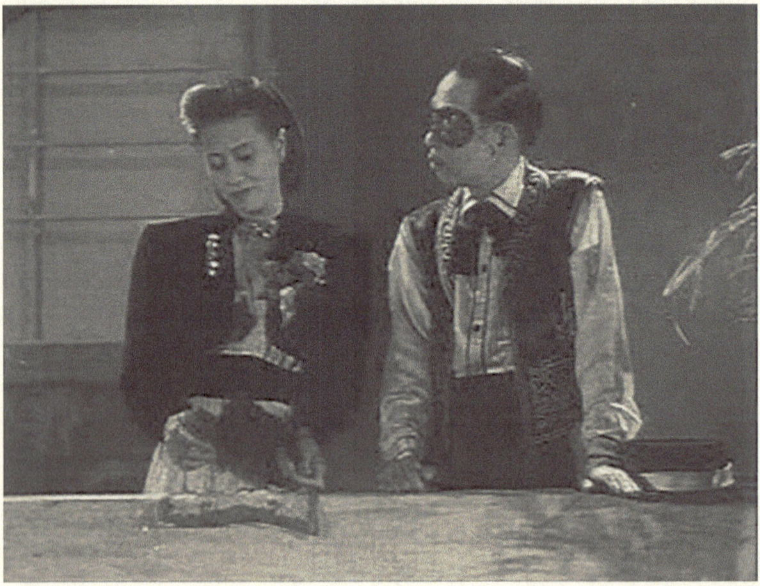

Figure 20.

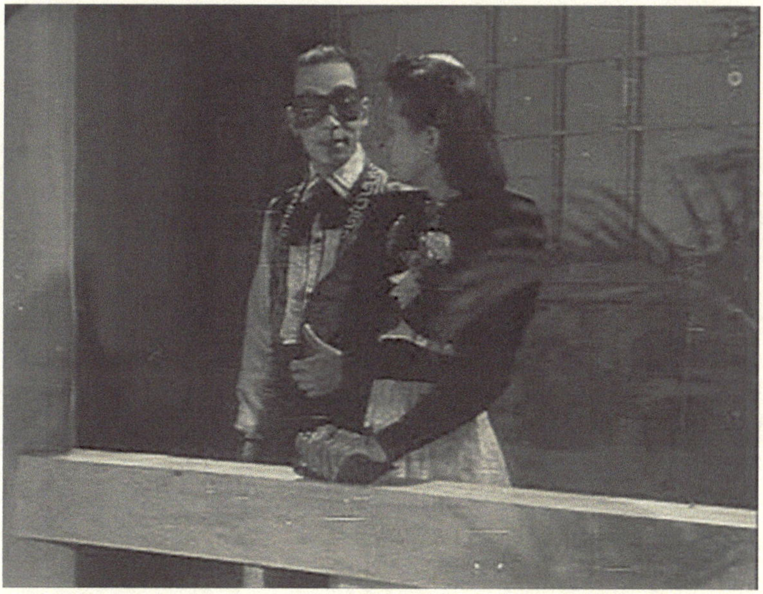

Figure 21.

the spectators' attention to the rhythm of the performers' recitations and musical structure. Moreover, these two-shots allow the audience to apprehend the dialectical relationship between the two lovers: a woman who pretends to be someone more aloof, wealthy, and sophisticated than she really is, and a man who seems to present himself as himself, but actually presents a performance of what he wants Yuk-neung to believe him to be, that is, a masquerade. In this sense, the Hollywood notions of spatiotemporal continuity are more or less abandoned or modified in favor of an editing style that preserves the musical rhythm and the integrity of the dialectics or relationships between the two characters.

White Golden Dragon next sings a *saipei soenggeoi,* in which he accuses Yuk-neung of being aloof. With the camera framing out the performers' legs, Sit Kok-sin uses *zauwai,* by changing his position from the right side of Yuk-neung to the left side, to substitute what would have been done on stage by his steps. In addition, with his mask on his face, Sit also cannot use his eyes to perform (*guanmu* or *gwaanmuk*). Instead, he is limited completely to his hand gestures (*zuoshou* or *zousau*). The camera then dollies back until it reaches the distance of a long shot (Figure 22), with the frame decorated by the foliage of a tree in the foreground. By distancing itself from the actors, the camera asks the spectators to focus on the vocal performance of Sit Kok-sin and Cheng Mang-ha, and again, the dialectical relationship between them. After Yuk-neung has finished her musical retort or *haageoi,* she walks to the left of frame; then, both White Golden Dragon and the camera (on a dolly) follow (Figure 23). He then starts singing the second *saipei soenggeoi.* Each musical phrase mirrors the previous one in syntactic structure and its penchant for repeating certain phrases—a strategy foreshadowed by Yuk-neung's repeated "I don't care." In addition, in the beginning of the tune, White Golden Dragon accuses Yuk-neong of being passive aggressive. Then, by her second *haageoi* in this shot, Yuk-neung uses the same words against White Golden Dragon.

After her second *haageoi,* White Golden Dragon's singing transitions into an extended *liushui* (*lauseoi* or unmetered passage), to which Yuk-neung responds with her own *lauseoi.* White Golden Dragon closes the improvisatory passage with a double cadence, which Yuk-neung repeats with the words *daamjau* (worries). The camera is then motivated by the paradigmatic and musical change to cut to a medium shot of the two bickering lovers as White Golden Dragon begins a new *saipei* by constructing a phrase that ends with the word *daamjau* (Figure 24). After a brief transitional phrase in which White Golden Dragon tells Yuk-neung how handsome he thinks he is (with hand gestures pointing to his facial features), Yuk-neung walks forward with a big smile and suggests that he should be ashamed of his vanity (Figure 25). The camera in fact reframes subtly to accommodate her move. As White Golden Dragon replies with his new *soenggeoi,* Yuk-neung walks to the right of frame and the camera reframes them again (Figure 26). Between Figures 25 and 26, a visual structure close to the Hollywood notion of shot-reverse-shot is achieved not through editing, but by staging (in relation to the camera) and *zauwai.* In so doing, the musical rhythm is clearly indicated by the fluid changes of these characters' physical positions, but their dialectical relationship is carefully preserved within the same composition. After this point, the couple continues to bicker as White Golden Dragon boasts about his wealth. Here, Yuk-neung provides a subtle variation to break the consistent musical exchange between the two by singing her cadence to a high *pinghau* (tenor voice) and by tentatively employing the *fuhau* (bitter tone), thus introducing an unexpected lower register to her part of the music and the semitones. In fact, this launches a new series of musical exchanges that are sung in the *fuhau.*

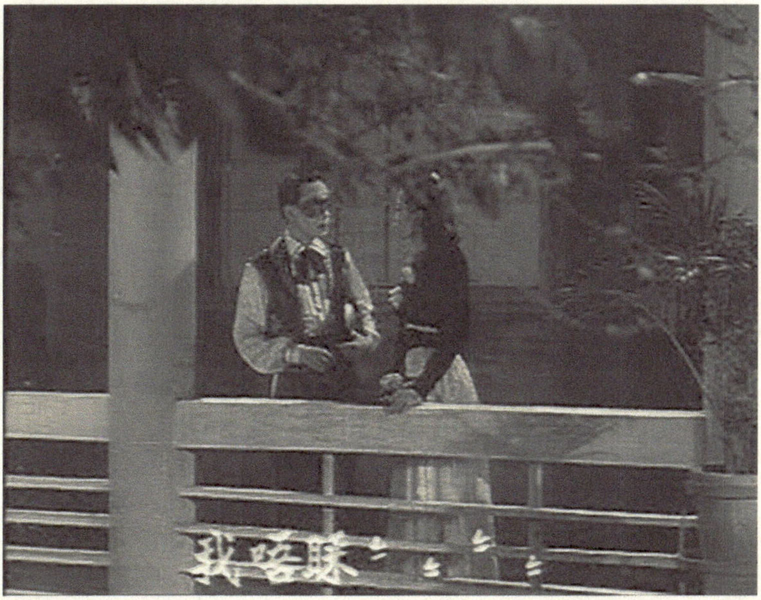

Figure 22.

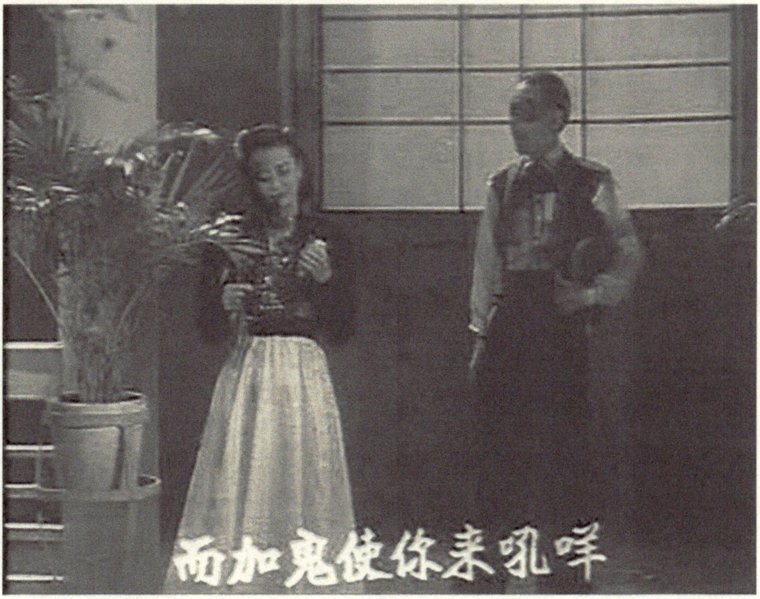

Figure 23.

This shot-by-shot analysis reveals to us that the sequence is not shot and edited simply to preserve the theatrical spatiotemporal unity of the performance. Rather, its framing, staging, and editing are motivated by the musical structure of the vocal performance and the human relationship it seeks to convey. The editing, together with the various manipulations of the musical forms (lyrical repetition, extended cadence, tonality shift, etc.), allows the spectators to enjoy the pleasure of the vocal performance as a pure performance. In fact, narratively, the entire point of this musical sequence is to show the multilayered performances of White Golden Dragon. However, the performance and the lyrics themselves are gleeful. In this sense, the spectators are put into a state of pure play, that is, playing for the sole purpose of playing. In fact, the spectators are not encouraged to pay attention to the meaning of the lyrics word-by-word. Rather, the entire auditory experience is foregrounded by the film's formal manipulation and apprehended in its totality and immediacy as a spark of life that is perpetually suspended in a state of play.

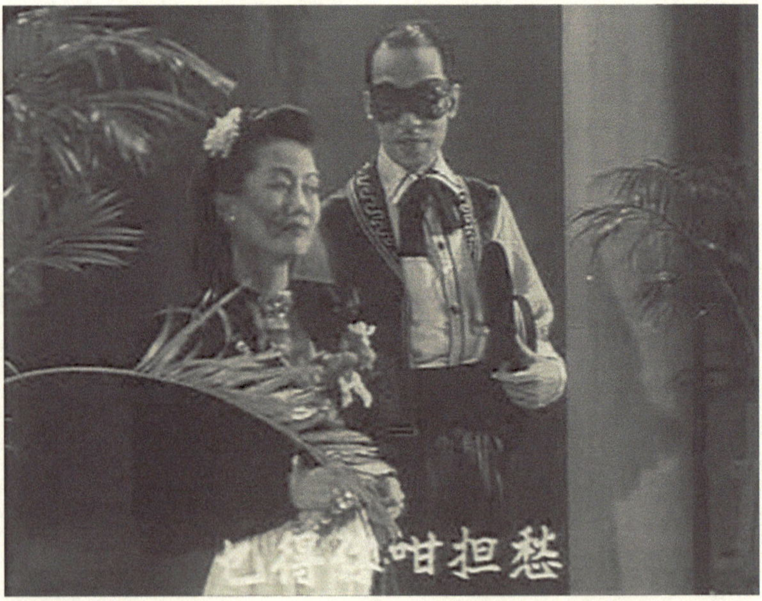

Figure 24.

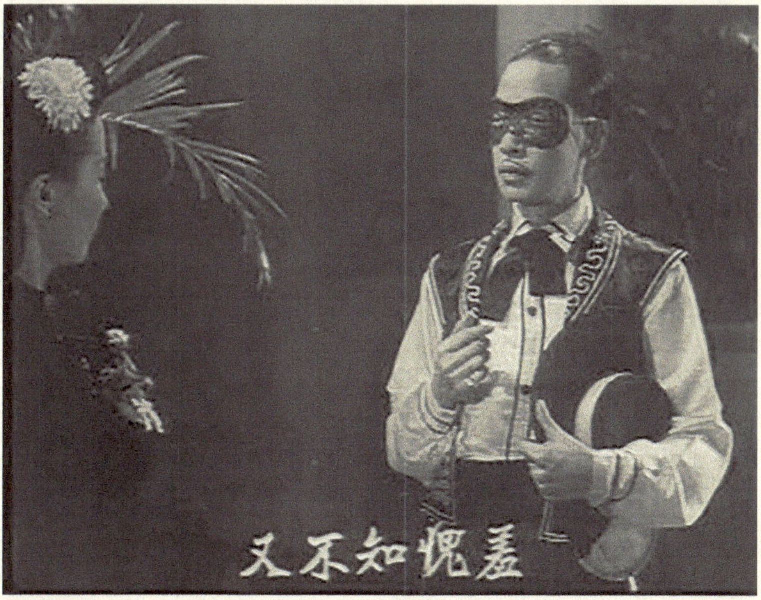

Figure 25.

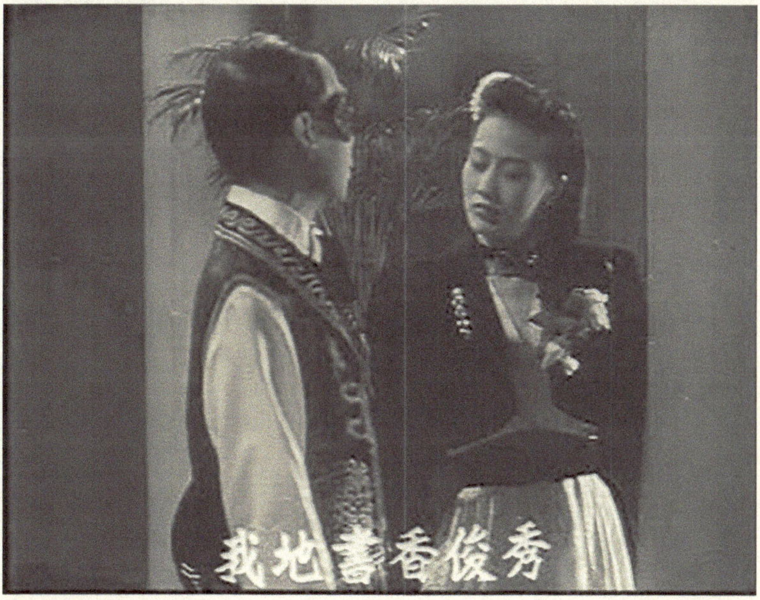

Figure 26.

Cinema at Play: Theorization and Politicization

For the early Cantonese filmmakers, the delicate distance between the cinematographic image and reality is the process of ideation itself. Yet, what the cinematographic experience aims to achieve is not to bring this idea to its fruition; rather, it engages the spectators in this very process of informing so that contesting relationships in life and the conflicting modes of *cing* can be put at play. What is left in a flux of statelessness and indeterminacy is best understood as a potentiality. The Cantonese idea of *hei* or play in fact forms a comparative space with a similar set of arguments proposed by Walter Benjamin and Giorgio Agamben. It was also used as a political tool to put into play the Shanghai-Nanking–centric idea of national culture and cinema.

In her reading of Benjamin's second version of "Das Kunstwerk im Zeitalter seiner technischen Reproduzierbarkeit" ["The Work of Art in the Age of Its Technological Reproducibility," 1935], Miriam Hansen argues that Benjamin pushes further his thesis of the mechanical reproduction by thinking of the cinema as a "room for play."[86] In his essay, Benjamin is in fact rethinking his earlier thesis with the rise of National Socialism. Here, Benjamin identifies two "technologies." First is what he calls the "prehistoric art," which uses "certain fixed notations in the service of magical practice." This type of art ultimately serves a ritualistic purpose: the "contemplation of an ancestral figure [that] strengthens the occult powers of the beholder." What Benjamin calls "prehistoric art" can in fact be understood as a reference to the art of the Third Reich. For Benjamin, the "subjects for these notations were humans and their environment, which were depicted according to the requirements of a society whose technology existed only in fusion with ritual," and the result of this first technology is the reduction of the human beings to objects of "sacrifice." This first technology sets for itself the aim of mastering nature. The second technology, namely, the cinematographic technology of mechanical reproduction, distances itself from nature not by mastering it, but by maintaining an interplay between nature and humanity.[87] He continues:

> The primary social function of art today is to rehearse that interplay. This applies especially to film. *The function of film is to train human beings in the apperceptions and reactions needed to deal with a vast apparatus whose role in their lives is expanding almost daily.* Dealing with this apparatus also teaches them that technology will release them from their enslavement to the powers of the apparatus only when humanity's whole constitution has

> adapted itself to the new productive forces which the second technology has set free.[88]

Benjamin explains this further in a footnote:

> This second technology is a system in which the mastering of elementary social forces is a precondition for playing [*das Spiel*] with natural forces. Just as a child who has learned to grasp stretches out its hand for the moon as it would for a ball, so humanity, in its efforts at innervation, sets its sights as much on currently utopian goals as on goals within reach. For in revolutions, it is not only the second technology which asserts its claims vis-à-vis society. Because this technology aims at liberating human beings from drudgery, the individual suddenly sees his scope for play, his field of action [*Spielraum*] immeasurably expanded. He does not yet know his way around this space. But already he registers his demands on it.[89]

Benjamin's "prehistoric art" can be read as an allegory for the collective aestheticization of life under National Socialism. In this sense, what he hints at is the fundamental principle that gives rise to Nazism and collective dictatorship: the mobilization of a highly aestheticized state of life—that is, the reduction of human beings to highly aestheticized, mathematicized, rationalized, and mechanicized bare lives—as a reaction against the ever-expanding social apparatus that invokes fear, anxiety, and dystopia. Alternatively, such a reaction can be seen as a temporary paralysis when the collective comes face-to-face with the crisis of modernity. What the cinema does, as Hansen argues in her analysis, is to set free again the human sensorium by re-engaging it in an interplay not between humanity and nature, but between nature and the machine, or *physis* and *civilization*.[90]

The Cantonese cinema can therefore be regarded as a cultural discourse that has a political mission: it momentarily sets free the cinema from being mobilized by the CCoP for the purpose of aestheticizing life. It does so by opening a "room for play" between the national and the regional, the mechanical reproduction and the human performance—and in the context of *White Golden Dragon*, truthfulness and masquerade. This question is in fact embodied in the debate on the legitimacy of the Cantonese cinema as a regional or dialect art form. This debate reveals two different imaginations of the nation, and two approaches to reality. On the one hand, the Shanghai producers and those film critics who took their side imagined the nation and national cinema as a unified entity, with linguistic unification as its ultimate sign and destiny. In this sense, the political reality that the cinematographic image approaches is supposed to be properly directed in accordance with a national *telos*. On the other hand, the Cantonese filmmakers saw the national space as a public sphere where collective affects were cultivated through a constant negotiation among various political focal points, regional interests, and linguistic practices. In this light, what constitutes reality are the diverse linguistic, cultural, or even ideological deposits that made up the imaginary Chinese nation as a pluralistic sphere.

The dialect problem, as I mentioned earlier, is in fact two-fold. On the one hand, the Shanghai filmmakers and Nanking policymakers argue that as a dialect cinema, the Cantonese sound film failed to inculcate its audience with the national ideal of linguistic unity. On the other hand, they accused the Cantonese sound films of being coarsely made and excessively produced, which in turn promoted vulgar or even erotic contents and ideas. The dialect issue was in fact debated in the Nanking Conference in 1937, where Cantonese directors Li Hua (Lee Fa) and Runje Shaw met with Luo Gang, Li-tzu Shao, and Li-fu Ch'en, who represented the position of the KMT authorities, as well as film executives Lo Ming-yau (UPS) and Zhou Jianyun (Star), who represented the interests of the Shanghai film industry. At the meeting, the Cantonese delegates claimed that they fully understood and supported Nanking's policy of unifying the Chinese language. However, since not everyone could understand Mandarin, Cantonese films were instrumental in cultivating national consciousness among viewers in Canton, Hong Kong, and overseas.[91] The Cantonese position was best exemplified by a speech made by Li-fu Ch'en, who, despite his position as a Nanking-based policymaker, was sympathetic to the Cantonese argument. Ch'en suggested that national consciousness was best promulgated by educating people from various regions with dialect cinemas. He argued that the CFCC should focus less on censoring Cantonese films than on dubbing Hollywood films into different dialects.[92]

Along the same vein, director Feng Zhigang (Fung Chi-kong) argued:

> If we recognize the cinema as a tool that can effectively instill a consciousness into the sentient bodies of the spectators, and can use films to inspire them to think about intellectual issues, the language used in a film is a medium of intervention in one's consciousness. Hence, [the state] ought to put a film's consciousness under scrutiny. However, putting limitation

> on a film's linguistic choice is, at this historical juncture, premature. It is because a regional dialect best bears the political responsibility of a specific region. . . . The Cantonese-language film can make tangible the feudal system of beliefs in the Cantonese region. Such beliefs are best expressed and turned into knowledge, at least for the time being, by the Cantonese language itself.[93]

Among the Cantonese filmmakers and critics, those who were primarily trained in the new theater tended to side with the Shanghai-Nanking position, whereas those who came from the Cantonese theater preferred a more pluralistic and playful approach to the question of national consciousness. For example, film critic Jichen (Chiksan) argues that the three-year postponement of the KMT's ban on the Cantonese cinema should persuade its filmmakers to "pay attention to art and elevate its political consciousness." And he proposed that the Cantonese filmmakers should do so by making more national-revolutionary dramas and moral plays.[94] Meanwhile, film critic Ling Mei (Ling Mui) also proposes the making of educational films specifically for teaching the Cantonese audience the national language. Yet, Ling argued, banning the Cantonese film would simply open the Cantonese market to Hollywood films. While the Cantonese language could "help the Mandarin film industry to propagate its national policy in the Cantonese regions," Hollywood films would simply perpetuate colonialism during China's national crisis.[95]

In a similar manner, an anonymous editor of *Art Lane* argued that the national language as heard in Shanghai cinema was a myth: nobody really spoke the way these actors speak on film. Banning the Cantonese film without problematizing the English-language film suggested that in the eyes of the KMT policymakers, the "Cantonese and the Cantonese language are in fact inferior to the foreigners and their foreign languages. Our own fellow nationals now look down upon us with such unequal legal measures; we have no one but ourselves to blame for the kind of unequal treatments we receive from the foreigners." For the editor, therefore, the CCoP's position was best understood as a form of internalized colonialism, which would have the effect of opening the Cantonese market not to the Shanghai productions, but to Hollywood.[96]

Some filmmakers and critics, however, believed that the only way to rectify the dialect issue was to detheatricalize the Cantonese sound film. For example, film director Xu Xiaogu (Hui Siu-kuk) argues that the "cinema uses action and affection to dissect dramatic logic; it does not rely on dialogues to explicate the causal relationships that motivate it." However, for Hui, while the theater is a *mofang yishu* (*moufong ngaiseot* or mimetic art), the cinema is *rensheng yishu* (*jansang ngaiseot* or life art); it uses "affections and sensations" to engage the spectators in life itself, and in the larger sociopolitical progression.[97] In a similar manner, director Chan Pei defended the Cantonese theatrical comedy by arguing that the comedic art form "stimulates the spectators' interests in life"; it encourages its audience to think about ethical and political questions not by means of didactic inculcation, but by engaging them in an aesthetic experience.[98]

In 1937, novelist Song Wanli (Sung Man-lei) supported Tsai Chu-sang's idea of promulgating a mode of national defense cinema in the south. In fact, he argued that these national defense films should promote what he called the *Guangdong jingshen* (*Gwongdung zingsan* or the spirit of Kwangtung). For Sung, it was erroneous for anyone to imagine the Chinese nation as a monolithic cultural sphere; rather, regional and ethnic cultures should manifest themselves as parts of the larger pluralistic national whole.[99] In fact, the works of Tsai Chu-sang and most of the Cantonese national defense films do not focus on a single personal objective. Instead, these films use a group of people to illustrate a cross section of the Cantonese-Hong Kong society at the time. Each of them faces a different set of problems because of her or his gendered position and social class. In the end, these characters all realize that the current state of capitalism has taken the human dignity away from the lives of the middle and working classes. And they are determined to rebuild the Chinese society from their immediate family units, often by going to the front to contribute their efforts to the war cause.

Retrospectively, the criticisms of the early Cantonese sound cinema could also be seen as a difference between the Shanghai filmmakers' notion of approaching reality and that of their Cantonese counterparts. Film historian Po Fung argues that the claim about the South Sea productions being roughly produced and coarsely made may not be entirely ungrounded, but not through a lack of artistic vision or aesthetic sensibility. Upon watching *Nüxing zhi guang* [*Neoising zi gwong* or *The Light of Women,* Gao Lihen or Ko Lei-hen, South Sea, 1937], a film rediscovered and restored in 2013, Po pointed out that the camerawork, lighting, and production design of the early Cantonese sound films might have been severely limited by the sound recording systems of the time. In these films, the musical numbers were usually recorded in studios using the RCA Victor technology. However, the dialogue scenes were recorded on the set with incomplete equipment purchased from American newsreel camera operators. From the changing perspectives of the location sound, one can deduce that a microphone was planted at the center of the set. As a result, most of the actors would need to line up around the microphone and enunciate deliberately in order to deliver their lines comprehensibly. This explains the film's preference for the long shot and medium shot. In addition, lighting and production design in the long and medium shots is usually kept simple and generic, whereas expressive high-contrast lighting is used in close-ups, thus producing what the Shanghai filmmakers regarded as lighting inconsistencies and continuity problems. Po also observes that with the exception of the main actors, supporting actors in *The Light of Women* sometimes speak regional dialects like the Amoy, Hokkien, and Hakka, and one of the actors, possibly Chinese-American, speaks with an English accent.[100] Some of these "continuity problems" can also be seen in *Twin Sisters*. Therefore, from the perspective of the Shanghai filmmakers, these early Cantonese sound films fail to conform to the Hollywood standard of technological and stylistic seamlessness—or, in other words, the Hollywood notion of describing reality.

A more culturally biased complaint raised by the Shanghai filmmakers and critics was that the Cantonese sound films were vulgar.[101] Again, some of their complaints were perhaps not entirely ungrounded, but the perception of vulgarity invokes a deeper question of how reality is supposed to be approached. It is important to remember that Shanghai cinema in the 1930s attracted many literati and intellectuals as screenwriters and directors. Thus their screenplays tend to be crafted in accordance with the classical Hollywood standard. Vulgar dialogues or behaviors, especially those made by characters who are supposed to be from the lower classes, are narratively framed for the purpose of giving the intellectual urban viewers a taste of the socially othered. In the Cantonese sound film, dialogues are usually less polished and more colloquial. In Shanghai cinema, intellectual characters are supposed to be linguistically articulate and eloquent. They give literary speeches and deliver high-sounding dialogues, and never run out of words in any circumstances. In Hong Kong cinema however, intellectuals employ a mixture of literary and colloquial languages, and at times they even run out of words and look embarrassed. Meanwhile peasants and workers are not afraid of using bawdy language to express social frustration or in moments of sisterly or brotherly bonding.

For example, by the end of the opening scene in *Twin Sisters,* the urban intellectual Ching (Ng Cho-fan) and his helper Fatty (Liu Guikang or Lau Kwai-hong) watch Ching's love object Siu-tip (Wu Tip-ying) walking away. In a medium shot, the two young men smile at each other. Fatty asks Ching what he thinks about Siu-tip. Ching replies with a blush, "*Gogtak hoenghaa di nuizai tinzan di; gokdak kui hou holin*" (I find these country girls very naive; I feel sorry for her). Ching's condescending view on country girls not only fails to fit the politically-correct prototype of a young Chinese intellectual as imagined by the Shanghai filmmakers, the unapologetic and naturalistic way in which Ng delivers his line turns this supposedly bright young man into a sexist figure. Then, Ching taps Fatty's shoulder and says, "*Zapye laa, gong laa*" (Wrap things up, [don't] talk). The line is entirely unmotivated by any narrative logic, and Ng's embarrassment—for running out of words and for delivering a line that does not quite make sense narratively and grammatically, is visible in his body gesture and facial expression. The result is a more naturalistic performance and a less pretentious representation of an intellectual character.

In this sense, the early Cantonese sound films might have been coarsely or hastily made; but perhaps because of these economic and technological limitations, they developed a form that values contingencies over control, integrity of performance over illusion of continuity, playfulness over seriousness. In a sense, while Shanghai cinema took itself seriously as an educational ritual, the Cantonese cinema took itself playfully as a game. In *Infanzia e storia* [*Infancy and History,* 1978], Agamben considers play as the binary opposite of ritual. For Agamben, the ritual turns a secular object sacred. In fact, it attaches particular linguistic functions and symbolic meanings to every step one takes in the ritual. Meanwhile, the play returns the sacred object to the secular, that is, it appropriates every sacred object not only for human use, but also for the fun of it, as the player strips all the linguistic functions and symbolic meanings that are attached to the object. Yet the ritualistic naming and sanctioning of various objects as sacred, in many different cultures, is often preceded by, or undertaken in the same process as, the conversion of these objects into play things.[102] In fact, the Cantonese theater itself is at once impregnated with sacred meanings and taken by its human audience as playful entertainment. Hence, for Agamben:

> Indeed, to be more precise, *we can regard ritual and play not as two distinct machines but as a single machine, a single binary system, which is articulated across two categories which cannot be isolated and across whose correlation and difference the very functioning of the system is based.*[103]

Thus for Agamben, in the act of play, the act of appropriating a sacred object for the purpose of suspending its sacredness is in fact an act of abandoning the object's history and signifying function. An infant that turns every sacred object into play, or a ghost that inspires human beings to turn every object sacred, in fact puts into action the same *signifying difference*: it abandons an object's relationship with time, thus suspending the "difference between diachrony and synchrony, between *aiōn* and *chrónos,* between living and dead, between nature and culture."[104] In other words, cinema of play is in fact a cinema of potentiality—one that approaches reality by sketching an idea in its process of becoming.

Conclusion

The early Cantonese sound film is therefore best understood as a cinema of ideation, that is, it sketches an affective state or an outline of life that invites the spectators to engage in the process of ideation. It sketches thoughts so that the spectators can appreciate not a fictional representation of life, but life itself as it is instantiated in a network of human relationships. The Cantonese filmmakers did this not by turning the cinema into an aesthetic experience that engages the spectators in a philosophical process; rather, they did so by putting life at play, and together with it, its ontological and political existence, thus making visible the inconsistencies, contingencies, playfulness, and gleefulness of life—in its pure immanence.

The vernacular Cantonese maxim *jansang jyu hei; hei jyu jansang* (life is like a play; a play is like a life) therefore acquires a new meaning here. The maxim is usually understood to mean that drama is simply the mimesis of life, although very often, life imitates drama. In the context of Sit Kok-sin's cinema, however, a play manifests life in all its immanence, whereas life is also put into a perpetual state of play in the cinema. In this sense, the cinema is best understood as a site where the process of approaching reality is put into a perpetual state of play. Yet, it is in this state of playfulness that reality becomes perpetually desirable. It is both a myth that is yet to be achieved and a ritual that never fulfills its potential to actualize the myth itself. Nonetheless, life in all its presence and concreteness—which is ironically absent in the formal mechanism of cinema—manifests itself precisely as an aftertaste, an indescribable energy, or a potentiality that is always ready to spark off multiple acts of creation.

CONCLUSION

FILM THEORY IS NOT EXCLUSIVELY a Western practice and the task of rethinking film theory as a global discourse is not simply a matter of adding more works from other parts of the world to the Euro-American canon. As the previous chapters demonstrated, filmmakers, critics, and intellectuals in Shanghai and Hong Kong between the 1920s and 1940s participated actively in the global discourse on film theory and criticism. Yet their participation in the inter- or intraregional circulation of knowledge and intellectual concepts often took the form of unrequited love. No doubt, these Chinese writers imagined themselves conversing with their Euro-American counterparts on an equal footing. In the intellectual dialogue they constructed, these thinkers not only responded to the theoretical ideas proposed in the West, but also reconfigured these notions and invented new conceptual frameworks in accordance with the semicolonial or colonial conditions of their politically and culturally extraterritorial spaces. Yet with Europe and North America as the imagined centers of knowledge production, these highly original, politically provocative, and philosophically thoughtful contributions to world film theory have so far remained untranslated and ignored.

This book therefore argues that a global understanding of film theory requires rewriting our approaches to major issues by highlighting the conceptual and intellectual connections between major theorists around the world. Most of the books and articles I have discussed were in fact intended to be parts of an inter- or intraregional dialogue. What I have done is not only make these texts and discussions available to their intended audience, but also put the intellectual confabulations between China and Euro-America—conversations that these Chinese writers had once imagined—back together both as a renewed understanding of the history(ies) of film theory(ies) and as a source of inspiration for us to rethink what cinema is today. In order to undertake this task, I focus on the example of how Chinese and Euro-American film theorists think about reality and the cinema, especially how Chinese film theories during the Republican period may help us locate the aporia within Bazinian ontology.

The goal of opening a comparative space between Chinese and Euro-American film theories, therefore, is not only to reconstruct an international, intracontinental, or empire-wide conversation that film theorists between the 1920s and 1940s missed the opportunity to have. More important, this book suggests a new dimension of cinematographic reality at a time when our discipline perceives an ontological crisis. As I mentioned in the beginning of this book, this crisis was first thought to be caused by the emergence of the digital image, which no longer seems to guarantee any direct referentiality to physical reality, and in fact, any direct relationship between an object and the image-consciousness the spectators apprehend. Unquestionably, with the advent of the digital image and the various new modes of image dissemination, mediation, and participation, the relationships between physical reality, the image, and our sense-perception have undergone serious changes. Yet, instead of abandoning Bazin altogether or revising Bazin as a response to the digital image, I want to use this comparative space between Chinese and Euro-American theories to rethink, retrospectively and retroactively, what Bazin might have been missing—or, alternatively, what we might have always missed between the lines in Bazin's ontology. In short, I will suggest possible ways by which we may use our understanding of approaching reality to reconfigure the various ontological, teleological, sociological, and ethical questions related to the digital image and media today.

But as the demand for knowing and understanding non-Western film theories continues to grow, this book should also serve to remind us of the ever-present danger of replicating the colonial production of knowledge. As scholars, researchers, and students who are interested in studying Chinese film theory, our task is not simply to introduce—as native informants—theoretical ideas that are assumed to be fundamentally different from their Euro-American counterparts, and leave the task of reconceptualizing them—which often means incorporating them within the epistemological space of Western theory—exclusively to scholars of Euro-American film theory. Studying Chinese film theory is not a matter of examining a fundamentally exotic object. Rather, we need to put these concepts into the global process of knowledge production by—once again—reconstructing their intended dialogues in history and by critiquing both of these epistemological spaces in all their vulnerability and fallibility. Hence, this book does not recruit Chinese film theory to prove that "Bazin was always right all along." Rather, it uses this comparative opportunity to uncover and wrestle with a philosophical aporia that Bazin himself—and the many Chinese writers that I have mentioned—tried to negotiate.

In our effort to reconstruct this cross-cultural dialogue, we need to remember that the term "theory" cannot simply be transferred from the Euro-American episteme to the Chinese intellectual debate. The term *lilun,* often employed in an academic context to indicate theory, is a composite term made up of the words *li* (ontological, social, or ethical principles derived from the classics) and *lun* (argumentation or debate). In the introduction, I trace the etymological history of the term, and the historical problem of the play-drama, theater, and later on, cinema, as "minor vehicles," being excluded from academic studies from the imperial period into the early 1940s. The critical debates that I have outlined here were called *pinglun* (evaluation and critique). This term suggests that a discursive space on the cinema during the Republican period was not necessarily constructed out of formal investigation, academic referencing, and systematized ratiocination. Rather, filmmakers, critics, and intellectuals discussed and conversed about current cinematic practice and individual films, and exchanged their private opinions on the cinema. Because most of these intellectual groups consisted of writers who published their works in the same magazines or filmmakers who worked for the same studios, theoretical vocabularies and paradigms—and by extension, conceptual and epistemic spaces—began to emerge out of their critical discourse.

What fascinates me here is the vernacularity of the term *pinglun,* and of the process by which theoretical spaces were developed. The term brings us back to the historical moment, between the 1920s and 1940s, when discussions on film around the world were conducted primarily on the colloquial level, and when the boundary between *lixing* (rationality) and *ganxing* (affectivity) was—and to some extent, still is—not sharply demarcated. The idea of generating a conversation by having writers mutually critique each other's private opinions has the potential to reconfigure the Enlightenment mode of knowledge production, which often assumes a binary relationship between a transcendental subject and an object of study. Instead, the notions of critiquing and talking suggest a more vernacular form of knowledge discussion that admits, and at times privileges, the coexistence of multiple private and potentially contesting opinions, each carrying its own subjectival position and contributing to the negotiation and mediation of conflicting affectivities. Yet, the historical practice of *dianying pinglun* (film criticism) did not hand us systems of theories. Rather, threads of theoretical thought emerged as these mutual critiques and discussions began to generate shared paradigms, sociopolitical interests, and common understandings of how we approach the cinema.

From Historical Interventions to Posthistoricity

The concept I have been wrestling with in this book is encapsulated in the term "approaching reality." What the Chinese film theorists meant by the term was that the cinematographic image, within its technological limitations, has yet to be a form of total reality, though it allows the spectators to apprehend an affect as though they had been there at the time the event actually happened. I have argued that this term suggests a delicate distance between the image and reality, one that was negotiated by Bazin in his body of work when he defined the cinematographic image as a trace of reality, which makes present the absence of reality itself. In a similar manner, screenwriters and critics Gu Kenfu and Hou Yao used the term approaching reality in the 1920s to suggest that there is a certain gap between the spectator's affective state and the image-consciousness it apprehends. In fact, this gap is best understood as a site where multiple potentialities are configured when the spectator, in the process of apprehending the image, forms a specific relationship with time.

Understanding the cinematographic image as a site of potentialities requires one to think beyond the notion of photographic indexicality and referentiality. In the course of my discussion, I focused on the deeper ontological implications underneath Bazin's fascination with the photographic imprint. The philosophical aporia Bazin negotiates in his writing lies in the camera's capability to snatch life from the physical reality and preserve it as a trace. What interests Bazin, however, is not the day-to-day life-process, but a spark of life that manifests itself when a piece of time-passed is preserved on film, and in the process of reactivating this passage of time, the absence of life is made present. Each time the film calls this life-undead back from the abyss of time, it reenacts this process of un-dying. What the cinematographic image crystalizes is therefore neither life nor death; past nor present. Rather, it is the very potentiality—the precise zone of indiscernibility—between these poles, what Deleuze calls life in its absolute immanence.

In the mid-1980s, through a series of mistranslations and misinterpretations, Chinese film scholars Chen Xihe and Zhong Dafeng completely missed the term approaching reality in their discussions of Gu Kenfu and Hou Yao's film theory from the 1920s. Instead, Chen and Zhong argued that Gu and Hou considered the cinema to be ontologically based on the play-drama. Such a missed opportunity, to a certain degree, was the result of Chen and Zhong's eagerness to construct a cinema ontology specific to the artistic and industrial developments of Shanghai cinema in the 1920s. It was also a response to the political urgency in the 1980s to build a body of knowledge that Chinese film scholars could nationalize. Upon closer examination, I argue that Gu Kenfu, in his attempt to theorize the cinema in relationship to the play-drama, was in fact deeply fascinated with how the camera snatches a piece of performance from a life-process, preserves it, and replays it in such a way that the spectator is put into an affective state as though she or he had been there. Each unique performance is undead, as though it were an echo from the end of time that constantly instantiates the potentiality between life and death—what Agamben would call the *kairos,* or the time it takes for time to end. In this sense, the digital image, with its potential disjunction, resequencing, and reshuffling between space and time, affectivity and consciousness, can inspire us to rethink temporality beyond the binary poles of beginning and end, past and present. Instead, the digital image makes us even more aware of the multiple dimensions of time that are embedded in the cinematographic image.

With this in mind, one may argue that the Marxist film theory in the 1930s brought our attention from the depth of time and the immanence of life back to the mundane—but perhaps more politically urgent—notion of the life-process. For Lenin, consciousness is not only a form of apprehension, but also an acquisition. Hence, the focus of Marxist film theory in Shanghai, via the debates on Leninism in Japan, is how consciousness is politically directed under the modalities of capitalism, imperialism, and feudalism. In Marxist terms, approaching reality is best understood as the way a group of spectators, under the deliberate direction of the bourgeoisie, apprehends a consciousness that is ideologically inflected. From the Marxist perspective, the capitalist film image can be seen as an indicator of the political reality, which the ideological apparatus of the bourgeoisie has carefully concealed from its viewers.

However, Marxist film theorists in Shanghai in the 1930s were interested not only in critiquing the mode of politically directed cinema under capitalism, imperialism, and feudalism, but also in the active construction of a new form of cinema, by seizing control of the means of production and rewriting its paradigm of narration. Such a socially progressive cinema embodies its own political consciousness; it thinks, feels, and activates political actions by instilling a mode of consciousness in the sentient bodies of its viewers, which makes tangible the ideological work that informs the modality of their political existence. Nonetheless, it does so not by instilling a completely new consciousness in the spectators' bodies; rather, it makes palpable the distance between the image-consciousness these viewers apprehend and the political reality that has been concealed from them, thus allowing a *yishi*—a yet-to-be-defined schema that permits the audience to be aware of the intricate distance itself, but has yet to take the form of a consciousness—to be engendered. In this sense, Marxist cinema is supposed to be a form of sensorial intervention. Such an intervention, or vocation, calls a group of spectators to a state where those sociopolitical relationships and historical conditions that constitute and propel capitalism, imperialism, and feudalism are momentarily interrupted. In other words, these viewers become aware of a potential end to this historical process. When they return to their day-to-day life-process, they form a "class," for which the time that remains is the time it takes for the existing historical process to end, a perpetual state of potentiality for renewal and reinvigoration to be activated by political actions.

Nevertheless, it may not be too presumptuous to ask: If the digital image no longer refers to a sensory-motor schema, but constructs both a physical memory and a sense of temporality that constantly puts into question the human sense-certainty, i.e. a kind of time that is built upon the assumption that time is already undead, can it still provide the form of sensual shock or violence that is necessary to politicize cinema—and, more importantly, to make life manifest itself? In 2002, Jean Baudrillard pondered this question by focusing on the referentiality between the image and reality. His sociopolitical "diagnosis" resonates with the discussion of posthistoricity proposed by Alexandre Kojève (1902–68). Kojève's starting point is the Hegelian and Marxist presupposition that the end of history is the "disappearance of Man," a state in which the distinction between humanity and nature, or animality, is dissolved. In a humorous way, Kojève reassures his readers that history will not end in such a catastrophic way. Rather, it is a state in which "Man remains alive as animal in *harmony* with Nature or given Being." He further theorizes: "What disappears is Man properly so called—that is, Action negating the given, and Error, or, in general, the Subject *opposed* to the Object." When the material praxis of History comes to a "conclusion," an individual "has 'nothing more to do.' " But this does not mean that history and action end. Rather, time suspends itself as an opening that perpetuates as an "epilogue."[1] For Kojève, social relations in the posthistorical state are reduced to their pure forms, performances that seem to mean nothing but for the sheer purpose of performing them. After his return from a visit to Japan, he declared sarcastically that Japan had already arrived in its posthistorical state:

> "Post-historical" Japanese civilization undertook ways diametrically opposed to the "American way." No doubt, there were no longer in Japan any Religion, Morals, or Politics in the "European" or "historical" sense of the words. But *Snobbery* in its pure state created disciplines negating the "natural" or "animal" given which in effectiveness far surpassed those that arose, in Japan or elsewhere, from "historical" Action—that is, from warlike and revolutionary Struggles or from forced Work. To be sure, the peaks (equally nowhere else) of specifically Japanese snobbery—the Noh theatre, the ceremony of tea, and the art of bouquets of flowers—were and still remain the exclusive prerogative of the nobles and the rich. But in spite of persistent economic and social inequalities, all Japanese without exception are currently in a position to live according to totally *formalized* values—that is, values completely empty of all "human" content in the "historical" sense.[2]

As Agamben argues, Kojève's humor suggests that such a socioeconomic state is not really "post-history." Rather, it implies that human beings are way too stubborn to allow themselves to succumb to it. Kojève's satirical reading of "Japanese snobbery" implies that all these social performances serve no specific purpose other than maintaining one final line that would define humanity: a collective performance of the ritual of being human.[3] In other words, posthistorical cinema, in Marxist terms, will continue to perform acts that instantiate existing social relations not for any historical purpose, but for the sole aim of maintaining the very notion of humanity apart from animality.

In 2002, Jean Baudrillard argued that this type of posthistorical media has already arrived:

> In September 1987, in Madrid, a Real Madrid-Naples European Cup match took place at night in a completely empty stadium, without a single spectator, as a consequence of disciplinary action taken by the International Federation in response to the excesses of the Madrid supporters at an earlier game. Thousands of fans besieged the stadium, but no one got in. The match was relayed in its entirety via television.
>
> A ban of this kind could never do away with the chauvinistic passions surrounding soccer, but it does perfectly exemplify the terroristic hyperrealism of our world, a world where a "real" event occurs in a vacuum, stripped of its context and visible only from afar, televisually. Here we have a sort of surgically accurate prefigurement of the events of our future: events so minimal that they might well not need take place at all—along with their maximal enlargement on screens. No one will have directly experienced the actual course of such happenings, but everyone will have received an image of them. A pure event, in other words, devoid of any reference in nature, and readily susceptible to replacement by synthetic images.[4]

Baudrillard's passage is often read in the light of his apparent fear that the digital image will bring us a mode of mediation in which the image is completely detached from any natural referents. But Baudrillard's fear is more profound than that. What the European Cup match points towards is the potentiality that in posthistoricity, consciousness will not return to what Marx and Engels would call a pure or animal state. Instead, a "pure event . . . devoid of any reference in nature" suggests that posthistorical consciousness can exist without any reference to either humanity or animality. Instead, social events or relationships are carried on for the purpose of maintaining humanity not as a category opposite to nature or animality, but as an imaginary absolute value.

In the case of the European Cup match, the actual event (the match itself) is performed in a spatial and temporal dimension that is completely detached from those spectators who apprehended it on television. In fact, the spectators had no guarantee that the actual event happened in the first place other than a belief that such a consciousness must be grounded in some form of reality. Yet this constructed belief generated real affective responses from the viewers, responses that confirmed their "chauvinistic passions," their sense of in-group loyalty and nationalistic sentiments. Nonetheless, these passions were mobilized commercially by the football clubs, the television companies, and the global sponsors for the purpose of maximizing their profits. These companies utilized these human affects because their brands and self-certainty relied on the perpetuation and continuation of these sentiments among their fan bases. In this sense, a consciousness can be completely fabricated for the purpose of grafting it onto the spectators' sense-certainty in order to maintain a set of social relationships. In other words, Baudrillard's fear is that the digital image allows a global dissemination of an image that is apprehended by an ever-increasing number of lives as a directed consciousness, and the directedness lies in the global corporations' manipulation of their consumers' last hope for being human.

What the Digital Image Thinks . . .

Baudrillard's imagination of the digital image and mediation, nonetheless, maintains a number of assumptions that my discussion on the concept of approaching reality has problematized. In terms of the Shanghai Marxist film theories from the 1930s, the directed consciousness molded by high capitalism can be seen as so powerful that the dissociation between the image and reality is not only unquestioned by the televisual viewers, but also reinstated as a myth by the structure of knowledge that refuses to admit its referential detachment from reality. However, what Baudrillard "predicted" is the mode of corporate television or cinematographic productions, which aim at persuading their viewers to think the way the image does. In this sense, Baudrillard has not departed from the premise that the Shanghai Marxist intellectuals, and Iwasaki before them, have already identified. The digital technology may make it easier for the sociopolitical apparatus to instrumentalize the image for the purpose of directing a collective consciousness, but it does not automatically transform the ideological work that sustains its ontological integrity.

A key question that gradually emerges here is whether the digital image can still be regarded as a body that thinks. Towards the end of the first chapter, I pointed out that the digital image is not a trace (as in an analogon) of the physical appearance of an object or a human being; rather, the camera maps out the thermal algorithm of an overall image and stores it as a set of data scrambled and scattered among other data in a chip or hard drive. Each time an image is "recalled" to a screen, the viewer is not witnessing a reactivation of an analogon, together with a passage of time snatched from a life-process. Instead, each time an image reappears, it is already a reconstruction and recomposition.

The ideas of reconstruction, recomposition, and regeneration are keys to our understanding of the mode of temporality and life in the digital image. Let us return to Sartre's example in *The Imaginary.* When Sartre looks at a photograph of his friend Pierre, he sees the image as a lifeless analogon of Pierre. It lacks life. His mind therefore comes up with an image-consciousness of Pierre (what Bergson would call a sensory-motor schema), which brings to life the living Pierre he knows. Bazin argues that the mental process described by Sartre has already been built into the cinematographic machine, as the cinema snatches the very passage of time that Pierre has once lived, and the cinematographic image draws the viewer into the temporal reality of Pierre, whose transformation was carefully preserved and mummified. A digital image of Pierre, however, does not reanimate Pierre in the very passage of time-passed that the cinematograph preserved. Rather, based on a mathematical record of the thermal energy the camera captured and analyzed, Pierre is given a new body, a new temporal existence, and a new set of relationships with the beholder of the image—even though the image convinces the viewer that this is a trace of Pierre. What the digital image potentially restores is the mental process that Sartre has identified. For the spectator, this digital image of Pierre lacks life, and a mental analogon must be produced in order to convince the viewer that this is indeed a reanimation of Pierre from a passage of time-passed.

What is opened up in this viewing process is a gap between a passage of time-passed, which cannot be conceived otherwise, and a digital recomposition whose existence is always present. Yet via a mental analogon, this digital recomposition is conveniently taken by the viewer as an index or referent of the passage of time-passed. This question is often taken as one about the digital image's mimetic faithfulness—not indexicality—to the image, and the degree to which the digital image faithfully (or in some cases, authentically) reproduces the likeness of the object being recorded has been a subject of debate or concern among filmmakers, critics, and scholars. When the digital image first appeared as a technology, filmmakers complained about its imperfection—its lack of life and warmth, i.e. its failure to disguise itself as an imprint or trace of a passage of time-passed. Today, the digital image is equally praised and vilified for its hyperperfection: it surpasses the way the viewers sense, perceive, remember, and fantasize the actual event or object, but it exceeds the perceptual limitations of the human eyes and brain. In other words, the digital image is always one step behind or ahead of its photographic counterpart.

Nonetheless, I want to avoid concentrating on the digital image's degree of mimetic faithfulness. Instead, I want to bring our attention to the widening gap between the irretrievable loss of time-passed and the ever-renewing sense of present that the digital image generates. What the digital technology makes palpable is precisely the measurement between the chronometric present and the time it takes for time to end, and politically, the structure of knowledge and technology that configures the temporal potentiality embedded in the cinematographic image (be that optical or digital). The result is a renewed critical space. On the one hand, the reality that the various corporate- or state-sponsored images, such as the cinema of Feng Xiaogang, offers its spectators is "so hyper-real" that it begins to provoke critical thought among the viewers about the believability of the image's mimetic appearance, affect, and ideological work. On the other hand, the reality that the new independent Chinese documentary filmmakers like Zhou Hao, Huang Weikai, and Pan Zhiqi offer their spectators is so unprecedented in cinema history that a gap of knowledge, or a thought, is opened between the directed consciousness devised by the state apparatus, i.e. what the state wants its citizens to believe, and what their film images embody, that is, what the state apparatus wishes to conceal from the viewers.

Preindividuation

The actual technicalities of the production and reproduction of the digital image challenge a deeper ontological presupposition maintained by Marxist film theories. In Marxist criticisms, an ontological dyad is set up between the individuals, who exercise a degree of political agency under the directed consciousness of the larger sociopolitical apparatus, and the collective, which informs in each individual its ontological consistency. The Bazinian notion of the mechanical trace is in fact based on the assumption that an individual life leaves its trace on a piece of film by means of mechanical reproduction. Yet, what the digital image does is to absorb the thermal energy from an individual body and reimmerse it in the larger algorithm of what Gilbert Simondon would call preindividual life, i.e. a preindividual state in which all lives and objects, beings and machines, are predistinguished—not that they are "all the same" ontologically, but that they share a common ontogenetic existence.[5] Each process of image recomposition is best understood as a moment at which a new operation of individuation takes place, that is, when an affect—or *qing* (*cing*)—is transduced within a given domain, thus giving definitions to physical, biological, psychic, and collective individuations.

For Simondon, transduction is defined as "a physical, biological, mental, or social operation, through which an activity propagates from point to point within a domain, while grounding this propagation in the structuration of the domain, which is operated from place to place: each region of the constituted structure serves as a principle of constitution for the next region."[6] In other words, a technical structure—for example a social media network or a digitally mediated community—is best understood not as a collection of individuals who interact intersubjectively. Instead, it can be seen as a preindividuated structure. As this structure undergoes information, or affectivity, the process of transduction individuates beings who believe that they are stand-alone agents, but at the same time know that they are ontogenetically related to other beings and objects within a given domain, an existence that exceeds those boundaries that define their own bodies, subjectivities, and social spaces.

Simondon's philosophy could in fact help us reconfigure the soft film theory for the purpose of rethinking the impact of the digital image in our understanding of cinema ontology. The soft film theory, proposed by screenwriters and critics Liu Na'ou and Huang Jiamo, was a poetically articulated and philosophically complex discussion on how the spectator beholds the cinematographic image and approaches the reality of life in all its presence and concreteness. On the one hand, the soft film theory is indebted to Kantian aesthetics and the contemporaneous debate on cinematic beauty and the sublime in France and Germany. On the other hand, it is also best understood as a pluralistic semantic field inherited from several decades of debate on the definitions of life among Chinese intellectuals, and Wang Guowei's reconfiguration of Kantian aesthetics in Buddhist terms. Between the 1890s and 1930s, through a series of translations, reconfigurations, and inventions, the Chinese intellectuals came up with three interrelated notions of life: *rensheng* (human life), *shengtai* (life form or biological life), and *minsheng* (national life). In such an intellectual imagination, life manifests itself in each individual life form, and all life forms are intricately tied to the larger political life that constitutes and propels the nation as a production machine. In this sense, the cinema as an aesthetic experience allows the beholders to approach the reality of life, satisfy their biological desire, and instill a collective will in their sentient bodies.

In such a debate of life, individual life forms and political lives are both seen as expressions of life-in-itself, best understood in Spinozian terms as *conatus* or the pure desire to subsist in the universe as one substance. In this sense, the cinematographic image can be seen as an appearance or manifestation of this universal substance. Yet, Wang Guowei's aesthetics complicates this matter. For him, an aesthetic experience is a process of *wudao*, or arriving at *dao*, in three *jingjie* or stages: (1) living in the appearance; (2) not living in the appearance; (3) living in the appearance as not living in it. In other words, the ultimate objective of seeing through the transparency of the image (i.e. into life) is not to negate its appearance and look for something beyond it; rather, the beholder is supposed to dwell fully in the image while realizing that the difference between dwelling in it and negating it can be suspended into a pure difference.

For Wang Guowei, based on his understanding of Kant, such an aesthetic experience can be considered neither as beauty nor the sublime, but as *guya*: an elegance or sense of interest aroused by a trace through a passage of time-passed. But what interests Wang Guowei is not really a passage of time in the linear sense of it; rather, for Wang, an aesthete who searches for *dao* will also look "back" to a passage of time-passed as though it were all laid out in an instant, that is, time passes as not passes. In my discussion of the digital image, an aporia emerges: if the digital image is technically not a trace of a passage of time, but a regeneration of it that tries to convince its viewer to recall a past, the digital image is constantly a crystal that mirrors the past and the present, the present and the future, as though they were all laid out on an equalizing plane. This is what Deleuze would call a crystal image.

This means that a cinematographic image, be that photographic or digital, is a potentiality that manifests itself on an equalizing plane, and it makes tangible the substantiality of life. But such interpretation may still be too "easy." For Spinoza, the universal substance is not a thing; rather, it is a substantiation of *conatus*. Muriel Combes, based on the philosophy of Simondon, argues:

> A substance appears when a term absorbs into itself the relation that gave rise to it, thus obscuring it. As long as being is understood substantially, relation appears as nothing but a mental connection between a substance

> and attributes or qualities conceivable outside it. . . . Yet Simondon shows that the characteristics of individuation that appear when we study the formation of crystalline forms of a same type . . . are not "qualities" insofar as "such characteristics are prior to any idea of substance (since we are dealing with the same body)." Transparency and opacity in particular can characterize the same form . . . in succession as a function of the temperature imposed on the metastable system at the moment of crystallization. Transparency and opacity thus cannot be thought of as qualities of a substance, but as characteristics appearing in a system undergoing a change of state.[7]

In other words, what Spinoza calls a substance, for Simondon is "an extreme instance of relation, that of the inconsistency of relation."[8] It is an appearance or instantiation not only of a set of relations, but of their very inconsistency that gives rise to further potentialities to restructure these relations into different modes of connection and appearance.

Bazin's idea of the photographic image as a trace of time is often understood literally as an index of time. Reconfigured in Simondon's terms, the Bazinian trace can be reinterpreted as a crystallization of a structural inconsistency in time within a given domain of relations. One may even say that the photographic image is the "substance" of time. In this sense, it would be too easy for one to argue that the digital image is by definition insubstantial. The difference between a trace produced by a chemical reaction and one reproduced by a thermal algorithm is a technical relation between two structures that are ontogenetically connected. But in the mind of the beholder, there is indeed a perceptual difference in the way these two different technologies approach this process of substantiation: the photographic image produces, and the mechanical reproduction, after all, continues to copy the same trace and retain the originality of the trace itself; the digital image, by definition, regenerates, and the process of recomposition is best considered as a process of resubstantiation. What the digital image does, from the perspective of reception, is take away the "aura" by resubstantiating a trace by a means (in this sense, ocular and tactile) not historically trusted by the spectators. What film scholars conceive of as a digital crisis, in this specific regard, is to some degree an anxiety about a renewed ontogenetic relationship between humans and the machines.

Here, I refer to Benjamin's notion of the aura, however, with a critical distance. My use of the term aura here to describe the photographic image, as opposed to its digital counterpart, might be regarded by some

Benjaminian scholars as borderline blasphemous, for Benjamin seems to argue that what the cinema lacks is precisely the aura a beholder has historically associated with the plastic arts. Remember what Benjamin claims:

> In even the most perfect reproduction, *one* thing is lacking: the here and now of the work of art—its unique existence in a particular place. It is this unique existence—and nothing else—that bears the mark of the history to which the work has been subject. This history includes changes to the physical structure of the work over time, together with any changes in ownership. Trace of the former can be detected only by the chemical or physical analyses (which cannot be performed on a reproduction), while changes of ownership are part of a tradition which can be traced only from the standpoint of the original in its present location.[9]

One could say that Benjamin's idea of the aura is associated with the materiality and material history of a piece of art. In this regard, film archivists and historians have long contested that the celluloid medium does have its materiality and material history. By the same token, until recently, digital restoration of cinematic works had been viewed askance because digital media no longer carry any traces of the art object's material historicity.

However, Benjamin also defines the aura on an ontological level:

> This process is symptomatic; its significance extends far beyond the realm of art. *It might be stated as a general formula that the technology of reproduction detaches the reproduced object from the sphere of tradition. By replicating the work many times over, it substitutes a mass existence for a unique existence. And in permitting the reproduction to reach the recipient in his or her own situation, it actualizes that which is reproduced.*[10]

What Benjamin critiques here is the tendency of mass culture in the 1930s to reproduce works of art—in this case, the cinematographic image—in mathematically and mechanically precise forms that could be delivered to individuals who no longer require an appreciation of the material history of the art object. For Benjamin, a mass-produced image reactualizes a time-passed as though it were here and now, thus erasing the very materiality and historicity that inform an aesthetic experience. The idea of "reproduction" is usually interpreted in this context as the process of mass copying; but what Benjamin hints at is that there is a second register in this process of reproduction: the process of reproducing a life-process, i.e. a process of regeneration and reanimation of time that erases the very technological, or in fact, ideological work that goes into it. But for Benjamin, the cinematographic apparatus is "only" a symptom of the larger social apparatus, which serializes and mechanizes human lives by means of the same process, replicating and reproducing modes of sociopolitical existence for mass consumption—existence that claims an ontological consistency on its own that the masses come to believe in as the actual condition of their reality.

Aura and a Renewed Distance between Art and Reality

In ontological terms, aura can be understood as what remains concealed from the spectators as they misrecognize the cinematographic image as a reproduction of the chronometric present. In this light, Bazinian ontology can be seen as an effort—though not a conscious one—to restore cinematographic aura by turning the viewers' attention not to the illusion of presence in cinema, but to the presence of an absence to which the cinematographic image draws its viewers. Fey Mou shared a similar view. Borrowing ideas from his interpretations of Chinese painting and the Chinese theater, Fey consciously resists the use of narrational devices to persuade his audience to generate narrative inferences, and by extension, an illusion of reality. Instead, he uses the long take and deep staging to capture the boredom of life and the mundanity of the everyday. In so doing, desire, which is a potentiality absent in form but made present as an object or event activates it, hangs in the air as the presence of its absence. In *Spring in a Small Town,* desire is not only inferred by the narrative's cause-and-effect chain, but is also made present as an absence by the profound boredom life arouses in the spectator's suspension-imagination—an erotic and frustrating sensation that is released through the perpetual frustration of desire.

Nonetheless, Fey's film theory also has a Confucian ontological and ethical dimension. What *Spring in a Small Town* offers is not a cinematographic experience in which desire manifests itself rampantly. Instead, desire is constantly regulated within an overall air of *qing,* which informs the various human relationships and individual personalities. Meanwhile, *qing* is adjudicated upon by *ren,* the principles of being human, or for some, benevolence. In *Spring,* what manifests itself in the cinematographic air is not simply the characters' amorous desires, but also being human or life-itself as a potentiality from which desires are substantiated.

Likewise, in *Confucius,* Fey chose not to inculcate his audience with *ren* rhetorically and didactically. Rather, by showing the everydayness of the before and after in Confucius' key moments in life, *ren* hangs in the air as a mode of suspension-imagination.

The conversation between Bazin, Benjamin, and Fey that I reconstruct here brings one to a little aporia. On the one hand, cinematographic reality manifests itself in the absolute immanence of life. On the other hand, it can be produced by means of the film's syntagmatic structure (Metz's cinematographic syntagm) and the filmmaker's paradigmatic choices (Bordwell and Thompson's narrational devices). The former suggests that reality is an ontological ground that is self-evident. The latter nonetheless implies that reality is an artifact. In "Le Réalisme cinématographique et l'école italienne de la libération" ["An Aesthetic of Reality: Cinematic Realism and the Italian School of the Liberation," 1948], Bazin wrestles with this dilemma. In the article, he argues that before the total cinema becomes technically possible, reality is as much an aesthetic as an ontological issue. Yet the cinema would not exist if the threshold between presence and absence was completely taken away:

> Every form of aesthetic must necessarily choose between what is worth preserving and what should be discarded, and what should not even be considered. But when this aesthetic aims in essence at creating the illusion of reality, as does the cinema, this choice sets up a fundamental contradiction which is at once unacceptable and necessary: necessary because art can only exist when such a choice is made. . . . Unacceptable because it would be done definitely at the expense of that reality which the cinema proposes to restore integrally. . . . Actually the "art" of cinema lives off this contradiction. It gets the most out of the potential for abstraction and symbolism provided by the present limits of the screen, but this utilization of the residue of conventions abandoned by technique can work either to the advantage or to the detriment of realism.[11]

Bazin's idea can in fact be further elaborated by the term I have been pondering over and over again in this book: approaching reality. In a sense, before the total cinema is technically possible, filmmakers always need to employ artistic or narrational devices to approach reality. Yet, paradoxically, once any artistic devices are used, cinematic reality is reduced to a form. In this sense, what Bordwell and Thompson teach us is how the classical Hollywood film, within its technological limits and social expectations, offers one possible form of reality whose primary concern is to preserve the spectator's sense of causality and unity—albeit at the expense of its aura.

Art and reality, however, are not necessarily dichotomized in the way Bazin believes, and the spectator's proximity to reality is not technologically predetermined. In some ways, Andy Warhol's portrait films challenge some of these Bazinian assumptions. Many of these films consist of a close-up or medium close-up of a person, who was either asked to look at the camera lens or was supposed to be in a somewhat vulnerable position. In *Blow Job,* 1964, for example, the filmed subject, DeVeren Bookwalter (1939–87), was supposed to be receiving fellatio while the camera observed his face. Warhol allowed the camera to run through the entire roll of film, and then he replaced it with another roll. He then spliced together these camera rolls, including the flash frames. In an exhibition, these portrait films are presented as "portraits." According to David James, these film portraits:

> do not document their subjects' ability to manifest an autonomous, unified self so much as narrate their anxious response to the process of being photographed. The camera is a presence in whose regard and against whose silence the sitter must construct himself. As it makes performance inevitable, it constitutes being as performance. The simple activities proffered as the subject of documentation are insufficient fully to engage the sitter and merely establish an alternative area of attention, momentarily allowing self-consciousness to slip away. The sitter oscillates between his activity and awareness of the context in which it is taking place.[12]

In other words, what threatens the spectator's viewing comfort is that the cinematographic reality of these moving portraits challenges the passivity of the spectator's viewing position. In fact, instead of absorbing the spectator into the portrait, it extends itself by looking at the spectator. And such a direct contact between the spectator's eyes and the performer's hinders the spectator's construction of an imaginary. Instead, the spectator must confront what Metz would call the presymbolic: this is not a hero who is symbolically articulated as *my* imaginary self; rather, it is a woman or man whose existence comes face-to-face with *mine.* But to complicate matters, the flash frames from time to time restore the presence of the cinematographic apparatus by reminding the spectator that she or he is after all seeing an image that is symbolically articulated by a mechanical device.

Warhol's portrait films do not make a cinematic experience more or less aesthetic on the one hand, nor do they make the cinematic reality more or less real on the other. Instead, they make clear to the spectator that she or he is occupying the threshold between cinematic presence and absence, art and reality, all of which are codependent in the cinema. In fact, approaching reality is made possible by approaching art. Likewise, approaching cinematic presence is made possible precisely by approaching its absence.

One might argue that Warhol's portrait films were constructed deliberately for the purpose of making clear the threshold between presence and absence, reality and art. In this sense, the spectators are left with no choice but to confront this threshold. In our day-to-day viewing experience, nevertheless, we are left to exercise the freedom not to take what we see as total reality or total art. This is because what we take as a cinematic experience precisely hinges upon this threshold between reality and art, presence and absence. In *Inception* (Christopher Nolan, Warner Brothers, 2010), Dom Cobb (Leonardo DiCaprio) has the ability and technology to enter another person's mind, in which he can construct a dream where he and his "dream team" can extract information embedded in this person's unconscious. Mr. Saito (Ken Watanabe) employs Dom Cobb to enter the mind of Robert Michael Fischer (Cilian Murphy). But Dom Cobb's mission is not to extract information from Fischer, but to rebuild the initiating memory (i.e. the Oedipal complex) that forms and supports Fischer's ontological consistency (inception), so that Fischer will come out of his dream a different person. The difficulty is that Fischer was trained to resist invaders to his dream, and Dom Cobb must convince Fischer to allow the dream team to locate the core of his subjectivity.

When the dream team has successfully initiated a dream in which Fischer finds himself in a bar, a safe place where Dom Cobb can actively begin a conversation with Fischer's mind, Dom Cobb asks Fischer to reexamine what he sees and try to discern certain hints that reality as he sees it "is not real." As Cobb speaks, the spectators are already aware that all the objects in the room appear to be tilted and the glass tinkles as the space begins to shake. In two long shots, the film shows the customers around Dom Cobb and Fischer stopping what they are doing and staring at the camera, a sign that Fischer has become self-conscious of his act of dreaming. This point-of-view shot is both an image from Fischer's perspective and a direct-address utterance to the viewer. It demonstrates that what the viewer might have taken as reality (the bar) a moment ago is in fact carefully composed—both physically and digitally—as an artifact (a digitally constructed image). In the scene, Fischer admits that he has been trained to say "no" to any invader's attempt to recompose the symbolic components of his dream so as to preserve the imaginary integrity of his subjectivity. What Dom Cobb tries to do—at least at this moment of the film—is to convince Fischer not to say no to the dream team's attempt to recompose his dream by pretending that they are in his dream as his dream's protector. The ethical dilemma is this: By not saying no to Dom Cobb, what he sees is indeed an artifact that can be reconfigured, remolded, invaded, and resymbolized as an imaginary that has real impact on Fischer's subjectivity. To the spectators, Fischer's not saying no to Dom Cobb also pushes them deeper into the film's constructedness and artificiality—yet the film's realism hinges upon how far the spectator is willing not to say no to the artistic-artificial construct and the game we are invited to play in it.

In the digital debate, some scholars consider the search for a new ontology a form of disciplinary hysteria, that is, the fear that the digital image has fundamentally challenged our established notion of photographic indexicality is only a fear, for it remains a potentiality that has yet to be actualized. What I want to point out, however, is that potentiality is not a technological issue. In the scene from *Inception* I have just discussed, the reality and artificiality of the scene itself and the series of cinematographic syntagmas that follow do not hinge upon the distinction between the digital and the optical but upon our decision to say no or not to say no. In a parallel storyline in the film, Mal Cobb (Dom Cobb's wife; Marion Cotillard) commits suicide by jumping off a building, for she refuses to admit that the world in which she lives is real, and she believes that by jumping off the building, she will enter another layer of dream or reality. We later on learn that the world where Mal Cobb lives is in fact a dream constructed by Dom Cobb. Dom wants Mal to believe that this is the ideal world where they can live and grow old, thus he locks Mal's totem (an object that allows the dreamer to test whether she or he is in a dream or in reality; in this case, Mal's totem is a top, which, once spun in a dream, would never fall) into a safe so that Mal can never verify her reality. This has the effect of taking away Mal's freedom to say no or not say no to the reality in which she finds herself. However, as suggested towards the end of the film, the inception that Dom Cobb does to Fischer's subjectivity may in fact be part of a larger inception that he does to himself, i.e. what the spectators take for granted as the film's "reality" is ultimately a dream within a dream. In this sense, the entire film is precisely about the threshold of cinema: At what point does one say no to an illusion of reality that is dependent on a constant reconfiguration of its dream contents? The ending shot of the film which shows Dom Cobb's token (also a top) spinning perpetually, thus suggesting that Dom Cobb, who believes himself to be back in reality where he is reunited with his children, is in fact in another layer of dream. This shot symbolizes precisely the cinematographic image as a potentiality, and in it, our saying no to any attempt to leave the threshold and enter either into total reality or total art.

Returning to the example of how the U.S. military uses the digital image to construct a virtual battlefield for its home-based special mission agents (see chapter 1), one can see how the cinema can be taken out of the threshold between art and reality. The virtual battlefield is at once packaged as an artifact that has no physical effect on the special mission agent, but does in fact remotely control what happens in a physical space elsewhere at the time the soldier carries out her or his quasi-virtual mission. Likewise, this piece of art produces a hyperreal impact on these soldiers' mental and moral integrity, all precisely because of its very irreality. In this particular case, the virtual battlefield is not constructed out of a direct indexicality of the real people in Iraq or Afghanistan; it simulates the actual situation almost to the point of direct indexicality. But interestingly enough, such virtual experience leaves an indelible indexical trace in the brains of these soldiers while they execute lives elsewhere.

By maintaining the cinema's threshold between presence and absence, reality and art, we do not necessarily need to conform to the classical Hollywood mode of narration (as Warhol's film or even *Inception* demonstrate), or to resist any attempt to unlock cinema's potential to activate political actions. What we see from the virtual battlefield is an example of how we can potentially say "yes" to a higher level of reality achieved precisely by its apparent total abstraction (in some sense, it corresponds to Baudrillard's dystopia). The threshold is the zone at which our freedom to say "no" is unlocked, and it folds back to itself where dreams can continue to be reconfigured, trespassed, mutually interfered, transduced, and deactivated, among political communities that would otherwise find nowhere to put it into a discourse—let alone practice.

Joculogy, Social Media, and Contemporary Cinema

To a certain extent, the idea of cinema as *play* may offer us an answer to the question of how cinema can continuously reinvent itself as an image, and as an institution that constantly puts into an interplay the distance between art and reality. In the 1930s, the Hong Kong Cantonese theater and cinema were industrially and artistically combined. What first appeared to be an industrial and business opportunity had in fact a profound impact on the question of cinema ontology. The fact that cinema merged with the theater does not imply—as Chen Xihe and Zhong Dafeng would have argued—that the cinema is a kind of play-drama. Rather, it implies that the Cantonese filmmakers in the 1930s imagined the cinema as a site of negotiation between reality and play, the sacred and the profane. To start with, the Cantonese *hei* is best understood not simply as drama or theater. Rather, for theater artist and critic Mak Siu-ha, *hei* is a musical performance that negotiates the relationship between the sacred and the symbolic on the one hand, and the profane and the end of signification on the other. It does so not by means of mimesis, but biomimesis, that is, it emulates not the appearance of life, but the principle of life. A Cantonese *hei* is therefore engendered by *cing,* and *cing* is in turn engendered by music. As an art form, the Cantonese theater does not describe reality, but instead sketches ideation.

In fact, Cantonese theater artist Sit Kok-sin does not see the cinema as a narrational medium. Rather, he sees a film, via the body of a *siusang* (versatile male actor who can play multiple leading or supporting roles), as an instantiation of human relationships in their various manifestations. In this sense, his film is characterized by a lack of ethical determination and point of identification. Instead, scenes of life are put together as an interplay between dramatic vignettes and musical numbers, while shots are edited together not in accordance with drama, but with a creative rhythm internal to the music itself. Therefore, watching the theater-cinema of Sit Kok-sin is a process of appreciating life at play. And in the context of the KMT's attempt to nationalize cinema as an educational instrument, Sit and other Cantonese filmmakers offered an opportunity to keep the cinema in its zone of indiscernibility by putting life and its political existence as play; it challenges the Shanghai-Nanking notion of national cinema by privileging humor over seriousness, human relations over narrative continuity, presentation over representation, contingency over directorial control, and regional sensibility over any form of top-down national unity.

Putting life at play has the effect of suspending the semiotic differences in a zone of indiscernibility, allowing new existential, ethical, and political meanings to go through renegotiation and regeneration. The digital turn is in fact often marked by a shift from the narratological to the ludological.[13] This can be understood in two perspectives. From one perspective, social media like Facebook, Weibo, YouTube, and Tudou are no longer characterized by storytelling or constructing any form of narrative logic. Rather, they thrive on an interplay between narrative making and the accumulative act of gaming, participating, and playfulness. One clicks on the links on YouTube not for the purpose of making any narratological sense out of one clip after another. Rather, clips are suggested mechanically based on users' feedbacks (not actual feedback, but the cookies that allow an individual user's information to feed into the YouTube's server as a way to recommend a set of clips that would most likely generate more clicks). Yet, as Thomas Elsaesser argues, these clicks are somewhat causally related as each of them is the consequence of the previous viewing experience. Each click therefore hinges upon an indistinction between intentioned narrativizing and untinentioned gaming.[14]

It is tempting to say that Facebook and YouTube are public rituals as much as gaming. Yet, in these social media, "rituals" do not carry a signifying function, i.e. they are not always performed for the purpose of constructing a narrative collectively. They are often pure actions performed for the fun of creating new chances to connect discrete word plays, statements, images, and events into somewhat playful situations—situations that can sometimes, often by accident, be translated into a narrative event. Likewise, myths that articulate historical events (personal convictions, news items, political opinions) are translated into words alone without necessarily being actualized into action. In other words, as Agamben would argue, these social media are less ludological than *jocus*, that is they divorce myth and ritual (the confirmation and invocation of the myth), patience and action, words and deeds.[15]

But even within the realm of social media, not every domain of the social network offers the same experience of approaching reality. Social media are not "cinema" as understood historically; yet they are sites where the cinematographic institution and experience are renegotiated. Facebook, now used primarily by subscribers between the age of 30 and

50, has a tendency to move towards narrativization, continuity, and subjectival integrity. As a Facebook user, I am given a site and I make connections with other members in the social network, thus forming a certain domain. The way I foster relationship and affective connections with my friends and acquaintances, or members who share a set of similar social, political, or cultural interests, is to post a composed thought, a piece of news, a link to an image or website that would invite other individuals to like or comment. These likes and comments would then appear in these individuals' walls, which have the effect of reposting and disseminating my ideas and creative productions. After a period of time, my opinions and posts gradually take the form of my personality, and the agreements I gather from my friends reinforce my sense of membership in the communities to which I belong. In fact, the Facebook likes can be fetishized by individual users as signifiers of their personality and popularity. Over a period of time, a Facebook page can be read as a narrative of an individual's "subjectivity," as manifested by her or his thoughts, concepts, writings, photographic works, interactions with other individuals—a personality constructed as a narration.

Twitter changes this idea by focusing on pithy thoughts (with character limits), instantaneous transmissions of news, and transient sharing of affects and information within a given domain. On Twitter, ideas, thoughts and affects are circulated not necessarily among friends, but among followers, who can be other individuals who may or may not know me, or organizations and corporations that wish to pick up opinions and affects to help promote their popularity and brands. On Twitter, spontaneity and contingency take over continuity, consistency, and subjectivity. Each tweet can be seen as a transduction of social, physic, mental, or even physical operations within a given domain, which sparks off a new wave of individuations. Ultimately, I am not interested in constructing a narrative about myself, nor have I built up a performative subjectivity through my tweets. Instead, individual subjectivities are replaced by ontogenetic connections and separations; meanwhile, substantiality is replaced by relations and potentialities. These are indeed features reconfigured by more personalized devices such as WeChat, Whatsapp, and Line, which aim at sharing spontaneous thoughts, contingent plans, and instantaneous affects mostly among friends who have already known each other in physical spaces. One can see that while Facebook caters increasingly to its subscribers' desire to narrativize and mythologize,

Twitter and other mobile apps are designed to involve their subscribers in a perpetual state of play. In this sense, Weibo, which incorporates all of these functions in a mega media structure, is supposed to offer its subscribers a site where an interplay between their narratological and joculogical desires are negotiated, state interference notwithstanding.

In the cinema, the emergence of the mind-game film also privileges gaming. Yet, such gaming is once again less ludological than jocus. In a mind-game film, the spectators apprehend pure actions that are performed for the fun of creating multiple accesses to versions of a film's narrative. Yet, narrativization—that is, the fabrication of myths—is no longer a necessary guarantee of pleasure. Rather, the process of signifying is enjoyed as a game. In fact, the mind-game is best enjoyed as a somatic experience: a total divorce of the image from its signifying function.[16] But as Gary Bettinson argues, despite the popularity of the 1970s Shaw Brothers' mind-game *wuxia (*martial arts) films based on the novels of Gu Long (pseudonym of Xiong Yaohua, 1938–85), mind-game narratives are not as popular in Chinese cinemas as in Hollywood, with the exception of *Wuxia* [reedited and released in the United States as *Dragon,* Peter Chan, We Pictures, Stellar Mega Films, Dingsheng Cultural Investment, Jiangsu Broadcasting Corporation, and the Yunnan Film Group, 2011] and *Mangtan* [*Maangtaam* or *Blind Detective,* Johnnie To, Media Asia, Emperor Film Production, Sil-Metropole, Milkyway, and Beijing Roast Film and TV Production, 2013]. In fact, both *Wuxia* and *Blind Detective* were considered by their viewers not as playful films or games, but as films that provoke serious thoughts on cinematographic reality and narrative credulity.[17]

However, perhaps joculogical cinema has already been the dominant mode of cinematographic genres in the Hong Kong-Canton region. The Mandarin or Cantonese Hong Kong musicals in the 1950s and 1960s, the Cantonese theater-film, the *wuxia* and gangster films, the comedic films from the 1980s, the *wulitou* (*mouleitau*) or nonsensical comedies of Stephen Chow, and the various independent comedic flicks produced in Hong Kong for a specifically Hong Kong Cantonese audience: these genres and film forms inherit the idea of cinema as play believed in and advocated by the early Hong Kong Cantonese sound filmmakers, which has left an indelible mark in the larger national discourse on Chinese cinema and popular culture. Culturally, socially, politically, and linguistically, these films form a critical space, a vernacular public sphere where contesting opinions on the relationship between politics and life, the national and the regional, art and reality, are interplayed and remediated.

What Is Cinema Ontology?

Approaching reality therefore has the effect of shifting our locus of discussion from what cinema is to what cinema can be. By saying that cinema can be reality, but has yet to be, we in fact invoke Bazin's famous notion that "cinema has not yet been invented." Bazin's statement is often read teleologically, that cinema, as a perfect manifestation of reality, has yet to be technologically possible. However, I want to suggest that we read this statement ethically, and consider that a complete state of indistinction between the cinematographic image and reality, where life and death are perpetually actualized, is in fact precisely something that we do not want to have, something that would take away both the mystical and playful indiscernibility between life and death, good and evil, past and present, something that we treasure both in cinema and in our increasingly complex social media.

For this purpose, I want to return to the *Vajracchedikā Prajñāpāramitā Sūtra,* and to discuss briefly an idea that I mentioned at the end of chapter 3: what could be a Buddhist ontology of cinema? A special feature of the Kumārajīva translation is the extensive use (41 occurrences) of the phrase *rushi* (like/as is). In fact, the *Sūtra* opens with a narrator framing the entire text by writing, *Rushi wo wen* (Like/as what I heard).[18] As I argued in chapter 3, the phrase *rushi* preserves an indeterminacy between likeness and being, and is first and foremost understood as "the way it is." In fact, in the text, a Buddha is often referred to as *rulai* (like-approaching or as though [it were] approaching). What it signifies is an appearance that *is* there, but has yet to be fully actualized.

The term *rushi,* in its different linguistic variations, is considered the core concept in the philosophical system conveyed by the *Sūtra.* In §2, the Venerable Subhuti asks the Buddha, "*yun he ying zhu, yun he hangfu qi xin?*" (tell me how one should *zhu,* how one should conquer one's heart). The term *zhu* literally means "to live." But here, Subhuti does not mean to ask the Buddha how one should live. Rather, the term *zhu* is understood as "living like/as is" or "living the way it is." In fact, one may not even consider the idea of "living" as we understand it on a day-to-day basis. It is in fact closer to the idea of "being in the state it is" or "being/like." In this light, when Subhuti asks how one should conquer one's heart, he does not have in mind the idea of conquering one's desire. Rather, he is asking how one should reconcile a state of being that is not a state (*zhu*), with a constant process of approaching that seems to resist any attempt *to be in the state it is* (*xin*). The terms *zhu* and *xin* in some ways are juxtaposed as two poles here: to hold onto a state; to move towards or away from a state.

To this question, the Buddha replies, "*rushi hangfu qi xin*" (conquer one's heart like/as is or the way it is). At first glance, the Buddha does not seem to answer Subhuti's question. In fact, what he implies is that Subhuti has already answered his own question, and he does so by keeping the indiscernibility between likeness and being, reality and the approach to reality undisturbed.

As Nan Huai-chin argued, the idea of *zhu* (pinning oneself down to a state) is to actualize a potentiality and *live* in an appearance, or, alternatively, to *not live* in an appearance. In fact, if the idea of *not to "zhu"* were to be considered a potentiality, any attempt to actualize it is a departure from absolute immanence and an approach to a state of transcendence. In this sense, appearances—all we see, sense, perceive, or even imagine—are by definition informed by our transcendent values—or in fact, our constant desire to transcend what is immanent by actualizing, or not actualizing, the potentiality of life. In this sense, to reckon with the difference between actualizing and not actualizing, that is, to zero out the indiscernibility between the two modes of approaching reality until no remainder is left, as Agamben suggests, is one way of not pinning oneself down to a state. But for Nan, our attempt to hold onto the very idea of potentiality is in itself a form of *zhu.*[19]

Asking what ontology is in Buddhist term is therefore a precarious question. The term *ontology* in the Chinese language is *benti* (the body itself or the body in its form). In this sense, what is the *benti* of cinema, a form of *xiang* or appearance that is mechanically reproduced, institutionalized, and apprehended like/as reality? The first Buddhist answer that would come to my mind is *rushi* (like/as is). The *benti* of cinema is/is like reality, or reality as the way it is, but has yet to be fully actualized. However, if we push this question further, one may argue that *benti ben wu ti* (the body itself/in itself/[does not have or is] not a body). This is not to say that ontology is not ontology. Rather, the idea of *benti ben wu ti* maintains the very indiscernibility between a body and *not a body.* In this light, *approaching reality* is/is like *not approaching reality,* as cinematographic reality is at a threshold between here and there, present and past, presence and absence. It is neither virtual nor actual, being or becoming. It is neither a state nor a nonstate. It neither proliferates nor distinguishes. As stated in the *Heart Sūtra (Prajñāpāramitā Hṛdaya)*:

> O, Sariputra, form does not differ from voidness, and voidness does not differ from form. Form is voidness and the void is form; the same is true for feeling, conception, volition and consciousness.
>
> Sariputra, the characteristics of the voidness of all dharmas are non-arising, non-ceasing, non-defiled, non-pure, non-increasing, non-decreasing.
>
> Therefore, in the void there is no form, feeling, conception, volition or consciousness.
>
> No eye, ear, nose, tongue, body or mind; no form, sound, smell, taste, touch, mind-object, or eye realm, until we come to no realm of consciousness;
>
> No ignorance and also no ending of ignorance, until we come to no old age and death and no ending of old age and death.[20]

What *is not* cinema. . . .

NOTES

Introduction

1 For a discussion of this problem, see, for example, Hu Ke, "Contemporary Film Theory in China," trans. Ted Wang, Chris Berry, and Chen Mei, *Screening the Past,* no. 3 (March 25, 1998), http://tlweb.latrobe.edu.au/humanities/screeningthepast/reruns/hkrr2b.html, first published in *Dangdai dianying* [Contemporary cinema], no. 2 (1995): 65–73. Throughout the book, the terms "the West" and "Western" and their counterparts "the East" and "Eastern" are treated as historical and sociopolitical constructions.

2 See, for example, Chen Xihe, "Xuni xianshizhuyi he houdianying lilun" [Virtual realism and post-film theory] (2001), in Ding Yaping, ed., *Bainian Zhongguo dianying lilun wenxuan* [One hundred years of Chinese film theory and criticism] (Beijing: Wenhua yishu chubanshe, 2002), 2:720–36.

3 Dudley Andrew, "The Core and the Flow of Film Studies," *Critical Inquiry* 35, no. 4 (Summer 2009): 879–85.

4 The proposed anthologies are *The Chinese Film Theory Reader,* eds. Victor Fan, Guo-Juin Hong, and Jason McGrath; and a parallel volume in Japanese film theory to be edited by Aaron Gerow and Abé Mark Nornes.

5 Kim Soyoung, "A Theory on the Desk? Or a Theory of Yearning?" (paper presented at the Permanent Seminar on Histories of Film Theories: Histories of Film Theories in East Asia, University of Michigan, Ann Arbor, September 28, 2012).

6 The working title of Aaron Gerow's book is *A Historical Introduction to Japanese Film Theory.* For his published articles, see for example "Introduction," in *Decentering Theory: Reconsidering the History of Japanese Film Theory,* special issue, *Review of Japanese Culture and Society,* no. 22 (December 2010): 1–13; "The Process of Theory: Reading Gonda Yasunosuke and Early Film Theory," in *Decentering Theory,* 37–43; "A Retrospective of Japanese Retrospectives," *Undercurrent* 6 (April 2010), http://www.fipresci.org/undercurrent/issue_0609/gerow_retro.htm; "Critical Receptions: Historical Conceptions of Japanese Film Criticism," in *Oxford Handbook of Japanese Cinema,* ed. Miyao Daisuke (New York: Oxford University Press, 2014), 61–78; "Japanese Film Theory, Gonda Yasunosuke, and Another Film Civilization," in *In the Beginning, and the Very End: Film Theories in*

Perspective, eds. Francesco Casetti, Jane Gaines, and Valentina Re (Udine: Forum, 2010), 553–60.

7 André Bazin, "Ontology of the Photographic Image" (1945), in *What Is Cinema?,* trans. Hugh Grey (1968; repr., Berkeley: University of California Press, 2005), 1:15; Dudley Andrew, *What Cinema Is!: Bazin's Quest and Its Charge* (Malden, Mass.: Wiley-Blackwell, 2010), 9. Andrew also refers to Serge Daney, "André Bazin," in *Cahiers Critique* (Paris: *Cahiers du cinéma,* 1986), 174, first published in *Cahiers du cinéma* 1983.

8 Thomas Elsaesser, "A Bazinian Half-Century," in *Opening Bazin: Postwar Film Theory and Its Afterlife,* eds. Dudley Andrew and Hervé Joubert-Laurencin (New York: Oxford University Press, 2011), 7–8. For discussions on the digital problem, see, for example, Jean Baudrillard, *Simulacra and Simulation* (1981), trans. Sheila Faria Glaser (Ann Arbor: University of Michigan Press, 1994), 6; Baudrillard, *The Transparency of Evil: Essays on Extreme Phenomenon* (1990), trans. James Benedict (London: Verso, 1993), 4; William Brown, "Man without a Movie Camera—Movies without Men: Towards a Posthumanist Cinema?" in *Film Theory and Contemporary Hollywood Movies,* ed. Warren Buckland (New York: Routledge, 2009), 66–85; D. N. Rodowick, *The Virtual Life of Film* (Cambridge, Mass.: Harvard University Press, 2007); Vivian Sobchack, "The Scene of the Screen: Envisioning Electronic 'Presence'," in *Materialities of Communication,* eds. Hans Ulrich Gumbrecht and K. Ludiwg Pfeiffer (Stanford, Calif.: Stanford University Press, 1994), 83–106; see also Francesco Casetti, "The Filmic Experience," *Screen* 50, no. 1 (Spring 2009): 56–66.

9 The phrase "opening Bazin" comes from the title of Andrew and Joubert-Laurencin, eds., *Opening Bazin,* cited in note 8.

10 Elsaesser, "Bazinian Half-Century," 4.

11 See, for example, Gu Kenfu, "Fakanci" [Inaugurating preface], *Yingxi zazhi* [*The Motion Picture Review*] 1, no. 1 (1920): 10; Hou Yao, *Yingxi juben zuofa* [Methods of writing a shadow play] (Shanghai: Taidong shuju, 1926), 13–23.

12 Daney, "André Bazin," 174; quoted in Andrew, *What Cinema Is!,* 9.

13 Bazin, "An Aesthetic of Reality: Cinematic Realism and the Italian School of the Liberation" (1948), in *What Is Cinema?,* 2:26–27; Bazin, "The Myth of Total Cinema" (1946), in *What Is Cinema?,* 1:21.

14 Li Yanshou and Li Dashi, *Bei shi* [History of the Northern Dynasties] (Beijing: Beijing tushuguan chubanshe, 2003), *juan* 44, no page, first published in the seventh century.

15 Mai Xiaoxia (Mak Siu-ha), *Guangdong xiju shilue* [*Gwongdung heikek siloek* or Brief history of the Cantonese theater] (Hong Kong: Zhongguo wenhua xiejinhui or Zunggwok manfaa hipzeonwui, 1940), 1.

16 Charles Laughlin, *Literature of Leisure and Chinese Modernity* (Honolulu: University of Hawaii Press, 2008), 1–23.

17 Sun Mingjing, "Boyin jiemu xuan: dianying yu dongyuan minzhong" [Radio program select: cinema and the mobilization of the masses], *Dianying yu boyin* [*Film & Radio*] 1, no. 5 (September 1942): 2–9.

18 See Wu Di (Wu Qizhi), ed., *Zhongguo dianying yanjiu ziliao: 1949–1979* [Research

materials on Chinese cinema: 1949–1979], 3 vols. (Beijing: Culture and Art Publishing House, 2006).

19 See *Zhongguo xuesheng zhoubao* [*Zunggwok hoksang zaubou* or *Chinese Students Weekly*] nos. 1–1128 (1952–74); *Da texie* [*Daai dakse* or Close-up] nos. 1–64 (1975–78); see also *Dianying shuangzhoukan* (*Dinjing soengzauhon*) [*City Entertainment Magazine*] nos. 1–618 (1979–2002).

20 George S. Samsel, Xia Hong, and Hou Jianping, eds., *Chinese Film Theory: A Guide to the New Era* (New York: Praeger, 1990).

21 See Jiang Yasha and Chen Zhanqi, eds., *Zhongguo zaoqi dianying huakan* [Early film magazines of China], 12 vols. (Beijing: Quanguo tushuguan wenxian suowei fuzhi zhongxin, 2004); Bao Weihong, *Dances of Fire: Aesthetic Affect and the Intermediation of Chinese Cinema, 1884–1945* (Minneapolis: University of Minnesota Press, 2014); Fan, Hong, and McGrath, eds., *Chinese Film Theory Reader;* Yiman Wang, *Remaking Chinese Cinema: Through the Prism of Shanghai, Hong Kong, and Hollywood* (Honolulu: University of Hawaii Press, 2013); Yingjin Zhang, *Chinese National Cinema* (New York: Routledge, 2004), 51–56; Zhang Zhen, *Amorous History of the Silver Screen: Shanghai Cinema, 1896–1937* (Chicago: University of Chicago Press, 2005).

22 Ding Yaping, ed., *Bainian Zhongguo dianying lilun wenxuan,* 2 vols.; Hu Ke, *Zhongguo dianying lilun shiping* [Commentaries on the history of Chinese film theory] (Beijing: Zhongguo dianying chubanshe, 2005).

23 Lydia Liu, *The Clash of Empire: The Invention of China in Modern World Making* (Cambridge, Mass.: Harvard University Press, 2004), 12–13.

24 Aaron Gerow, "Theorizing the Theory Complex" (keynote address at the Permanent Seminar on Histories of Film Theories, University of Michigan, Ann Arbor, September 27, 2012); Dudley Andrew, *Concepts in Film Theory* (New York: Oxford University Press, 1984), 12.

25 Gilbert Cohen-Séat, *Essai sur les principes d'une philosophie du cinéma* [Essay on the principles of a philosophy of cinema]. (Paris: Presses universitaires de France, 1946); Edward Lowry, *The Filmology Movement and Film Study in France* (Ann Arbor: University of Michigan Research Press, 1985).

26 Andrew, "Core and the Flow of Film Studies," 888–93.

27 See *Xiandai dianying* [*Modern Screen*], nos. 1–7 (March 1933–June 1934).

28 See, for example, Mak Siu-ha, *Gwongdung heikek siloek*; Ouyang Yuqian, "Shitan Yueju" [An attempted discussion on the Cantonese theater], in *Zhongguo xiqu yanjiu ziliao chuji* [A preliminary anthology of research materials on the Chinese theater and music], ed. Ouyang (Hong Kong: Xiju yishu chubanshe or Heikuk ngaiseot ceotbaanse, 1954), 109–57; Yang Chuntang (Yeung Chun-tong), ed., *Zhen shan mei: Xue Juexian yishu rensheng* [*Zan sin mei: Sit Kok-sin ngaiseot jansang* or Honesty, goodness, and beauty: the artistic life of Sit Kok-sin] (Hong Kong: University Museum and Art Gallery, University of Hong Kong, 2009).

29 I would like to thank Jason McGrath for this summary.

30 Chen Xihe, "Zhongguo dianying meixue de zai renshi: ping *Yingxi juben zuofa*" [Understanding again the Chinese film aesthetics: On *Methods of Writing a*

Shadow Play] (1986), in Ding Yaping, ed., *Bainian Zhongguo dianying lilun wenxuan,* 2:202–03 [citation at note 2]; Gu Kenfu, "Fakanci," 10; Hou Yao, *Yingxi juben zuofa,* 13–23; Zhong Dafeng, "Lun yingxi" [On the shadow play] (1985), in Ding, ed., *Bainian Zhongguo dianying lilun wenxuan* 2:200; Zhong Dafeng, "'Yingxi' lilun lishi suoyuan" [On the historical origin of the shadow play theory] (1986), in Ding, ed., *Bainian Zhongguo dianying lilun wenxuan* 2:224–25.

31 My understanding of the term *potentiality* comes from Aristotle, *De anima,* trans. R. D. Hicks (Cambridge, U.K.: Cambridge University Press, 1907), 417 a 2–5; quoted in Agamben, "On Potentiality," in *Potentialities: Collected Essays in Philosophy,* trans. Daniel Heller-Roazen (Stanford, Calif.: Stanford University Press, 1999), 178–79.

32 Bazin, "Ontologie de l'image photographique," in *Qu'est-ce que le cinéma?* (1958; repr., Paris: Les Éditions du Cerf, 2002), 14; "Ontology of the Photographic Image," 1:15.

33 Vladimir Lenin, *What Is to Be Done?* (1902), trans. Joe Fineberg and George Hanna (New York: The Lenin Internet Archive, 1999), 16–31.

34 Aono Suekichi, "Shizen seichō to mokudeki ishiki" [Naturally generated and directed consciousness], pts. 1 and 2, *Bungei sensen* [Frontline of art and literature] (September 1926 and January 1927), no page; Iwasaki Akira, *Eiga to shihon shugi* [Cinema and capitalism] (Tokyo: Ōraisha, 1931), 97–124.

35 Iwasaki, "Xiandai dianying yu youchan jieji" [Modern cinema and the bourgeoisie], trans. Lu Xun, *Mengya yuekan* [Seeding monthly] 1, no. 3 (March 1930): 1–33.

36 Feng Wu (A Ying), "Lun Zhongguo dianying wenhua yundong" [On the Chinese film cultural movement], *Mingxing yuebao* [Star monthly] 1, no. 1 (May 1, 1933): 12–18; Wang Chenwu, "Zhongguo dianying zhi lu (shang)" [The road of Chinese cinema: part 1], *Mingxing yuebao* 1, no. 1 (May 1, 1933): 48–53; Xi Naifang (or Zheng Boqi), "Dianying zuiyan—bianxiang de dianying shi ping" [A critique on cinema—or, a criticism on contemporary cinema], *Mingxing yuebao* 1, no. 1 (May 1, 1933): 20–25; Zhang Shichuan, "Chuanshengtong li" [From the loudspeaker] (1933), in Ding, ed., *Bainian Zhongguo dianying lilun wenxuan,* 1:133–37; Zheng Zhengqiu, "Ruhe zoushang qianjin zhi lu" [How to follow the progressive path?], *Mingxing yuebao* 1, no. 1 (May 1, 1933): 28–30.

37 Shen Xiling, "Zhongguo dianying zhi weiji yu xin lujing" [The crisis and new path of Chinese cinema], *Dianying yishu* (Film art) 1, no. 1 (1932): 1–2.

38 Huang Jiamo, "Yingxing yingpian yu ruanxing yingpian" [Hard film and soft film], *Modern Screen* 1, no. 6 (December 1, 1933): 3; "*Xiandai dianying* yu Zhongguo dianyingjie" [*Modern Screen* and the Chinese film profession], *Modern Screen* 1, no. 1 (March 1, 1933): 1; Liu Na'ou, "Dianying jiezou jian lun" [On film rhythm], *Modern Screen* 1, no. 6 (December 1, 1933): 1–2; "Écranesque," *Modern Screen* 1, no. 2 (April 1, 1933): 1; "Guanyu zuozhe de taidu" [On the author's attitude], *Modern Screen* 1, no. 5 (October 1, 1933): 1; "Zhongguo dianying miaoxie de shendu wenti" [Problems with the depth of description in Chinese cinema], *Modern Screen* 1, no. 3 (May 1, 1933): 2–3.

39 Ricciotto Canudo, "The Birth of a Sixth Art" (1911), in Richard Abel, ed., *French Film*

Theory and Criticism: A History/Anthology, 1907–1939 (Princeton, N.J.: Princeton University Press, 1988), 1:58–66; Louis Delluc, "Beauty in the Cinema" (1917), in Abel, ed., *French Film Theory and Criticism*, 1:137–39; "Le Beauté," in *Cinéma et cie. Confidences d'un spectateur* (Paris: Grasset, 1919), 2; Jean Epstein, "Le Cinématographe vu de l'Etna" (1926), trans. Stuart Liebman, in *Jean Epstein, Critical Essays and New Translations*, eds. Sarah Keller and Jason N. Paul (Amsterdam: Amsterdam University Press, 2012), 288; Immanuel Kant, *Critique of the Power of Judgement* (1790), trans. Paul Guyer and Eric Matthews, ed. Guyer (Cambridge, U.K.: Cambridge University Press, 2000), §18–28; Siegfried Kracauer, "Cult of Distraction: On Berlin's Picture Palaces" (1926), in *The Mass Ornament: Weimar Essay*, trans. and ed. Thomas Y. Levin (Cambridge, Mass.: Harvard University Press, 1995), 323–25; "The Mass Ornament" (1927), in *Mass Ornament*, 76–78 and 83–84; Wang Guowei, *Renjian cihua* [On human literature] (1910; repr., Beijing: Pushe, 1926), §6.

40 Gilles Deleuze, *Cinema 2: The Time-Image* (1985), trans. Hugh Tomlinson and Robert Galeta (1989; repr., Minneapolis: University of Minnesota Press, 2001), 68–69; Deleuze, *Expressionism in Philosophy: Spinoza* (1968), trans. Martin Joughin (New York: Zone Books, 1990), 67; Agamben, "Absolute Immanence," in *Potentialities*, 226.

41 Susan Daruvala, "The Aesthetics and Moral Politics of Fei Mu's *Spring in a Small Town*," *Journal of Chinese Cinemas* 1, no. 3 (September 2007): 173; Carolyn FitzGerald, *Fragmenting Modernisms: Chinese Wartime Literature, Art, and Film, 1937–49* (Leiden: Brill, 2013), 169–216.

42 Fey Mou, "Guanyu jiuju dianyinghua de wenti" [On the question of cinematizing the old theater] (1942), in Ding, ed., *Bainian Zhongguo dianying lilun wenxuan*, 1:292.

43 Fey, "Lue tan 'kongqi'" [Let's talk about 'air' briefly] (1934), in Ding, ed., *Bainian Zhongguo dianying lilun wenxuan*, 1:216–17.

44 Fey, "'Daoxu fa' yu 'xuanxiang' zuoyong" ["Inverse narration" and the functions of "suspension-imagination"] (1934), in Ding, ed., *Bainian Zhongguo dianying lilun wenxuan*,1:214.

45 My discussion of *ren* is based on a discussion of the term in Mengzi (Mencius), "Jinxin xia," in *Mengzi yizhu* [Mencius, with annotations and modern translations], annotated and trans. Yang Bojun (Beijing: Zhonghua shuju, 2010), *juan* 14.1–5, first written around the fourth century BCE.

46 Wong Ain-ling, ed., *Fei Mu's* Confucius (Hong Kong: Hong Kong Film Archives, 2010).

47 Fei Mu (Fey Mou), "Confucius and His Time" (1945), trans. Agnes Lam, in Wong, ed., *Fei Mu's* Confucius, 147.

48 David Bordwell, *Narration in the Fiction Film* (Madison: Wisconsin University Press, 1985), 51–53 and 150–52; Bazin, "An Aesthetic of Reality: Cinematic Realism and the Italian School of the Liberation," in *What Is Cinema?*, 2:26–27; Christian Metz, "The Cinema: Language or Language System?" (1971), in *Film Language: A Semiotics of the Cinema*, trans. Michael Taylor (New York: Oxford University Press, 1974), 61–91; "*The Imaginary Signifier* [Excerpts]" (1975), trans. Ben Brewster, in *Narrative,*

Apparatus, Ideology: A Film Theory Reader, ed. Philip Rosen (New York: Columbia University Press, 1986), 259; Kristin Thompson, *Breaking the Glass Armour: Neoformalist Film Analysis* (Madison: Wisconsin University Press, 1985), 3–45.

49 Mak, *Gwongdung heikek siloek,* 2.

50 Li Yizhuang and Zhou Chengren, *Zaoqi Xianggang dianying shi: 1897–1945* [History of early Hong Kong cinema: 1897–1945] (Shanghai: Shanghai renmin chubanshen, 2009), 131.

51 Mak, *Gwongdung heikek siloek,* 1.

52 A summary of this historical period could be seen in Zhiwei Xiao, "Constructing a New National Culture: Film Censorship and the Issues of Cantonese Dialect, Superstition, and Sex in the Nanjing Decade," in *Cinema and Urban Culture in Shanghai, 1922–1943,* ed. Yingjin Zhang (Stanford, Calif.: Stanford University Press, 1999), 187–90; Li Hua (Lee Fa), "Shang Jing qiangjiu Yueyu pian lizhan Hu yingshang jingguo" ["Soeng Ging cinggau Jyutjyu pin likzin Wu jingsoeng gingguo" or The Nanking visit: how we fought against the Shanghai studio executives in order to save the Cantonese film], in *Ling xing* [*Ling Sing*], no. 203 (1937): 2–4.

53 Mak, *Gwongdung heikek siloek;* Ouyang, "Shitan Yueju," 109–57; Xue Juexian (Sit Kok-sin), "Nanyou zhiqu" ["Naamyau geiceoi" or Afterthoughts on my visit to Southeast Asia] (1930), in Yeung, ed., *Zan sin mei,* 168; "Wo de fendou" ["Ngo dik fandau" or My struggle] (1940), in Yeung, ed., *Zan sin mei,* 179–82; "Zhuyan he daoyan *Xu Bai Jinlong* de houhua" ["Zyujin wo doujin *Zuk Baak Gam-lung* dik hauwaa" or After playing the lead in and directing *White Golden Dragon: The Sequel*] (1937), in Yeung, ed., *Zan sin mei,* 169.

54 Walter Benjamin, "The Work of Art in the Age of Its Technological Reproducibility: Second Version" (1936), trans. Edmund Jephcott and Harry Zohn, in *Selected Writings,* eds. Marcus Bullock and Michael Jennings (Cambridge, Mass.: Belknap Press, 2006) 3:107–108; Miriam Hansen, "Room-for-Play: Benjamin's Gamble with Cinema," *October,* no. 109 (Summer 2004): 23–24; Agamben, "In Playland: Reflections on History and Play," in *Infancy and History: Essays on the Destruction of Experience* (1978), trans. Liz Heron (London, Verso, 1993), 65–88.

55 My discussion refers to concepts of individuality by Gilbert Simondon; see Muriel Combes, *Gilbert Simondon and the Philosophy of the Transindividual* (1999), trans. Thomas LaMarre (Cambridge, Mass.: MIT Press, 2013).

56 Nan Huai-jin (Nan Huai-chin), Jingang Jing *shuo sheme?* [What does the *Vajracchedikā prajñāpāramitā sūtra* say?] (Shanghai: Fudan daxue chubanshe, 2001; first published Taipei: Laogu wenhua shiye gongsi, 1992).

1. Approaching Reality

1 "China" and "the West" (and "China" and "the World") are put within quotation marks here to emphasize that they are not supposed to be taken for granted as naturalized historical terms. Rather, they are both historically constructed concepts that are often pitted against each other as opposites. See Haun Saussy, "China and the World: The Tale of a Topos," *Modern Language Quarterly* 68, no. 2 (June 2007): 145–71; Eric Hayot, Haun Saussy, and Steven Yao, eds., *Sinographies:*

Writing China (Minneapolis: University of Minnesota Press, 2008); see also Teemu Ruskola, *Legal Orientalism: China, the United States, and Modern Law* (Cambridge, Mass.: Harvard University Press, 2013), 1–59.

2 Chen, "Zhongguo dianying meixue de zai renshi," 2:202–03.

3 Ibid., 2:208–09; Zhong, "Lun yingxi," 2:200; Zhong, "'Yingxi' lilun lishi suoyuan," 2:224–25.

4 Cecile Lagesse, "Bazin and the Politics of Realism in Mainland China," in Andrew and Joubert-Laurencin, eds., *Opening Bazin*, 316–23. According to Lagesse, Bazin's writings were first introduced into the Chinese academy with the translation of his essay "Montage Interdit" ["The Virtues and Limitations of Montage"] (1953 and 1957) in 1962, 316.

5 Andrew, *What Cinema Is!*, 10.

6 See Henri Bergson, *Creative Evolution* (1907), trans. Arthur Mitchell (Mineola: Dover Publications, 1998); Jean-Paul Sartre, *The Imaginary* (1940), trans. Jonathan Webber (London: Routledge, 2004); Maurice Merleau-Ponty, *Phenomenology of Perception* (1945), trans. Colin Smith (London: Routeldge, 2000). About the totality and immediacy of a subject's apprehension of an image, Bergson, Sartre, and Merleau-Ponty have different opinions. For Bergson, between representation and action there lies a cause that transforms a potentiality (in representation) to an actuality (in action), a "step" that Deleuze has famously developed into the idea of the sensory-motor schema, comparable to a sketch that has yet to be fully formed into an image (145). For Sartre, each moment of re-actualization contains within itself its potentialities, its possible outcomes, and its actualization in one total state of consciousness. In this sense, what we call a movement within an image is in fact a reimage in its totality (13–14). Merleau-Ponty argues that the subject is aware of a certain progression towards the image-consciousness, but such an imaginary movement is always synthesized as a whole (233). The phrase "here and now" is usually attributed to Roland Barthes, *Camera Lucida: Reflections on Photography* (1980), trans. Richard Howard (New York: Hill and Wang, 1981), 84. However, it was in fact used earlier in Walter Benjamin, "A Small History of Photography" (1931), in *One Way Street and Other Writings*, trans. Edmund Jephcott and Kingsley Shorter (London: NLB, 1979), 243. See Graeme Gilloch, "Pictures of the Past: Benjamin and Barthes on Photography and History," *European Journal of Cultural Studies* 5, no. 1 (2002): 5–25. Andrew also discusses this problem in the "Preface to the Revised Edition," in *André Bazin* (1978; repr., New York: Oxford University Press, 2013), xii.

7 Elsaesser, "A Bazinian Half-Century," 7–8.

8 Lagesse, "Bazin and the Politics of Realism in Mainland China," 316–17; Bai Jingsheng, "Tantan mengtaiqi de fazhan" [Discussion on the evolution of montage], *Dianying yishu* [Film art], no. 1 (1979), no page; Li Tuo, "Yige zhide zhongshi de dianying meixue xuepai—guanyu 'chang jingtou lilun'" [A school of thought on film aesthetics worth paying attention to: on the "long take theory], in *Dianying wenhua chongkan* [Film culture series] (Beijing: Zhongguo shehui kexue chubanshe, 1980), 1:148–60.

9 Li Tuo and Zhang Nuanxin, "Tan dianying yuyan de xiandaihua" [On the

modernization of film language] (1979), in Ding, ed., *Bainian Zhongguo dianying lilun wenxuan*, 2:11–13 and 30–36.

10 Lagesse, "Bazin and the Politics of Realism in Mainland China," 317; Brian Henderson, "Two Types of Film Theory," *Film Quarterly* 24, no. 3 (Spring 1971): 33–42.

11 Michael S. Duke, *Blooming and Contending: Chinese Literature in the Post-Mao Era* (Bloomington: Indiana University Press, 1985), 24–27.

12 Siegfried Kracauer, *Theory of Film: The Redemption of Physical Reality* (New York: Oxford University Press, 1960); translated into Chinese by Shao Mujun as *Dianying de benxing: wuzhi xianshi de fuyuan* [Nature of film: the redemption of physical reality] (Beijing: Zhongguo dianying chubanshe, 1981).

13 Hao Jian, "Andelei Bazan zai Zhongguo: bei yanshuo yu bei xiaojian" [André Bazin in China: spoken and forgotten], *Dangdai dianying* [*Contemporary Cinema*] 4, no. 145 (December 2008), no page; quoted in Lagesse, "Bazin and the Politics of Realism in Mainland China," 317.

14 Mao Zedong (Mao Tse-tung), "Talks at the Yenan Forum on Art and Literature (May 23, 1942)," in *Selected Works of Mao Tse-tung* (Beijing: Foreign Languages Press, 1977), ed. Foreign Languages Press, http://www.marxists.org/reference/archive/mao/selected-works/volume-3/mswv3_08.htm; Cheng Jihua, Li Shaobai, and Xing Zuwen, *Zhongguo dianying fazhan shi* [History of the development of Chinese cinema], 2 vols. (1963; repr., Beijing: Zhongguo dianying chubanshe, 1980).

15 Xia Yan, *Xie dianying juben de jige wenti* [On several questions about screenwriting] (Beijing: Zhongguo dianying chubanshe, 1959).

16 Warren Sun and Frederick C. Teiwes, *End of the Maoist Era: Chinese Politics During the Twilight of the Cultural Revolution, 1972–1976* (Armonk, N.Y.: M. E. Sharpe, 2007), 382–461.

17 Bazin, "Le mythe du cinéma total," in *Qu'est-ce que le cinéma?*, 23; Bazin,"The Myth of Total Cinema," 1:21.

18 Gu Kenfu, "Fakanci," 10; Hou, *Yingxi juben zuofa* [Methods], 13–23.

19 Lu Xun, "Yizhe fuji" [Translator's notes], *Mengya yuekan* 1, no. 3 (March 1930): 27–33.

20 Zheng Zhengqiu, "Ruhe zoushang qianjin zhi lu," 28–30.

21 Ye Yiqun, "Jianli Zhongguo dianying fengge" [Establish a Chinese film style] (1949), in Ding, ed., *Bainian Zhongguo dianying lilun wenxuan*, 1:383–86.

22 Xia Yan, *Xie dianying juben de jige wenti.*

23 See Poon Wai-ming, "Bo Xilai de tuyang" [The soil that nurtured Bo Xilai], in *Ming bao yuekan* [*Ming Pao Monthly*] 48, no. 9 (September 2013): 1.This official position has been renewed recently by Xi Jinping (b. 1953), General Secretary of the Central Committee of the CCP (in office since November 2012): "We cannot use the thirty years since the 'reform and open' policy has been implemented to refute those thirty years prior to that moment" (quoted in 1).

24 Wang Hui, "Zhengzhi yu daode ji qi zhihuan de mimi" [Politics and ethics, and the secret about their inter-changeability] (1990), in Ding, ed., *Bainian Zhongguo dianying lilun wenxuan*, 2:353–78.

25 Zhong, "Lun 'Yingxi,'" 157; Zhong's historical claim has more recently been con-

tested by film scholars, who now believe that terms including the shadow play, the *dianying* (electric shadows)—the name that is now in use in the Chinese language to signify film and cinema—and other nominations emerged more or less around the same time. Here, I put the term "left-wing" within quotation marks to indicate that the term itself is a debatable one, a problem I will discuss in chapter 2.

26 Bao Tianxiao, *Chuanying Lou huiyilu* [Memoir from the House of Jade and Shadows] (Hong Kong: Dahua chubanshe or Daaiwaa ceotbaanse, 1973), 93, qtd. ibid. 158.

27 Hou, *Yingxi juben zuofa,* 5, quoted in Zhong, "Lun 'Yingxi'," 158.

28 Xu Zhuodai, "Yingxi zhe xi ye" [The shadow play is a play], *Minxin tekan* [Special issue of the China Sun magazine] 3, *Sannian yihou* [Three years later] (1926), no page, quoted in Zhong, "Lun 'Yingxi,'" 158.

29 See the discussion of a similar problem in relation to Walter Benjamin's use of the term "mimesis" in Hansen, "Room-for-Play," 3–46.

30 Hou, *Yingxi juben zuofa,* 5.

31 Bazin, "Théatre et cinéma" (1951), in *Qu'est-ce que le cinéma?,* 129–79; Bazin, "Death Every Afternoon" (1958), trans. Mark A. Cohen, in *Rites of Realism: Essays on Corporeal Cinema,* ed. Ivone Margulies (Durham, N.C.: Duke University Press, 2003), 29.

32 Zhong, "Lun 'Yingxi,'" 159.

33 Ibid., 159–62; Andrew Jones also discusses this issue in *Yellow Music: Media Culture and Colonial Modernity in the Chinese Jazz Age* (Durham, N.C.: Duke University Press, 2001), 12.

34 Iwasaki, "Xiandai dianying yu youchan jieji," 1–33, first published as "Senden • sendō shudan toshite no eiga" [Propaganda: film as a tool for incitation] in the Marxist magazine *Shinkō geijutsu* [Burgeoning arts], then incorporated into *Eiga to shihon shugi,* 97–124. For the historical background of the hard film theory, see, for example, Cheng, Li and Xing, *Zhongguo dianying fazhan shi,* 1:200–03 and 1:271–72; see also Hu Jubin, *Projecting a Nation: Chinese National Cinema before 1949* (Hong Kong: Hong Kong University Press, 2003), 79–83, 90–97, and 109–13.

35 Iwasaki, "Xiandai dianying yu youchan jieji," 5–7; Iwasaki, *Eiga to shihon shugi,* 102–03.

36 Lu Xun, "Yizhe fuji," 27–33.

37 Zhong, "Lun 'Yingxi'," 162–64. This definition of *quwei* was probably borrowed from the popular discussion of the same term, pronounced in Japanese as *shumi*; see Liang Qichao, "Xuwen zhi quwei" [The joy of scholarship] (1922), in *Liang Qichao jingdian wencun* [Collection of the classic essays by Liang Qichao], ed. Hong Zhigang (Shanghai: Shanghai Daxue chubanshe, 2003), 278–79.

38 Zhong, "Lun 'Yingxi'," 164–193. That being said, this impression of Shanghai cinema in the 1920s has been somewhat questioned by the recent discovery of two films released during this decade, *Ersun fu* [*Mother's Happiness,* Shi Dongshan, Great China, 1926] and *Pansi dong* [*The Cave of the Silken Web,* Dan Duyu, Shanghai Yingxi Company, 1927].

39 Kristine Harris, "'The Romance of the Western Chamber' and the Classical Subject

Film in 1920s Shanghai," in Yingjin Zhang, ed., *Cinema and Urban Culture in Shanghai*, 53–54.

40 Hou, *Yingxi juben zuofa,* Preface 1.

41 Ibid., qtd. Chen, "Zhongguo dianying meixue de zai renshi," 206–207.

42 Hou, *Yingxi juben zuofa,* 48–49; Chen, "Zhongguo dianying meixue de zai renshi," 206–07.

43 Hou, *Yingxi juben zuofa,*1–2 and 15–23.

44 Ibid., 2–3.

45 For the impact of German philosophy on the pluralistic idea of life debated among Chinese intellectuals during the Republican period, see Lydia Liu, "Life as Form: How Biomimesis Encountered Buddhism in Lu Xun," *The Journal of Asian Studies* 68, no. 1 (February 1, 2009): 21–54; see also Xiaoqing Lin, "Historicizing Subjective Reality: Rewriting History in Early Republican China," *Modern China* 25, no. 1 (January 1999): 3–43.

46 Chen, "Zhongguo dianying meixue de zai renshi," 217–18.

47 Ibid., 209.

48 Lagesse, "Bazin and the Politics of Realism in Mainland China," 317.

49 Gu, "Fakanci," 11.

50 Hou, *Yingxi juben zuofa,* 2.

51 Ibid., 3–4 and 19.

52 Gu, "Fakanci," 7.

53 Ibid.

54 Compare my reading with Zhang Zhen's observation that if we focus on the other parts of Gu's arguments, we get a much more materialistic, educational, and disciplinary notion of cinema. See Zhang, *Amorous History of the Silver Screen,* 134–35.

55 Gu, "Fakanci," 7.

56 Ibid.

57 Ibid., 8–10.

58 Wen C. Fong, "Why Chinese Painting Is History," *The Art Bulletin* 85, no. 2 (June 2003): 258–80.

59 Andrew, "The Core and the Flow of Film Studies," 891–92; Elsaesser, "A Bazinian Half-Century," 4–5.

60 Andrew, *What Cinema Is!,* 9.

61 Ibid., 12–13.

62 Sartre, *Imaginary,* 17–18 and 20.

63 Andrew, *What Cinema Is!,* 13.

64 Hou, *Yingxi juben zuofa,* 5.

65 Ibid., 2–5.

66 Agamben, "Absolute Immanence," 229.

67 See, for example, Baudrillard, *Simulacra and Simulation,* 6; *Transparency of Evil,* 4; Sobchack, "The Scene of the Screen," 83–106; see also Gilberto Perez, *The Material Ghost: Films and Their Medium* (Baltimore: Johns Hopkins University Press, 1998).

68 Brown, "Man without a Movie Camera," 66–85.

69 Elsaesser, "The Bazinian Half-Century," 7–8.

70 Sartre, *Imaginary,* 75–77.

71 Bazin, "Death Every Afternoon," 30.

72 Gilles Deleuze, *Cinema 1: The Movement-Image* (1983), trans. Hugh Tomlinson and Barbara Habberjam (Minneapolis: University of Minnesota Press, 1986), 1–11.

73 Ibid., 87–122.

74 Agamben, *The Time That Remains: A Commentary on the Letter to the Romans* (2000), trans. Patricia Dailey (Stanford, Calif.: Stanford University Press, 2005), 59–87.

75 Gu, "Fakanci," 10.

76 Hou, *Yingxi juben zuofa,* 7.

77 See, for example, Lev Manovich, *The Language of New Media* (Cambridge, Mass.: MIT Press, 2001).

78 Sobchack, "Scene of the Screen," 83–106; Rodowick, *Virtual Life of Film.*

79 P.W. Singer, *Wired for War: The Robotics Revolution and Conflict in the Twenty-First Century* (New York: Penguin Press, 2009).

2. Cinema of Thought

1 I put the term "left-wing" within quotation marks here to indicate that its historical definition is debatable.

2 See Mu Shiying, "Dangjin dianying piping jiantao (yingping)" [Contemporary film criticisms: a reevaluation (film criticism)], *Furen huabao* [Women pictorial], no. 31 (August 1935): 7–8; see also Cheng, Li and Xing, *Zhongguo dianying fazhan shi,* 1:200–03, 271–72, and 413–20.

3 Hu, *Projecting a Nation,* 79–83, 90–97, and 109–13; Laikwan Pang, *Building a New China in Cinema: The Chinese Left-Wing Cinema Movement: 1932–1937* (Lanham: Rowman & Littlefield Publishers, 2002), 131–41; Vivian Shen, *Origins of Left-Wing Cinema in China, 1932–37* (New York: Routledge, 2005).

4 Huang, "Yingxing yingpian yu ruanxing yingpian," 3.

5 Ibid.; Liu, "Daoyan jianta le Zhongguo dianying" [Our directors stepped upon Chinese cinema], in *Furen huabao,* no. 31 (August 1935): 4–6; "Zhongguo dianying miaoxie de shendu wenti," 2–3; Mu, "Dangjin dianying piping jiantao," 8; Wang Chenwu, "Yintan xiaozhan" [A little dip into the cinematic alter], *Lianhua huabao* [UPS pictorial] 8, nos. 5–6 (1937): 4–5.

6 Fang Zhi, "Zhongyang dianying shiye gaikuang" [An overview of Central's film business], in *Zhongguo dianying nianjian: 1934* [China film year book: 1934], ed. Zhongguo jiaoyu dianying xiehui (National Educational Cinematographic Society of China or NECSC) (Beijing: China Radio and Television Publishing House, 2008), 555–56.

7 Matthew Johnson, "International and Wartime Origins of the Propaganda State: The Motion Picture in China: 1897–1955" (Ph.D. thesis, University of San Diego, 2008), 83–156.

8 See the "Zhongguo dianying xingzheng" section in *Zhongguo dianying nianjian,* 555–89.

9 Zhang, *Chinese National Cinema,* 50.

10 The executive board of the UPS included Hong Kong businessman Robert Hotung (1862–1956), former Premier of the Republic of China (in office 1913–14, during the Presidency of Yuan Shikai, 1913–15) and prominent politician Xiong Xiling (1867–1937), wife of Zhang Xueliang (1901–2001), Yu Fengzhi (1897–1990), as well as other businessmen, judges, and diplomats; see "Lianhua dashi ji" ["UPS Events"] in *Lianhua nianjian: Minguo 22–24 nian* [*UPS Year Book: 1933–34*] (Shanghai: United Photoplay Service, 1935), 12–18; Zhong Baoxian (Chung Po-yin), *Xianggang yingshi ye bainian* [*Hoenggong jingsijip baaknin* or One hundred years of Hong Kong film and television industry] (Hong Kong: Joint Publishing, 2007), 60–64; Johnson, "International and Wartime Origins of the Propaganda State," 112.

11 "Lianhua dashi ji," 12–18.

12 "Guonei ge gongsi chupin shuliang tongjibiao" [Total number of films produced by domestic companies], in *UPS Year Book: 1933–34,* no page.

13 Cheng, Li and Xing, *Zhongguo dianying fazhan shi,* 1:179–83; "Mingxing Gongsi shi'er nian jingli shi" [History of the twelve-year experiences of the Star Film Company], in NECSC, ed., *Zhongguo dianying nianjian,* 906.

14 Cheng, Li and Xing, *Zhongguo dianying fazhan shi,* 1:183–85 and 201.

15 Chen Gongbo (Ch'en Kung-po), "Muqian zenyang jianshe guojia ziben" [How do we build up our national capital now?] (1928), *Chen Gongbo xiansheng wenji* [Anthology of essays written by Master Ch'en Kung-po] (Hong Kong: Yuandong tushu gongsi or Jyundung tousyu gungsi, 1967), 39–66; Margherita Zanasi, "Chen Gongbo and the Construction of a Modern Nation in 1930s China," in *Nation Work: Asian Elites and National Identities,* eds. Timothy Brook and André Schmid (Ann Arbor: The University of Michigan Press, 2000), 125–58.

16 Jiang Jieshi (Chiang Kai-shek), *Xin shenghuo yundong yaoyi* [The principles of the New Life Movement] (1939) (Nanchang: Zhongguo Guomindang, Zhongyang zhixing weiyuanhui, Xunlian weiyuanhui, 1940), 32.

17 Ibid.

18 Zhang, *Amorous History of the Silver Screen,* 267–79; Hansen, "Fallen Women, Rising Stars, New Horizons: Shanghai Silent Film as Vernacular Modernism," *Film Quarterly* 54, no. 1 (Fall 2000): 15. Variations of this trope are discussed in Chris Berry and Mary Farquhar, *China on Screen* (New York: Columbia University Press, 2006), 108–34; Hu, *Projecting a Nation,* 75–113; Pang, *Building a New China in Cinema,* 131–41; Paul Pickowicz, "The Theme of Spiritual Pollution in Chinese Films of the 1930s," *Modern China* 17, no. 1 (January 1991): 48–52; Xiao, "Constructing a New National Culture," 198; Zhang, "Prostitution and Urban Imagination: Negotiating the Public and the Private in Chinese Films of the 1930s," in Zhang, ed., *Cinema and Urban Culture in Shanghai,* 160–82.

19 "Mingxing Gongsi shi'er nian jingli shi," 906; Cai Dengshan, "*Tixiao yinyuan* nao shuangbao de neimu" [Behind the double production of *Fate in Tears and Laughter*], in PChome online, http://news.pchome.com.tw/magazine/print/cl/unitas/4952/1304179200586710150 06.htm.

20 Cheng, Li and Xing, *Zhongguo dianying fazahn shi,* 1:200–03.

21 Mu, "Dangjin dianying piping jiantao," 8.

22 Liu, *The Clash of Empire*, 11–12.

23 Iwasaki, "Xiandai," 1–33.

24 Iwasaki, *Eiga to shihon shugi*, 97–124.

25 Gerow, *A Page of Madness: Cinema and Modernity in 1920s Japan* (Ann Arbor: Center for Japanese Studies, University of Michigan, 2008), 100–01; Nornes, *Japanese Documentary Film: The Meiji Era through Hiroshima* (Minneapolis: University of Minnesota Press, 2003), 19–47 and 125–30.

26 Iwasaki, "Xiandai," 1; Iwasaki, *Eiga to shihon shugi*, 97.

27 Iwasaki, "Xiandai," 5–7; Iwasaki, *Eiga to shihon shugi*, 102–03.

28 Iwasaki, "Xiandai," 6–7; Iwasaki, *Eiga to shihon shugi*, 102–03.

29 Iwasaki, "Xiandai," 7; Iwasaki, *Eiga to shihon shugi*, 103.

30 Aono, "Shizen seichō to mokudeki ishiki," pts. 1 and 2.

31 Lenin, *What Is to Be Done?*, 16–31.

32 Ibid., 17; Lenin's emphasis.

33 Ibid., 7.

34 Aono, "Shizen seichō to mokudeki ishiki,"pt. 1, no page.

35 Aono, "Shizen seichō to mokudeki ishiki," pt. 2, no page.

36 Iwasaki, "Xiandai," 19; Iwasaki, *Eiga to shihon shugi*, 116.

37 Lu Xun, "Yizhe fuji," 28.

38 Ibid., 29.

39 Ibid., 30–31.

40 "Dianying gonghui zhi Fan Pengke han" [Letter to Douglas Fairbanks by the Shanghai Film Union], in *Shen bao* [*Shun Po* or *Shanghai News*], December 19, 1929, 15. Quoted in Lu Xun, 31–32.

41 Lu Xun, "Yizhe fuji," 33.

42 If we wish to push this question to the neo-Lacanian register, the political irony that Lu Xun points out is very close to Slavoj Žižek's recent notion of "believing through the Other," in which the subaltern assigns its belief (about the self) to the Other, despite its knowledge of itself that is contradictory to the Other's belief. See Žižek, "The Interpassive Subject" (lecture, Traverses series, Centre Georges Pompidou, 1988), http://www.lacan.com/zizek-pompidou.htm.

43 Liu Na'ou, "Zhongguo dianying miaoxie de shendu wenti," 2.

44 Huang, "Yingxing yingpian yu ruanxing yingpian," 3; Mu, "Dangjin dianying piping jiantao," 8.

45 Jean-Louis Baudry, "The Apparatus" (1975), trans. Jean Andrews and Bertrand Augst, *Camera Obscura* 1, no. 1 (Fall 1976): 120 and 123; "Ideological Effects of the Basic Cinematographic Apparatus," trans. Alan Williams, *Film Quarterly* 28, no. 2 (Winter 1974–1975): 40. Jean-Louis Comolli and Jean Narboni, "Cinema/Ideology/Criticism," in *Movies and Methods: An Anthology*, ed. Bill Nichols (Berkeley: University of California Press, 1976), 1:22–30.

46 Shen Xiling, "Zhongguo dianying zhi weiji yu xin lujing," 1–2.

47 Ibid., 1.

48 Ibid., 2.

49 Lenin, *Materialism and Empirio-Criticism*, trans. David Kvitko (New York:

International Publisher, 1927); David B. Myers, "Marx's Concept of Truth: A Kantian Interpretation," *Canadian Journal of Philosophy* 7, no. 2 (June 1977): 315–26.

50 Sergei Eisenstein, "The Cinematographic Principle and the Ideogram," in *Film Form: Essays in Film Theory,* ed. and trans. Jay Leyda (1949; repr., San Diego: Harcourt Brace Jovanovich, 1977), 28–44; "Montage of Attractions, An Essay," in *The Film Sense,* trans. and ed. Leyda (1942; repr., San Diego: Harcourt Brace Jovanovich, 1975), 230–32; Dziga Vertov, "From the History of the Kinoks," in *Kino-Eye: The Writings of Dziga Vertov,* trans. Kevin O'Brien, ed. Annette Michelson (Berkeley: University of California Press, 1984), 94; "Kinoks: A Revolution," in Michelson, ed., *Kino-Eye,* 17; "WE: Variant of a Manifesto" (1919), in Michelson, ed., *Kino-Eye,* 7. For an interpretation of Vertov's notion of "life caught unaware," see Yuri Tsivian, commentary, *Man with the Movie Camera,* directed by Vertov (1929; Chatsworth: Image Entertainment, 2002), DVD.

51 *Xiyuan zazhi* [*Heijyun zaapzi* or Movie theater magazine], no. 6 (1932), back cover. For a Chinese translation of Pudovkin's works, see, for example, Tian Shi, trans., "Yanyuan de gongzuo: yinmu yu mutai" [The work of an actor: screen and stage], *Modern Screen* 1, no. 6 (December 1, 1933): 4–5. Most translations of Pudvokin's works in China are no longer extant, several of them are referenced in Zheng Junli, "Zailun yanji" [Again, on the techniques of performance], prt. 1, *Lianhua huabao* 5, no. 9 (May 1, 1935): 12; prt. 4, *Lianhua huabao* 6, no. 2 (July 16, 1935): 12; prt. 5, *Lianhua huabao* 6, no. 4 (August 16, 1935): 13 and 16.

52 Pudovkin, "From *Film Technique* [On Editing]" (1926), trans. Ivor Montagu, in *Film Theory and Criticism,* eds. Leo Braudy and Marshall Cohen, 6th ed. (New York: Oxford University Press, 2004), 7.

53 Ibid., 11–12.

54 Mu, "Dangjin dianying piping jiantao," 7.

55 Zheng, "Ruhe zoushang qianjin zhi lu?," 28.

56 Huang, "Yingxing dianying yu ruanxing dianying," 3.

57 Zheng, "Ruhe zoushang qianjin zhi lu?," 28.

58 Ibid., 29.

59 Timothy Brook, "Capitalism and the Writing of Modern History in China," in *China and Historical Capitalism: Genealogies of Sinological Knowledge,* ed. Brook (Cambridge, UK: Cambridge University Press, 1999), 149–50.

60 Zheng, "Ruhe zoushang qianjin zhi lu?,"30.

61 Wang, "Zhongguo dianying zhi lu (shang)," 48.

62 Iwasaki, *Eiga to shihon shugi,* 3–33, translated by Yi Wen as "Dianying yu ziben zhuyi" [Cinema and capitalism], *Mingxing yuebao* 1, no. 2 (June 1, 1933): 8–13.

63 Wang, "Zhongguo dianying zhi lu (shang)," 48–49.

64 Iwasaki, *Eiga to shihon shugi,* quoted in ibid., 49.

65 Wang, "Zhongguo dianying zhi lu (shang)," 50.

66 Zheng, "Ruhe zoushang qianjin zhi lu?," 30.

67 Zhang, "Chuanshengtong li," 1:135–36.

68 Zheng, "Dianying zuiyan," 20–21.

69 Ibid., 23–24.

70 The term "petite urbanite" is generally understood to refer to salaried urban dwellers, who may or may not own property, and are indifferent to the larger semicolonial conditions in which they live.

71 Zheng, "Dianying zuiyan," 24–25.

72 The term "imaginary solution" was coined by Thomas Elsaesser. It describes the process in which Hollywood cinema constructs a narrative to negotiate actual sociopolitical problems, with a denouement that often provides "imaginary" solutions so that the spectators will believe that the "real" problem that the film tries to negotiate can be, or even has been, resolved. See Elsaesser, *Fassbinder's Germany: History, Identity, Subject* (Amsterdam: Amsterdam University Press, 1994), 199.

73 Wang, "Zhongguo dianying zhi lu (shang)," 51–52.

74 A Ying, "Lun Zhongguo dianying wenhua yundong," 12–18. For a discussion on *Daybreak,* see Victor Fan, "The Cinema of Sun Yu: Ice Cream for the Eye . . . but with a *Homo sacer," Journal of Chinese Cinemas* 5, no. 3 (November 2011): 233–40.

75 A Ying, "Lun Zhongguo dianying wenhua yundong," 13.

76 "Dianying faze zhi guiding" [Film regulations], in *UPS Year Book,* 63; see also Hu, *Projecting a Nation,* 87–88.

77 A Ying, "Lun Zhongguo dianying wenhua yundong," 13.

78 Ibid.

79 Zanasi, *Saving the Nation: Economic Modernity in Republican China* (Chicago: University of Chicago Press, 2006).

80 A Ying, "Lun Zhongguo dianying wenhua yundong,"14.

81 Ibid., 17–18.

82 Pudovkin, "From *Film Technique* [On Editing]," 7.

83 Tian Shi, trans., "Yanyuan de gongzuo: yinmu yu mutai," 4–5; Moussinac's theory is discussed in Liu, "Dianying jiezou jianlun," 1–2.

84 Jessica Ka Yee Chan, "Translating 'Montage': The Discreet Attractions of Soviet Montage for Chinese Revolutionary Cinema," *Journal of Chinese Cinemas* 5, no. 3 (November 2011): 197–218.

85 Zheng Junli, "Zailun yanji," pt. 5, 16.

86 Baudry, "Ideological Effects of the Basic Cinematographic Apparatus," 40–43.

87 Ibid., 44; Baudry's emphasis.

88 Ibid., 44–46.

89 Baudry, "Apparatus," 120 and 123; Baudry's emphasis.

90 Fan Yufei, "Dianying de tezhi" [The special quality of cinema], *Qingqing* [*Chin Chin*], no. 25 (1939): 18.

91 Deleuze, *Cinema 2,* 158.

92 Ibid., 163, Deleuze's emphasis.

93 Ibid., 158.

94 Pier Paolo Pasolini, "Cinema of Poetry," trans. Bill Nichols from the French version, trans. Marianne de Vettimo and Jacques Bontemps, in *Movies and Methods,* ed. Nichols (Berkeley: University of California Press, 1976) 1:544.

95 Ibid., 1:544–45, 548.

96 Henri Bergson, *The Creative Mind: An Introduction to Metaphysics,* trans. Ma-belle L.

Adison (New York: Carol Publishing Group, 1992), 118, quoted in David Rodowick, *Gilles Deleuze's Time Machine* (1997; repr., Durham, N.C.: Duke University Press, 2003), 124.

97 Rodowick, *Gilles Deleuze's Time Machine,* 124, Rodowick's emphasis.

98 Deleuze, *Cinema 2,* 81.

99 Rodowick, *Gilles Deleuze's Time Machine,* 82.

100 Deleuze, *Cinema 2,* 98.

101 Agamben, *The Time that Remains,* 29–32.

102 Zheng, "Dianying zuiyan," 21.

103 Deleuze, *Cinema 2,* 98.

3. Soft Film Theory

1 Huang, "Yingxing yingpian yu ruanxing yingpian," 3. The term *xianshi* is usually translated as reality. In chapter 2, I argued that the term is in fact composed of two words, *xian* (presence) and *shi* (concreteness). Hence philosophically, the term *xianshi* can be understood as presence and concreteness.

2 Liu, "Zhongguo dianying miaoxie de shendu wenti," 3.

3 See the film-related articles in *Chin Chin* 1, nos. 2 to 11, no. 7 (1933–39); *Lianyou* [*Good Companion*] 1, nos. 1 to 26, no. 172 (1926–45); *Linglong* [*Ling Lung*], nos. 1–298 (1931–37); *Lianhua huabao* 5, nos. 4 to 7, no. 8 (1935–36).

4 See *Diantong banyue huabao* [*Denton Gazette: Semi-Monthly Pictorial*], nos. 1–13 (May–November 1935).

5 Zhang, *Amorous History of the Silver Screen,* 244–97.

6 Cheng, Li and Xing, *Zhongguo dianying fazhan shi,* 1:395–412, 1:494–501, and 2:94–118.

7 Fan, "Cinema of Sun Yu," 220–21.

8 The term "life-process" originally came from Marx, *The German Ideology* (Amherst, N.Y.: Prometheus Books, 1998).

9 Lothar Ledderose, *Ten Thousand Things: Module and Mass Production in Chinese Art* (Princeton, N.J.: Princeton University Press, 1998), 7; Ledderose's emphasis.

10 Liu, "Life as Form," 24.

11 Ibid., 22.

12 Liu, "Life as Form," 22; Susan Brownell, *Training the Body for China: Sports in the Moral Order of the People's Republic* (Chicago: University of Chicago Press, 1995), 44–45; Liu Dong, "Yan Fu's Translation of *On Liberty* by John S. Mill" (unpublished manuscript, December 2009); Benjamin Schwartz, *In Search of Wealth and Power: Yen Fu and the West* (Cambridge, Mass.: The Belknap Press of Harvard University Press, 1964), 15; Hoyt Cleveland Tillman, "Yan Fu's Utilitarianism in Chinese Perspective," in Paul A. Cohen and Merle Goldman, eds., *Ideas across Cultures: Essays on Chinese Thought in Honor of Benjamin I. Schwartz* (Cambridge, Mass.: Harvard University Asia Center, 1990), 63–84.

13 Yan Fu, *Tianyan lun* [Discussion on natural evolution, 1896–98] (Beijing: Zhongguo qingnian chubanshe, 2009), a translation of Thomas Huxley, "Evolution and Ethics," in *"Evolution and Ethics" and Other Essays,* ed. Eastbourne Hodeslea (1893; repr.,

New York: D. Appleton and Company, 1902), 46–116; *Qunji quanjie lun* [On the boundaries between social and individual rights, 1903], in *Yan yi mingzhu congkan* [Series of translations of famous works by Yan Fu], vol. 4 (Shanghai: Shanghai shangwu yinshuguan, 1931), translation of John Stuart Mill, *On Liberty* (1859; repr., London: Longmans, Green, Reader, and Dyer, 1869); *Qunxue yiyan* [On the study of the collective, 1903], in *Yan yi mingzhu congkan,* vol. 6, a translation of Herbert Spencer, *Principles of Sociology* (1864; repr., New York: D. Appleton and Company, 1898).

14 Yan, "Yuan qiang" [On the origin of strength], *Zhi bao,* March 4, 1895, 1.

15 Yan, *Tianyan lun,* 96 and 98.

16 Schwartz, *In Search of Wealth and Power,* 15.

17 Liu, "Yan Fu's Translation of *On Liberty* by John S. Mill," 2.

18 For an interpretation of this concept in pre-Warring States China, see, for example, Michael Puett, *To Become a God: Cosmology, Sacrifice, and Self-Divinization in Early China* (Cambridge, Mass.: Harvard University Asia Center for the Harvard-Yenching Institute, 2002), 289–315.

19 Zhou Zuoren, "Humane Literature," trans. Ernst Wolfe, in *Modern Chinese Literary Thought: Writing on Literature, 1893–1945,* ed. Kirk A. Denton (Stanford, Calif.: Stanford University Press, 1996), 153, quoted in Liu, "Life as Form," 26.

20 For the distinction between *zoë* and *bios* in the pre-classical European context, see Agamben, *Homo Sacer: Sovereign Power and Bare Life* (1995), trans. Daniel Heller-Roazen (Stanford, Calif.: Stanford University Press, 1998), 1–2.

21 Liu, "Life as Form," 50–51.

22 Zhang Taiyan, "Qiwulun shi" (1908) [On equalizing things: an exegesis], in *Zhang Taiyan quanji* [Complete collection of works by Zhang Taiyan] (Shanghai: Shanghai renmin chubanshe, 1980), 6:4.

23 Zhang, "Qiwulun shi," 6:5–6. For a study of Zhang Taiyan's thoughts, see, for example, Su Meiwen, *Zhang Taiyan* Qiwulun shi *zhi yanjiu* [A study of Zhang Taiyan's *On Equalizing Things*] (Taipei: Hua-Mu-Lan Culture Publishing, 2007).

24 Liu, "Life as Form," 41 and 50.

25 Nan Huaichin, *Jingang jing shuo shenme,* 62–83.

26 Liu, "Life as Form," 41; Zhang Junmai, Ding Wenjiang, et al., *Kexue yu renshengguan* [Science and *Weltsschauung*] (Taipei: Wenxue chubanshe, 1977), 94–135; Bergson, *Creative Evolution* (1907), trans. Arthur Mitchell (Mineola: Dover Publications, 1998), 87, Bergson's emphasis.

27 Ch'en, "Muqian zenyang jianshe guojia ziben," 39–66.

28 Ibid.; Zanasi, "Chen Gongbo and the Construction of a Modern Nation in 1930s China," 125–58.

29 Chiang, *Xin shenghuo yundong yaoyi,* 32.

30 Fan, "The Cinema of Sun Yu," 223–34.

31 Delluc, "Le Beauté," 2.

32 Louis Charney, "In a Moment: Film and the Philosophy of Modernity," in *Cinema and the Invention of Modern Life,* ed. by Charney and Vanessa R. Schwartz (Berkeley: University of California Press, 1995), 279–96. Charney argues that the French

critics' celebration of the *photogénie* is symptomatic of their attempt to come to terms with a "fleeting, fragmentary, and shocking" art form while trying to hold onto the more traditional modes of aesthetic experience in painting and sculpture (281), quoted in Tracy Cox, "Consuming Distractions in *Prix de beauté*," *Camera Obscura* 17, no. 2 (2002): 63.

33 Epstein, "Le Cinématographe vu de l'Etna," 288.

34 Ibid., 291.

35 Michael Cowan, "The Heart Machine: 'Rhythm' and Body in Weimar Film and Fritz Lang's *Metropolis*," *Modernism/Modernity* 14, no. 2 (2007): 231.

36 Ibid., 231–32.

37 Siegfried Kracauer, "The Mass Ornament," 76–78 and 83–84; Temenuga Trifonova, "From Distraction to Indeterminacy to Distraction: Kracauer and Contemporary Film Realist Discourse," in *European Film Theory*, ed. Trifonova (New York: Routledge, 2009), 271–85.

38 Cowan, "The Heart Machine," 240.

39 Thomas LaMarre, "The Biopolitics of Companion Species: Wartime Animation and Multi-Ethnic Nationalism," in *The Politics of Culture: Around the Work of Naoki Sakai*, eds. Richard F. Calichman and John Kamjun Kim (London: Routledge, 2010), 72–90.

40 "*Huashen guniang* benshi" [*Tomboy*: synopsis] (Shanghai: Guolian dianyingyuan, 1938); Shen, *Origins of Left-Wing Cinema in China*, 4; Zhang, *Amorous History of the Silver Screen*, 284–90.

41 See, for example, Shen Xiling, "Yijiusan'er nian Zhongguo dianyingjie de zong jiezhang yu yijiusansan nian de xin qiwang" [Review of the Chinese film industry in 1932 and my expectations for 1933], *Modern Screen* 1, no. 1 (1933): 7–8; Cheng Bugao, "*Kuangliu*" [*Raging Torrent*], *Modern Screen* 1, no. 1 (1933): 22.

42 "Lianhua diyipian xuanyan" ["The First UPS Manifesto"], in *UPS Year Book*, 19.

43 "Wu Bangfan xiegan qiyi: Lianhua daju zhuchi yiren" [The uprising of Wu Bangfan: the changing face of UPS' executive board], *Diansheng zhoukan* [*Movietone*] 5, no. 2 (January 10, 1936): 46.

44 "Lianhua dashi ji," 12–18.

45 Huang, "*Xiandai dianying* yu Zhongguo dianyingjie," 1.

46 Ibid.

47 Liu, "Écranesque," 1.

48 Riciotto Canudo, "The Birth of a Sixth Art" (1911), in Abel, ed., *French Film Theory and Criticism*, 1:61–62.

49 Liu, "Écranesque," 1.

50 Another European example of this line of thinking can be seen in Guido Seeber and Julius Pinschewer's *Kipho* film. See Cowan, "Rhythm, Advertising, and the Filmic Avant-Garde in Weimar," *October*, no. 131 (Winter 2010): 23–50.

51 Liu, "Écranesque," 1.

52 Liu, "Dianying jiezou jianlun," 1–2.

53 Fan, "Cinema of Sun Yu," 228; René Clair, "Rhythm" (1925), in Abel, ed., *French Film Theory and Criticism*, 1:268–70.

54 Fan, "Cinema of Sun Yu," 228; Léon Moussinac, *Le cinéma soviètique* (Paris: Gallimard, 1928).

55 Moussinac, "On Cinegraphic Rhythm" (1923), in Abel, ed., *French Film Theory and Criticism*, 1:281, Moussinac's emphasis.

56 Liu, "Dianying jiezou jianlun," 2.

57 Ibid.

58 Zhang, *Amorous History of the Silver Screen*, 284–90.

59 Liu, "Zhongguo dianying miaoxie de shendu wenti," 2.

60 Ibid.; Fan, "Cinema of Sun Yu," 230.

61 Ibid., 230, n. 6.

62 Ibid., 230.

63 However, Liu is not criticizing only the Star productions here. Rather, he had in mind two UPS productions: *Chengshi zhi ye* [*Night in the City*, Fey Mou, 1933] and *Duhui de zaochen* [*Dawn over the Metropolis*, Tsai Chu-sang, 1933]. Liu, "Zhongguo dianying miaoxie de shendu wenti," 2–3.

64 Liu, "Guanyu zuozhe de taidu," 1.

65 Arthur Schopenhauer, *The World as Will and Presentation* (1818–19), trans. Richard E. Aquila (New York: Pearson Longman, 2008), 1:31, Book 1, §1.

66 Bazin, "Ontologie de l'image photographique," 14.

67 Fan, "Cinema of Sun Yu," 231. The phrase "let the being of the object unconcealed" is paraphrased from Martin Heidegger, *Being and Time: A Translation of* Sein und Zeit (1953), trans. Joan Stambaugh (Albany: State University of New York Press, 1996). According to him, "letting be" means to "discover something that is already a 'being' in its handiness and thus let it be encountered as the being of this being." In his footnote, he adds, "Thus to let it presence in its truth" (79).

68 Bazin, "De la politique des auteurs," in *Cahiers du cinéma*, no. 70 (1957): 2–11.

69 For the concept of preindividuation, see the explanation of Simondon's philosophy in Combes, *Gilbert Simondon and the Philosophy of the Transindividual*, 28–33.

70 Deleuze, "Immanence: A Life" (1995), in *Pure Immanence: Essays on a Life*, trans. Anne Boyman (New York: Zone Book, 2005), 26–27.

71 Huang, "Yingxing yingpian yu ruanxing yingpian," 3; Fan, "Cinema of Sun Yu," 229.

72 Huang, "Yingxing yingpian yu ruanxing yingpian," 3.

73 This idea was suggested by Thomas LaMarre in a private conversation we had in 2011.

74 Kant, *Critique of the Power of Judgment*, §1, 5:203, 89, Kant's emphasis.

75 Ibid., §17, 5:236, 120.

76 Ibid., §19–20, 5:237–38, 121–22.

77 Ibid., §84, 5:435, 302, Kant's emphasis.

78 Wang, "Guya zai meixue shang de weizhi" [The position of *guya* in aesthetics] (1907), in *Wang Guowei yishu* [Essays left by Wang Guowei] (Shanghai: Shanghai guji shudian, 1983), 3:620–21; for a discussion of this essay, see Luo Gang, "Wang Guowei de guya shuo yu Zhong Xi shixue chuantong" [Wang Guowei's theory of *guya* and the poetic traditions of China and the West] (December 30, 2013), http://www.douban.com/group/topic/47633124/.

79 Wang, *Renjian cihua, Renjian cihua zhu ping* [On human literature; annotations and commentaries on *On Human Literature*] (Nanjing: Jiangsu guji chubanshe, 2002), 213.

80 See, *Dao yuan* [On the origin of *dao*], in *Mawangdui Hanmu boshu* [Silk scrolls from the Han tombs of Mawangdui], ed. Huang Ti (Beijing: Wenwu chubanshe, 1980), 87–88.

81 Nan, *Jinggang jing shuo shenme?*, 50–53 and 93–97.

82 Wang, *Renjian cihua* (1926 edition), chapter 6; the poem was originally from Yan Shu, "Die lian hua" [A butterfly loves its flower].

83 Ibid.; the poem was taken from Liu Yong or Ouyang Xiu, "Die lian hua."

84 Ibid.; the poem was extracted from Xin Qizhi, "Qingyu'an, yuanxi" [Desk of green jade; new year's eve].

85 Wang, *Renjian cihua, renjian cihua zhuping*, 281.

86 Nan, *Jinggang jing shuo shenme?*, 17.

87 Baruch Spinoza, *Ethics* (1677), trans. and ed. G. H. R. Parkinson (Oxford: Oxford University Press, 2000), Propositions 1–8, 76–78, Scholium 2, 80–81, Part 3, Propositions 6 and 8, 171–72, Part 2, Proposition 19, 135, and Part 5, 287–318. For a detailed analysis and discussion of Spinoza's *Ethics*, see Deleuze, *Expressionism in Philosophy: Spinoza*, trans. Martin Joughin (New York: Zone Book, 1990).

88 Deleuze, *Expressionism in Philosophy*, 67, quoted in Agamben, "Absolute Immanence," 226, Deleuze's emphasis.

89 Agamben, "Absolute Immanence," 234–235; the original discussion can be found in Spinoza, *Opera*, ed. Carl Gebhardt (Heidelberg: C. Winter, 1925), 3:361.

90 Agamben, "Absolute Immanence," 236, Agamben's emphasis.

91 Ibid., 238–39.

92 Foucault, *Histoire de la sexualité 1. La volonté de savoir [History of Sexuality: The Will to Knowledge]* (1976; repr., Paris: Gallimard, 2002), 178; this is also the foundation of Agamben's thesis in *Homo Sacer.*

93 Deleuze, *Cinema 2*, 68–69, Deleuze's emphasis.

4. Fey Mou

1 Daruvala, "The Aesthetics and Moral Politics of Fei Mu's *Spring in a Small Town*," 173; Yingjin Zhang, *Chinese National Cinema*, 81 and 101; see also Chen Mo, *Liuying chunmeng • Fei Mu dianying lungao* [Flying warbler in a springtime dream: on the cinema of Fei Mu] (Beijing: Zhongguo dianying chubanshe, 2000), 3.

2 Wong Ain-ling, "Introduction: The Vicissitudes of History," in Wong, ed., *Fei Mu's* Confucius, 90.

3 Ibid.

4 In UPS' administrative structure, Wu Xingzai was a senior executive of the Great China Lilium Film Company. He was crucial in supplying the necessary funding when the UPS was in a financial crisis in 1936. And during this crisis, he eventually replaced Lo Ming-yau as UPS's CEO. Wu had always considered Fey Mou a talent whom the UPS had to keep regardless of its financial difficulties. In some ways, Fey's joining Wen Hwa after the war could be regarded as a fulfillment of his con-

tract with the UPS. See "Qianyejie zuzhi yintuan; xiang Lianhua touzi sanshiwan yuan: Tichu tiaojian feichang keke, neibu daquan jun gui tongzhi" [Group formed by bankers invested ¥300,000 in the UPS: with the harsh condition of centralizing control over the studio], *Movietone* 5, no. 27 (July 10, 1936): 647.

5 Fey, "Daoyan • ju zuozhe—xie gei changji" [Director; screenwriter: to production assistants], in Ding, ed., *Bainian Zhongguo dianying lilun wenxuan,* 1:373.

6 See Chen, *Liuying chunmeng,* 3–4.

7 See Wong Ain-ling, ed., *Shiren daoyan: Fei Mu* [Poet-director: Fey Mou] (Hong Kong: Hong Kong Film Critics Society, 1998).

8 Daruvala, "The Aesthetics and Moral Politics of Fei Mu's *Spring in a Small Town,*" 173.

9 Wong, "Introduction," 93.

10 Sam Ho, "Beauty in *Ren,* Poetry in Images: Confucian Aesthetics in *Confucius,*" in Wong, ed., *Fei Mu's* Confucius, 128–29.

11 Ibid.; FitzGerald, *Fragmenting Modernisms,* 169–216; Koo Siu-sun, "Exploring Film as a Literary Form in *Confucius,*" in Wong, ed., *Fei Mu's* Confucius, 118–22.

12 Daruvala, "The Aesthetics and Moral Politics of Fei Mu's *Spring in a Small Town,*" 173.

13 FitzGerald, *Fragmenting Modernisms,* 196–97.

14 Ho, "Beauty in *Ren,* Poetry in Images," 123; Koo, "Exploring Film as a Literary Form in *Confucius,*" 122.

15 Bazin, "An Aesthetic of Reality," 2:26–27.

16 Bazin, "Theater and Cinema," prt. 2, in *What Is Cinema?,* 1:96–98.

17 Deleuze, *Cinema 2,* 1–24.

18 Fey, "'Daoxu fa' yu 'xuanxiang' zuoyong," 1:214–15; "Lue tan 'kongqi,'" 1:216–17.

19 Ho, "Beauty in *Ren,* Poetry in Images," 125.

20 My discussion of *ren* is based on a discussion of the term in Mencius, "Jinxin xia," *juan* 14.1–5.

21 Fey, "'Daoxu fa' yu 'xuanxiang' zuoyong," 1:214.

22 The works of Viktor Shklovsky and Yuri Tynianov were translated and circulated among the Chinese intellectuals during the Republic era. See, for example, Q. S. Tong and Xiaoyi Zhou, "Comparative Literature in China," *CLCWeb: Comparative Literature and Culture* 2, no. 4 (2000), http://dx.doi.org/10.7771/1481-4374.1092. For neoformalism, see Bordwell, *Narration in the Fiction Film,* 51–53 and 150–52; see also Thompson, *Breaking the Glass Armour,* 3–7.

23 Thompson, *Breaking the Glass Armour,* 3–7.

24 Ibid., 3–45.

25 Ibid.; Bordwell, *Narration in the Fiction Film,* 51–53 and 150–52.

26 Metz, "On the Impression of Reality in the Cinema," in *Film Language,* 4, Metz's emphasis.

27 Metz, "The Cinema," 61–91.

28 Metz, "The Cinema: Language or Language System?" (1968), in *Film Language: A Semiotics of the Cinema,* trans. Michael Taylor (Chicago: Chicago University Press, 1974), 67.

29 Roland Barthes wrestles with this problem in "The Photographic Message," "Rhetoric of the Image," and "The Third Meaning," in *Image, Music, Text*, trans. Stephen Heath (New York: The Noonday Press, 1977), 15–68.

30 Metz, "*The Imaginary Signifier*," 259, Metz's emphasis.

31 Thompson, *Breaking the Glass Armour*, 3–7.

32 Bordwell, *Ozu and the Poetics of Cinema* (Princeton, N.J.: Princeton University Press, 1988), 51.

33 Agamben, *The Man without Content* (1994), trans. Georgia Albert (Stanford, Calif.: Stanford University Press, 1999), 68–93.

34 Fey, "'Daoxu fa' yu 'xuanxiang' zuoyong," 1:124.

35 UPS, "*Xiang xuehai* benshi" [Synopsis of *Sea of Fragrant Snow*], 1934.

36 Metz, "*The Imaginary Signifier*," 262–66.

37 See, for example, Jin Zhaozi, *Shiyong Guowen xiuci xue* [Practical poetics of the national language and literature] (Shanghai: Zhonghua shuju, 1934).

38 Ibid.

39 Fey, "'Daoxu fa' yu 'xuanxiang' zuoyong," 1:125.

40 Ibid.

41 Fu Hiu, "Foxue yu kexue duihua de butong lichang" [The different topoi between Buddhist studies and the sciences], in *Foxue yu kexue* [Buddhist studies and the sciences] (2011): 20–31.

42 Bordwell, *Figures Traced in Light: On Cinematic Staging* (Berkeley: University of California Press, 2005), 238.

43 Fey, "Lue tan 'kongqi,'" 1:126–27.

44 Ibid., 1:127.

45 For the details of the suture theory, see Mary Ann Doane, "The Voice in the Cinema: The Articulation of Body and Space" (1980), in Rosen, ed., *Narrative, Apparatus, Ideology*, 335–48; Steven Heath, "Narrative Space" (1976), in Rosen, ed., *Narrative, Apparatus, Ideology*, 379–420; Julia Kristeva, "Ellipsis on Dread and the Specular Seduction" (1975), trans. Kristeva (1979), in Rosen, ed. *Narrative, Apparatus, Ideology*, 236–43; Kaja Silverman, "'Suture' (excerpts)" (1983), in Rosen, ed., *Narrative, Apparatus, Ideology*, 219–35.

46 Grace Fong, *Wu Wenying and the Art of Southern Song Ci Poetry* (Princeton, N.J.: Princeton University Press, 1987), 105.

47 Li Zhongming, "Kang Ri Zhangzheng shiqi Jingju fazhan shilue" [A brief narrative history of the development of the Peking Opera during the Anti-Japanese War], in *Kangzhan shiqi de Zhongguo wenhua* [Chinese culture during the Anti-Japanese War] (Beijing: Renmin chubanshe, 2006).

48 Fey, "Guanyu jiuju dianyinghua de wenti," 1:292.

49 Ibid., 1:192.

50 Ibid.

51 Bazin, "Theater and Cinema," prt 2, 1:96–97.

52 Ibid., 97.

53 Ibid., 99.

54 Aristotle, *De anima*, 417, a 2–5; Agamben, "On Potentiality," 178.

55 Deleuze, *Cinema 2*.

56 Metz, "*Imaginary Signifier*," 266–67.

57 See, for example, "Zheng luan" [Rectifying disorder], in the *Shiliu jing* [Sixteen classics], in Huang Ti, ed., *Mawangdui Hanmu boshu*, 67.

58 Ibid.

59 "Zhongyong" [Doctrine of the mean], in *Li ji yizhu* [Book of rites with translations and annotations], trans. and annotated Yang Tianyu (Shanghai: Shanghai guji chubanshe, 2004), 2:691–713.

60 An explication of the relationship between *qing* and *li* can be seen in the "Yue ji" [Records of music] and "She yi" [Rites of archery] chapters in the *Li ji*, 1:467–508 and 2:833–40.

61 FitzGerald, *Fragmenting Modernisms*, 193.

62 Ho, "Beauty in *Ren*, Poetry in Images," 125.

63 Ibid., 123.

64 Wong, "Introduction," 93. Wong also explains her ideas in her interview in "*Kongfuzi* de meixue tese" [*Hungfuzi* dik meiseot daksik or Some special characteristics in the aesthetics of *Confucius*], special feature in *Confucius*, directed by Fey Mou (1940; Hong Kong: Hong Kong Film Archive, 2012), DVD.

65 Wong, "*Hungfuzi* dik meiseot daksik."

66 Ibid.

67 Koo siu-sun, "Exploring Film as a Literary Form in *Confucius*," in Wong, ed., *Fei Mu's* Confucius, 118–22.

68 Ho, "Beauty in *Ren*, Poetry in Images," 124–28; Tan Jiazhe, *Lunyu yu Zhongguo sixiang yanjiu* [Study of the *Analects* and Chinese thoughts] (Taipei: Tonsan Bookstore, 2005), 252–73.

69 *Lunyu yizhu* [*Analects* with translations and annotations], trans. and annotated Yang Bojun (2009; repr., Beijing: Zhonghua shuju, 2010), 2.

70 *Laozi*, ed. and annotated Zhang Zhen (1989; repr., Changsha: Yuelu shushe, 1991).

71 See, "Jing fa" [Eternal law], in Wong, ed., *Mawangdui Hanmu boshu*, 43.

72 Fey, "Confucius and His Time," in Wong, ed., *Fei Mu's* Confucius, 148.

73 Li Ling, "History and Literature," in Wong, ed., *Fei Mu's* Confucius, 106.

74 See, Žižek, *Enjoy Your Symptom!: Jacques Lacan in Hollywood and Out*, 2nd ed. (New York: Routledge, 2001), 165–86; see also Fan, "The Unanswered Question of *Forrest Gump*," *Screen* 49, no. 4 (Winter 2008): 460–61.

5. Cinema of Ideation, Cinema of Play

1 Mak, *Gwongdung heikek siloek*, 2.

2 Ibid., 1.

3 Liu Ping, *Zhong Ri xiandai yanju jiaoliu tushi* [An illustrated history of the exchange between the Chinese and Japanese theaters] (Beijing: Joint Publishing, 2012), 20–145; Li Jian (Lai Kin), *Xianggang Yueju xulun* [*Hoenggong Jyutkek zeoileon* or A discourse on the Hong Kong Cantonese theater] (Hong Kong: Joint Publishing, 2010), 172–73.

4 Lai, *Hoenggong Jyutkek zeoileon*, 176–77.

5 Ouyang, "Shitan Yueju," 124–30.

6 Lai, *Hoenggong Jyutkek zeoileon*, 173.

7 See, for example, Charles Musser, "Rethinking Early Cinema: Cinema of Attractions and Narrativity," in *The Cinema of Attractions: Reloaded*, ed. Wanda Strauven (Amsterdam: University of Amsterdam Press, 2006), 389–416.

8 Chen Feinong (Chan Feinung), *Yueju liushi nian* [*Jyutkek luksap nin* or Sixty years in the Cantonese theater] (Hong Kong: The Cantonese Opera Research Programme of the Music Department, the Chinese University of Hong Kong, 2007), 155–57; Lai, *Hoenggong Jyutkek zeoileon*, 34–51; Mak, *Gwongdong heikek siloek*, 17; Ouyang, "Shitan Yueju," 150.

9 Lai, *Hoenggong Jyutkek zeoileon*, 179; Li and Zhou, *Zaoqi Xianggang dianying shi*, 33–44.

10 Li and Zhou, *Zaoqi Xianggang dianying shi*, 45–50; Ouyang, "Shitan Yueju," 124–30.

11 Lai, *Hoenggong Jyutkek zeoileon*, 145.

12 Zhiwei Xiao, "Constructing a New National Culture," 184; Ng Kwan-yuk, ed., *Xianggang Xiayu dianying fangzong* [*Hoenggong Haamun dinjing fongzung* or *In Search of the Hong Kong Xiamenese Cinema*] (Hong Kong: Hong Kong Film Archive, 2013); "Xiamen youren choushe, zhuan she Xiayu shengpian gongsi" [Some people in Amoy are setting up a production company specialized in making sound films in the Amoy dialect), *Movietone* 5, no. 35 (September 4, 1936): 884.

13 Both the Queen's Theatre and the Lee Theatre stopped screening silent films by mid-1930. See *Huanghou dianying* [*Wonghau dingjing* or *The Queen's Theatre Gazette*], no. 511 (December 1930): 1; "Xianggang yingtan zhi weilai guan" ["Hoenggong jingtaan zi meiloi gwun" or The future of Hong Kong movie theaters], *Xiyuan zazhi* [*Heijyun zaapzi* or *The Theatre Guide*], no. 2 (February 1, 1932): 11–12; *Zhongyang Xiyuan Shengguang zhoukan* [*Zungyoeng Heijyun Singgwong zauhon* or *Central Theater Weekly*] 1, no. 28 (December 14, 1930).

14 Li and Zhou, *Zaoqi Xianggang dianying shi*, 62–79.

15 Ibid., 83–87.

16 Conversation with Po Fung, Hong Kong Film Archive, summer 2012; Lai, *Hoenggong Jyutkek zeoileon*, 188–89.

17 Yao Dehuai, "'Guifan Putonghua' yu "Dazhong Putonghua'" ["Regulated Putonghua" and "Mass Putonghua"], *Yuwen jianshe tongxun* [*Language Construction News*], no. 57 (October 1998).

18 Xiao, "Constructing a New National Culture," 184.

19 The policy is explicated in "*Tianlun* jiazhi Yingwen shuoming: Lianhua Gongsi chufa liubaiyuan" [English subtitles added to *Song of China*: UPS was fined six hundred yuan], *Movietone* 5, no. 2 (January 10, 1936): 50.

20 Zhi Qing, "Tianyi Gongsi Yueyu youshengpian wenti" [On the sound films of Unique], *Movietone* 3, no. 17 (1934): 327.

21 Xiao, "Constructing a New National Culture," 184–85.

22 Li and Zhou, Zaoqi Xianggang dianying shi, 141–66.

23 Xiao, "Constructing a New National Culture," 184–85; "Guangzhou zhi dianying

jiancha wenti" [On film censorship in Canton], *Movietone* 4, no. 47 (November 22, 1935): 1017.

24 Lai, *Hoenggong Jyutkek zeoileon,* 186.

25 Teemu Ruskola, *Legal Orientalism: China, the United States, and Modern Law* (Cambridge, Mass.: Harvard University Press, 2013), 60–107.

26 These films are available in the Hong Kong Film Archive. See also the *Daguan zazhi* [*Grandview Magazine*] (1936).

27 Lai, *Hoenggong Jyutkek zeoileon,* 188; Li and Zhou, *Zaoqi Xianggang dianying shi,* 95–100; Ouyang, "Shitan Yueju," 126–27.

28 "Xue yu Nanyue Gongsi hezuo guocheng baogao" ["Sit jyu Naamjyut Gungsi hapzok gwocing bougou" or Report on the collaboration between Sit Kok-sin and South China], *Youyou* [*Jaujau*], no. 2 (August 18, 1935): no page.

29 See, for example, "Yueyu pian zhengming yundong" ["Jyutpin zingming wandung" or Cantonese film rectification movement], *Lingxing* [*Ling Sing*] 7, no. 15 (June 27, 1937): no page; Jichen (Chiksan), "Yueyu pian gexin yundong" ["Jyutjyu pin gaaksan wandung" or Cantonese film reform movement], *Yilin* [*Art Lane*], no. 11 (1937): no page.

30 "Shao Zuiweng liangnianlai de xinxie huawei wuyou" ["Siu Zuijung loengninloi dik samhjyut faawai wuyau" or Runje Shaw's two years' worth of work were all gone], *Movietone* 5, no. 33 (August 21, 1936): 826; Ge'an (Kak'on), "Xianggang Tianyi zhipianchang shana cheng zhaotu" or "Hoenggong Tinjat Zaipincong saatnaa sing ziutou" or In an instant, Unique's Hong Kong Studio became a ruin], *Jaujau,* no. 24 (1936): 5; Zhao Zhao (Chiu Chiu), "Yishi yingxiong er jin anzai: Shao Zuiweng zhi chenggong yu shibai jingguo" ["Jatsai jinghung ji gam ngonzoi: Siu Zuijung sing-gung jyu satbaai ginggwo" or The life-long hero is still here: the success and failure of Runje Shaw], *Jaujau,* no. 24 (1936): 6–7.

31 Li and Zhou, *Zaoqi Xianggang dianying shi,* 100–11.

32 Xiao, "Constructing a New National Culture," 185–86.

33 "Qiao Gang shenshang jiaoyu xinwen gejie hezu Huanzhu Yueyupian lianhe hui" ["Kiu Gong sansoeng gaaujuk sanman gokgaai hapzou Wunzo Jyutpin lyunhap wui" or Gentry, businessmen, educators, and journalists in Hong Kong put together the United Association for Rescuing Cantonese Cinema], *Ling Sing* 7, no. 15 (June 26, 1937): 8.

34 Ibid.

35 Lee Fa, "Soeng Ging cinggau Jyutjyu pin likzin Wu jingsoeng ginggwo," 2–4; Xiao, "Constructing a New National Culture," 187–90; Song Jianchao (Sung Kim-chiu), "Yuepian you sannian huanjin shuo" ["Jyutpin yau saamnin wungam syut" or The ban against the Cantonese film may be postponed for another three years], *Art Lane,* no. 9 (July 1937): no page.

36 Chiksan, "Guanyu jinying Yueyu yingpian mianmian guan" ["Guaanjyu gamjing Jyutjyu jingpin minmin gwun" or Different ways to think about the ban against Cantonese cinema], *Art Lane,* no. 3 (April 1937): no page; Lo Ming-yau, "Guonan jinggao tongren" ["Gwoknaan ginggou tungjan" or To comrades: in our national crisis], *Art Lane,* no. 17 (November 1, 1937): no page.

37 Wang Mao (Wong Mau), "Zhonghua minzu yi daole zuihou guantou: Huanan dianyingjie dongyuan qilai!" ["Zungwaa manzuk douliu zuihau gwaantau: Waanaam dinjinggaai dungjyun heiloi" or The Chinese nation is at a critical juncture: let's mobilize the South China film industry!], *Ling Sing* 7, no. 20 (August 22, 1938): 1.

38 "Nanhua dianyingjie zhenzai hui shezhi zhi *Zuihou guantou* zai chongfeng diyixian zhi Nanyue gongzuo suxie" ["Waanaam dinjinggaai zanzoi wui sipzai zi *Zuihau gwaantau* zoi cungfung daijatsin zi Naamjyut gungzok cukse" or *At This Critical Juncture*, a joint production by the South China Filmmakers' War Relief Association: notes from the frontline at the South China Studio], *Nanyue* [*Naamjyut* or *South China*], no. 2 (September 1, 1937): no page.

39 "Yueyu pian zhengming yundong" ["Jyutjyu pin zingming wandung" or Rectification of the Cantonese film movement], *Ling Sing* 7, no. 15 (June 27, 1937): 2; "Dianying qingjie yundong" ["Dinjing cinggit wandung" or Film cleansing movement], *Movietone* 4, no. 41 (October 11, 1935): 1015; Maotu (Maautou), "Suowei yingpian qingjie yundong" ["Sowai jingpin cinggit wandung" or So-called film cleansing movement], *Jaujau*, no. 10 (November 15, 1935): 9.

40 "Pumie shenguaipian! Pumie Hanjian!" ["Pokmit sangwaaipin! Pokmit Hongaan!" or Eliminate the gods and demons film! Eliminate the traitors!], *Ling Sing* 8, no. 14 (August 15, 1938): 1; "Wuhu! Shenguaipian" ["Wufu! Sangwaaipin" or Alas! Gods and demons films!], *Ling Sing* 8, no. 14 (August 15, 1938): 2–3.

41 "Cai Chusheng xiansheng fangwen" ["Coi Cosang sinsaang fongman" or An interview of Tsai Chu-sang], *Ling Sing* 7, no. 28 (December 25, 1937): 20–21.

42 "Wu Chufan tan Yuepian" ["Ng Chofaan taam Jyutpin" or "A Talk on Cantonese Cinema by Ng Cho-fan"], *Zhonglian huabao* [*Zunglyun waabou* or *Union Film Pictorial*], no. 8 (April, 1956): 8–9.

43 Mak, *Gwongdung heikei siloek,* 1.

44 Ibid., 9.

45 Ibid., 1.

46 Ibid., 2.

47 Huang Peijie, *Gongbi renwu hua yanjiu* [A study of the meticulous stroke in portraits] (Lanzhou: Gansu renmin meishu chubanshe, 2003).

48 See, for example, Su Shu, *Weilu shihua* [Poetry talks around a coal burner] (Jinan: Qi Lu shushe, 1997), first published circa seventeenth century.

49 Ibid.

50 Ouyang, "Xuyan" [Introduction], in *Zhongguo xiqu yanjiu ziliao chuji,* 3.

51 Mak, *Gwongdung heikek siloek,* 4–5.

52 Ibid., 4–5.

53 Ibid.

54 Chan, *Jyutkek luksap nin,* 53; Lai, *Hoenggong Jyutkek zeoileon,* 2.

55 Ouyang, "Shitan Yueju," 111.

56 Ibid., 131–32.

57 Chen Shouren (Chan Sau-yan), *Yishi, xinyang, yanju: shengong yueju zai Xianggang* [*Jisik, seongyoeng, jinkek: sangung Jyutkek zoi Hoenggong* or Rites, religion,

and dramatic performance: *sangung Jyutkek* in Hong Kong] (Hong Kong: The Cantonese Opera Research Programme of the Music Department, the Chinese University of Hong Kong, 2008), 55–74.

58 Lin Niantong (Lam Nin-tung), "Wushi niandai Yueyu dianying yanjiu zhong de jige wenti" ["Ngsap nindoi Jyutjyu dinjing jingau zung dik geigo mantai" or Several questions on the studies of the Cantonese cinema of the 1950s], *Daai dakse,* no. 59 (June 9, 1978): 4.

59 See, for example, Jin Bingxing (Kam Bing-hing), "Zhongguo xin dianying de qiwang" ["Zunggwok san dinjing dik keimong" or Hopes for the new Chinese cinema], *The Chinese Student Weekly,* no. 794 (October 6, 1967): 11; Luo Ka (Lo Kar), "Yueyu pian • ganxiang • qiwang" ["Jyutjyu pin • gamsoeng • keimong" or Cantonese cinema: thoughts and expectations], *Daai dakse,* no. 63 (August 18, 1978): 11–12.

60 Lam, "Ngsap nindoi Jyutjyu dinjing jingau zung dik geigo mantai," 47–50.

61 Chan, *Jyutkek luksap nin,* 104–05; Mak, *Gwongdung heikek siloek,* 21–22.

62 Mak, *Gwongdung heikek siloek,* 24–25; Ouyang, "Shitan Yueju," 132–36.

63 See Wang Shaoxia (Wong Siuhap), *Yuequ jiben zhishi* [*Jyutkuk geibun zisik* or Fundamental knowledge of the music in the Cantonese theater] (1999; repr., Hong Kong: Yixuan yueyuan, 2011).

64 Mak, *Gwongdung heikek siloek,* 1 and 23.

65 Wong, *Jyutkuk geibun zisik,* 14–15.

66 Conversation with Po Fung in Hong Kong on July 23, 2013.

67 Pui-Chee Leung, *Nanyin yu Yue'ou zhi yanjiu* [A study of nanyin and yue'ou] (San Francisco: Asian American Studies and School of Ethnic Studies, San Francisco State University, 1988), 24–27 and 146–48.

68 Chan, *Jyutkek luksap nin,* 104–06; Mak, *Gwongdung heikek siloek,* 21–22, qtd. Lai, *Hoenggong Jyutkek zeoileon,* 109–11.

69 Lai, *Hoenggong Jyutkek zeoileon,* 40–48.

70 Mak, *Gwongdung heikek siloek,* 1.

71 Lu Dun (Lo Duen), "Lun biaoyan yishu"["Leon biujin ngaiseot" or On the art of performance], prt. 1, *Art Lane,* no. 44 (December 15, 1938): no page.

72 Ibid.

73 Sit, "Wo de fendou" ["Ngo dik fandau" or My struggle, 1940], in Yeung, ed., *Zan, sin, mei,* 179–82.

74 Chan Fei-nung, "Xue Juexian yanxi jiyou tianfen" ["Sit Goksin jinhei gikjau tinfan" or Sit Kok-sin has an exceptional talent in performance], in Yeung, ed., *Zan, sin, mei,* 43.

75 Ibid.

76 Yin Mantao (Yan Mun-to), "Xue Juexian changqiang yishu tese" ["Sit Goksin choenghong ngaiseot daksik" or The special characteristics of the vocal style of Sit Kok-sin], in Yeung, ed., *Zan, sin, mei,* 62; Wong Siu-hap, *Jyutkuk geibun zisik,* 151–52.

77 Yan, "Sit Goksin choenghong ngaiseot daksik,"63.

78 Ibid., 63–64.

79 Sit, "Ngo dik fandau," 181.

80 Ibid.

81 Sit, "Nanyou zhiqu" ["Naamjau ziceoi" or Afterthoughts on my visit to Southeast Asia, 1930], in Yeung, ed., *Zan, sin,mei,* 168.

82 Ibid.

83 Sit, "Zhuyan he daoyan *Xu Bai Jinlong* de houhua" ["Zyujin wo doujin *San Baak Gamlung* dik hauwaa" or After playing the lead in and directing *White Golden Dragon: A Sequel,* 1937], in Yeung, ed., *Zan, sin, mei,* 169.

84 Yingzi, "Bai Jinlong xiajuan xi zhong you xi; Xue Juexian yu Shao Zuiweng danao yijian" ["Baak Gamlung haagyun hei zung jau hei; Sit Goksin jyu Siu Zuijung daainaau jigin" or The sequel of *White Golden Dragon* has a play within a play: Sit Kok-sin started an argument with Runje Shaw], *Jaujau,* no. 22 (July 28, 1936): 7.

85 Lam, "Ngsap nindoi Jyutjyu dinjing jingau zung dik geigo mantai,"4.

86 Hansen, "Room-for-Play," 3–46.

87 Benjamin, "The Work of Art in the Age of Its Technological Reproducibility," 107.

88 Ibid., 107–08, Benjamin's emphasis.

89 Quoted in Hansen, "Room-for-Play," 19. Here, Hansen refers to ibid., 124, n. 10.

90 See Hansen, "Room-for-Play," 23–24.

91 Lee Fa, "Soeng Ging cinggau Jyutjyu pin likzin Wu jingsoeng ginggwo," 3–4; "Yueyu pian shifou gai jin" ["Jyutjyu pin sifau goi gam" or Shall we ban the Cantonese film?], *Art Lane,* no. 7 (June 1937): no page.

92 Lee Fa, "Soeng Ging cinggau Jyutjyu pin likzin Wu jingsoeng ginggwo," 3–4.

93 Feng Zhigang (Fung Chi-kong), "Yueyu pian de cun jin wenti" ["Jyutjyu pin dik cyun gam mantai" or On the preservation of and ban on the Cantonese film], *Art Lane,* no. 3 (April 1937): no page.

94 Chiksan, "Yueyu pian gexin yundong" ["Jyutjyu pin gaaksan wandung" or The Cantonese film reform movement], *Art Lane,* no. 11 (August 1, 1937): no page.

95 Ling Mei (Ling Mui), "Jin Yueyu shengpian zhi wojian" ["Gam Jyutjyu singpin zi ngogin" or My opinions on the ban on the Cantonese sound film], *Art Lane,* no. 1 (February 1937): no page.

96 "Jyutjyu pin sifau goi gam," no page.

97 Xu Xiaogu (Hui Siu-guk), "Cong xiju tandao dianying" ["Cung heikek taamdou dinjing" or From the theater to the cinema], *Art Lane,* no. 48 (February 15, 1939): no page.

98 Chen Pi (Chan Pei), "Dianying ye zhong zhi biandaozhe yingyou zhi renshi" ["Dinjing jip zung zi pindou ze jingjau zi jingsik" or What screenwriters should know in our film industry], *Art Lane,* no. 1 (February 2, 1937): no page.

99 Song Wanli (Sung Manlei), "Huanan dianying yu Guangdong jingshen" ["Waanaam dingjing jyu Gwongdung zingsan" or South China cinema and its Kwantung spirit], *Art Lane,* no. 35 (August 1, 1938): no page.

100 Conversation with Po Fung. I watched this film in the summer of 2014.

101 See, for example, "Jyutjyu pin gaaksan wandung," no page.

102 Agamben, *Infancy and History,* 65–88.

103 Ibid., 74, Agamben's emphasis.

104 Ibid., 84–85.

Conclusion

1 Alexandre Kojève, *Introduction to the Reading of Hegel*, trans. James Nichols, ed. Allan Boom (New York: Basic Books, 1969), 158, n. 6.

2 Ibid., 161–62.

3 Agamben, *The Open: Man and Animal*, trans. Kevin Attell (Stanford, Calif.: Stanford University Press, 2004), 11–12.

4 Jean Baudrillard, *The Transparency of Evil*, 79–80.

5 Combes, *Gilbert Simondon and the Philosophy of the Transindividual*, 4–5.

6 Gilbert Simondon, *L'individu et sa genèse physico-biologique* (1964; repr., Grenoble: Éditions Jérôme Millon, 1995), 30; *L'individuation à la lumière des notions de forme et d'information* (Grenoble: Éditions Jérôme Millon, 2005); these passages are trans. and quoted in ibid., 6.

7 Combes, *Gilbert Simondon and the Philosophy of the Transindividual*, 16–17. Here, Combes refers to Simondon, *L'individu et sa genèse physico-biologique*, 75; and *L'individuation à la lumière des notions de forme et d'information*, 77.

8 Combes, *Gilbert Simondon and the Philosophy of the Transindividual*, 17.

9 Benjamin, "The Work of Art in the Age of Its Technological Reproducibility," 103, Benjamin's emphasis.

10 Ibid., 104, Benjamin's emphasis.

11 Bazin, "An Aesthetic of Reality," 26–27.

12 David E. James, *Allegories of Cinema: American Film in the Sixties* (Princeton, N.J.: Princeton University Press, 1989), 69.

13 Hansen, "Room-for-Play," 40–45.

14 Elsaesser, "Tales of Epiphany and Entropy: Paranarrative Worlds on YouTube," in Buckland, ed., *Film Theory and Contemporary Hollywood Movies*, 150–172.

15 Agamben, *Infancy and History*, 70.

16 Elsaesser, "The Mind-Game Film," in Buckland, ed., *Puzzle Films: Complex Storytelling in Contemporary Cinema* (Malden, Mass.: Wiley-Blackwell, 2009), 13–40; David Bordwell, *The Way Hollywood Tells It: Story and Style in Modern Movies* (Berkeley: University of California Press, 2006), 72–103.

17 Gary Bettinson, "*WuXia* Ethos in Wong Kar Wai's Martial Arts Film," keynote speech (Herstmonceux: Bader International Study Centre, Queen's University [Canada], December 10, 2013).

18 *Vajracchedikā Prajñāpāramitā Sūtra*, §1.

19 Nan Huai-chin, Jingang Jing *shuo sheme?*

20 *The Prajna Paramita Heart Sutra*, trans. Lok To (1995; repr., New York: Buddha Dharma Education Association Inc., 2000), 7–8.

FILMOGRAPHY

All Quiet on the Western Front. Dir. Lewis Milestone. Prod. Carl Laemmle, Jr. Universal, USA, 1930. 35 mm (1080p HD). 138 minutes.

Bai Jinlong [*Baak Gamlung* or *White Golden Dragon*]. Dir. Sit Kok-sin. Prod. Runje Shaw. Unique, Hong Kong, 1934. 35 mm (Print lost). Duration or reel number unknown.

The Big Heat. Dir. Fritz Lang. Prod. Robert Arthur. Columbia, USA, 1953. 35 mm (DVD). 89 minutes.

Blow Job. Dir. and Prod. Andy Warhol. USA, 1964. 16 mm at 16fps (1080p HD; Museum of Modern Art). 35 minutes.

Boxing [*Bokhang* or *Tragedy of Love*]. Dir. and Prod. Li Beihai. Chung Wah Sound and Silent Movies Production Company, Hong Kong, 1934. Print lost. Format and duration unknown.

Brief Encounter. Dir. David Lean. Prod. Noël Coward, Anthony Havelock-Allan, and Ronald Neame. Cineguild, UK, 1945. 35 mm (DVD). 86 minutes.

Chengshi zhi ye [*Night in the City*]. Dir. Fey Mou. Prod. Lo Ming-yau. United Photoplay Service, China, 1933. 35 mm (Print lost). 65 minutes.

Ersun fu [*Mother's Happiness*]. Dir. Shi Dongshan. Prod. Wu Xingzai. Great China Lilium, China, 1926. 35 mm (EYE Film Institute Netherlands). 8 reels.

Genü Hongmudan [*The Sing-Song Girl Red Peony*]. Dir. and Prod. Zhang Shichuan. Star Film Company, China, 1931. 35 mm (Print lost). 180 minutes.

The Grand Duchess and the Waiter. Dir. Malcolm St. Clair. Prod. Jesse L. Lasky and Adolph Zukor. Paramount, USA, 1926. 35 mm. 70 minutes.

Gudao tiantang [*Gwudou tintong* or *Orphan Island Paradise*]. Dir. Tsai Chu-sang. Prod. Lo Jingyu. Tai Tei Film Company, Hong Kong, 1939. 35 mm (VCD). 100 minutes.

Huang Feihong zhengzhuan shangji zhi bianfeng miezhu [*Wong Fei-hung zingzyun soengzaap zi binfung mitzuk* or *The True Story of Wong Fei-hung, Part 1*]. Dir. Wu Pang. Prod. Cheung Chok-hong. Yongyao Film Company, Hong Kong, 1949. 35 mm (DVD). 72 minutes.

Huang Feihong zhengzhuan xiaji zhi huoshao Bawangzhuang [*Wong Fei-hung zingzyun haazaap zi fosiu Baawongzong* or *The True Story of Wong Fei-hung, Part 2*]. Dir. Wu

Pang. Prod. Cheung Chok-hong. Yongyao Film Company, Hong Kong, 1949. 35 mm (DVD). 80 minutes.

Huashen guniang [*Tomboy*]. Dir. Fang Peilin. Prod. Yan Chuntang. Yee Hwa, China, 1936. 35 mm (Print lost). 10 reels.

Kipho. Dir. and Prod. Julius Pinschewer. Werbefilm GmbH Julius Pinschewer, Germany, 1925. 35 mm (DVD). 5 minutes.

Kuangliu [*Raging Torrent*]. Dir. Cheng Bugao. Prod. Zhang Shichuan. Star Film Company, China, 1933. 35 mm (Print lost). 8 reels.

Kongfuzi [*Confucius* or *Master Kung*]. Dir. Fey Mou. Prod. Jin Xinmin and Tong Lian. Min Hwa Film Company, China, 1940. 35 mm (DVD). 97 minutes.

Inception. Dir. Christopher Nolan. Prod. Nolan and Emma Thomas. Warner Brothers, UK and USA, 2010. 75 mm IMAX. 148 minutes.

Langdie [*Longdip* or *Butterflies of the Waves*]. Dir. and Prod. Sit Kok-sin. Fei Fei Film Company, Hong Kong, 1934. 35 mm (Print lost). Duration or reel number unknown.

Liangxin [*Loengsam* or *Conscience*]. Dir. Mak Siu-ha. Prod. Li Beihai. Chung Wah Sound and Silent Movies Production Company, Hong Kong, 1933. 35 mm (Print lost). Format and duration unknown.

Mangtan [*Maangtaam* or *Blind Detective*]. Dir. Johnnie To. Prod. Johnnie To and Wai Ka-fai. Media Asia, Emperor Film Production, Sil-Metropole, Milkyway, and Beijing Roast Film and TV Production, Hong Kong and China, 2013. 35 mm (Blu- ray). 129 minutes.

Nanguo zimeihua [*Naamguok zimuifaa* or *Twin Sisters of the South*]. Dir. Lai Ban. Prod. Wu Tip-ying. Wu Tip-ying Film Company, Hong Kong, 1939. 35 mm (VHS; Hong Kong Film Archive). 85 minutes.

Nüxing de nahan [*Cry of Women*]. Dir. Shen Xiling. Prod. Zhou Jianyun. Star Film Company, China, 1933. 35 mm (VCD). 80 minutes.

Nüxing zhi guang [*Neoising zi gwong* or *The Light of Women*]. Dir. Ko Lei-hen. Prod. Runje Shaw. South Sea, Hong Kong, 1937. 16 mm (DVD; Hong Kong Film Archive). 84 minutes.

Pansi dong [*The Cave of the Silken Web*]. Dir. and Prod. Dan Duyu. Shanghai Yingxi Company, China, 1927. 35 mm (EYE Film Institute, Netherlands). 10 reels (incomplete).

La passion de Jeanne d'Arc [*The Passion of Joan of Arc*]. Dir. Carl Theodor Dryer. Prod. Unknown. Société générale des films, France, 1928. 35 mm (2K). 97 minutes.

Potomok Chingiskhana [*Storm Over Asia*]. Dir. Vsevold Pudovkin. Prod. Unknown. Mezhrabpomfilm, USSR, 1928. 35 mm (DVD). 127 minutes.

Qiancheng wanli [*Cincing maanlei* or *Ten Thousand Li Ahead*]. Dir. Tsai Chu-sang. Prod. Luo Xuelian and Zheng Yingshi. San Sang Film Company, Hong Kong, 1941. 35 mm (VHS; Hong Kong Film Archive). 102 minutes.

Rensheng [*Life*]. Dir. Fey Mou. Prod. Lo Ming-yau. United Photoplay Service, 1934. 35 mm (Print lost). 10 reels.

Sange modeng nuxing [*Three Modern Women*]. Dir. Bu Wancang. Prod. Lo Ming-yau. United Photoplay Service, China, 1933. 35 mm (China Film Archive). 110 minutes.

Shazai dongfang [*Sozai dungfong* or The idiot's wedding night]. Dir. and Prod. Li Beihai.

Chung Wah Sound and Silent Movies Production Company, Hong Kong, 1933. 35 mm. Duration unknown.

Shanghai Express. Dir. Josef von Sternberg. Prod. Adolf Zukor. Paramount, USA, 1932. 80 minutes.

Sunrise. Dir. F. W. Murnau. Prod. William Fox. Fox, USA, 1927. 35 mm (1080p HD). 95 minutes.

The Thief of Bagdad. Dir. Raoul Walsh. Prod. Douglas Fairbanks. United Artists, USA, 1924. 35 mm (HD 1080p). 140 minutes.

Tianming [*Daybreak*]. Dir. Sun Yu. Prod. Lo Ming-yau. United Photoplay Service, China, 1933. 35 mm (DVD). 98 minutes.

Tou shaoya [*Tau siungaap* or Stealing a roast duck]. Dir. Lay Min-wai. Prod. Benjamin Brodsky. Asia Film and Theatre Company, Hong Kong and USA, 1909. No further information.

Tsivian, Yuri. Commentary on the DVD release of *Man with the Movie Camera* (1929). Image Entertainment, USA, 2002. 68 minutes.

Wapan shenyuan [*Ngaapun sanjyun* or Vindicated by the earthenware basin]. Hong Kong and USA, no other information.

Wuxia [reedited and released in the United States as *Dragon*]. Dir. Peter Chan. Prod. Peter Chan, Huang Jianxin, and Jojo Hui. We Pictures, Stellar Mega Films, Dingsheng Cultural Investment, Jiangsu Broadcasting Corporation, and the Yunnan Film Group, Hong Kong and China, 2011. 35 mm (Blu-ray). 116 minutes.

Xiang xuehai [*Sea of Fragrant Snow*]. Dir. Fey Mou. Prod. Lo Ming-yau. United Photoplay Service, China, 1934. 35 mm (Print lost). Duration or reel number unknown.

Xiaocheng zhi chun [*Spring in a Small Town*]. Dir. Fey Mou. Prod. Wang Wanbin. Wenhua Film Company, China, 1948. 35 mm (DVD). 94 minutes.

Xin Bai Jinglong [*San Baak Gamlung* or *New White Golden Dragon*]. Dir. Yeung Kungleung. Prod. Tse Bing-kwan. Great China Film Company, Hong Kong, 1947. 35 mm (VCD). 87 minutes.

Xu Bai Jinlong [*Zuk Baak Gamlung* or *White Golden Dragon: A Sequel*]. Dir. Sit Kok-sin. Prod. Runje Shaw. South Seas, Hong Kong, 1937. 35 mm (Print lost). Duration or reel number unknown.

Zhuangzi shi qi [*Zongzi si cai* or Zhuangzi tests his wife]. Dir. and Prod. Lay Man-wai. China-America Film Company, Hong Kong and USA, 1913. 35 mm (Print lost). 2 reels.

Zuihou guantou [*Zeoihau gwaantau* or *At This Critical Juncture*]. Dir. Chan Pei, Lee Chi-ching, Nam Hoi Sap Sam Long, So Yee, Chiu Shu-sun, and Ko Lei-hen. Prod. Huanan yingjie zhengzaihui (Waahnaam jinggaai zanzoiwui). Grandview Film Company, Qiming Production Company, South China Film Company, South Sea Film Company, and Globe Film Company, Hong Kong, 1938. 35 mm (Print lost). Duration unknown.

INDEX

VICTOR FAN is lecturer of film studies at King's College London.

MIX
Papier | Fördert gute Waldnutzung
FSC® C083411

Zeitfracht Medien GmbH
Ferdinand-Jühlke-Straße 7
99095 Erfurt, Deutschland
produktsicherheit@kolibri360.de